kamera
BOOKS

GW00645014

kamerabooks.com

OTHER BOOKS BY SEAN MARTIN

Sean Martin

NEW WAVES IN CINEMA

kamera
BOOKS

First published in 2013 by Kamera Books
an imprint of Oldcastle Books,
PO Box 394, Harpenden, Herts, AL5 1XJ
www.kamerabooks.com

ISBN
978-1-84243-254-9
978-1-84243-446-8 (epub)
978-1-84243-246-4 (mobi)
978-1-84243-447-5 (pdf)

Typeset by Elsa Mathern
Printed and bound by CPI Group (UK) Ltd, Croydon, CR0 4YY

If cinema has a social function, it's really to make people confront other systems of thought, or other systems of living than the ones they habitually know.

– Jacques Rivette

I went to the Béla Balázs Studio, which at that time was a very open place. Anyone who had a sensible idea received some money to make a film, even if they just walked in off the street. They gave so little money, though, that I had to shoot my first film in five days...There are two kinds of behaviour: either you kick the door in or you knock politely. I wanted to kick it in.

– Béla Tarr

The problem is not to make political films, but to make films politically.

– Jean-Luc Godard

ACKNOWLEDGEMENTS

I would like to thank Ion Mills and Hannah Patterson for their patience and support during the writing of this book. Thanks also to Louise Milne for sagely advice, always gratefully received, and for the loan of certain ancient tomes. Thanks to the staff of the National Library of Scotland in Edinburgh for continual help, to the staff at Edinburgh Central Library, and also to the staff of the British Library in London. Thanks to Nick Harding and Andrea Bertorelli for help with some Italian translations. Finally, a few acknowledgements are due regarding the origins of this book: thanks must go to Professor Nigel Mace, who introduced me to many of the films discussed in this book on his film course at University College Plymouth; and to my friend, the late Lukáš Tomin, with whom I first enthused about the Czech New Wave and *The Party and the Guests*.

CONTENTS

INTRODUCTION:
OLD GUARDS, NEW WAVES

At the Cannes Film Festival in 1959, the knives were out for François Truffaut. The 27-year-old firebrand critic, whose outspoken reviews for the magazine *Cahiers du cinéma* had earned him the nickname 'The Gravedigger of French Cinema', had decided to turn his hand to directing. After making a couple of shorts, he was now presenting his debut feature film, *The 400 Blows*, in Competition. It was quite a turnaround for Truffaut: only the year before, he had been banned from attending Cannes, such was the hostility aroused by his incendiary journalism, and, at the 1959 festival, a number of the more conservative critics were quietly hoping that Truffaut had finally bitten off more than he could chew. Unfortunately for them, *The 400 Blows* proved to be a masterpiece, earning Truffaut the Best Director prize, and demonstrating with seemingly effortless ease that he was just as skilled behind the camera as he was behind the typewriter.

The success of the film catapulted Truffaut and his young star, Jean-Pierre Léaud, into the international spotlight, and critics began to acknowledge Truffaut and his contemporaries as the *Nouvelle Vague*, or New Wave, of French cinema. Indeed, the New Wave seemed to dominate the 1959 Cannes Festival: Marcel Camus won the top prize, the Palme d'Or, for his *Orfeu Negro*, while Alain Resnais' *Hiroshima mon amour*, presented out of Competition, still managed to win the International Critics' (FIPRESCI) Prize, and sold well internationally. However, while Cannes marked the symbolic birth of the New Wave, it had in fact been evolving over the course of the previous few years.

Agnès Varda made what is arguably the first French New Wave film, in 1954, with the independently financed *La pointe courte*, followed in 1956 by Roger Vadim's *And God Created Woman*, featuring his then wife, Brigitte Bardot. 1957 saw the premiere of Louis Malle's *Lift to the Scaffold* and, in the following year, Claude Chabrol completed his debut feature, *Le beau Serge*. Like Truffaut, Chabrol was a critic-turned-filmmaker, who had also written for *Cahiers du cinéma*, and their colleagues at the magazine, Eric Rohmer, Jean-Luc Godard and Jacques Rivette, would all follow them over the next two years with their respective first features, *Le signe du lion*, *Breathless* and *Paris nous appartient*.

The so-called '*Cahiers* group' would form the nucleus of the French New Wave, although the likes of Malle, Vadim, Varda and Resnais – who never wrote for the magazine – showed that the movement was a very loose-knit affair, and the term 'new wave' almost became shorthand for any exciting new French film, whether made by a 'New Wave' filmmaker or not. Indeed, the period from the late 50s to the mid 60s saw hundreds of new French films get made. Liberated from the studio environment by lightweight cameras and young, frequently non-professional casts, the French New Wave changed the way films were made. Nothing would ever quite be the same again.

In order to clarify which of the myriad films emerging from France during this period can be termed as 'new wave', we need to examine what exactly constitutes a new wave, and how it differs from the 'old guard' it rebelled against.

DEFINITIONS OF NEW WAVE

New waves in cinema tend to have certain characteristics that set them apart from the 'old guard' (although, it should be noted, such an 'us and them' view of film production is not always strictly accurate).[1]

New Waves can be characterised, or facilitated by, the emergence of new equipment, such as lightweight 16mm cameras, Nagra sound recorders, faster film stocks that allowed filmmakers to shoot in available light and in real locations rather than remaining studio-bound, and they also tended to use non-professional actors. New equipment became widely available during the 1950s, with filmmakers starting to use the new Éclair Cameflex 16mm camera, or the Arriflex, which had been widely used during the Second World War as a news camera and whose use in drama had been hitherto frowned upon. In terms of film stock, Kodak Tri-X, launched in 1954, was fast enough to allow filmmakers to shoot in available light; again, the truckloads of equipment − literally − that films had employed up to that point could now be happily dispensed with. The lightweight Nagra III tape recorder was launched in 1958, which freed filmmakers from having to use cumbersome studio recorders and meant that sound could easily be recorded on location.

It was not all problem-free, however. There were initial problems in that the handheld cameras proved too noisy to record simultaneous (synchronous) sound at first, which meant that filmmakers were forced to shoot handheld sequences mute, adding the sound later. The development of proper blimps, which muffled the magazines, became a huge step forwards and meant that, from the early 60s, handheld shots could now safely have sync sound without the unwelcome presence of the camera's rattle. (Early attempts at handheld with sync sound were achieved through the cameras being equipped with DIY blimps in the form of sleeping bags, blankets or coats.)[2]

The styles and subjects of the films themselves changed, veering sharply away from what Truffaut dubbed '*le cinéma du papa*' towards new narrative approaches ranging from the factual to the self-reflexive. Scripts dealt with issues that had either not been attempted before, or, if they had, were now treated with a frankness absent from earlier treatments of the same material. At the other extreme, film itself became the essential subject, both through the appropriation of genres (e.g. Truffaut's post *Jules et Jim* films of the 1960s, Chabrol's thrillers) or the experimentation of Godard, Marker, Straub/Huillet and pre-*Heimat* Edgar Reitz.

New sources of funding also played a key role in bringing fresh voices to the cinema. Early French New Wave films such as *La pointe courte* and *Le beau Serge* were frequently financed with private investment that came from the filmmakers' friends or families. When *The 400 Blows* and *Breathless* became international hits in 1959/60, distributors began to take notice, and started to offer New Wave filmmakers advances to make further films. There was even state involvement: the New German Cinema, for instance, which announced itself with a declaration made at the 1962 Oberhausen Short Film Festival, later benefitted greatly from the financial involvement of West German television, and some of its most notable films, such as Fassbinder's *Berlin Alexanderplatz* (1980) were made for television (although it did receive later theatrical releases in various countries).

Distribution and exhibition had their part to play as well, particularly in the guise of the film clubs which began to appear after the end of the Second World War in cities across Europe. In addition to these were fully fledged independent cinemas, such as Cinémathèque Française in Paris, which opened in 1948 and was to prove so crucial to Truffaut and his collaborators, not just as a place to view films they had been unable to see up to that point – during the Nazi Occupation of France, the import of foreign films had been banned – but also as a place to meet like-minded people.

The impassioned debates about cinema that were a frequent feature of life at the Cinémathèque help define one of the other main features of the French New Wave, and which other new waves also adopted: an ideology. That Truffaut and his colleagues were all contributors to the journal *Cahiers du cinéma* further refined their thinking (both Rohmer and Rivette edited the magazine at different times), as did their close relationship with the critic André Bazin. Central to the French New Wave's thinking, and to many of those that came after them, was the notion of auteur cinema, in which films were seen as effectively the work of the director, as opposed to the producer, screenwriter or studio. The director 'wrote' his or her films using the caméra-stylo (camera pen) as much as a novelist would write their novels; everything in an auteur film was informed and shaped by the director's outlook, morality and personal experience.

NEW WAVES AND WORLD CINEMA

This book is intended to be a short survey of some key New Waves. The main focus will be the major movements of the 1950s, 60s and

70s – using the years 1959 to 1979 as rough bookends – finishing with a brief look at digital cinema and suggestions for further viewing. These were years of momentous cultural change, and it could be argued that cinema has never been as vital since. Film mattered in a way it no longer seems to.

In a book of this size, it is unfortunately not possible to examine every single new wave, group or trend. Neither will it be able to cover many aspects of world cinema, with which new wave cinemas often have much in common. (For more on the distinction between the two terms, see the Epilogue.) Indeed, the boundaries are somewhat blurred, highlighted by the fact that there has always been a crossover between new waves and rejuvenated national cinemas. The Czech New Wave is a case in point, being made up of two generations of filmmakers who came to international attention at exactly the same time; the older we could dub the rejuvenated national cinema, the younger, the New Wave.

But new waves, new world cinemas – our definitions may be a little slippery – did not emerge ex nihilo. New waves need old guards to react against, and the old guard, in the shape of classical Hollywood forms of narrative and each country's respective national film industry, became established fairly early on in film history. The first new waves, therefore, also emerged early on, and, like the French New Wave after them, came to prominence in a world recovering from war. The year was 1919, and the country was Germany.

PIONEERS

SLEEPWALKERS & EVIL GENIUSES:
GERMAN EXPRESSIONISM

Expressionism was a term first used to describe certain trends in art and theatre around the turn of the twentieth century: emotions were exaggerated, reality distorted, subjectivity favoured over critical distance. 'Expressionist art in practically every way seemed to suggest a protest against the norm.'[3] Although it was never an official group, Expressionism came to be associated with such painters as Edvard Munch and Egon Schiele, and dramatists such as August Strindberg and Georg Kaiser. Although there were also expressionist architects, writers and composers, it was expressionist theatre and painting which had the greatest influence on what was to become known as German Expressionist cinema.[4] The cultural milieu of postwar Germany – with all its hedonism, liberalism and despair – allowed it to flourish and achieve international recognition. It was a period which, it might be possible to suggest, also somehow needed these dark, disturbing films, after what was, up until that time, the worst war history had ever recorded.

Expressionist cinema reflected its era well: the films featured an assortment of antiheroes, evil genii, monsters and magicians whose lives are touched by madness, paranoia and heightened emotional states. Such is either the weakness of the 'hero', or the strength of the evil genius, that reality becomes nightmarish and their environments – frequently urban – take on all the characteristics of a George Grosz painting, or a story by Kafka. Set design and art direction played an important role, with strange angles, mirrors and shadows predominating. Expressionist filmmakers were indeed to get such a huge amount of mileage out of the latter two devices that the eminent film critic and historian Lotte Eisner, whose *The Haunted Screen* remains one of the classic books on the subject, wrote that expressionist cinema was a 'world of shadows and mirrors'.[5]

There were several key players who influenced the movement, perhaps foremost among them the theatre director Max Reinhardt and the producer Erich Pommer. Reinhardt (1873–1943) dominated German theatre before his eventual flight to England in 1938, and amongst his repertory company were such figures as F W Murnau, Ernst Lubitsch, Max Schreck, Emil Jannings, Conrad Veidt and Paul Wegener, all of whom would go on to become important in expressionist cinema and, in the case of the first two, cinema history. Reinhardt's stage productions were notable, among other things, for their chiaroscuro lighting, which highlighted key areas while leaving much of the stage darkened. Not only would this technique later be employed by the likes of Murnau and Fritz Lang, it echoed one of the main themes of expressionist cinema, that of a small light struggling to remain lit – not always successfully – against the prevailing dark.

Whilst Reinhardt was busy on the stages of Berlin, Erich Pommer was pursuing his vision of a German cinema that could not only be great art, but also good business. He was instrumental in developing and promoting a German national cinema, and produced the earliest expressionist classic, Robert Wiene's *The Cabinet of Dr Caligari* (1919). Although strictly speaking not the first expressionist film – *The Student of Prague* (1913), *The House Without a Door* (1914) and *The Golem* (1915) all employed expressionist themes and stylistic techniques – Wiene's film became the first major expressionist success, both critically and commercially. With its story of an evil doctor manipulating a somnambulist to commit a series of murders played out on sets designed by expressionist artists Hermann Warm, Walter Röhrig and Walter Reimann, *Caligari* can also be seen as the archetypal film of the movement.

The film was originally intended to be a critique of the 'Old Europe' mindset that had led to the Great War, with the character of Cesare, the somnambulist, representing the millions of ordinary men who had been led to their deaths in the trenches. The climactic exposure of the supposedly respectable psychiatrist Caligari as the instigator of Cesare's crimes was meant to represent the triumph of reason over the insanity of the politicians, aristocrats and military leaders who were directly responsible for the conflict. As it turned out, the main action of the film was presented as a flashback told by the character of Francis (a device suggested by Fritz Lang, who was originally assigned to direct). The end of the film reveals that Francis is a patient in a mental asylum, undermining the revolutionary intent of the original script: has Francis imagined the whole thing? That his cell at the asylum looks very similar to the ones in which Caligari and Cesare are imprisoned in the flashback suggests that society is indeed out of control, all the old certainties are dead, and nothing is quite as it seems.

Themes of somnambulism, dreams and monsters quickly established themselves as the stock-in-trade of expressionist films. Paul Wegener's *The Golem* (1920) was in fact his third film treating the Jewish legend, but is the only one to survive (the first two films being made in 1915 and 1917). The film's full title, *The Golem: How He Came into the World*, informs us that this is actually a prequel to the earlier films, and traces the creation of the golem by Rabbi Loew (1525–1609), a semi-legendary figure in the mythology of Prague, who intends the monster to both serve him and defend the Jewish quarter from the city's rulers. The creature comes under the control of the Rabbi's assistant, who uses it for his own ends. The golem's reign of havoc is only brought to an end by a small girl, who removes the magic star from the monster's chest, thus disabling it.[6] The theme of anti-Semitism in the film seems, from this vantage point in time, oddly prophetic and ominous: after the downfall of the Weimar government, there would be no magic stars to protect Germany's Jewish population.

Henrik Galeen's *The Student of Prague* (1926) is, like Wegener's *Golem* of 1920, a remake. Galeen's film follows the original, made in 1913, fairly closely. (The first version, on which Galeen was assistant director, can fairly claim to be, if not the first expressionist film, then certainly a prototype of the school.) Balduin, an impoverished student, strikes a deal with the money-lender Scapinelli: in return for a large sum in gold and the chance to meet a rich heiress with whom Balduin is in love, Scapinelli can take anything in Balduin's room. The money-lender orders the student's reflection to step out of the mirror, and this doppelgänger then begins to undermine Balduin's attempts to woo the heiress. Driven almost mad, the student shoots his reflection, only to die himself.

Scapinelli is a worthy expressionist villain, but pales in comparison to Count Orlok in F W Murnau's adaptation of Bram Stoker's *Dracula: Nosferatu, A Symphony of Horrors* (*Nosferatu, eine Symphonie des Grauens*, 1922, written by Galeen). Here, the evil genius is the vampire Count Orlok, memorably personified by the seemingly genuinely inhuman Max Schreck. The countryside around the Count's castle is memorably animate: the horses that stand in the twilit field as Hutter enters the village seem to be frightened by the mere mention of dark forces, while the villagers cower at the inn. Schreck's Orlok – like all good vampires – can be read in a variety of ways; given the time in which the film was made, he could personify the blood that has been drained out of old Europe by the Great War, or the dark political undercurrents of Weimar Germany. *Faust* (1926), the last film Murnau made before he went to Hollywood,[7] takes this image to an extreme: at one point, Faust is shown looming over the entire town as if he were a giant bird, as if nineteenth-century Romanticism had become infected and inflated with twentieth-century paranoia.

Fritz Lang's Dr Mabuse was arguably the character who embodied this paranoia better than any other in the expressionist canon. He is first seen in *Dr Mabuse, the Gambler* (*Dr Mabuse – der Spieler*, 1922, produced by Pommer), originally a four-hour epic that followed Mabuse's career as a criminal mastermind who, like Caligari, uses hypnosis to achieve his ends. And, also like Caligari, he uses agents to commit his crimes for him. At the end of the film, he is caught and sent to an insane asylum, but that does not stop his scheming. *The Testament of Dr Mabuse* (*Das Testament des Dr Mabuse*, 1933) picks up where the first film ended. The imprisoned Mabuse spends his days writing his 'testament' while a gang in the outside world commits the crimes that are detailed in Mabuse's writings. When Mabuse apparently dies, his ghost seems to confer with Professor

Baum, who runs the asylum. Mabuse's ghost speaks of an 'unlimited reign of crime' and, from then on, Baum seems to be possessed by the Doctor's spirit. At the end of the film, Baum, believing himself to be Mabuse, is seen incarcerated in one of his own cells, tearing the testament to pieces. According to one rumour, the film came to the attention of Joseph Goebbels, who called Lang into his office for a chat one day in 1933. Goebbels was apparently unhappy about the film, perhaps feeling that references to an 'unlimited reign of crime' were perhaps too close for comfort (the Nazis had only been in power for a few months at this time, but had already opened their first concentration camp, at Dachau). Lang was offered the post of head of UFA, the German film industry's main studio, but he declined and fled first to Paris, and then later the US. Goebbels banned *The Testament of Dr Mabuse* anyway.

Expressionism's high-water mark – at least in Germany – was in the early to mid twenties. It was not universally popular – German audiences, like those elsewhere, loved Chaplin and flocked in their droves to see home-grown melodramas – but the influence of expressionism seeped out like a dark miasma. Lang's *Metropolis* (1927) successfully exported expressionist values to science fiction, while G W Pabst's *Pandora's Box* (*Die Büchse der Pandora*, 1929) and von Sternberg's *The Blue Angel* (*Der blaue Engel*, 1930) were both melodramas with an expressionist edge, pitting Louise Brooks and Emil Jannings against fates they ultimately cannot wriggle out of. Expressionism crossed international boundaries, too. Still in France after making his silent masterpiece, *The Passion of Joan of Arc*, Carl Dreyer went on to make his first sound film, the eerie *Vampyr* (1932), loosely based on Sheridan Le Fanu's story 'Carmilla'. *Vampyr* is perhaps the most dreamlike and psychologically subtle of all expressionist films, and the most important early vampire film after *Nosferatu*.

Expressionism's influence reached Hollywood, hardly surprising since many of Weimar Germany's biggest talents ended up there by the time Hitler rose to power. Karl Freund, who had shot both Murnau's *The Last Laugh* (*Der letzte Mann*, 1924) and Lang's *Metropolis*, directed *The Mummy* (1932) and *Mad Love* (1935), both of which clearly showed that their director was still spiritually at UFA.

James Whale's Frankenstein movies also clearly owed a debt to the Germans, as did the later film noirs. Fritz Lang returned to Germany at the end of his career and made a third Mabuse film, *The Thousand Eyes of Dr Mabuse* (*Die tausend Augen des Dr Mabuse*, 1960), by which time the 'unlimited reign of crime' had transformed the world, and cinema itself was undergoing the revolutions of the late 1950s and 1960s. The newcomers were to acknowledge the expressionist pioneers with various tributes and homages, and Lang appeared – as himself – in Godard's *Contempt* (*Le Mepris*, 1963).

REALISM & EXPERIMENT: SOVIET FORMALISM

Cinema came to Russia in May 1896, when the Lumière brothers screened their works in Moscow and St Petersburg; the first Russian film – of Tsar Nicholas II's coronation at the Kremlin – was made the same month. By the time Nicholas fell and the Bolsheviks seized power, the Russian film industry was producing over 100 films a year in the face of lively competition from French, German, Danish, British and Italian companies, in addition to a fledgling Hollywood. Although the first film released in Russia after the Revolution was anything but revolutionary – Protazanov's *Father Sergius*, adapted from the Tolstoy story – the Bolsheviks were quick to seize upon film as a valuable propaganda tool and, in doing so, effectively created the first 'post-colonial' or, more properly, 'post-imperial' cinema.

Central to Bolshevik cinema was the theory of montage – from the French, 'putting together' – which was given its first major demonstration in 1918 by the filmmaker and theorist Lev Kuleshov (1899–1970). Due to a lack of funds with which to make their own films, Kuleshov and his students began recutting D W Griffith's *Birth of a Nation*, a print of which had been smuggled into Russia, in order to study how Griffith had achieved his dramatic effects. In doing so, Kuleshov helped establish the world's first film school, Moscow's All-Union State Institute of Cinematography (VGIK for short, pronounced 'vuh-geek'), and it was here that his most important editing experiment was undertaken, the so-called Kuleshov Effect. Footage from pre-Revolutionary films was put together with shots of the actor Ivan Mozzhukin alternating with shots of a bowl of soup, a little girl playing, and a dead woman in her coffin. When the film was shown to an audience, they believed that the expression on Mozzhukhin's face was different each time, showing, respectively, hunger at seeing the soup, joy at seeing what they took to be his daughter, and grief at seeing what they took to be his mother; indeed, people raved about how good Mozzhukhin's acting was. What they didn't realise was that the shots of Mozzhukhin were in fact a single shot used repeatedly, and it was they themselves who were imputing values to his 'reactions' to the soup, the girl and the dead woman. For Kuleshov, it proved two things: that editing was the most important aspect of filmmaking, more so than what the camera had originally captured, and that, for a film to work properly, the audience had to be active in interpreting what it was they were seeing. Others were quick to develop their own theories of montage, including two of Kuleshov's most brilliant pupils, Sergei Eisenstein (1898–1948) and Vsevolod Pudovkin (1893 –1953).

Eisenstein called his theory the 'montage of attractions' and, for him, film was all about dynamism and conflict. A film comprises a collision of images, where an individual shot should be seen as coming not *after* the preceding shot, but *on top* of it. In this way, Eisenstein argued, the meaning of a film would alter and deepen with each successive shot, the way a symphony might build. His montage contained five main strands: Metric, Rhythmic, Tonal, Overtonal and Intellectual. Metric montage is created by making each shot within any given sequence precisely the same length, regardless of what is happening in the shot; Eisenstein believed this to be the most basic form of montage. Eisenstein's own *Battleship Potemkin* (1925) contains a classic example, where he uses shots of different statues of lions to give the appearance that a single stone lion is standing up to cheer the crew of the *Potemkin* on.[8] Rhythmic montage is also determined by time, but uses the visual components of a shot to convey yet deeper meanings; *Potemkin* again includes a classic example of this, in the celebrated Odessa Steps sequence in which shots of a mother and her baby's pram are intercut with shots of the advancing imperial guard, bayonets drawn. Tonal montage employs the emotional content of a shot to convey meaning, such as in the languid, mournful sequence – again from *Potemkin*, something of a showcase for Eisenstein's theories – showing the death of the sailor Vakulinchuk.

Overtonal montage – sometimes referred to as associational montage – is the overall effect gained by using metric, rhythmic and tonal montage, although Eisenstein seems to have not been too clear in his mind about what this actually meant. While he claimed that his 1929 film *The General Line* contained examples of overtonal montage, the Odessa Steps sequence can also be viewed as an overtonal sequence. Intellectual montage, meanwhile, utilised shots which, when combined, conveyed an intellectual meaning. In his first full-length film, *Strike* (1924), Eisenstein presents us with shots of factory workers being attacked, intercut with shots of a bull being slaughtered. There is nothing to link the two events, except in our minds: the workers are being slaughtered as if they were no better than cattle. Eisenstein regarded this as the highest form of montage, and yet, of his theories, it was the one that came in for the most flak from both fellow filmmakers and the Party.

The famous Winter Palace sequence in *October* (1928) highlights one of the main problems of intellectual montage, namely its interpretation. Eisenstein repeatedly intercuts shots of Alexander Kerensky with a mechanical peacock, which has frequently been interpreted as meaning that Eisenstein wants to make us see the head of Russia's Provisional Government of 1917 as vain and arrogant. However, this reading seems too simplistic, as it cannot explain the presence of the shot of the padlock in the sequence. It has been suggested[9] that the sequence is really supposed to represent the Winter Palace and all it stands for swallowing Kerensky via the peacock's rear end, the padlock supposedly representing the fact that Kerensky is now trapped within the Winter Palace, both physically and in terms of his thinking. Kerensky, in other words, is really no better than the tsar. Despite its intellectual brilliance, however, the sequence is mainly remembered for the peacock standing for vanity, and Eisenstein's message was lost.[10]

Pudovkin had his own ideas about montage. While he wrote in praise of Eisenstein, and *October* in particular, the two men frequently argued. Where Eisenstein saw montage as being about conflict, Pudovkin saw it as a means to link shots and unify scenes, which in turn act as building blocks to tell the whole story of the film. And where Eisenstein's films of the 1920s generally don't have one central character around whom the story revolves, Pudovkin lyrically celebrates individuals' struggles against tsarist oppression, most memorably in his masterpiece, *Mother* (1926), which depicts an ordinary woman's realisation of the need for revolution when her son, a trade union activist, receives a prison sentence. The final sequence shows the mother joining a demonstration that is marching on the prison where her son is held. Pudovkin's camera cuts to shots of a frozen river and, as the demonstrators advance on the prison, the ice begins to crack. The son, sprung from his cell, escapes on a block of ice, and we return to the crumbling floes again at the end of the film; the long freeze of tsarist rule is over.

Despite the spats between Eisenstein and Pudovkin over montage, and the international success of *The Battleship Potemkin* – Hollywood mogul David O Selznick, of all people, described it as 'unquestionably one of the greatest motion pictures ever made'[11] – there were other sides to the Soviet wave of the 1920s that, while apparently in the service of the Revolution, seem to strain at the leash a little more, testing Soviet ideology, young as it was, with daring experimentalism. At the forefront of this trend was the filmmaker who, along with Eisenstein, is arguably the most influential of all Soviet filmmakers from the period, Dziga Vertov.

Vertov (1896-1954) was born Denis Kaufman to a family of Jewish intellectuals living in the Polish town of Białystok, then in Russia. He had two brothers, Mikhail (1897–1979) and Boris (1906–80), both of whom would go on to become successful cameramen (Boris would work with Jean Vigo and also won an Oscar for *On the Waterfront*). He adopted his pseudonym, which means 'spinning top', in 1917, by which time he had become interested in sound collages and, after the October Revolution of that year, newsreel. Vertov edited the first newsreel series in Russia, *Kino-Nedelya*, whose name translates as the rather bland-sounding 'Film Weekly', and, by 1919, was directing his own films, beginning with *The Anniversary of the Revolution* (1919), *The Battle of Tsaritsyn* (1920), *The Agit-Train Vsik* (1921), and a 13-reel *History of the Civil War* (1922). During this period, Vertov worked on the Agit-trains and continued to refine his ideas, assembling a small group of collaborators around him, including his future wife, the editor Elisaveta Svilova (1900–75), and his brother Mikhail; Vertov dubbed the group the Kinoks (derived from 'kino-oki', 'cinema eyes'). In various Kinok manifestos, Vertov argued that drama was a bourgeois fairytale, and that real cinema was documentary footage of 'life caught unawares'. Despite agreeing with his montage colleagues on the importance of editing, Vertov also stressed the importance of the camera, which he saw as an impartial recorder of reality, superior to human vision, calling it the 'cine eye'. And, in what was virtually a blueprint for new wave filmmakers of the 1950s and 60s, Vertov called for his fellow Kinoks to use fast film stock, light, handheld cameras and equally portable lighting equipment.

Armed with both theories and collaborators, between 1922 and 1925, Vertov directed his first major work, the 23-episode newsreel series, *Kino Pravda*. The title was a pun: 'pravda' not only means 'truth', but was also the name of the official party newspaper, and it reflected Vertov's faith not only in the camera and the editing table, but also in Marxism (he was much more of a dogmatist than Eisenstein). As the series progressed, the films became ever more avant-garde, which displeased the party, which was coming to see Vertov as a bit of a tiresome crank. Fortunately, his reputation was given a boost by the European avant-garde, who applauded his 1924 film *Kino Eye – Life Caught Unawares*, awarding it prizes at the 1925 Paris World Exhibition. The film, a feature-length documentary, centres around the activities of a group of Young Pioneers in a Soviet village. The children are busy making posters, handing out leaflets encouraging the villagers to buy from the co-operative, visiting widows and promoting temperance. Vertov intercuts scenes showing the children evidently having a good time with experimental sections shown in reverse of the un-killing of a bull, and the un-baking of bread. The success of *Kino Eye* led to Vertov being able to make two more feature-length films, *A Sixth of the World* and *Stride, Soviet!* (both 1926). The authorities, however, balked at supporting what was to become Vertov's masterpiece, *The Man with the Movie Camera* (1929).

The Man with the Movie Camera fits into the 'city symphony' genre that was popular at the time (Walter Ruttmann's 1927 film *Berlin: Symphony of a Great City* perhaps being the most well known today), but at the same time transcends it. Supposedly depicting a day in the life of a Soviet city, Vertov actually shows three cities – Moscow, Odessa and Kiev (the film was a Ukrainian production). Where the film differs from the likes of Ruttmann's is in the character of the cameraman, 'played' by Mikhail Kaufman. He is shown filming city life, and later editing it, so the film becomes not just a collage of city life, but also a film about itself, about the process of making a film, and of watching it. Using every trick in the book – a book largely written by Vertov himself – the film uses split screens, dissolves, Dutch angles, tracking shots, double exposure, freeze frames, jump cuts, footage shown in either reverse, sped up or slowed down, and even animation. The film divided audiences both at home and abroad, but Vertov was able to continue working, producing as a follow-up his first sound film, *Enthusiasm: Donbass Symphony* (1931). Also filmed in the Ukraine, the film celebrates the transformation of the Donbass region during the first Five Year Plan. Workers are shown busy in steel mills, locomotive yards and in the mines, fields are harvested and churches are converted into political and social clubs, all to the accompaniment of a collage of industrial and agricultural sounds. Like *The Man with the Movie Camera*, the film was plotless, and it received an even cooler reception at home, although it was a great success abroad, with Charlie Chaplin marvelling at the complexity of the soundtrack and declaring it the film of the year.

The Ukraine was also home to the other great name from the era, Alexander Dovzhenko (1894–1956). While his colleagues experimented with montage, documentary and the avant-garde, Dovzhenko's films often took their inspiration from Ukrainian folklore and nature and, as a result, are arguably among the most poetic and visually beautiful of all Soviet films from the 1920s and early 1930s. His greatest achievement remains his 'Ukrainian Trilogy' comprising *Zvenigora* (1928), *Arsenal* (1929) and *Earth* (1930). *Zvenigora* – about a treasure hidden deep inside a mountain – is suffused with Ukrainian folklore and superstition, and established Dovzhenko as a major filmmaker. *Arsenal*, by contrast, seems much more Soviet in that it depicts a valiant civil war struggle between Bolshevik and White Russian troops at a munitions plant. *Earth*, widely regarded as Dovzhenko's masterpiece, tells the story of an insurrection by peasants against an unjust landlord.

Could films so rooted in Ukrainian culture be revolutionary? The party evidently thought not, and saw counter-revolutionary tendencies in *Earth*. Furthermore, *Arsenal*, in its depiction of an attack on an empty trench, seems at times anti-war, and, given the context of the times, anti-revolution. *Earth* fared badly at home – although, as might be expected by now – was lauded abroad, and Dovzhenko opted to produce what he thought would be more mainstream and acceptable fare in the shape of *Ivan* (1932) and *Aerograd* (1935), both of which saw him successfully making the transition to sound films.

If the Soviet 'new wave' of the 1920s started in political upheaval, then it is true to say that it ended in precisely the same circumstances. A cinema that began in necessity – filmmakers too impoverished to shoot, so they recut found footage – flourished to produce some of the most groundbreaking and influential films of all time (the work of Eisenstein and Vertov in particular), but was then effectively crippled when Stalin assumed sole power and his influence grew in the 1930s. The experimentalism of the 1920s was replaced with the turgid 'socialist realism' of the 1930s, which, despite its name, wasn't particularly realistic, instead being largely given over to bland portrayals of farm collectives and factory workers living happily under the benign Uncle Joe.[12] Although all the main figures in Soviet cinema survived Stalin's purges – the writers and poets, for instance, were not so lucky – many of them found themselves unable to continue working as they had done in the 1920s: Vertov was forced to work on run-of-the-mill newsreels, Dovzhenko found his only work as a wartime documentarist and, later, as a novelist, while Eisenstein came closest of them all to official censure. Only his premature death in 1948 at the age of 50 spared him a trip to the Gulag. It would take yet another political turnaround, the Party Congress of 1956 and its denunciation of Stalin, to reinvigorate Russian cinema.

'IT WAS JUST LIFE': ITALIAN NEOREALISM

Like the Soviets, the neorealists emerged under a regime, only this time it was not Communist, but Fascist. For Mussolini, however, films had more cultural and entertainment value than they did propagandist value. As a result, he founded the Venice Film Festival in 1932; a film school, the Centro Sperimentale di Cinematografia, in 1935; and then, perhaps most importantly of all, Cinecittà Studios in Rome in 1937. His son Vittorio (1916–97) would work as a film producer and also edited the influential journal *Cinema* for a number of years. The journal was important, not just for its news content, but also for its role in disseminating new ideas from abroad, such as Soviet montage theory. It would also become a platform for critics calling for the renewal of Italian cinema, a renewal that would become neorealism. Such calls had been made, in fact, as early as 1933, with the journalist Leo Longanesi appealing for films to be shot on location with non-professional actors. And one of the Fascist era's most important filmmakers, Alessandro Blasetti (1900–87), was doing just that in films such as *1860* (1934) and *The Old Guard* (1935).

Obsession (*Ossessione*, 1943), directed by Luchino Visconti (1906–76), is generally seen as the first neorealist film proper. Based on James M Cain's novel *The Postman Always Rings Twice* (incidentally, like *Nosferatu*, without paying for the rights), Visconti largely adheres to Cain's plot concerning infidelity and murder, but brings his own sensibility to bear on it. The film doesn't shy away from showing the harshness of Italian rural existence, which Visconti captures largely in wide and mid-shots. This, combined with long takes, deromanticises both passion and Italy, which outraged both the Church and the Fascists, neither of whom wanted such sordidness onscreen. The Church made its position known by having an archbishop sprinkle holy water in the auditorium after a screening, while Vittorio Mussolini declared 'this is not Italy' after viewing the film. The Cultural Ministry announced that it was a 'film that stinks of latrines' and destroyed the negative. It was only due to Visconti's having made a duplicate negative in secret that the film survived at all.

The end of the war saw Italian filmmakers freed from the harassments, thematic constraints and censorship under which they had worked during Mussolini's regime. This desire to tackle previously taboo subjects, such as poverty and social injustice, came at the same time as calls from the likes of screenwriter Cesare Zavattini (1902–89) for a new cinema, one that would dispense with Hollywood values and concentrate on the realities of life in the immediate aftermath of the war. His views were shared by a number of critics writing for *Cinema*, including emerging directors Michelangelo Antonioni (1912–2007) and Giuseppe De Santis (1917–97), as well as Visconti. With the appearance of films such as Roberto Rossellini's *Rome, Open City* (1945) and Vittorio De Sica's *Shoeshine* (1946), neorealism came into its own as a movement.

Although only a group in the loosest sense of the word, the neorealists were defined by shared concerns and working principles. They strived for an air of authenticity in their films, using largely non-professional actors and shooting on location. The lives of ordinary people formed the plots, often emphasising the collective over the individual and the promise of a better future symbolised by children. Emotions were favoured over intellectual abstraction; the films were simple, almost documentary in style, preferring to show events in real time rather than in contrived Hollywood fashion; a lot of the plotting, therefore, was quite loose in order to emphasise the 'reality' of the story. Ideologically, the neorealists were Marxist-humanists (although some, like Visconti, were paid-up communists – but perhaps that's splitting hairs). And between the end of the war and the early 1950s, they made some of cinema's most enduring and influential films.

Roberto Rossellini (1906–77) began directing under Mussolini, and was in fact using neorealist principles in films he made for the regime, such as the wartime trilogy of *A Pilot Returns* (1942), *The White Ship* (1942) and *The Man with the Cross* (1943), but it was not until his great postwar trilogy that he made his mark internationally. *Rome Open City* (*Roma, Città Aperta*, 1945) was shot under difficult conditions in the last days of the war in Europe: film stock had to be acquired on the black market, Rossellini couldn't watch any of the material until the shoot was over, and the entire soundtrack had to be post-synched. The film depicts the struggle of Italian partisans against the Nazis, featuring the infamous scene where the partisan Manfredi is tortured as Nazis listen to music and enjoy a cigarette in the next room, and culminates with the execution of the priest, Don Pietro. Hope for the future is suggested by the children who witness this atrocity.

Paisan (*Paisà*, 1946) deals with the Allied invasion of Italy in 1943, and is arguably a greater film. In a break with conventional narrative, Rossellini tells the story in six episodes, incorporating actual documentary footage into each. The theme of an initial culture clash but eventual kinship between the American GIs and the Italians they have come to liberate is reflected in the way Rossellini uses non-professional actors, an omnipotent voiceover and the mixing of actuality footage with dramatic; two different strands seemingly working against each other, but overall working in harmony.

Germany Year Zero (*Germania, Anno Zero*, 1947) takes a similar approach, in mixing a situation that is classic neorealist fare with a strand that could almost be described as expressionist. Shot largely on location amid the ruins of Berlin, the film tells the story of 12-year-old Edmund, who lives with his ailing father and sister Eva, who is forced by circumstance into working as a prostitute. Edmund's brother, Karlheinz, is in hiding, fearing that his Nazi past will catch up with him. Edmund becomes involved in various black market activities as a means of survival. So far, so neorealist. However, it is the presence in the story of the former schoolteacher, Herr Enning, that hints at the dark world of prewar expressionism, suggesting that the nightmares of one era had survived into the succeeding one, the spirit of Mabuse blossoming darkly into Hitler. Enning is not only an unrepentant Nazi – he sells records of Hitler's speeches on the black market – but also has designs on Edmund, suggesting to the boy that he murder his father. Edmund's carrying out of Enning's plan provides the film with one of the bleakest endings in the neorealist canon. Children in neorealism generally embody hope for the future, despite sometimes encountering danger; Edmund is perhaps the most tragic of them.

Vittorio de Sica's first major contribution to the neorealist canon, *Shoeshine* (*Sciusica*, 1946) also has a tragic undercurrent to the central relationship between the boys Giuseppe and Pasquale. The two, who work as shoeshine boys, dream of buying a horse, but their plans of a happy future are dashed when they are convicted of handling stolen goods and sent to a borstal run by 'inhumane state officials and priests'.[13] Pasquale is tricked into betraying Giuseppe in borstal, but, when Giuseppe takes his revenge and dies while trying to escape, Pasquale is wrongly held responsible. The bittersweet ending shows the horse bolting for the freedom denied the boys. *Shoeshine* is a textbook example of the 'little man against the system', told with what is arguably a more sophisticated technique than, say, Rossellini's trilogy, but one that is still markedly more 'realistic' than most Hollywood product of the time (Orson Welles once remarked that *Shoeshine* was a great film because it so successfully concealed its artistry: 'The camera disappeared, the screen disappeared; it was just life.'[14]).

De Sica's follow-up, *Bicycle Thieves* (*Ladri di Biciclette*, 1948), is perhaps the archetypal neorealist film. Antonio (Lamberto Maggiorani) secures a job as a bill poster, a position that requires him to own a bicycle. Just as he is about to start, the all-important bicycle is stolen, and he begins a quest around Rome with his small son, Bruno (Enzo Staiola), to retrieve it. The film was made with a relatively large budget, and, as per usual neorealist practice, was played largely by non-actors. De Sica had trouble casting the two leads, and actually started shooting without having found a boy to play Bruno. He found Antonio when Maggiorani brought his son to audition for the part of Bruno, but De Sica was struck by Maggiorani's appearance ('his hands, covered in calluses, a workman's hands, not an actor's'[15]) and offered him the part straightaway. Aware of the dangers of stardom and of how films can pollute and mislead those who make them as much as those who watch them, De Sica asked Maggiorani that he give up cinema after filming was over and return to his normal job, a promise the non-actor kept. (Ironically, Maggiorani lost his job at the factory where he worked – *Bicycle Thieves* being made at a time of record unemployment in Italy – and he returned to acting, appearing in over a dozen further films.) One day early in the shoot, De Sica, annoyed at the large crowd that had gathered to watch them at work, turned round to see the eight-year old Enzo Staiola amongst the onlookers: he had found his Bruno.

Bicycle Thieves was based on a novel by Luigi Bartolini, and adapted by Cesare Zavattini, who was to become one of De Sica's main collaborators during this period. Concerned with portraying the daily existence of an Italian everyman, Zavattini and De Sica took major liberties with Bartolini's text, simplifying the action so that the entire film was about the quest to retrieve the stolen bike. Dramatic conflicts, too, were largely eradicated, and the film spends much time showing Antonio and Bruno *not* searching for the bicycle, watching them instead engaged in simple actions such as sheltering from the rain, eating or just hopelessly sitting on the kerbside. The plot found favour with the critic André Bazin, who observed that 'plainly there is not enough material here even for a news item: the whole story would not deserve two lines in a stray dog column'.[16] Despite occasional mawkishness – especially lingering shots of the doe-eyed and sometimes annoying Staiola – and a poor performance at the box office, the simplicity of the story would have a huge influence on future filmmakers, and Bazin's praise was important: his enthusiasm for the film would be passed on to his protégé, François Truffaut.

AGAINST A CERTAIN TENDENCY: THE FRENCH NEW WAVE

THE *POLITIQUE DES AUTEURS*

The year 1946 proved to be a momentous one for French cinema. With the war finally over, American films could once again play in the cinemas of Paris. In comparison with the largely moribund state of French filmmaking, the influx of Hollywood product was a revelation: films by Alfred Hitchcock, Howard Hawks, Nicholas Ray, John Ford and Orson Welles appeared and caused a sensation among the capital's cinéphiles. (Truffaut later claimed to have seen *Citizen Kane* over 30 times.) In addition, French films that had previously been banned were now finally available, perhaps the two most important being Jean Vigo's *Zéro de Conduite* (*Zero for Conduct*, 1933) and Jean Renoir's *La Règle du Jeu* (*The Rules of the Game*, 1939). In both there was a freedom and a poetry – and a healthy disrespect for authority – which proved highly influential. If the Americans showed what cinema was capable of, Vigo and Renoir showed it was possible to make great films in France: all that was needed were the right conditions and the right people.

They were not long in coming. Ciné-clubs began springing up all over Paris, where the film intelligentsia could watch and discuss the latest releases, while magazines such as the Communist *L'Ecran* and *Revue du Cinéma* denounced or praised the influx of American films that were now lighting up Paris every night. The Cinémathèque Française, which had been set up in 1936 by Henri Langlois, Georges Franju and Jean Mitry with the aim of collecting and preserving films (a task made all the more important during the war when many films faced destruction at the hands of the Nazis), received a government grant enabling it to move to a permanent address. The Cinémathèque began to hold daily screenings, both of the newly released American films, and also of films from its own collection. Such was the dedication of Langlois to the cause that it made him a guru-like figure, 'the dragon who guards our treasures'.[17]

New criticism was also in the air. While *Revue du Cinéma* often wrote in praise of the new American films, *L'Ecran* frequently fulminated against them. Arguably the most important article the magazine ever ran, however, was Alexandre Astruc's 'The Birth of a New Avant-Garde', published in March 1948, which called for filmmakers to 'write' their films with the 'caméra-stylo' (camera pen) in much the same way that a writer would write with a real pen; it was, in other words, a call for a new kind of cinema, in which the vision of the 'author' – or *auteur* – of the film was central.[18] Astruc would also become involved with the ciné-club called Objectif-49, which included filmmakers and critics such as Jean Cocteau, Robert Bresson, Réné Clément and Raymond Queneau, all of whom supported the idea of a cinema of auteurs. As if to underline their independence from mainstream cinema, they held a Festival of Rejected Films at Biarritz in 1949,[19] showing films that had variously been banned or not taken by Cannes. Amongst the films screened were Visconti's *Ossessione* and Kenneth Anger's *Fireworks*, with the Grand Prix going to Jean Rouch for *Initiation à la danse*, a documentary about an initiation ceremony in Niger.

Arguably the real turning point came in 1951, when André Bazin co-founded a new magazine called *Cahiers du cinéma*, along with fellow critics Jacques Doniol-Valcroze and Joseph-Marie Lo Duca. The magazine drew on a second ciné-club, which met in the Latin Quarter under the aegis of Eric Rohmer, for some of its writers. These included the young François Truffaut and Jean-Luc Godard, who would go on to cut their teeth as critics and theorists at Bazin's new magazine. They were quickly joined by Rohmer, Jacques Rivette and Claude Chabrol. The combined effect of seeing and discussing a wealth of films at the Cinémathèque and writing about them in

Cahiers gave each future filmmaker a unique education in the history and theory of film. Bazin dubbed them 'the Young Turks'.

Bazin was developing his own theories about cinema during this time in such essays as 'The Evolution of Film Language', 'The Ontology of the Photographic Image' and 'In Defence of Mixed Cinema'. Bazin's theories were diametrically opposed to those of the Soviet filmmakers of the 1920s. He rejected the stress placed on montage by Eisenstein, and instead argued for a realism that employed long takes and deep focus (where both background and foreground are in focus at the same time). Deep focus was particularly important for Bazin, as he believed that it made the viewer more active and enabled them the better to interpret what they were seeing. Bazin also encouraged the 'Young Turks', despite the fact that he didn't always agree with them. Between them, they thrashed out a new theory of cinema, developing Astruc's and Bazin's ideas to come up with what was called the *politique des auteurs*, which was to become central to the New Wave.

Although Truffaut is often credited with the *politique des auteurs* – auteur policy – it was really a group effort by the Young Turks. They held that the director is the main author of a film, a somewhat perverse notion given that many of the films they had been watching at the Cinémathèque had been Hollywood movies, in which the directors were nearly always hired hands, answerable to the studio. But this, they argued, was precisely the point: given the strictures of both the Hollywood system and genres, it was only the director who could add that certain *je ne sais quoi* which would make a film stand out from the crowd. Other major contributors to a film – such as screenwriter, director of photography, editor, composer – were all secondary to the vision of the auteur. If a film could be likened to a ship, they were the crew hauling the sails and working the oars; there could only be one captain, and that was the director.

The *politique* insisted that it was very selective: Renoir, Ophüls, Bresson, Hawks, Hitchcock, Ford, Ray, Vigo and Welles all made the list, but certain other directors could never be auteurs as they lacked an overarching vision that informed all their work, although it could be possible for them to make a good film – by accident, one assumes; Claude Autant-Lara's *Four Bags Full* (*La Traversée de Paris*, 1956) being one such example. Conversely, a film by an auteur that didn't really work would always be more interesting than a more accomplished piece of work by a non-auteur. 'There are no works,' *Cahiers* proclaimed, 'there are only auteurs.'

The final principal aspect of the *politique* was the notion that a film is a conversation between the auteur and his or her audience. Godard expected his audience to be able to read significance into his casting of Brigitte Bardot in *Le Mépris* (*Contempt*, 1963), for instance. Bardot was not merely being Bardot in a film about film, but implicit in her onscreen presence was every other film she had made, and all the attendant cultural and critical baggage. Likewise, viewers following Truffaut's Antoine Doinel films over the course of the 20 years in which they were made would be expected to have kept abreast of Jean-Pierre Léaud's career in order to be able to appreciate the films fully. Likewise, a familiarity with the new novel and developments in cultural theory and criticism would help audiences read films by Godard, Rivette or Resnais. The filmmakers were acutely conscious that they were not making films in a vacuum, despite their fanatical cinéphilia.

THE NEW WAVE

The term 'nouvelle vague' or 'new wave' first appeared in the French magazine *L'Express* in October 1957, and referred to the post-World War II generation of French youth, who were seen as somewhat rebellious, given to listening to jazz and discussing films in cafés, and who had enough disposable income to make going to the cinema a regular cultural activity. During the course of the following year, the term began to be used to designate the new generation of filmmakers who were starting to emerge and, by the time of Truffaut's success at Cannes in 1959, 'new wave' was synonymous with the new cinema. Like the new wave of youth culture, the new-wave filmmakers adopted an antagonistic and at times openly critical stance against the older generation, perhaps most famously encapsulated by Truffaut's 1954 article, 'A Certain Tendency of the French Cinema', in which he attacked what he termed the 'tradition of quality' – tired, staid studio films directed by ageing jobbing directors; by 1958, even the head of the French society of ciné-clubs, Pierre Billard, was complaining about the stagnant condition of French filmmaking. Something, it was hoped, was just around the corner.

That something had, in fact, been brewing for some time. Not only were there sea changes afoot in the shape of the ciné-clubs and magazines like *Cahiers* and its rival, *Positif,* but a handful of filmmakers had managed to produce a small number of feature films outside of traditional industry routes. One of the problems the French film industry faced, apart from a large-scale creative *impasse*, was a lack of subsidies from the government body, Centre National de la Cinématographie (CNC). If a film was to be regarded as 'official', it had to be made along CNC guidelines, and with their permission. Such permission was flatly ignored by the precursors of the New Wave proper, filmmakers such as Jean-Pierre Melville (1917–73) and Agnès Varda (b. 1928).

Unable to enter the industry by normal routes – for example, as someone's assistant – Melville decided to go ahead and make films anyway. Melville shot his first feature, *Le Silence de la Mer* (*The Silence of the Sea*) in 1947 for the then seemingly impossibly low sum of $18,000 (roughly 10 per cent of the average feature budget of the time). He shot the film without the permission of the CNC, as a result of which he had to effectively make the film on an amateur basis, buying his stock, like Rossellini, on the black market. He also cut costs by not paying for the rights to adapt the novel on which the film was based. But it was a relatively easy story to film: a three-hander set largely in one location, it told the story of a somewhat naive Nazi officer billeted with an elderly man who lives with his niece. The officer tries to make friends, but is met with a wall of silence. Granted a short leave in Paris, the officer finally realises the true nature of the Nazi regime, and decides the only decent thing to do is to volunteer for the front. Before he departs, the old man leaves an Anatole France book out for him to look at, which contains the lines, 'It is good for a soldier to disobey criminal orders.' It is the nearest thing to real communication between the two characters in the entire film.

Melville shot the film in an austere manner, with long takes, deep focus and inventive use of sound (he later claimed it influenced Bresson). Once completed, it took Melville well over a year to get the film released. The author of the novel on which it was based, Vercours, liked the film so much that he only charged Melville a nominal sum for the rights, and fellow ex-Resistance members helped Melville lobby the CNC to get the film released, upon which it garnered very favourable reviews, and showed that one did not need official industry permission to make a film: all it took was great deal of determination, and a little ingenuity.

Agnès Varda took a similar approach, shooting her first film – a feature – in 1954 after receiving an inheritance. She had no film training, other than being a photographer. *La pointe courte* (1954) followed a young Parisian couple (Philippe Noiret and Silvia Monfort) as they try to sort out their marriage problems in a small Mediterranean fishing village. Their discussions alternate with scenes from village life: government inspectors arrive to check that all the fishermen have the correct licences to fish, a child dies, a marriage is arranged. Like *Le Silence de la Mer*, it was shot on location with non-professional actors (except the two leads), while its mixture of drama and documentary recalls Visconti's *La Terra Trema*. Varda's budget was even smaller than Melville's with the film finally costing $14,000 (in other words 25 per cent of the two signature films of the French New Wave, *The 400 Blows* and *Breathless*), with everyone working for a percentage. And, like Melville, Varda fell foul of the CNC, being branded an 'amateur', as the film was made without their permission.

The film may have disappeared completely, had it not been for the fact that Varda asked Alain Resnais – by then an Oscar-winning documentarist – to edit it. Resnais then showed the finished film to Bazin, who loved it and secured a screening for the film in Cannes, and afterwards a brief release at a small cinema called the Studio Parnasse – due to CNC restrictions, no major distributor would touch it – where, fittingly, it played alongside another classic, independently made take on Mediterranean life, Vigo's *A propos de Nice*.

THE *CAHIERS* DIRECTORS

Cahiers du cinéma had been, along with the Cinémathèque, at the forefront of Parisian cinéphilia during the early and mid-1950s, and the magazine was to produce the New Wave's central group of directors, François Truffaut (1932–84), Jean-Luc Godard (b. 1930), Claude Chabrol (1930–2010), Eric Rohmer (1920–2010) and Jacques Rivette (b. 1928). Through discussing films at the Cinémathèque and writing about them for *Cahiers* with the encouragement of Bazin, the *Cahiers* group epitomised everything the French New Wave stood for: personal films that were both stylish and self-conscious; that were concerned with new ways of telling a story onscreen; that had fresh approaches to genre; that were often shot quickly and cheaply; that spoke to the newly enfranchised audience of young people; and that would help redefine what cinema was capable of.

'The French New Wave,' observed Richard Neupert, 'changed for ever the whole notion of how movies could be made. [It is] perhaps the richest and most exciting period in world film history.'[20] And central to this cinematic and cultural seismic shift were the *Cahiers* directors, who were to be to film what The Beatles would become to music a few years later. 1959 was the *annus mirabilis* of this revolution, and François Truffaut was at its epicentre.

François Truffaut

Born in 1932, Truffaut had a troubled childhood, often finding himself in borstal. After the war, he was taken under the wing of Bazin, who was to become almost a surrogate father to the teenage Truffaut, and Bazin encouraged his young charge to attend the cinema in order to help keep him out of further trouble. The result was fortuitous: at the Cinémathèque he met Godard and Rivette, and they became avid filmgoers, watching everything they possibly could. Indeed, they developed a friendly rivalry as to who could see the most, with Rivette coming out as the most hardcore *cinéphile* (although he once did admit that Godard attended more films, 'although Jean-Luc doesn't always stay to the end'; Rivette, of course, always stayed to the end).

Bazin also secured a job for Truffaut at *Cahiers*, and Truffaut's landmark essay, 'A Certain Tendency in the French Cinema', appeared in issue 31 in January 1954 and became something of a rallying cry for the *Cahiers* group. In addition to attacking the moribund state of French filmmaking, the so-called 'tradition of quality', Truffaut also lambasted unfaithful literary adaptations, holding Bresson's *Diary of a Country Priest* to be one of the few successful examples. From 1956, Truffaut's tirades continued in a weekly column for the larger-circulation magazine *Arts*, which brought him wider notoriety. This was to culminate in his 1957 essay, 'You are Witnesses in this Trial: the French Cinema is Being Crushed Under the Weight of its False Legends', which was little short of a manifesto. It declared, amongst other things, that:

- The excuse of directors that they have no control over subject matter is cowardice.
- The crisis of French cinema is a lack of courage.
- One can make an excellent film for $10,000.
- Rossellini proves that risk pays.
- There are no bad films, only mediocre directors.
- Tomorrow's films will be made by adventurers.

This essay, together with a subsequent piece attacking Cannes, led to Truffaut's being banned from attending the 1958 festival. By that time, though, it didn't matter: Truffaut had already begun making short films, the best of them being *Les Mistons* (*The Brats*, 1957), about a group of boys obsessed with sabotaging the courtship of a young couple; it seems very much like a dry run for *The 400 Blows*. Truffaut also collaborated with Godard on *Histoire d'eau* (*The Story of Water*, 1958), an essay film about the floods of January 1958. And, perhaps in answer to Truffaut's call, government subsidies became available, encouraging producers to take more risks. In addition, the weakness of the franc in 1959 meant that French films were suddenly cheap for international distributors to pick up.

The 400 Blows (*Les Quatre Cent Coups*, 1959) was the first in what would become known as the Antoine Doinel cycle, which saw Truffaut work with his lead actor, Jean-Pierre Léaud, five times over the course of 20 years; they remain a landmark in world cinema. *The 400 Blows* owes much to Truffaut's own delinquent adolescence, with the rebellious Antoine turning against teachers, parents and social workers; the famous freeze-frame ending, showing Antoine looking directly in the camera, almost suggests that, although tired after his escapes from Paris and then borstal, he is still willing to take on all comers. The city itself is arguably the other star of the film: unlike the studio-bound 'cinéma du papa', Truffaut's camera glides through Paris, celebrating its streets and buildings in the thin wintery light. It is here – and in the famous schoolroom opening – that one senses Truffaut paying homage to Vigo. The rebellious boys – cinematic sons of Vigo's school rebels in *Zéro de Conduite* – also allow Truffaut to flex his comedic muscles, culminating in moments such as Antoine's excuse for missing a lesson due to his mother 'dying'. Needless to say, his mother is not amused to hear about this. What sets Truffaut's film apart from the 'certain tendency in French cinema', and which exemplified the New Wave spirit, is its lyrical humanism and the empathy it evokes for Antoine in the audience. Truffaut celebrates the rebellious Doinel, and does so without condemning him.

Truffaut once commented that 'a film director's total work is a diary kept over a lifetime'[21], a comment that would be apposite for the four sequels he would make over the next two decades, whose stories share much with Truffaut's own biography. He did not return to Antoine straightaway but, after making *Shoot the Piano Player* (*Tirez sur la pianiste*, 1960) and the celebrated *Jules and Jim* (*Jules et Jim*, 1962), Truffaut contributed a Doinel episode to the portmanteau feature *Love at Twenty* (*L'amour à vingt ans*; other directors included Andrzej Wajda). 'Antoine and Colette' recounts the story of Antoine's first love affair, and, after the confident, cocky character of *The 400 Blows*, Truffaut portrays him as an increasingly nervous and fumbling adolescent. His love for Colette, a musician, is not reciprocated; she treats him with indifference and is the first in a series of *femmes fatales* who would recur frequently in Truffaut's films of the 1960s. Although he loses the girl, Antoine gains her family: Colette's parents become his surrogate parents by the film's end. (In reality, these roles were played by André and Janine Bazin.)

Stolen Kisses (*Baisers Volés*, 1968) shows Antoine finishing his military service and becoming a private detective, and continuing his romantic pursuits (including visits to a prostitute). The film marks the end of the congruence with Truffaut's own life, and sees Léaud contributing more to the character of Antoine. Its follow up, *Bed & Board* (*Domicile Conjugal*, 1970), was more openly farcical: Antoine sets up another doomed business (as a flower dyer, 'improving' nature), then gets married and fathers a child, only to leave his wife for an enigmatic Japanese woman who declares, 'If I ever commit suicide with someone, I'd like it to be you.' Antoine returns to his wife.

The final film in the cycle, *Love on the Run* (*L'amour en fuite* 1979), uses outtakes from the earlier films to deepen the sense of real time passing and loss (something Truffaut had explored in his previous film, *The Green Room* [*Le chambre vert*, 1978]). Although perhaps the weakest of the four Doinel features, its elegiac tone suggests that Truffaut knew his own glory days, and those of the New Wave, were long gone. He and Antoine had grown up, cinema had changed, and 1959 suddenly seemed like a very long time ago.

The reference in *The 400 Blows* to cinema – Antoine steals a poster of Ingmar Bergman's muse Harriet Andersson – is arguably Truffaut's first onscreen acknowledgement of his own cinéphilia. Indeed, aside from the Doinel films and *Jules et Jim*, he would spend most of the remaining decade concentrating on genre films, all bar one of which were films noirs: *Shoot the Piano Player* (*Tirez sur le pianiste*, 1960), *The Soft Skin* (*La Peau Douce*, 1964), *The Bride Wore Black* (*La Mariée était en noir*, 1968) and *Mississippi Mermaid* (*La Sirène du Mississippi*, 1969); the exception was an adaptation of Ray Bradbury's classic science-fiction novel *Fahrenheit 451* (1966). One could argue that Truffaut's own light touch was in itself a genre – a trademark, certainly – and the relative lack of success, both critically and commercially, of his genre films seems to have signalled the end of this phase of his career.

But it would be a mistake to dismiss them: genre was, after all, one of the keystones of the *politique des auteurs*, and Truffaut's 1960s' films can be seen as a prolonged dialogue with genre, but a very different one to that conducted by Godard. Indeed, not wishing to be typecast as an 'autobiographical' director, the first thing Truffaut did after his initial success was to make *Shoot the Piano Player*, which both adheres to the genre of the detective film and also undercuts it through the use of stylistic devices not normally associated with noirs, such as handheld camerawork that sometimes lets its characters leave the frame as if by accident and comedic interludes in the plotting (Charlie taking so long to ask Léna out for a drink that, by the time he does so, she has gone off with someone else). Such generic revisions would be a feature of the later films as well.

In addition to the genre films, Truffaut also authored a book on Hitchcock, *Le Cinéma selon Hitchcock* (1966). (An English version was published as *Hitchcock-Truffaut* the following year.) Unlike the book on Hitchcock by Rohmer and Chabrol, Truffaut's took the form of an extended interview that revealed as much about himself as about Hitchcock. He groups Hitchcock with Chaplin, von Stroheim and Lubitsch – who for him represent the 'era of quality' as much as Renoir did – and praises the master of suspense for undertaking to 'delve into [cinema's] potential, and to work out its rules, rules more demanding than those pertaining to the writing of a novel'.[22]

Hitchcock is also important for the simple reason that it is a book: they were almost as important to Truffaut as films, and he celebrates their ability to captivate and inspire. Antoine writes an essay about Balzac in *The 400 Blows* and, later, in his enthusiasm for the writer, lights a candle to him that nearly burns down the house, while in *Fahrenheit 451* books symbolise revolt against the system and hope for the future. *Jules and Jim* (*Jules et Jim*, 1962), Truffaut's celebrated film of a three-way love affair, was based on one of his favourite novels, by Henri-Pierre Roché. Obsessed with also filming Roché's only other novel, Truffaut finally did so a decade later with *Anne and Muriel* (*Les Deux Anglaises et le continent*, 1971), a film that owed something to Welles's *The Magnificent Ambersons* (1942) with its concerns about regret and loss. Later films *Such a Gorgeous Kid Like Me* (*Une Belle Fille comme moi*, 1972) and *The Story of Adèle H* (*L'histoire d'Adèle H*, 1975) reveal the ability of the written word to oppress and imprison; Truffaut might have been a romantic, but he was not a naive one.

The end of the 1960s saw the end of Truffaut's explorations of genre.[23] The new decade brought a remarkable study of adult-child relationships in *The Wild Child* (*L'Enfant sauvage*, 1970), in which a feral boy (Jean-Pierre Cargol) is brought up by Doctor Itard (played by Truffaut himself). The boy finds the stability that always eludes Antoine Doinel; perhaps in tacit recognition of this, Truffaut dedicated the film to Jean-

Pierre Léaud. In 1973, Truffaut celebrated cinema once more, although this time not with a genre film. *Day for Night (La nuit americaine)*[24] follows the shooting of *Meet Pamela*, a melodrama positively reeking of *fromage*. Truffaut again stars – as the director, naturally – and the film also features Léaud in a rare non-Doinel role. If any one film of the New Wave shows their collective love of cinema, it is *Day for Night*. Truffaut said that films and filmmaking provided him with the family he never had as a child, and watching this almost effortlessly joyous film – which ranks alongside *The 400 Blows* and *Jules and Jim* as one of his masterpieces – one easily understands why. The film also won Truffaut an Oscar, for Best Foreign Language Film.

Jean-Luc Godard

Although Godard's name, like that of Truffaut, is synonymous with the New Wave, the two filmmakers had little in common other than their apprenticeship at the Cinémathèque and *Cahiers*. As Kristin Thompson and David Bordwell note, 'Truffaut and Godard usefully define the poles of the New Wave. One proved that young cinema could rejuvenate mainstream filmmaking; the other that the new generation could be hostile to the comfort and pleasure of ordinary cinema.'[25] Such hostility would be more marked in Godard's work as the 1960s wore on and, by the mid-1970s, had retreated from 'ordinary cinema' altogether. By that time, Godard had proved himself one of the most influential of all filmmakers, and his work had been compared to a variety of canonical artists, from Picasso to Joyce to Schoenberg.

Godard started as a critic, and he is perhaps best appreciated as the New Wave's premier critic-philosopher. Beginning in 1950, he wrote for various magazines, including *Cahiers* and a small magazine, *Les Amis du Cinema*, and, from 1956, also for the larger-circulation *Arts*. Although his criticism from this period was overshadowed by the more high-profile – and volatile – pieces written by Truffaut, the essays Godard wrote for these magazines reveal him as already trying to get to grips with what cinema actually is, how filmmakers construct meaning, and the symbiotic relationship between a film and its audience. In addition to the theories that were then being trashed out by his fellow Young Turks, Godard's thinking was also influenced by ethnology and semiotics, while his style was often poetic, gnomic and hermetic. An early essay, 'Towards a Political Cinema',[26] is a case in point: whilst discussing recent Soviet cinema, Godard quotes Rimbaud, alludes to Racine and brings in the structuralist philosopher Brice Parain in a footnote. Such density would be repeated in Godard's cinema: as he notes in this article, 'a political cinema is always rooted in repetition'.[27]

This is not to suggest that Godard was repeating himself as a result of a paucity of ideas, rather the opposite, that he was struggling to articulate the problems that faced anyone trying to make films that were at once new and relevant to the times they were made in, whilst also acknowledging the history of cinema and the forces that shaped it. Over time, Godard cultivated the image of an iconoclast and agitator, coming out with numerous statements, such as 'a film should have a beginning, a middle, and an end... but not necessarily in that order', 'the cinema is truth twenty-four times per second' and 'all you need for a movie is a girl and a gun'.

Godard's landmark first feature, *Breathless* (*A bout de souffle*, 1960), was precisely that. In telling the story of the small-time gangster, Michel (Jean-Paul Belmondo), and his relationship with an archetypal American in Paris, Patricia (Jean Seberg), Godard manages to '[synthesise] film-aesthetic currents as different as neorealist naturalism and B-movie melodramatics'.[28] The neorealism is embodied in scenes of Michel and Patricia walking through Paris or joking in her apartment, the B-movie melodrama in Michel's fondness for cliché – 'Don't move or I'll shoot!' – and in his killing of the traffic cop and theft of the car. The film is both iconic and ironic: Michel models himself on Humphrey Bogart (specifically Bogart's signature noir roles such as Sam Spade, Rick Blaine and Philip Marlowe) and acts as if he were conscious of being the lead in a movie, which of course he is. Godard pays further homage to 1940s America in cinema by dedicating *Breathless* to Monogram Pictures, who produced such films as *Cosmo Jones*, *Crime Smasher*, *I Killed That Man* and *Suspense*;[29] in so doing, he was acknowledging where film had been, but was also pointing in the direction that it could go in the future by using innovative techniques such as jump cutting and getting performances out of Belmondo and Seberg that were at once spontaneous and self-conscious.

Godard's production methods also took cues from his colleagues Truffaut and Chabrol, both of whom had already made the move into directing features by the time *Breathless* was shot in the August and September of 1959. The script – such as it was – was based on an outline written by Truffaut, who at one time considered it as a possible sequel to *The 400 Blows*,[30] while Chabrol lent his name to the project as 'technical advisor', giving the project the credibility that producer Georges de Beauregard required. As Richard Neupert notes, 'The mode of production for *Breathless* was more unconventional and "personal" even than most of its contemporaries,' with improvisation '[affecting] every aspect of the *mise-en-scène*'.[31] The script stuck surprisingly close to Truffaut's outline, although Godard arrived on set every day with notes written down on scraps of paper rather than a full script, asking Belmondo and Seberg to do a lot of improvising around his notes. (So much so that they began to suspect that 'Godard had no idea what he was doing'.[32])

Although lightweight Nagra sound recorders were by then in use, enabling filmmakers to shoot sync sound with handheld cameras, Godard and his cinematographer Raoul Coutard elected to shoot most of the film silent, and with a skeleton crew. There was no tripod, no lights, and, for tracking shots, Coutard was pushed in a wheelchair or even a mail pushcart. As he himself later noted, 'Little by little we discovered a need to escape from convention and even run counter to the rules of "cinematographic grammar".'[33] Such a need to escape from convention even extended to the choice of stock the film was shot on: Godard and Coutard used a fast Ilford stock that was designed for still cameras, forcing Coutard to make up all the spools himself. 'The goal was to capture a rough documentary quality, following the characters as if Coutard were a reporter out to get a story.'[34]

The way the film was edited broke new ground as well, with Godard famously opting to use the jump cut on a number of occasions in the film, the one stylistic device that the film is most associated with. Going against traditional filmmaking methods, Godard's images jump from one moment to the next, without a matching break in the soundtrack, thus stressing style at the expense of realism. Various theories have been put forward as to why Godard chose to use the jump cut. Detractors claimed that Godard knew the film to be second-rate, and decided to put in the jump cuts in an attempt to either sabotage it completely, or to try and save it from a critical mauling.[35] The film's supporters argued that the cuts were visual expressions of Poiccard's state of mind, his innate restlessness and propensity for casual violence, or an attempt to bring a new sensibility to cinematic form. (The film has been compared to both jazz and cubism.) Godard himself claimed that the film was simply too long in its original version, and they introduced the jump cuts as a solution to both shorten the film and to make it stylistically interesting.

There were additional aspects of *Breathless* that announced it as something new. While improvised dialogue itself was not new, the extent to which the dialogue was improvised here (especially for a feature-length film) was unprecedented. Godard critic David Sterritt sees an affinity with the Beat Generation, who championed improvisation as a key creative method, while Robert Frank shot *Pull My Daisy* – with an improvised narration by Jack Kerouac – at around the same time as Godard shot *Breathless*.[36] The story itself, although linear, has numerous gaps between scenes, and it's impossible to tell how much time has elapsed between one scene and another, such as when Michel shoots the traffic cop on the country road: the next scene has him in Paris, as if Godard is suggesting we don't need to know what happened between the two scenes, or is inviting us to invent something of our own. Likewise, many of the scenes in the film have an 'unfinished' quality to them – perhaps a result of the improvising, but maybe also due to Godard's editing – that do not rely on traditional dramatic development or characterisation. Richard Neupert's description of *Breathless* as being made up of 'incomplete shards of action'[37] summarises Godard's approach very well. He also draws attention to the fact that not only are the characters not fully fleshed out, but also that their actions often remain unjustified. ('The characters remain fascinatingly complex and incomplete.'[38]) Furthermore, the characters' eyelines frequently don't match, giving the sense that they are not communicating with each other, or are in a space which remains opaque to the viewer. Continuity is 'rejected in favour of discontinuity',[39] the 'soundtrack is emphasised as an artificial construction'[40] in the sense that, when a jump cut is used, the soundtrack doesn't have a matching jump, thereby reminding the viewer that what they are seeing is wholly artificial. 'Style disrupts rather than clarifies Godard's story,'[41] continues Neupert, who also notes that, 'The result would prove stunningly "unprofessional" to some critics but historically monumental to others.'[42]

Breathless was released on 16 March 1960, and was a huge commercial success. As James Monaco points out, '*The 400 Blows* was fresh and new but it was also perceived to exist within certain broad traditions. *Breathless*, on the other hand, was clearly revolutionary';[43] the film's release was a decisive moment in French, New Wave and, indeed, world cinema. For many people, especially other filmmakers, things would never quite be the same again. Godard would continue to carve his own singular niche as filmmaker-theorist-agitator, but would never again enjoy the success that he did with his first feature. But such was the impact of *Breathless* that perhaps he didn't need to. The lines between *le cinéma du papa* and the New Wave had clearly been drawn; Godard had thrown the gauntlet down.

Claude Chabrol

Genre fascinated Truffaut and Godard. Truffaut was respectful; Godard's approach, on the other hand, involved liberal amounts of irony and iconoclasm. Claude Chabrol was the revisionist and classicist in the *Cahiers* group.

American films had been a major concern for the *Cahiers* directors, citing Welles, Hawks and Ray – to name but three – as authors and poets; auteurs. Hitchcock, too, came to obsess them, with Chabrol collaborating with Eric Rohmer on a book about him, published in 1957 (Chabrol covered Hitchcock's English period). Chabrol was the first of the *Cahiers* group to get a feature off the ground, with *Le Beau Serge* (*Handsome Serge*, 1958), which was funded independently, with money his wife inherited. (It also received money from the CNC, as subsidy rules had just been changed.) The film won a prize at the Locarno Film Festival in 1958, and it did good business when it was released in February 1959. By then, Chabrol had shot his second feature, *Les Cousins*, which was released a mere month later. That, too, was a box-office hit, and Chabrol was able to help other rising directors get their own films made, producing shorts for Rivette and Rohmer, as well as their first features.

Le Beau Serge is, in many ways, atypical Chabrol. It was shot in the village he grew up in, 150 miles south of Paris, and follows François (Jean-Claude Brialy) as he returns to the village to recover from illness. He is shocked to see that his old friend Serge (Gerard Blain) has fallen on hard times. Serge and his wife have had a Downs Syndrome child which died; now his wife is pregnant again, Serge fears that the new baby will be similarly afflicted, and turns to drink. The film immediately calls attention to its use of real locations in an opening title which informs us that it was shot entirely 'in the parish of Sardent', a fact which earned the film praise when it was released. The film's use of non-professionals (many villagers take the smaller roles in the film) and the 'socially conscious' elements of the script (Serge's alcoholism, the loss of a disabled child) were also singled out for praise. On the basis of *Le Beau Serge*, it could have been assumed that Chabrol was masterminding a French revival of neorealism, but his second film put paid to that idea once and for all.

Les Cousins (*The Cousins*, 1959) once again features Brialy and Blain, but this time the situation is reversed: Blain's country boy comes to the city to study law, and falls in with Paul (Brialy), a bohemian student. Chabrol adds significant new elements, which were to become his trademarks: a love triangle is introduced in the shape of Juliette Mayniel's character, the milieu is definitely bourgeois, and a murder is committed. Chabrol would return to these elements time and time again, even using the same character names (Charles and Paul, with the female character usually being called *Hélène*.)

Despite the success of these early films, a string of flops in the early 1960s – both his own films and also ones he had produced, such as the debut features by Rivette and Rohmer – led to the forced sale of AJYM, his production company, and Chabrol opted to work as a jobbing director; better to be making a bad film than no film at all, he reasoned. *Variety* picked up on this and declared in a headline 'Vital to Keep Making Pictures, and What Sort Not Relevant; Chabrol No "Doctrinaire" Type'.[44] *Cahiers* – then under the editorship of Jacques

Rivette – was aghast at the prospect of one of the key players in the New Wave selling out and making commercial dreck, and didn't interview Chabrol again until 1982. And bad films there were – most of his 'hired hand' period from 1964 to 1967 is fairly silly – spy spoofs in the main – and it is to Chabrol's credit that he took it all in his stride, describing the films of these years as 'drivel' and admitting that, if he was being paid to make drivel, he would give the producers all the drivel they could hope for; as Chabrol himself said, 'Let's not do things by halves.'[45]

Arguably the best of this period was a Second World War movie called *La Ligne de demarcation* (1966), which was written by a former Resistance fighter by the name of Colonel Rémy. Chabrol realised too late that the Colonel was, as he tactfully put it, 'a man of the right', and 'one of the most appalling characters I know', who believed that the real troublemakers were the Gestapo, while the Wehrmacht 'was very fair'. To make matters worse, Rémy frequently visited the set to helpfully provide Chabrol with modifications to the script that would help serve his Gestapo theory. 'The only effort I had to make,' Chabrol later explained, 'was to stop the film from turning into German propaganda,' and he decided the most tactful way to appease the Colonel was to shoot some of the new 'German propaganda' scenes with no film loaded in the camera. Rémy was satisfied, and Chabrol delivered the picture. Perhaps as a coping strategy, he also directed most of the film drunk.[46]

Chabrol bounced back in 1968, the year France underwent meltdown. With overtones of Hitchcock and Lang, and an obsession with the after effects of murder rather than the crime itself, Chabrol would really hit his stride with a series of ten films made between 1968 and 1973 that have been dubbed his 'Decameron' (although sometimes they are referred to as the 'Hélène Cycle', given the recurrences of the name – one of Chabrol's favourites – in the series). Amongst them are *Les Biches* (*The Does, The Girlfriends*, 1968), *La Femme infidèle* (*The Unfaithful Wife*, 1968), *Le Boucher* (*The Butcher*, 1969), *La Rupture* (*The Rupture* 1970), *Juste avant la nuit* (*Just Before Nightfall*, 1971) and *La Décade prodigieuse* (*Ten Days' Wonder*, 1972). Chabrol found his mature style in these films, his style being 'not only self-conscious but spring[ing] from past film traditions as he mixes genres, authorial and intertextual reference... to create a new mixture for film language. And that is certainly one central aesthetic trait for defining a New Wave film.'[47]

The combination of a bourgeois milieu for many of these films, the mid-sixties potboilers that preceded them and Chabrol's own ambiguous political affiliations led to a number of critics being confused as to his importance as a filmmaker. As a producer, he was invaluable in getting the New Wave off the ground as a commercial viability; as a director, he has played the role of a trickster, ready to reveal the shortcomings not only of the bourgeoisie but also of the entrenched critical positions that were unable to appreciate Chabrol's diversity and his self-proclaimed love of 'reveal[ing] opacity'.[48] But this opacity often hides Chabrol's 'unwilling[ness] to affirm belief in anything: [he] rejects the bourgeois world yet finds all alternatives empty and ridiculous'.[49]

Chabrol took this bleak worldview into the mainstream. It was, after all, mainstream Hollywood directors such as Howard Hawks who had inspired the *Cahiers* group in the first place. And, like Truffaut, he was not content to make elitist fare for a small audience, but wanted to remake French cinema, to reinstate the quality of Renoir or Hitchcock at their peak. And at what better time to begin remaking the national cinema than when the old guard – the Colonel Rémys of this world – was apparently in dire trouble and about to breathe its last? Chabrol, like Truffaut and Godard, was caught up in the events of 1968, becoming actively involved in the Etats-Généraux du Cinéma, a cross-industry group formed to discuss the ramifications of the sacking of Langlois as head of the Cinémathèque in February of that year. 'Not a few historical commentators regard those February demonstrations as the first manifestation of the spirit that was to bloom in May and June of that year,' James Monaco later wrote. 'A political revolution had begun with an argument over film! That is another reason why the New Wave is important.'[50]

Eric Rohmer

Eric Rohmer was the most secretive of the *Cahiers* directors (although Rivette was almost equally self-effacing), so secretive that, as the story goes, his own mother did not know he was an award-winning filmmaker for many years. His date of birth is likewise unknown, although the generally accepted year is 1920. And Eric Rohmer was not his real name: he was born Jean-Marie Maurice Schérer, his pseudonym being a conflation of the names of two of his heroes, film director Erich von Stroheim and *Fu Manchu* writer Sax Rohmer. In fact, it is his second pseudonym, having first been 'Gilbert Cordier', under which name he wrote a novel, *Les Vacances*, in 1946.[51] As with the other *Cahiers* directors, he began by writing film reviews, then joined the staff at *Cahiers*, eventually editing the magazine from 1957 to 1963. He made a series of self-funded shorts during the 1950s, before making his feature debut in 1959 with *La Signe du Lion* (*The Sign of Leo*), which was produced by Chabrol's production company, AJYM Films. This was their second major collaboration, the first having been a book on Hitchcock that was published in 1957, predating Truffaut's by nearly a decade.

La Signe du Lion, unlike the first features by Truffaut, Godard and Chabrol, was not well received. And also unlike them, Rohmer showed Paris as a squalid city in which desperate people eke out desperate lives, centring around the figure of Pierre, a composer who, when he doesn't receive his expected inheritance, is forced out into the streets. Much of the film follows Pierre as he tramps his way around the city, sinking into a seemingly irreversible decline. He ends up as one half of a song-and-dance act with a tramp; these scenes would not have looked out of place in Renoir. Character and place – two of Rohmer's major preoccupations – are evident here: as with *The 400 Blows*, *Breathless* and *Paris nous appartient*, the city itself is a character, here seen during the August heat (the title being a reference to the astrological sign), and it is against this backdrop that Rohmer observes the chatter of Pierre and his circle. Talk is important for Rohmer: his characters endlessly debate their actions and motives, and reflect his interest in literature and philosophy. (In this sense, he resembles Godard and, to a lesser extent, Truffaut, while seeming to adopt a position opposite to Chabrol's.)

Pierre's struggles to survive almost seem to foreshadow Rohmer's own: Chabrol was forced to sell AJYM, and Rohmer's film was caught in the middle, ending up being recut and rescored, finally seeing a release in 1962. Rohmer was forced to return to making shorts for the best part of the next decade, in addition to working as a jobbing director in educational television. Perhaps most importantly during this period, which must not have been easy for Rohmer, he began working with the producer Barbet Schroeder and his company Les Films du Losange, which produced the six shorts Rohmer made after the critical and commercial failure of *La Signe*, two of which began a series entitled *Six Moral Tales*, which would establish his reputation. (The New Wave, for all their auteurist assumptions, needed equally talented producers to get their films off the ground, and in such figures as Schroeder, Georges de Beauregard and Chabrol himself, happily got them.)

The 'Moral Tales', or '*Contes Moraux*', all have the same basic premise: a man in a relationship becomes infatuated with another woman, is forced to choose between the two, ultimately returning to his original partner. The first film, *La Boulangère de Monceau* (*The Girl at the Monceau Bakery*, 1962), is relatively straightforward: a young man (played by Schroeder) becomes infatuated with a girl he sees in the street one day. In the course of trying to find her again, the girl at the bakery he frequents becomes interested in him. Just when they have arranged a date, the first girl reappears and things between Schroeder's character and the bakery girl finish abruptly. *La Carrière de Suzanne* (*Suzanne's Career*, 1963), the second in the series (which really shouldn't be classed as a short, as it runs for an hour) is a more complex work, revolving around the relationship between two students, Bertrand and Guillame, and their interest in two girls, Suzanne and Sophie. Bertrand's interest in both girls remains unrequited, and the film ends with him realising, in a voiceover, that Suzanne has made him look foolish.

Although *Suzanne's Career* seems very much like prentice work, the use of voiceover was a key device for Rohmer, and helps explain why the series is called *Six Moral Tales*. As he explains, 'moral' is based on the French word *moraliste*, which doesn't have an equivalent in English:

It doesn't really have much connection with the word 'moral'. A *moraliste* is someone who is interested in the description of what goes on inside man. He's concerned with states of mind and feelings... So *Contes Moraux* doesn't mean that there's a moral contained in them, even though there might be one... But 'moral' can also mean that they are people who like to bring their motives, the reasons for their actions, into the open... They are not people who act without thinking about what they are doing. What matters is what they think about their behaviour, rather than their behaviour itself. They aren't films... in which physical action takes place, they aren't films in which there is anything very dramatic, they are films in which a particular feeling is analysed... That's what *Conte Moral* means.[52]

After a four-year gap – a period spent working in television – Rohmer intended to return to the series with *Ma Nuit Chez Maud* (*My Night at Maud's*). However, Jean-Louis Trintignant was not available for a year, so Rohmer decided to make the fourth Moral Tale, *La Collectionneuse* (*The Collector*, 1967), instead. The film centres around the love triangle between Adrien, Daniel and Haydée, the collector of the title (she collects men). Here the variation on the central theme is generational: the bohemian Haydée is younger than Adrien, who is very much a product of the bourgeoisie (he's an art dealer). There was also something of Haydée in the way the film was made: cast and crew lived together in the house in St Tropez where the story takes place, with everyone working for a percentage.[53] This was a practical necessity, as the film was financed entirely from the sale to television of two of Rohmer's non-Moral shorts, which gave them a very limited budget; they were also shooting in colour and on 35mm for the first time. The gamble paid off: *La Collectionneuse* was Rohmer's first major critical success, winning a prize at the Berlin Film Festival, and paving the way for the even greater success of *Ma Nuit Chez Maud*, which was premiered at Cannes in 1969.

Maud is the centrepiece of the series, and also the most thoughtful. The nameless narrator (Jean-Louis Trintignant) is introduced by his Marxist friend Vidal (Antoine Vitez) to Maud (Françoise Fabian), a beautiful recluse. Here the triangle is not one of love, but of intellect:

the narrator and Vidal discuss Pascal's wager – we can't be sure God exists, so it's better to hedge our bets and live as though he does, having everything to gain and nothing to lose – which in turn becomes a theoretical underpinning for the rest of the series. The narrator and Maud spend the winter's evening on which the film takes place (it is the only film in the series to take place in winter) talking about love (she's divorced, he's about to marry), religion (he's a Catholic, she's an atheist) and the nature of emotional commitment. At the end of the film, the narrator marries Françoise (Marie-Christine Barrault), a girl he met in church. Overall he seems less wise than Maud, who is the first of the series' women to be stronger and more mature than the man. Indeed, the narrator seems to have a very different opinion of himself to that which he presents to Maud and the viewer, and it is here that Rohmer makes the *Ma Nuit Chez Maud* (and the other *Contes Moraux*) more than mere filmed conversations, as the director explains:

> There is another factor that obliged me from the start to clothe the tales in literary garb. Here, literature – and this is my principal excuse – belongs less to form than to content. My intention was not to film raw, unvarnished events, but the *narrative* that someone makes of them. The story, the choice of facts, their organisation... not the treatment that I could have made them submit to. One of the reasons that these tales are called 'Moral' is that physical actions are almost completely absent: everything happens in the head of the narrator.[54]

The final two films in the series, *Le Genou de Claire* (*Claire's Knee*, 1970) and *L'amour, l'après-midi* (*Love in the Afternoon/Chloë in the Afternoon*, 1972) continue Rohmer's preoccupation with their narrators, and the versions they give of their relationships with the women they encounter. *Claire* features Jean-Claude Brialy (along with *Maud*, this is the only *Tale* to feature professional actors) as a middle-aged man who develops a crush on a teenage schoolgirl, in particular her knee. The ghost of Pascal lurks: Brialy's character knows how little control he has over his own life and passions, making his obsession with Claire and touching her knee all the more absurd.

Jacques Rivette

Like Rohmer, Jacques Rivette seemed to miss the boat of the first years of the New Wave and, also like Rohmer, didn't really find his feet until the late 1960s. This is ironic, as Truffaut acknowledged that 'without Rivette there would be no New Wave.' Godard, too, had a high regard for their reclusive colleague, saying in 1970:

> Someone like Rivette, who knows cinema so much better than I, shoots seldom, so that people don't speak of him... If he had made ten films, he would have gone much further than I.[55]

Rivette was the first of the *Cahiers* group to start making films; *Quadrille*, an early effort, focused for its 40 or so minutes on the people in a dentist's waiting room. There was no plot, no dialogue, just place and duration (themes that Rivette would return to); it also featured the acting talents of a young Jean-Luc Godard. His most important short, *Le Coup du Berger*, was made in 1956, with Chabrol producing. A simple love triangle is couched in chess metaphors, signs of the playful intellectualism that was to come in Rivette's features. Aside from being a near-permanent fixture at the Cinémathèque, Rivette wrote for *Cahiers*, worked as assistant to Jacques Becker and Jean Renoir, and shot early short films for Truffaut and Rohmer.

Rivette began shooting his first feature, *Paris nous appartient* (*Paris Belongs to Us*), in the summer of 1958. The film was shot piecemeal as and when stock, cast and locations became available. (The fact that the theatrical troupe in the film doesn't rehearse in the same place twice reflects this on-the-run approach to shooting.) When stock finally ran out, with the film still incomplete, Chabrol donated unused stock from *Les Cousins*. The film was finally completed in 1960, but had to wait until late the following year for a premiere. The film is somewhere between Rohmer, in its depiction of the 'other Paris' in the plot concerning a troupe of actors struggling to put on a production of *Pericles*, and early Godard with its story of a sinister world conspiracy. As with Rohmer, much of the plot seems to be going on in the characters' heads, in particular Gérard, the paranoid theatre director, who fears the conspiracy the most. The film met with a divided response when it appeared, although it was not without supporters:

> The life of Paris, in a cinematic sense, is put in a new light. For the first time, the stones and the streets have a secret grace which is that of the imaginary... Except with Bresson, the connection between image and sound has never been so striking, evocative or necessary.[56]

Rivette's second feature, La *Religieuse* (1966), was based on Diderot and starred Anna Karina as a nun, stifled in one convent, and then apparently liberated in another. It is this second convent, however, with its lesbian mother superior, which kills Karina's character off. The film was banned by the French government – surely such things never happened in convents – but, when the ban was lifted, it became one of Rivette's most successful films. It marks the first time a woman was the central character in a Rivette film; women would come to play central roles in many of his later features.

Rivette found his feet with his third feature, *L'amour fou* (1968). Unlike Godard, who wanted to dismantle traditional cinema by first establishing a theoretical (and later political) position, Rivette's cinematic discoveries seem to have come about through the process of improvisation. One thing the two filmmakers did have in common was in looking back to the Soviet formalists for inspiration, as Rivette explains:

> In my idea of cinema, all the stages should be totally interacting. I want to return, though with quite different methods, aims and end products, to the old Dziga-Vertov idea: that the montage should be conceived with the project and not merely with the exposed film. This may sound like a conceit, but you could say that the script is written in the montage, and that the montage is established before shooting.[57]

L'amour fou was the first product of this method. It charts the downward path of a couple, Claire (Bulle Ogier) and Sébastien (Jean-Pierre Kalfon), who are part of an actors' group rehearsing Racine's *Andromaque*. Inspired by his idea of a film evolving with all the elements interacting, Rivette let Kalfon direct the actors who are involved with the Racine; a second 'free' element took the shape of a 16mm TV crew, who film the rehearsals. Rivette then cuts between 'reality' (35mm, a largely static camera) and the rehearsal (16mm, handheld). Occasionally one format comments on the other, but Rivette was careful not to let the Racine footage comment too directly on the 'reality' scenes, especially once Claire quits and goes home.

The final element in Rivette's mature style was length. Even as early as *Quadrille*, he had been fascinated by the idea that 'nothing takes place but the place', and here his cameras watch Claire and Sébastien's marriage implode for four and a quarter hours. (The final scene in their apartment is a full hour in itself.) Rivette's belief is that, after a certain period, the audience, if it hasn't walked out, will give up fighting the film and become completely immersed in it. It will be then up to the audience to work out what is going on and, in Rivette, that essentially means solving a mystery. Mystery for Rivette is not a question of Agatha Christie plots; rather, he sees mystery as being inherently linked to the art of fiction, as plots will always leave us wondering what will happen next.

Duration, mystery and collaboration with his actors would be taken to extremes in his next film, *Out 1* (1971), which features two theatrical troupes, a conspiracy about a mysterious cabal of thirteen and a strange hippy boutique which functions as a sort of magic toyshop or phantom tollbooth. The film, shot on 16mm in just six weeks, stars Jean-Pierre Léaud, Juliet Berto, Michael Lonsdale, Bulle Ogier, Bernadette Lafont, Françoise Fabian and Michèle Moretti, and originally ran for over 12½ hours, having been conceived as a TV series. French television balked at such an elephantine monstrosity, and the original cut was only shown once[58] before Rivette decided to bring in a new editor and construct a shorter version. The result, *Out 1: Spectre* (1972), runs a mere four and a quarter hours, and concentrates less on the rehearsal sequences,[59] and more on the conspiracy, which is triggered when Léaud's fake deaf mute hustler, Colin, begins to receive mysterious messages that allude to both Balzac (*The History of the Thirteen*) and Lewis Carroll (*The Hunting of the Snark*). He tries to work out what is going on – do the mysterious thirteen exist in secret behind the scenes? Is the shop where Bulle Ogier's character works, called the Angle of Chance, actually a front for them? Will the two plays being rehearsed ever be performed? – but ultimately nothing is solved. However, Colin remains certain that there is *something* mysterious going on, despite his inability to fathom quite what. '[If the conspiracy didn't exist then] the magic world in which I live would suddenly grow dim!' At the end of the film, Bulle Ogier discovers a room full of mirrors; the film then finishes on shots of the deserted Place d'Italie in Paris. As with the empty stage that finished *L'amour fou*, it is as though Rivette is finally showing us the empty-yet-full totality out of which all fictions emerge: the world in which we live, and the places we inhabit. We tell stories about them – or do they about us? We can never be sure, but this quiet conundrum – one could almost call it mysticism of a sort, Zen perhaps – lies at the bedrock of Rivette's best films, and it would certainly be present in his next film, arguably his masterpiece.

Céline and Julie Go Boating (*Céline et Julie vont en bateau*, 1974) came into being suddenly, when a higher-budget project, *Phénix*, fell through.[60] Again involving his lead actors, Juliet Berto and Dominique Labourier, from the beginning Rivette came up with a delightful shaggy dog story about a librarian, Julie (Labourier), who befriends Céline, a magician (Berto). Céline reveals that she has been working in a mysterious house, but she can only remember what took place inside the house after sucking a strange boiled sweet. After Julie visits the house, and sucks a sweet of her own, they determine that a little girl is in danger in the house (the events at the house being modelled on two Henry James stories, 'The Romance of Certain Old Clothes' and 'The Other House'). They enter the house at the same time and prevent the little girl from being murdered. Returning to their apartment, they find that the little girl, Madlyn, has followed them. They then take the boat trip of the title, and pass another boat in which are the adult characters from the house (one of whom is the film's producer, Barbet Schroeder). Reality and fiction have merged. Or have they? The very last scene is a doppelgänger of the first, only the roles are reversed: now Céline watches Julie hurry past, then we cut to a cat as enigmatic as Carroll's Cheshire Cat looking into the camera.

Despite its improvised feel, the film is full of references to literature (James, Carroll, Proust, Cocteau) and film (Hitchcock, the old serials of Louis Feuillade). Nicole Lubtchansky's tight editing forms the backbone of the film, a film which could be seen as an allegory of storytelling, and filmic storytelling in particular: Rivette originally thought of making Céline and Julie film editors, but decided this might be too prosaic/obvious. In this case, as in much of Rivette, it is a story – stories – controlled by women. This led to the film being hailed as a feminist classic, and also 'the most innovative film since *Citizen Kane*'.[61] Its concern for narrative processes, its method of production (collaborative, low budget), and its story of smart, self-determining women in Paris in the summer make *Céline and Julie* a late but significant entry into the New Wave canon.

THE LEFT BANK GROUP

While the *Cahiers* group formed the nucleus of the French New Wave, there was another loose-knit cabal which was dubbed the Left Bank Group. They had links with the New Novel – including such writers as Alain Robbe-Grillet and Marguerite Duras, who would move into directing, their films falling under the Left Bank umbrella – and were sometimes thought of as being more intellectual than their *Cahiers* counterparts, with both Alain Resnais and Chris Marker exploring new narrative structures, film form and the boundaries between fiction and documentary. (Marker will be discussed in the chapter on documentary.) However, it would be wrong to assume that the group consisted solely of highbrow intelligentsia: among their number was Jacques Demy, who would achieve success with *Les parapluies de Cherbourg* (*The Umbrellas of Cherbourg*, 1964), the definitive New Wave take on the Hollywood musical. The Left Bank Group were not only important filmmakers in their own right, but had also been there from the beginning, perhaps the most important of them being Alain Resnais, whose *Hiroshima mon amour* had been part of the New Wave's breakthrough at Cannes in 1959.

Resnais was already an established filmmaker long before that momentous Cannes. He knew Chris Marker and the two of them helped Bazin run ciné-clubs in the late 1940s. Resnais enjoyed early success with a documentary about Van Gogh – which won an Oscar in 1950 – and *Night and Fog* (*Nuit et brouillard*, 1955), his revered short documentary about Nazi concentration camps. Deciding early on that such subject matter would make for a harrowing film, Resnais chose instead to film the deserted camps as they appeared in the 1950s; his deadpan voiceover further added to the sense of distance Resnais felt was necessary for such an unfilmable subject. These stylistic innovations led to *Night and Fog* becoming a far more influential film than *Van Gogh*, despite the earlier film's Oscar success. During the mid-fifties, Resnais also worked as an editor, cutting early films by Agnès Varda and Truffaut and acting as adviser to Chabrol.[62]

Hiroshima mon amour (lit: Hiroshima My Love, 1959) began as a documentary about the atomic bomb, but evolved, once Duras was on board as scriptwiter, into a film about a love story between a French woman (Emmanuelle Riva) and a Japanese man (Eiji Okada). In many ways it is a classic Left Bank film in its handling of narrative structure and form: past and present are seamlessly intertwined, suggesting that the past still exists in the latter in many, largely unseen, ways ('The past shouldn't be in flashback,' the director once remarked) and Resnais incorporates documentary footage into the film that serves to mirror the fiction. Undercutting the passion between Riva's Elle and Okada's Lui (we are never given their names) is Resnais' detached observation of the horrors of the bomb, a detachment he had used to great effect in the narration of *Night and Fog*. It is as if the filmmaker is retiring from the action to let us take his place, to dip our hands through the cinema screen, *Orphée*-like, and feel both the characters' emotions and the burning skies over Japan in August 1945.

Resnais followed *Hiroshima mon amour* with the almost equally celebrated *Last Year at Marienbad* (*L'année dernière à Marienbad*, 1961), whose script was written by Robbe-Grillet. Again dispensing with chronological narrative, the film takes place in a dream-like state in which X (Giorgio Albertazzi) tries to convince A (Delphine Seyrig) that they had an affair the previous year. Resnais once again explores memory and the past, using techniques – a mobile camera, mirrors, a pervading sense of somnambulism, even though the characters are portrayed as 'awake' – that recalls expressionist cinema. *Muriel*

(1963) was again a collaboration with a writer associated with the New Novel, in this case Jean Cayrol (1911–2005). Here the central mystery revolves around the memories of Bernard (Jean-Baptiste Thierrée), and the atrocities he witnessed during the (then recently ended) Algerian war. Resnais employs rapid cutting to suggest that reality is a kaleidoscope of moments and memories, and that piecing them together comes at a price. Bernard's notebooks and his film-within-the-film keep him rooted in the past, much as the identities of the characters in *Hiroshima* and *Marienbad* are defined – or blurred – by their problematic relationship to the past. Time and space, identity and memory are the central enigmas in Resnais' cinematic universe.

For Jacques Demy (1931–90), the essence of cinema was to be found in genre. Whilst Chabrol and Truffaut spent much of the 1960s experimenting with genres such as thrillers, sci-fi and war movies, Demy had an entirely different approach to the problem. His love of musicals informs his first features *Lola* (1961) and *The Umbrellas of Cherbourg*, which won the Palme d'Or at Cannes in 1964. The film manages to be at once a loving nod towards Hollywood musicals, and also a convincing melodrama about the strained relationship between a couple (Catherine Deneuve and Nino Castelnuovo) separated by circumstance. Unusually for a musical, all the dialogue is sung. A third film, *Les Demoiselles de Rochefort* (*The Young Girls of Rochefort*, 1967), completes a loose trilogy.

Although Agnès Varda has distanced herself from the New Wave, the success of Truffaut and Godard certainly played a part in helping her get her second feature, *Cleo from 5 to 7* (*Cléo de 5 à 7*, 1962), made (the film was produced by Georges de Beauregard, who had produced *Breathless*). Cleo follows its main character (played by Corinne Marchand) as she waits for the results from an important medical examination. Presenting the story in almost real time, Marchand wanders around a Paris that is just as much in tension as her character: she witnesses an attack in a bar and meets a soldier who is just about to return to Algeria. A recurring theme in *Cleo* is female identity. Marchand's character is a pop singer, who is frequently shown checking her appearance in mirrors; she is defined and restricted by her image. To combat this, she goes out in disguise in the second half of the film, all the while observing and listening, and this is where the film's core arguably lies. 'Thus Cléo changes from object to be looked at to subject who looks and interprets what she looks at,' the critic Alison Smith has noted, 'from woman seen to woman seeing.'[63]

THE AUTHOR AS AUTEUR

The work of Resnais, Godard and Rivette reflected developments in the fiction of the time, in particular the New Novel, as exemplified by Resnais' sometime screenwriters, Alain Robbe-Grillet (1922–2008) and Marguerite Duras (1914–96), both of whom were associated with the Left Bank group.

Robbe-Grillet turned to directing after *Marienbad*, beginning with *L'Immortelle* (1963). As with the Resnais, the characters here are known only by letters – L, N and M – and the plot is not so much a story as a meditation on the possibilities of a narrative. L (Françoise Brion) and N (fellow *nouvelle vague* director Jacques Doniol-Valcroze) meet in Istanbul and seem to begin a relationship. But it is not the 'real' Istanbul but 'a Turkey of legend', as L says, to which N replies, 'As in books.' In later scenes they appear to be acknowledging that they are in either a film or a dream: at one point, L says, 'It's not a real scene,' while N comments on the scenery: 'What does it matter if these are not real houses?' The sense of unreality (or non-reality) only increases after L disappears. Desperate to find her again, N searches for L, only to be told that she never existed, or that her name is actually Madame Yak, or Lucille. When N seems to find L again in a marketplace, he – like the viewer – can never be sure if this L is the same as the first L. Narrative sense is further undermined when N is involved, with the new L, in a car crash. L is then seen laughing, but no laughter can be heard on the soundtrack. Did she survive the accident? Did she ever exist at all, or was she only a figment of N's imagination?

Such themes recur in Robbe-Grillet's other two great films of the 1960s, *Trans-Europ-Express* (1966) and *L'homme qui ment/Muž, ktorý luže* (*The Man Who Lies*, 1968). *Trans-Europ-Express* is Robbe-Grillet's take on a crime film in which a film director (played by Robbe-

Grillet himself) boards the Trans-Europ Express with his producer and assistant. They discuss making a film set on board a train, and start to develop a plot based on another passenger, whom they dub 'Elias' (Jean-Louis Trintignant) and imagine to be a drug smuggler. The twist comes when 'Elias' starts to behave in ways his creators have not anticipated, mainly due to his having an 'unforeseen' sado-masochistic relationship with a prostitute, Eva (Marie-France Pisier). In *The Man Who Lies*, it is even more difficult, if not impossible, to separate the real from the imagined. Set during World War II, a young man (Trintignant again) is apparently on the run from the Nazis in a forest. He takes refuge in a chateau with the three women who live there, claiming to be Jean Robin, a war hero and the missing husband of one of the women. 'Robin' starts to seduce all three women who, it transpires, are involved in a lesbian *ménage à trois*. 'Robin's' identity is never clearly established, and when the 'real' Robin appears, it leads to an elliptical resolution in which the story of the film appears to be repeating.

Robbe-Grillet went further than Godard and at least as far as Resnais and Rivette in undermining narrative conventions and expectations. It would be more accurate to describe Robbe-Grillet's films as games rather than as conventional stories, games that call our attention to the processes of fiction. Robbe-Grillet was as much a cinematic radical as he had been a literary one, in that he asserted that '*nothing* exists outside of the world of images. A satisfactory explanation of the events cannot be constructed because nothing happens prior to the first images on screen.'[64] These films or games require the active participation of the viewer in order to complete them. Robbe-Grillet believed that the most important character in a film was the spectator, because the spectator was the only person who could possibly make 'sense' of what he or she had just seen, a sense that was entirely personal. A film's plot happened entirely within the head of the spectator; it could not possibly be anything 'external', the way it is in traditional films, or the classic Hollywood narrative.

For Marguerite Duras also, narrative was never resolved as it is in traditional, patriarchal structures, and a number of her films were based on works from other media. *India Song* (1975), for example, started out as a play, drawing on elements from her novel *The Vice Consul* (1966) as did another of her films, *Woman of the Ganges* (1974), which itself spawned a third film, *Son nom de Venise dans Calcutta désert* (1976). As M B White comments, 'This process of transformation suggests that all works are "in progress", inherently subject to being reconstructed.'[65] Duras also challenges the patriarchal tendency towards ordered narratives by creating dichotomies between the sound and the image in her films. She achieved this by rarely using synch sound; voiceover instead predominates. Images on screen are referred to by the narrator in the past tense, immediately causing problems for the viewer who is trying to reconcile the 'present' of the images on the screen with the implied 'past' of the narration. 'In this way the audience participates in the search for a story, constructing possible narratives.'[66]

ON THE MARGINS, IN THE MIRRORS

A number of other directors fell outside both the core *Cahiers* and Left Bank groups. Louis Malle (1932–95) worked as an assistant to both Bresson and oceanographer Jacques Cousteau before making his feature debut with *Lift to the Scaffold* (*Ascenseur pour L'Echafaud*, 1957), an ingenious thriller centred around one main location – a lift. (Or, rather, a man trapped in one.) He tested the bounds of censorship with *Les Amants* (*The Lovers*, 1958), in which Jeanne Moreau's character enjoys her lover performing cunnilingus on her, and made a gripping portrayal of a man in acute mental and physical decline in *Le Feu Follet* (*The Fire Within*, 1963).

Jacques Rozier's *Adieu Philippine* (1962) was hailed by Alain Resnais as 'a masterpiece worthy of Jean Vigo'.[67] The film was typically new wave in its approach, with its loose script, casual style, modern themes and fresh acting style; *Cahiers* held it up as the model New Wave film. As with their links to the New Novel, so the French New Wave established links with the new criticism of the 1960s. The theorist Christian Metz used Rozier's film as a test case in his 'Grand Syntagmatic' method of film analysis, thus *Adieu Philippine*'s unconventional structure 'strengthened the connections between New Wave filmmaking practices and new methods in film criticism.'[68]

Other *Cahiers* directors have since slipped into obscurity, at least in the English-speaking world: Jacques Doniol-Valcroze (1920–89) and Pierre Kast (1920–84) both made first features that were more successful at the time than Rohmer's and Rivette's, namely *Le coeur battant* (*The French Game*, 1960) and *Amour de poche* (*A Nude in his Pocket*, 1957) respectively. It says something of the vagaries of fashion in film that, when Truffaut died of a brain tumour on 21 October 1984, few noticed that Kast had died the day before.

EVERYTHING IS CAPSIZING:
60s ITALIAN CINEMA

Cannes 1960 was another watershed year, although for not quite the same reasons as 1959. Michelangelo Antonioni's sixth feature, *L'Avventura*, had just screened in Competition, and received one of the most infamous receptions ever accorded a film. People booed. They stamped their feet. They jeered. They walked out. They found the film boring; couldn't understand why Lea Massari's character, Anna, goes missing, a mystery which Antonioni doesn't seem interested in ever resolving. This was something new, and they hated it. Critics and filmmakers, on the other hand, realised that Antonioni *was* doing something new, and 35 of them clubbed together and issued a joint statement in support of the director. The film was awarded the Jury Prize. Almost immediately, it was recognised as a classic and, a mere two years later, it appeared at number two on *Sight and Sound*'s decennial poll to find the best film of all time.

Italian cinema in the 1960s was a byword for cool, almost as much as the *nouvelle vague*. With the country undergoing an economic revival, Italian producers were able to challenge Hollywood's domination of the marketplace as never before.[69] Yet it wasn't the same tight-knit scene as in France: there were no theoretical or critical underpinnings informing the movement and the various big-name directors seem a somewhat disparate group (it has to be said that even the French periodically denied that they were a movement, tired of the term 'New Wave' and media hype).[70] And art cinema certainly didn't dominate the domestic production scene: much Italian cinema of the 1950s and 1960s was made up of comedies and westerns.

And yet 'the decade 1958–68 was… of pivotal importance in both the economic and artistic history of modern Italian cinema.'[71]

The new Italian cinema was a development of, and reaction against, earlier filmmaking practices, neorealism in particular. What theory and criticism there were would all come from the political arena, rather than the cinematic, with Pier Paolo Pasolini, Bernardo Bertolucci and Gillo Pontecorvo being among the most vocal political voices of the era. What unites the Italian filmmakers of the 1960s was their epitomisation of auterist cinema.

ITALIAN CINEMA PRE-1960

The society Antonioni and his peers were reacting against was marked by the ghosts of the Mussolini era. Despite Mussolini's proclamation that 'cinema is the strongest weapon', very few films produced in Italy under Il Duce (1922–43) were fascist propaganda, and the country found itself inundated with American films during the 1920s and 1930s. The regime responded with protectionism, passing laws against the import of foreign films between 1927 and 1940, and also by founding the Venice Film Festival in 1932. The festival was intended as a showcase for Italian cinema, but became increasingly a show window for fascism as the decade wore on.[72] (The top prize was known as the Mussolini Cup.) Domestically produced films were, of course, subject to fascist approval, but the fact that films such as Visconti's *Obsession* got made, albeit with official censure, shows that Mussolini's cinema policy was, as with much else, largely one of rhetorical posturing and proclamation. (Visconti would almost certainly have been deported to the camps had he been in Hitler's Germany.)

The church was also aware of the power of cinema, and responded by founding the Centro Cattolico Cinematografico (CCC, or the Catholic Film Centre) in 1934. Pope Pius XI issued an encyclical in 1936 urging caution, especially when it came to morality and the need to protect the young. Church policy on the cinema was often indistinguishable from that of the fascists, agreeing that films such as *Ossessione* did indeed 'stink of latrines'. Visconti and other major directors of the 1960s, such as Fellini, Pasolini and Antonioni, would all find themselves under fire from the CCC and church apologists.

If there was little to distinguish Mussolini from the pope, then cinema in postwar Italy was likewise similar to that of the fascist era. The Andreotti law of 1949 required scripts to be submitted before shooting began in order to check that the films in question were not slandering the mother country or showing her in a bad light. One of the main areas in which the post-1945 years did differ was in cinema attendance, with 1955 being the peak year with 819 million admissions. The arrival of television was to cause a slow decline, but cinema going in Italy remained very popular: even in the early 1970s, there were still over 500 million admissions a year, more than the combined totals of France, Germany and Britain.[73] Films popular at home were the sword and sandal epics (a genre known as 'peplum' films, such as *Hercules* and its sequels), and comedy (*Big Deal on Madonna Street*, *The Great War*). But despite the proliferation of such essentially conservative fare, cultural shifts were beginning. As Robin Buss noted:

> The more Italy, and especially Northern Italy, moved into the second half of the twentieth century, the more its people, when they had time to stop and reflect on what was happening, feared that the ground might never stop shifting under their feet. The result of the ground shifting is a feeling of emptiness in the pit of the stomach, and a sense of emptiness, in some part or other, is conveyed by the great film directors of the 1960s.[74]

MICHELANGELO ANTONIONI

While neorealism did not make a major impression at the box office, it was, however, an enormous influence on filmmakers; it was a legacy almost all of the great Italian directors who came to international attention during the 1960s had to assimilate. In general, the trend was away from neorealism, although, as we will see, some directors had begun as neorealists and returned to the style to reinvigorate it. Antonioni, in his major work, moved away from neorealism into a territory that was altogether new and strange; modernism has claimed him, although it may well be that his work will outlast critical labels.

Antonioni started by writing scripts for directors such as Rossellini and De Santis, who would become leading lights in neorealism, and also worked as a critic, writing for the influential magazine *Cinema*. Indeed, it was an article he wrote for the magazine that led to the shooting of his first film, *Gente del Po* (*People of the Po*, 1943/47), a short documentary about fishermen in his native Po valley. His subsequent early films all fall very much within the neorealist tradition, including *N. U.* (*Nettezza urbana*, 1948), about city street cleaners, *Superstizione* (*Superstition*, 1949), about superstitions in rural southern Italy, and *Sette cani e un vestito* (*Seven Reeds, One Suit*, 1949), which examined the manufacture of rayon. There is little in these films to suggest the direction in which Antonioni would turn once he started making feature films, but the urban setting of *N. U.* betrays his interest in the contemporary Italian cityscape, frequently seen in his trademark medium and long shots, and the fashion models who appear at the end of *Sette cani e un vestito* would arguably not look out of place in his great films of the 1960s – *Blow-Up*, perhaps.

Cronaca di un amore (*Story of a Love Affair*, 1950) was Antonioni's first feature film, and it marked several major changes for the director. Gone are the neorealist tendencies and working-class milieu of the short documentaries; here we are firmly in the world of the middle classes, with the film charting the relationship of Guido and Paola, two ex-lovers who are temporarily reunited when Guido realises he's being investigated by Paola's husband, Enrico. Neorealism was, for Antonioni, a spent force by the time he made *Cronaca*: 'The only useful way of adhering to neorealism is to take an interest more in the interior than in the exterior – to express sentiments before choosing décors.'[75] There were a number of ways into the interior, and Antonioni was to explore several of them in his major work through his use of the camera, actors' performances, colour, sound and narrative structure.

The camera for Antonioni was almost another character. He avoided such conventions as shot/reverse shot for conversations and, under his direction, the camera was rarely dramatically tied to the action. In leisurely tracks around the actors, Antonioni's camera at once observes the characters and critiques them, such as in *Cronaca*'s scene between Guido and Paola on the bridge. This technique creates a distance between the film and the viewer that invites participation and contemplation. Antonioni also encouraged his actors to underplay, making their emotional states all the more enigmatic; the viewer becomes responsible for the creation of the characters' inner lives.

Scripts, too, would deviate from the traditional three-act structure favoured by Hollywood, in which the main character is plucked from their ordinary world into a quest which they successfully resolve and return home to their white picket fence and the resumption of the status quo. Antonioni reacted against the essential conservatism of this structure by introducing major gaps into his scripts (Anna's disappearance in *L'Avventura*), and combining that device with no traditional plot development or conflicts (*L'Eclisse*'s apparently inconclusive ending). In Antonioni's films, nothing is ever explained or proved. Everything is open.

The elliptical and allusive style of *L'Avventura* did not appear overnight. Rather, it was the development of a decade's work, through *Cronaca* and its follow-ups, *I Vinti* (*The Vanquished*, 1952), *La Signora senza camelie* (*The Lady without Camelias*, 1953), *Le Amiche* (*The Girlfriends*, 1955), and in the episode Antonioni contributed to the portmanteau feature *L'Amore in città* (*Love in the City*, 1953), in which Antonioni shows a suicide attempt after a failed love affair, but with no attempt to judge the character's actions. *Il Grido* (*The Cry*, 1957), set in a largely foggy Po valley, could be considered a landscape film, so central to the action is the location. The film charts the pained peregrinations of Aldo (Steve Cochran) after the failure of a long-term relationship. He tries to find solace with other women, but ultimately nothing can fill the void inside him. It is as if the fog in the valley is keeping him from what he most needs.

Antonioni's most celebrated period begins with his next film, *L'Avventura* (1960; lit: 'The Adventure'). The French New Wave demanded of their audiences that they be *au fait* with the likes of the New Novel and semiotics. The Italian filmmakers respected the audience's intelligence enough to make films that required more work on behalf of the viewer. These demands included patience – famously lacking in the Cannes audience which first saw *L'Avventura* – and a willingness to actively engage with the image. And no filmmaker made more demands on his audience than Antonioni, both in terms of measured pace and the general aura of enigma that cloaks his best work. And there was certainly no more taxing an enigma for audiences than what happens to Anna in *L'Avventura*. Antonioni simply isn't interested in her fate: she has somehow left the island, it would seem, leaving Claudia (Monica Vitti) to begin an affair with Anna's lover, Sandro (Gabriele Ferzetti). Anna's disappearance gradually diminishes in importance, while Anna and Sandro's relationship languishes. The film ends with them together, almost immobile, silent, not communicating.

L'Avventura made a star of Monica Vitti, who was also to appear in the director's next two films, *La Notte* (*The Night*, 1961) and *L'Eclisse* (*The Eclipse*, 1962), which form a loose trilogy of bourgeois alienation and silent despair. Vitti became closely identified with Antonioni's work, as much as, say, Jean-Pierre Léaud was with Truffaut's. In Monica Vitti, Antonioni found his perfect actor: her restrained performances speak volumes about her characters' sometimes uncertain emotional and mental terrain. With Vitti as his muse, Antonioni's work of the early 1960s was hailed as feminist. But what kind of liberation did Antonioni see for his female characters? *L'Avventura* ends with a relationship in impasse, a situation that *La Notte* explores further.

The film follows a day in the life of a Milanese couple. Giovanni (Marcello Mastroianni) is a successful writer married to Lidia (Jeanne Moreau). Their day involves visiting Tommaso, a terminally ill friend in hospital, then attending a launch party for Giovanni's latest book. Distressed by Tommaso's state of health, Lidia wanders around the neighbourhood she and Giovanni lived in as newlyweds. They later attend another party, learn that Tommaso has died, and each flirts with someone else. The following morning, Lidia tells Giovanni that she no longer loves him, and that she wants to die. Giovanni reassures her that they are in love and can make their marriage work. *La Notte* ends with Lidia reading out a love letter that Giovanni wrote to her just before they got married, which he does not remember.

Similarly inconclusive relationships form the narrative of *L'Eclisse*: Vittoria (Monica Vitti) leaves her lover and meets Piero (Alain Delon), a young stockbroker. She accompanies a friend to Verona, goes to a party, sees Piero again; a romance threatens to blossom. But, this being Antonioni, romance is the last thing that is likely to happen. Vittoria and Piero agree to meet again, but neither of them keeps the date: the celebrated ending of the film shows empty city streets for over seven minutes.

The Red Desert (*Il deserto rosso*, 1964) was Antonioni's first film in colour, and colour plays a prominent role in the film. Its storyline is similar to the trilogy films: Giuliana (Vitti again) is released from hospital after attempting suicide. She feels cuts off from her family and her husband, an industrialist. When Zeller (Richard Harris), a friend of the husband's, comes to town on business, there is the possibility that he may be able to draw her out of her malaise. It does not, and he leaves. She has a casual encounter with a sailor – a scene that Andrei Tarkovsky described as one of the very few love scenes in cinema that is a spiritual necessity (for Giuliana). But colour and the industrial landscape are at least as significant here: Antonioni painted locations and props (the red oil barrels, for instance) to make them almost too colourful. The effect startles and unsettles, making the film's post-urban landscapes at once beautiful – Antonioni wanted to find beauty in industry[76] – and oddly repellent.

Experiments with colour continued in his next film, *Blow-Up* (1966), his first film in English. Here the grass of Maryon Park in Charlton received extra coats of green paint to heighten and undermine its reality as Thomas (David Hemmings), a fashion photographer, thinks he has unwittingly photographed a crime in the park, and tries to uncover the mystery. He can't, of course. Audiences were by now getting accustomed to such open-ended films; *Blow-Up* was a huge hit and generated unprecedented amounts of acclaim, so much so that 'critics and reviewers reacted as if Antonioni had tackled – and solved – most of the weighty problems of Western metaphysics',[77] reinforcing the director as the fashionable-but-difficult auteur *par excellence*.

Such fleeting descriptions are, of course, inadequate for conveying the experience Antonioni was after. It would be wrong to think of these films as plotless, flat melodramas (just imagine what Douglas Sirk would have done with Monica Vitti). In his 1960s work, Antonioni is refining concerns that were evident as far back as *Cronaca*: questions of interpretation, of character, of place, of dealing with the problem that he identified in a press release at Cannes the year *L'Avventura* was shown, that 'modern man's technological capabilities have far outstripped his moral values'.[78] As Mary P Wood remarked, Antonioni's films are concerned with the psychological damage done to humans by the condition of modernity, 'damage done by casting people adrift in an alien environment. Fogs and mists recur in Antonioni's later films as metaphors of characters' inability to really see each other.'[79]

FEDERICO FELLINI

Fellini's reaction against neorealism – he had worked for Rossellini as a scriptwriter – was very different to that of Antonioni, almost its opposite. His early films, among them *The White Sheik* (*Lo sceicco bianco*, 1952), *I Vitelloni* (*The Young and the Passionate*, 1953),[80] *La Strada* (*The Road*, 1954), *Il Bidone* (*The Swindlers*, 1955) and *Nights of Cabiria* (*Le notti di Cabiria*, 1957) are all loosely neorealist, concerned with the lives of characters struggling on the margins of Italian society. They are frequently at odds with their circumstances: in *The White Sheik*, newlywed Wanda (Brunella Bovo) dreams of meeting her idol, the actor who plays the TV character 'the White Sheik' (Alberto Sordi), and interrupts her honeymoon to find him; Giulietta Masina's characters in *La Strada* and *Nights of Cabiria* seem otherworldly, almost too good for this world. Their stories are played out in an Italy as unscenic as Antonioni's: windswept beaches, ugly tenement blocks, urban wastelands, litter-strewn piazzas and rainy streets predominate. But this early period also contained the germ of Fellini's mature style, which would go from the neorealist to the semi-Bruegelian: carnivals and clowns, dreams and memories, fashionable socialites and paparazzi[81] would replace Fellini's earlier, simpler cinematic universe. *Variety Lights* (*Luci del varietà*, 1950, which Fellini co-directed with Alberto Lattuada) was set in the world of the theatre, *La Strada* in the circus, both of which would become favourite settings for the director, and, perhaps most Felliniesque of all – in what would become the accepted sense of the word – *Il Bidone* contains a sequence in which the gang dress up as priests in order to rob an old woman.

Fellini's early work enjoyed huge success, both at home and internationally, with both *La Strada* and *Nights of Cabiria* winning the Oscar for Best Foreign Film. *La Dolce Vita* (*The Sweet Life*, 1960), which won the Palme d'Or at Cannes, saw Fellini moving away from his neorealist roots into a more personal world that had only been hinted at in his earlier work. *La Dolce Vita* and its follow-up,[82] *8½*, are amongst his most successful films, both critically and commercially, and also announce the onset of his mature style. Indeed, these two films 'resulted in the virtual canonisation of Fellini as *the* archetypal genius, the auteur of auteurs'.[83]

La Dolce Vita broke new ground in its storytelling. There was no traditional three-act Hollywood structure; it was, rather, a picaresque – music-hall programme might be a better analogy – in which Marcello Rubini (Marcello Mastroianni) wanders through a prosperous Rome replete with movie stars, high fashion, the chattering classes; 'a fresco of existence that is at once luxurious and, at its core, without a soul.'[84] Fellini explained the approach he and his screenwriters took to writing the script:

> So I said: let's invent episodes, let's not worry for now about the logic or the narrative. We have to make a statue, break it, and recompose the pieces. Or better yet, try a decomposition in the manner of Picasso. The cinema is narrative in the nineteenth century sense: now let's try to do something different.[85]

The film relies on imagery, not plot, to convey its meaning. From the opening shot of a statue of Christ being carried by helicopter, to the famous Trevi fountain scene where the voluptuous Anita (Anita Ekberg) wades in the water, to the appearance of the Virgin being broadcast live on television (she is only visible to two small children), Fellini, as much as Antonioni, seems to be concerned with surface; what is, or is not, below it, has to be inferred by the viewer. Perhaps the nearest Fellini gets to judging his characters is in the aftermath of the suicide of Steiner (Alain Cluny) after he has murdered his own children: Marcello, seemingly little affected, continues partying and attends a party in which Nadia (Nadia Gray) performs a striptease.

Fellini described the Rome of *La Dolce Vita* as 'a city of the inner self... its topography is entirely spiritual'.[86] Opening with a shot of a statue of Christ being airlifted to a new location by helicopter, the film employed cultural and religious imagery with a certain degree of irreverence; the church interpreted the film as resolutely hostile to Catholicism, and it became the object of a crusade in the Catholic press. Indeed, 'many of the Catholic hierarchy... regarded it... as a work of art that was actually instrumental in pulling the faithful away from the church'.[87] There were even calls for Fellini's arrest on the grounds of 'outrage or derision of the Catholic religion' – a criminal offence at the time. Outrage occurred at the film's Milan premiere on 5 February 1960: an outraged member of the audience spat in Fellini's face.[88] The film offended political sensibilities as well, with it rapidly becoming a battleground between right and left. The left saw it as an attack on bourgeois indolence, indulgence and corruption, while the right saw it as a decadent assault on Italian cultural values. Fellini, however, positively thrived on decadence, commenting in an interview:

> I feel that decadence is indispensable to rebirth... So I am happy to be living at a time when everything is capsizing. It's a marvellous time, for the very reason that a whole series of ideologies, concepts and conventions is being wrecked... I don't see it as a sign of the death of civilisation but, on the contrary, as a sign of life.[89]

Fellini's next film, 8½, continued the director's quest for new narrative forms. Moving on from the episode-structure of La Dolce Vita, here Fellini used dreams and stream of consciousness as his guiding principles, partially due to his growing interest in dreams and Jungian psychology. (Fellini began keeping a dream diary around this time.[90]) 8½ also had an autobiographical element: the plot – such as it is – concerns itself with a film director, Guido Anselmi (Marcello Mastroianni), who can't decide on his next project. This reflected Fellini's own predicament as to how to follow up La Dolce Vita: after writing several versions of the script for 8½, Fellini still harboured doubts about the project. Even when shooting had started, Fellini had a crisis of confidence and began to write a letter to his producer, Angelo Rizzoli, asking him to call the shoot off. At that moment, 'everything fell into place. I got straight to the heart of the film... I would make a film telling the story of a director who no longer knows what film he wanted to make.'[91] Fellini wanted to show the process of creation, not explain it.

The indecision experienced by Anselmi is in fact the only piece of straightforward autobiography in the film; given Fellini's interest in Jung, one is almost tempted to say 'waking' autobiography: *8½* is really a dream autobiography, bringing Fellini's inner world onto the screen. The boundaries between reality and dream are constantly blurred. The film opens with the celebrated dream sequence of Guido being trapped in a car that is stuck in a nightmarish traffic jam. He manages to fly to freedom, only to be pulled to earth by a character we later learn is a press agent for one of the actresses he hopes will be in his film. We then cut to Guido in his hotel room, being examined by his doctor. This would appear to be 'reality', and yet there is a vaguely oneiric feel to the scene: why does the nurse spend most of the scene at Guido's desk, using his typewriter? And why does the doctor prescribe 'holy water'?

The following sequence, set in the gardens of the spa where Guido is staying, continues the delicate balance between dreaming and waking. People are queuing up to take the waters – mineral, not holy, we presume, although the scene is full of priests and nuns – with Guido among them. The opening of the scene is accompanied by Wagner's *Ride of the Valkyries* (played by an orchestra that is revealed to be playing on a terrace), and a number of older women smile and wave into the camera as it passes. Is the camera Guido's point of view? It is never made clear; he is first seen in the queue for water and, by the time he receives a full glass and meets the film critic, Daumier, we can assume that we are in waking reality, but it has taken well over two minutes of screen time to establish this and even then, the huge ruins in the background resemble nothing so much as a gigantic film set.

What Fellini so masterfully captured in the opening scenes of *8½* is a sense of what the critic Daumier (played by Jean Rougeul) calls 'ambiguous realism', a term that could easily be applied, not only to the rest of the film, but much of his subsequent work as well. *8½* marked a watershed in both his artistic development, and also in his profile as an artist. The film's success at the Academy Awards, where it won Fellini his third Oscar (for Best Foreign Film) entrenched his position as the real star of his films; subsequent releases often had his name added to their titles (*Fellini Satyricon, Fellini Roma, Fellini Casanova*). After the successes of *La Dolce Vita* and *8½*, Fellini was a brand.

LUCHINO VISCONTI

Luchino Visconti di Modrone, Count of Lonate Pozzolo, was born into an aristocratic family in 1906, but became a Communist in the 1930s after a period working in France as an assistant to Jean Renoir[92] (whose circle, were all Communists or Marxists associated with the Popular Front). Like Truffaut, Visconti admired Renoir's political and artistic convictions, which were to have a lasting impact upon him. Indeed, Visconti's communism was far from being a pose and he used his aristocratic standing to aid the Resistance during the Second World War: he hid caches of their arms in the garden of his villa in Rome, and also protected Resistance fighters by disguising them as members of his household staff. His political commitments are reflected in his film *Giorni di Gloria* (*Days of Glory*, 1945), a documentary about the show trials in Rome. When asked if a collaborator should be spared, Visconti was amongst those who voted not to spare the man; Visconti filmed his execution and included it in the film.

Visconti's second feature, *La Terra Trema* (*The Earth Trembles*, 1948), was an adaptation of Giovanni Verga's classic novel *The House by the Medlar Tree* (*I Malavoglia*, 1881). The film was originally intended to be part of a trilogy of films about the poor living conditions in southern Italy (the film was shot in Sicily); in the end, it was the only one of the three to be made (the other two films were to have been on miners and the peasantry). Like the earlier *Ossessione*, it was neorealist fare with real fishermen and villagers playing themselves and even contributing to the script. The choice of location was important: southern Italy was, for the left, emblematic of what was wrong with the country, as it was seen as being exploited by the rich north. In the village of Aci Trevi, where Visconti shot the film, 'the area's misery vibrated in their blood'.[93] Visconti also insisted on shooting the film in the local dialect, as Italian 'is not, in Sicily, the language of the poor'.[94] (It was a dialect so strong that most ordinary Sicilians couldn't understand it, let alone people on the mainland, so Visconti's assistant, Francesco Rosi, oversaw the dubbing of the film into standard Italian.) Recording sound on location was rare in Italy at this time, and also expensive. The film was made with the support of the Italian Communist party but, when funds ran low and nothing more was forthcoming from party coffers, Visconti had to sell family heirlooms – including paintings and his mother's jewels – to get the film finished.

Rocco and His Brothers (*Rocco e i suoi fratelli*, 1960) marked a return to neorealism of a sort,[95] being a study of a family which migrates from the poor south to the industrial north, and could almost be regarded as a sequel to *La Terra Trema*. The Parondi family, ruled by the matriarchal Rosaria (Katina Paxinou), struggles to maintain its southern values in the face of progressive Milanese culture. Vincenzo (Spiros Focas), the one brother already in the city with a job as the film opens, falls victim to the family's new urban environment: his old-fashioned views cost him his job and jeopardise his relationship with his fiancée, Ginetta (Claudia Cardinale). Central to the film is the love triangle between Rocco (Alain Delon), his thuggish boxer brother Simone (Renato Salvatori), and Nadia (Annie Girardot), a fellow immigrant who is forced to support herself working as a prostitute. In one scene, Simone rapes Nadia while Rocco looks on helplessly. Rocco relinquishes his pursuit of Nadia, and Simone – a thuggish boxer – ends up killing her. Rocco and Rosaria try to protect Simone – anything to keep the family together – but he is eventually shopped to the police by Ciro (Max Cartier), the one brother who seems to welcome his new life in Milan. The film caused a controversy upon its release similar to that created by Fellini's *La Dolce Vita*. Milanese objected to one of their own depicting their city as a place rife with foreigners, homosexuals, lowlife and criminals. The rape scene was darkened by the censor, on the grounds that it was 'intolerably realistic and brutal';[96] the producer, Goffredo Lombardo, thought this was preferable to having the scene cut altogether. Visconti was even forced to write to the Italian Minister of Culture to defend the film, noting that *Rocco* was 'the Italian motion picture industry's biggest box-office success of recent times, after *La Dolce Vita*'.[97]

Poor southerners and their misfortunes were not the only focus of Visconti's cinema. He turned his attention to the aristocracy and, more artist than party ideologue, his style shifted from neorealism to a kind of operatic melodrama: *Senso* (1954), *The Leopard* (*Il Gattopardo*, 1963, based on Giuseppe Tomasi di Lampedusa's novel) and *The Damned* (*La caduta degli dei*, 1969) were all historical films that demythologised the Risorgimento (in the case of the first two) or the country's fascist past (in the case of the third).

Senso was important for a number of reasons. As was his usual practice, Visconti, in adapting a short story by Camillo Boito (1836–1914), was not interested so much in being faithful to the source text as he was in bringing it into line with his own revisionist beliefs. Essentially a story of forbidden love set during the Italian wars of unification in the 1860s, the film examined the era through the relationship between Livia Serpieri (Alida Valli), an Italian countess, and Franz Mahler (Farley Granger), a young Austrian officer. The film was deemed too bleak by the censors, who charged Visconti with being unpatriotic: the film originally ended with Alida Valli's character being raped by drunken Italian soldiers, a scene Visconti was forced to scrap. The Ministry of Defence objected to the comparison Visconti drew between the failure of the Risorgimento and that of anti-Fascist resistance fighters; the film was re-cut after its Venice premiere, with this element toned down. But, despite these problems, Visconti took Italian cinema to new levels with *Senso*: it was the first major Italian colour film, and the first that could really compete with Hollywood in terms of its lavish scale.

The Leopard (*Il Gattopardo*, 1963) continued in a similar vein. The film starred Burt Lancaster, who was cast initially against Visconti's wishes, as Don Fabrizio Salina, a Sicilian prince who is powerless to stop his dynasty collapsing as Italy goes through the birth-pangs of unification under Garibaldi. His favourite nephew, Tancredi Falconeri (Alain Delon), runs off to the hills to join the rebels, but ends up a Piedmontese officer, a conservative married to a woman from a middle-class Mafia family. Visconti commented in an interview during shooting that what appeared to be a revolution for Sicily was a mirage: 'Garibaldi acted in good faith, but the opportunistic landlords were quick to exploit the changing situation for their own advancement, setting up a new bourgeois oppression.'[98] Visconti lamented the lack of change: 'Through centuries of servitude, Sicily today still lies in a kind of torpor and the Mafia persists like a gangrenous growth.'[99] (Local Mafia bosses had to be appeased during filming.) He also saw

The Leopard as a companion-piece to *Senso*, 'Only this time the vision is less cruel, the events viewed with more pathos.'[100]

The same could not be said of *The Damned* (*La caduta degli dei*, 1969; lit: 'The Fall of the Gods'), Visconti's treatment of Nazism which, at times, reaches levels of what could be described as hysterical, and almost surreal, cruelty, 'a highly stylised metaphor for Germany's descent into insanity'.[101] Set during the first 18 months of Hitler's regime, between the Reichstag Fire (27 February 1933) and the Night of the Long Knives (30 June 1934), the film follows the fortunes of wealthy steel magnates, the Essenbecks. Long thought to have been based on the real steel family of the Krupps, Visconti's fictitious clan was in fact a conglomeration of various families which had supported the Nazis: among them coal, steel and chemical magnates, and bankers.[102]

The film begins with the Essenbecks holding a birthday dinner for the Baron (Albrecht Schönhals), who is about to retire from the family firm. With a succession struggle for control of the steelworks looming between anti- and pro-Nazi elements within the company, a telephone call notifies the guests that the Reichstag is on fire. A surreal (or decadent) element of the film has already been introduced at this point, as the phone call interrupts a song being performed by a girl dressed as Marlene Dietrich – actually the troubled – to put it mildly – Martin Essenbeck (Helmut Berger) in drag. Later that night, the Baron is murdered by Bruckmann (Dirk Bogarde), general manager of the steelworks, who wants to gain control of the company with his lover, Sophie (Ingrid Thulin), Joachim's daughter-in-law and Martin's mother. Bruckmann frames the anti-Nazi Thalmann (Umberto Orsini) for the crime, and the film unfolds in increasingly operatic movements. Bruckmann is forced to kill again while Martin, living on a diet of drugs and delusion, commits rape and paedophilia (he abuses a little Jewish girl, who later commits suicide). The film climaxes with the Night of the Long Knives, which '[begins] with a pastoral scene of soldiers playing in a lake, then progress[es] into an almost surreal drunken orgy of soldiers, naked women, men in drag, finally leading to... brutal massacre'.[103] While all this is going on, Martin rapes his own mother.

From its opening shots of the steelworks to its finale, the mood of *The Damned* is apocalyptic, 'but [it] is an apocalyptic film because it is realistic, and this really is an apocalyptic period'.[104] The shoot, if not apocalyptic, was certainly difficult, with Italian money often not arriving on time, forcing the German hotels where cast and crew were staying to lock them in their rooms. That the film was reprising a period most Germans would rather forget didn't help. At one point Visconti himself went on strike as a protest at the financial situation. Ironically, the film was a huge success both critically and commercially, a classic instance of a European art film taking on Hollywood at the box office. *The Damned* may look like a Hollywood epic, but it is not. In Hollywood, nothing is allowed to threaten the status quo. Visconti's mature work – from *Senso* onwards, perhaps – is rooted in a desire to see that very same status quo disintegrate, in the hope that a new world may be born. As Visconti himself said, 'I do not weep because an old-fashioned world is collapsing. I would like the world to change faster.'[105]

THE AUTEURS OF POLITICS

Pier Paolo Pasolini

Pier Paolo Pasolini (1922–75) was a writer, poet and critic before he became a filmmaker. He experienced some success with his novels, *The Ragazzi* (lit: 'Boys of Life', in the sense of rent boys, 1955) and *A Violent Life* (1959), and, by 1957, was writing screenplays for Fellini, amongst others. (He contributed dialogue to *Nights of Cabiria*.) He was also writing film theory by this time, absorbing the ideas of contemporary linguistic and literary thinkers (as was happening in France with the likes of Robbe-Grillet, Rivette, Marker and Godard). For Pasolini, cinema expressed reality with reality itself, not with metaphors or semiotic codes; film's representation of physical objects, people and places was essentially poetic and metonymic. As Peter Bondanella has noted:

> The poetry of the cinema conserves not only reality's poetry but also its mysterious, sacred nature; in its most expressive moments, film is simultaneously realistic and anti-naturalistic. By communicating reality's mystery, its *sacralità*, cinema also succeeds in projecting reality's dreamlike quality, its *oniricità*.[106]

Pasolini was to explore the themes of sacredness and dream in much of his subsequent work, finding its political foundations in the work of Antonio Gramsci (1891–1937). Gramsci argued that the only way the working class could hope to rule was to first gain what he termed 'cultural hegemony' over other strata of society, and when he wrote of the Italian working class he had in mind the *lumpenproletariat* of the poorer south of the country, the *Mezzogiorno*. Pasolini, although a native of Bologna, was fascinated with the Italian south, and felt that the southern peoples had retained a 'preindustrial, mythical, and religious consciousness, a sense of mystery and awe in the face of physical reality' which he advocated, finding it 'prehistorical, pre-Christian, and prebourgeois'.[107]

Pasolini's first film as director, *Accattone* (1961),[108] focused on Vittorio, the 'accattone' (beggar) of the title, a pimp living in the *borgate*, the shanty town 'suburbs' of Rome, where Pasolini had himself lived in the early 1950s. He turned his lack of experience behind the camera into a stylistic advantage, often shooting scenes in long takes or as sequence shots, a style his assistant, Bernardo Bertolucci, called 'deliberately naïve',[109] and which, Gino Moliterno argues, 'in a sense, invented its own cinematic language to present the harsh reality of the *borgate*'.[110] Pasolini sought to escape from neorealism's long shadow through what he called 'pastiche construction', in which cultural extremes were brought together in order to draw attention to the disparity between them. Simply put, this frequently saw Pasolini accompanying shots of pimps and beggars in *Accattone*, or the ill and crippled in *The Gospel According to St Matthew*, with the music of Bach and Mozart. In addition to the pastiche technique, Pasolini further distanced himself from the neorealist model by investing *Accattone* with a number of Christ-like parallels: Vittorio's work (larceny) is termed 'divine services', one of his prostitutes is called Maddalena, he experiences a vision of his own death and ultimately fulfils that prophecy, dying with two thieves. This was not neorealism, nor social realism – despite employing the neorealist techniques of shooting on location, using non-professional actors – but:

> ... was ultimately less a denunciation of the existence of the *borgate*... than... a celebration of their radical otherness to the

culture of consumer capitalism that was rapidly replacing traditional values in Italy in the wake of the 'economic miracle' and which, for Pasolini, represented a social and cultural degradation.[111]

Pasolini confronted the Christ parallels head on with *The Gospel According to St Matthew* (1964), arguably an unusual choice of subject matter for an atheist, which nevertheless succeeds as one of the simplest and most powerful gospel films, with none of the overblown melodrama of Nicholas Ray's *King of Kings* (1961), whose movie posters had declared 'The Power, The Passion, The Greatness, The Glory!' For Pasolini, it is not a story about greatness and glory, but of the continuing struggles of the poor to overcome hardship imposed upon them by the power structures of the rich and powerful. He was keen to emphasise parallels between Christ's time and our own, shooting Pharisees and Roman soldiers as if they were modern-day aristocrats or riot police respectively. The film has been called 'quasi-Marxist', and Pasolini's Jesus is a man of the Italian south (where the film was shot), portrayed as a figure who 'came not to bring peace but to bring a sword'; it is significant that the word 'saint' was omitted from the Italian title of the film (*Il Vangelo secondo Matteo*). Yet the film did not ignore the spiritual aspects of the story, complete with miracles and angels, and angered some on the left for doing so, whilst pleasing Catholic bodies such as the OCIC (Office Catholique International du Cinéma).[112] Pasolini explained that the film was shown as if from the point of view of a believer, and who better to believe than a member of the southern sub-proletariat, with their ancient, mythical sensibility still intact?

A sense of myth seems to drive *The Hawks and the Sparrows* (*Uccellaci e Uccellini*, 1966; lit: 'Big Birds and Little Birds'),[113] a film which has been described as 'a fable, an essay, a confession, a pamphlet, a sub-titled lesson, a picaresque saga'.[114] The film was a response to Pasolini's growing sense of disenchantment with Italian Marxism, and makes for an interesting comparison with Godard's films of this period, who by 1966 was also undergoing crises of faith, turning to Maoism (see Chapters 2 and 7). Pasolini cites Mao in the opening titles, 'Where is the world headed?', and then spends the rest of the film trying to answer the question. The film follows the adventures of a father and son (played by the great Neapolitan comic actor Totò and Ninetto Davoli, who would go on to appear in many of Pasolini's later films) as they walk through an unidentified landscape, 'the exhausted periphery of a world beyond history'.[115] They befriend a talking crow that has Marxist leanings, and the bird from then on acts as a kind of Greek chorus as the trio become embroiled in various episodes, the most important of which is a mediaeval story the crow tells in which the two men appear as Franciscan monks, and attempt to learn the language of the birds in order to preach to them. After finally managing to impart a sermon to the birds which exhorts them to come to God and to stop the rich preying on the poor and weak, one of the hawks ignores the message and eats one of the sparrows. Back in the modern day, the father and son become so fed up with the crow's ideological hectoring that they eat it before continuing on their way. Until the hawks stop killing the sparrows, Pasolini seems to be saying, the world will never change.

The Hawks and the Sparrows marks the end of Pasolini's 'Gramscian' phase, and his films of the late 1960s move even further away from neorealism and more towards myth (but not the Jungian self-examination of Fellini). His 'mythological cycle' comprises four features, two based on ancient authors, and two on his own mythology. *Oedipus Rex* (1967) liberally reinterprets Sophocles' play as a parable about modern man's inability to 'know thyself' whilst Pasolini's take on Euripides' *Medea* (1969) saw Maria Callas in her first feature-film acting role. The clash between Jason and Medea reflects Pasolini's concerns about the first world's exploitation of the third world, with the latter coming off distinctly the worse. The third world, as epitomised in the film by Callas's queen and her tribal people, retains the 'prehistorical, pre-Christian, and prebourgeois' sensibility that Pasolini so admired and felt was vital in living a life both full of meaning and not dependent upon economic and political exploitation. The developed West, meanwhile, takes dramatic form as the pillaging Argonauts' quest for the Golden Fleece and Medea's separation from her homeland and traditional rituals.

In *Theorem* (1968), the first of the two mythic films based on original stories (Pasolini would later rework the screenplay into a novel), Terence Stamp plays a mysterious (and possibly divine) figure who visits a bourgeois family and becomes intimately involved with all of them in turn, exposing their bourgeois values as worthless. Only the servant Emilia (Laura Betti) comes out of this experience transformed for the better (she becomes a saint with healing powers, and is able to levitate). Pasolini is again attacking the cultural collapse that he saw all around him in Italy. Unlike Emilia, the family 'lack a sense of the sacred and the mysterious, a sense that manages to save the peasant woman from the fate experienced by the middle-class family'.[116] In *Pigpen* (*Porcile*, 1969), two storylines set centuries apart employ cannibalism and bestiality as metaphors for capitalism, and feature the kind of excesses for which Pasolini would become notorious (Julian, played by Jean-Pierre Léaud, has sex with pigs, which ultimately repay his affections by eating him).

Perhaps feeling that he had exhausted myth, and perhaps as a reaction against *Theorem* and *Pigpen*, which were both deliberately 'difficult' films, Pasolini decided to move into more mainstream cinema with the 'Trilogy of Life', comprising *The Decameron* (1971), *The Canterbury Tales* (1972) and *The Arabian Nights* (1974). The films are a celebration of narrative, stories 'told only for the pleasure of the telling', as Pasolini (playing Chaucer) writes at the end of *The Canterbury Tales*. The films all contained liberal amounts of exposed flesh (a requirement Alberto Grimaldi, the producer, insisted on), and were very successful at the box office. However, the films were not mere exploitation: Pasolini, at this time, viewed the sexual impulse as a way to free oneself from the confines of capitalistic consumerism, a sort of secular tantrism that embodied Pasolini's idea of the sacredness of life and the world:

> I made [the *Trilogy of Life*] in order to oppose the consumerist present to a very recent past where the human body and human relations were still real, although archaic, although prehistoric, although crude; nevertheless they were real, and these films opposed this reality to the non-reality of consumer civilisation.[117]

Pasolini changed his mind quite quickly about the Trilogy of Life, publishing an essay in which he retracted the films (much as Chaucer does at the end of the *Canterbury Tales*), and shifted to a despairing, almost nihilistic, perspective. His last film, *Salò, or the 120 Days of Sodom* (1975) was an adaptation of de Sade's novel, with the action being transposed to Mussolini's Republic of Salò in the closing stages of World War II. Four wealthy fascists kidnap a group of young people and graphically torture them, subjecting them to pain and humiliation, including a notorious meal sequence at which they are forced to eat human shit. At the end of the film, the victims are all killed. It was a return to the 'difficult parables' of *Theorem* and *Pigsty*, although far bleaker. The fact that Pasolini was murdered three weeks before the film was released only seems to make it bleaker still, almost as if his assassination was the only possible career move after a film such as this.

His death, allegedly at the hands of a rent boy, was felt by many at the time (and since) to have been a political murder. The case was reopened in 2005, but the judges felt they had too little evidence to convict anyone of a right-wing conspiracy. The world, for Pasolini, might have once been sacred, but, for all the beauty to be found in the *borgate*, it was still a dangerous place against whose inequalities one had no choice but to rail. His work – of which his cinema is an integral part – does just that, although his cinematic oeuvre ends in the nihilistic cul-de-sac of *Salò*.

Bernardo Bertolucci

Bernardo Bertolucci worked as an assistant to Pasolini on *Accattone*, and his father, Attilio, a well-known writer and poet, helped Pasolini get *The Ragazzi* published. Like his father and Pasolini, Bertolucci was also a poet but, unlike Pasolini, his film education did not come just from within Italy, but from the broader spectrum of what was happening elsewhere in the early 1960s. Crucially, he spent time in Paris as a young man, specifically at the Cinémathèque Française, where he discovered Godard and came to hero-worship Henri Langlois. His first feature, *The Grim Reaper* (*La commare seca*, 1962), was based on a story by Pasolini, and centres around the murder of an ageing prostitute. The film employs various time frames and points of view, in which all the suspects are interviewed about the night on which the nameless woman was murdered. No two accounts agree completely, but the killer is finally caught.

So far, so *Rashomon*. But if the film has any spiritual father, it is not Kurosawa, but Pasolini. The witnesses – among them a pimp, a small-time thief, a couple of delinquent teenagers, a hustler – are all denizens of the *borgate*, all of them at the scene of the crime due to economic necessity. The non-linear time sequence takes it out of Pasolini territory to some extent, and the reduction of the police commissar to a voice – recalling William Alland's virtually offscreen reporter in *Citizen Kane* – frees the film from having to conform to the police procedural. Bertolucci admitted that, during filming, he discovered that what he really wanted to film was something more abstract: the passing of time:

> This theme, so common to poetry, was rare in films. Naturally, there was Antonioni, but in his films, the passing of time takes on metaphysical dimensions… in my film, instead, the passing of time is whispered like a secret, with a low voice that almost passes unnoticed.[118]

But, like Antonioni, what makes Bertolucci modern or new wave is the ambiguity in his work; both this first film and many of the ones that were to follow portray people who are often lost, in some kind of limbo, or struggling with their past, or with history. Political systems ultimately do little to help Bertolucci's characters. Although a communist, Bertolucci never seems to have faith that it is politics alone that will save us. (His lifelong interest in Buddhism is perhaps significant here.) It is telling that, in the same year as he made *The Grim Reaper*, Bertolucci also published his first collection of poetry. The title was *In cerca del mistero*, or *In Search of Mystery*.

Ambiguity is certainly a major theme in Bertolucci's second feature, *Before the Revolution* (*Prima della rivoluzione*, 1964). Very loosely based on Stendhal's *The Charterhouse of Parma*, the film depicts the loves and confusions of Fabrizio, a young bourgeois living in the city (also Bertolucci's hometown). He breaks off his relationship with his fiancée, Clelia, wanders the streets reciting poetry, has discussions with his friends Agostino and Cesare, and has an affair with his aunt Gina, who is in Parma visiting her sister – Fabrizio's mother – for Easter. When the holiday is over, she leaves, and Fabrizio marries Clelia.

Rather than dwell on the taboo-breaking romance, the film seems more interested in conveying a sense of loss – Fabrizio is clearly not happy marrying Clelia, he loses Gina and also his friendship with Cesare, and Agostino drowns – played out in a city in which much was lost, first in the war, and then in postwar development. Bertolucci commented that he wanted to show the city in as beautiful a light as possible – the film was shot by L'Avventura's cinematographer, Aldo Scavarda – 'to give back to her all the style that she had lost... this tension that permeates the film makes it honest and false from the very beginning'.[119] This sense of honesty and falsehood is amplified by Fabrizio's comment that 'Clelia is the city, the part of the city that I have refused'; the part that he has refused is, of course, the comforts of bourgeois existence. It becomes clear from his friendship with Agostino and Cesare, however, that Fabrizio is temperamentally not a revolutionary type, despite his admiration for the ideals of the left. He wants revolution, which he sees as honesty, but settles for marriage and a bourgeois future (falsehood). Or is Fabrizio mistaken, and is it really the other way round?

In Stendhal's novel, Fabrizio gets to the battle of Waterloo, almost by accident, and in the commotion of battle is wounded by his own side. He later wonders if he really has the right to say he has been in the battle at all. Fabrizio in the film has the same problem: do his revolutionary ideals really count for anything if they don't bring about change? As Carl Jung once wrote, 'I asked myself whether these visions pointed to a revolution, but could not really imagine anything of the sort.'[120] And as the title of the film implies, if you lived before the revolution, you have not really lived. Agostino's comment to Fabrizio is most damning of all: 'What do you think you are doing? The revolution?'

But there seems to be something deeper going on: Claretta Tonetti comments that Fabrizio's predicament is one of 'am I really here, was I really there?'[121] Such a question goes beyond politics to the realms of philosophy, giving the film an unusual, almost metaphysical, depth. We must not forget that Bertolucci was from the same background as Fabrizio, making the film 'clearly autobiographical, in a way that is common in literature but very rare in the cinema before the 1960s'.[122] Such an introspective element would become a recurring feature in Bertolucci's work. (It might come as no surprise to learn that he began undergoing psychoanalysis in the late 1960s.)

Bertolucci dwelt upon the subject of failed idealisms for his next three films. *Partner* was based on Dostoyevsky's *The Double*, updated to the upheavals of 1968, and perhaps suggesting that revolutionaries suffer split personalities (or maybe it is Bertolucci's admission that he himself has one). In making a film about the political turmoil that was going on at the time, Bertolucci pays homage to Godard, who is a 'sometimes oppressive influence'[123] in the film: at one point, both protagonists, Jacob I and Jacob II (Pierre Clementi in both roles), turn to the camera and inform the audience that the biggest threat the world faces is American imperialism. While Bertolucci may indeed have a valid point, such rhetorical hectoring threatens the film with gravitational collapse. Luckily, Pythonesque humour comes to the rescue, as in the scene where the detergent saleswoman suffers death by washing machine. Stylistically, the film has something of a split personality, perhaps reflecting the two Jacobs, using long takes wherever possible (Bertolucci considered long takes and conventional cutting to be the mark of a conservative director), but is also shot in Cinemascope.

Bertolucci's next two films, shot back to back, were far more successful and are regarded as two of his best: *The Spider's Stratagem* (*La strategia del ragno*, 1969) and *The Conformist* (*Il conformista*, 1970). *The Spider's Stratagem* was made for RAI, the main Italian television network, at a time when the Italian television industry was undergoing major restructuring. The cultural importance of cinema was being recognised, and it was deemed a good investment to put TV money into movies by name directors (Fellini's *The Clowns* [*I Clowns*] was made for RAI at the same time as Bertolucci's film.) Such films would later receive their premieres on television, with some then receiving festival exhibition and theatrical release; they could be periodically rebroadcast in seasons devoted to the director, the film's genre, etc.[124] (TV money was also to provide a shot in the arm for the New German Cinema a year or two later – see Chapter 9.)

Based on Borges' story *The Theme of the Traitor and the Hero*, *The Spider's Stratagem* deals with the attempts of Athos Magnani (Giulio Brogi) to uncover the truth about his father, an anti-fascist activist, who was murdered in the 1930s. The film cuts between the present and the Mussolini era, sometimes blurring the distinction between the two with a fluidly operatic camera. (A device Theo Angelopoulos would use to great effect in films such as *The Travelling Players*, also dealing with the same period. See Chapter 6.) Bertolucci seems to be hinting that the mistakes of the past continue to be repeated in the present, an interpretation borne out by Athos's failure to uncover the truth about his father's death. He tries to leave town by train at the end of the film, but cannot: the tracks are overgrown with weeds. The ghosts of fascism continue to haunt both Athos and the world he lives in.

The Conformist was based on the 1951 novel of the same name by Alberto Moravia. Like its predecessor, the film confronts fascism and tries to find its root cause. Jean-Louis Trintignant plays Marcello Clerici, newlywed and honeymooning in Paris in 1938. Little does his wife know that her new husband is working for Mussolini's regime, and is in Paris to kill Professor Quadri (Enzo Tarascio), his former professor at university who has fled Italy but still continues to agitate against the Fascists. Moravia's novel relates the events of the mission chronologically; Bertolucci's film famously doesn't, with a dizzying Russian doll-like structure of flashbacks. Such chronological blurring gives the film an air of claustrophobia, conveying a sense of Fascism's reach. Even at the film's end, with the mission successfully accomplished, Clerici remains trapped by the system he has willingly given himself to.

The film is also a brilliant homage to film noir, beautifully lit by Vittorio Storaro, and Bertolucci has spoken of it as being influenced by the work of Orson Welles, Max Ophüls and Joseph von Sternberg. It marks Bertolucci's first attempt at making a more international, mainstream film – part of the money to make it came from Paramount. In order to do this, Bertolucci had to turn his back on his mentor, Jean-Luc Godard. In giving Professor Quadri Godard's address in Paris, Bertolucci is expressing his subconscious need to distance himself from his early influences. Bertolucci wondered whether 'I'm Marcello and I make Fascist movies and I want to kill Godard who's a revolutionary, who makes revolutionary movies and who was my teacher'.[125]

Francesco Rosi

Convoluted time frames also feature in the cinema of Francesco Rosi. Rosi had started out as an assistant to Visconti on *La Terra Trema*, and later supervised the Italian version of the film (the actors' thick Sicilian accents being incomprehensible to most Italian audiences). He later claimed that working with Visconti had taught him more than any film school ever could have (he'd been about to attend Centro Sperimentale di Cinematografia when Visconti hired him),[126] and then cemented his apprenticeship by working with established directors such as Raffaello Matarazzo and Mario Monicelli, as well as Antonioni (on *I Vinti*) and Visconti again (1951's *Bellissima* and *Senso*).

Rosi made his feature debut with *La Sfida* (*The Challenge*) in 1958. Like *La Terra Trema* before it, the film addresses the 'Southern Question', centring around Vito, a small-time gangster trying to muscle in on the fruit market in Naples, a trade already controlled by an established *camorra* syndicate. Indebted to both neorealism and Hollywood crime films, *La Sfida* progresses from both in Rosi's handling of narrative. Like the better-known *Salvatore Giuliano* after it, Rosi concentrates on the 'facts', although here we are dealing with a fictitious story, rather than one based on real events. This results in a very spare storyline, with no incidental characters or subplots, reminiscent of Bresson. Rosi's style here also has a tendency towards ellipsis, 'focus[ing] attention, often abruptly, on intense moments of violent confrontation between Vito and the other more powerful members of the syndicate'.[127]

I Magliari (*The Weavers*, 1959) continues to examine the Southern Question, but this time from the point of view of a group of Italian emigrants trying to survive in Germany by selling low-quality goods to better-off Germans. Although the film contains a love-story element, 'much of the film focuses on male groups exercising, challenging and negotiating power in a desperate effort to secure spoils and territory'.[128] Such themes were to be reworked in much of Rosi's later work, which were often films about 'cases involving power relationships between charismatic individuals, corporations, criminal organisations, and the state'.[129]

Rosi's third feature, *Salvatore Giuliano* (1962), was such a film, and was immediately hailed as a classic. Inspired by a true story that was ongoing at the time it was made, Rosi's film investigates the circumstances surrounding the death of the titular character, a 'Sicilian bandit turned political hero turned right-wing terrorist'.[130] Rather than being a traditional biopic or true crime film, *Salvatore Giuliano* mixes a neorealist approach with something that is closer to postmodernism. Rosi has spoken of the film being 'not a *documentary* way of making films, but a documented way'.[131]

The film investigates Giuliano's last few years, death and the subsequent investigation (roughly the years 1945–60) in a series of flashbacks, where 'respect for chronology is completely abandoned'.[132] Giuliano is mainly offscreen or shown in long shot and rarely speaks; his most memorable scene is his appearance as a corpse at the start of the film. That the film ends with another body – a Mafia go-between – shown in the same position as Giuliano's body, suggests that Rosi is intimating a conspiracy involving the political establishment and the underworld, but reserves final judgement.

Rosi dubbed this style of filmmaking *cine-inchiesta*, or investigative cinema. *Cine-inchiesta* films – and *Salvatore Giuliano* is the first film where Rosi masters this technique – are characterised, as we have noted, by their reliance on actual events, on being 'documented' films. Never interested in telling a story for the story's sake, Rosi instead avoids sensationalism and remains relatively neutral, although he admitted that his films could be described as being both a 'critical realism of overt ideological intentions' and 'a second phase of neorealism'.[133] In telling complex stories like *Salvatore Giuliano*, Rosi admitted that getting to the truth was difficult, that 'the impossibility of arriving at any one single truth regarding such complex situations and events, was part of what the film attempted to dramatise in its own structure'.[134] In a much later interview, Rosi meditated on what a film should do:

> To be effective, the questions the films ask must continue to live in the viewer even after the film is over. After my first few films, in fact, I stopped putting the words 'the End' at the conclusion because I think films should not end but should continue to grow inside us.[135]

THE SIGNIFICANCE OF THE EVERYDAY: THE BRITISH NEW WAVE

'Cinema' and 'Britain', François Truffaut once observed, are incompatible terms.[136] Britain was the home of the theatre, both serious drama and music hall, and later radio and television, but serious cinema, it seemed, lay forever outside the national ability. What world-class talent there had been in the UK – Hitchcock and Chaplin, for starters – had long since decamped to Hollywood, leaving only second-raters to run a seemingly ever-dull British film industry that had more in common with the civil service than the Cinémathèque.

FREE CINEMA

Truffaut was not alone in disparaging Britain's cinema. When the *Oxford Film Society Magazine* became *Sequence* in 1947, it was doing more than changing its name: under the new banner came the critical assaults of one of its new editors, Lindsay Anderson, who was to become as outspoken a critic in England as Truffaut was in France. Anderson believed that British cinema had lost its way, and that British filmmakers should look to Jean Vigo and the neorealists for inspiration. The only native director Anderson singled out for praise was the wartime documentarist Humphrey Jennings, whose films were imbued with the 'poetry of the everyday', a concept which would become something of a rallying cry for the British New Wave.

But when Anderson, together with Karel Reisz and Gavin Lambert, took over editing *Sequence* in 1947, a new wave seemed only a remote possibility: a more pressing concern was the establishing of some kind of theoretical position. As Lambert remembers, '*Sequence* was partly a series of love letters to directors we admired, partly a succession of hate mail against work we despised.'[137] One of Anderson's earliest pieces for the journal, 'A Possible Solution',[138] called for a specific kind of film: 'What is required is a cinema in which people can make films with as much freedom as if they were writing poems, painting pictures or composing string quartets.' At the same time, on the other side of the English Channel, Alexandre Astruc was formulating his 'caméra-stylo' theory, which essentially echoed the position called for by Anderson and his cohorts. As Gavin Lambert later noted, 'When Lindsay announced the need for "films of today" with more sense of national realities than *Doctor at Sea*, there was already a gap to be filled. Change, or the possibility of it, was in the air.'[139]

Sequence ceased publication in 1952 after only 14 issues, and Anderson began to write for *Sight and Sound*. The invective against staid British fare continued, culminating in what is perhaps his most famous article, 'Stand Up! Stand Up!',[140] in which Anderson attacked what he saw as 'the kind of philistinism which shrinks from art because art presents a challenge... By celebrating the merits of the trivial, we lower the prestige of the cinema and, indirectly, make it more difficult for anyone to make a good film.' Closely allied to this philistinism – indeed, in many respects, its bedfellow – is capitalism, whose film culture has produced films so artistically and intellectually bad that they should force any self-respecting critic to take a stand and defend his or her social, moral and aesthetic values. Anderson argues that while cinema does not create 'the significant social movements of our time, it intimately reflects them. And that it provides a reflection just as intimate – and just as significant – of social stagnation.' He rails against the closed minds which have created this stagnation, and sees hope in those whose imaginations have not yet stultified: 'Cinema makes its appeal above all to the youthful: that is to say, above all to those whose minds are unformed, and open to impression.'

By the time 'Stand Up! Stand Up!' had been published, two other key events had taken place. On 5 February 1956, Anderson organised a screening of films at the National Film Theatre in London that he dubbed 'Free Cinema'. 'Free Cinema was created for practical reasons,' Anderson later explained. 'The films existed before the group... journalists won't write about an independently made 16mm film of 20 minutes or about a 50-minute film about two deaf mutes in the East End. But if you put your films together and make a manifesto and call yourself 'Free Cinema' and make a lot of very challenging statements – then of course you write their articles for them and they're happy to print them.'[141] The 'very challenging statements' took the form of a manifesto that was printed in the programme for the screenings, signed by the filmmakers:

> Implicit in our attitude is a belief in freedom, in the importance of people and in the significance of the everyday.

> No film can be too personal. The image speaks. Sound amplifies and comments. Size is irrelevant. Perfection is not an aim. An attitude means a style. A style means an attitude.

In showing ordinary people in ordinary everyday settings, Free Cinema was the documentary embodiment of what would come to be known – sometimes disparagingly – as 'kitchen-sink' realism. The screenings of February 1956 featured work by the members of the rather loose-knit group, who at this point were Tony Richardson, Lorenza Mazzetti and Karel Reisz, who acknowledged Anderson as Free Cinema's driving force, dubbing him the group's 'publicist and priest'.[142] Richardson and Reisz's *Momma Don't Allow* captured a night in a jazz club in Wood Green, North London. The film was shot by Walter Lassally, who would go on to shoot a number of the key British New Wave films, on this occasion with a hand-held clockwork Bolex, which meant that no shot could last longer than 22 seconds (the maximum allowed by the camera's mechanism). As hand-held sync sound was still a few years away, the sound had to be synced in the studio afterwards. Mazzetti's film, *Together*, is the '50-minute film about two deaf mutes in the East End' (played by the artists Eduardo Paolozzi and Michael Andrews). It had actually been made in 1953 but, when Anderson first saw it, he realised it would be ideal for the Free Cinema screening. Also made that year was Anderson's own *O Dreamland*, which cast a critical eye over the amusement arcades and funfairs at Margate.

The films proved so successful that five further Free Cinema programmes were curated by Anderson over the next three years. As with the first programme, most of the films had not been made as Free Cinema films – they just happened to fit the bill. The next two programmes included works by Alain Tanner and Georges Franju, as well as Anderson's own documentaries *Wakefield Express* (about a newspaper, not a train), and *Every Day Except Christmas*, a portrait of market workers in Covent Garden. As would become standard new wave practice – any and all new waves, that is – there was an acute awareness of what was going on in other countries, and so the fourth Free Cinema event was devoted entirely to new Polish cinema, showcasing films by Polanski (*Two Men and a Wardrobe*), Lenica and Borowczyk, while the fifth was French (Truffaut's *Les Mistons* and Chabrol's *Le Beau Serge*). The final programme, shown in March 1959, brought things full circle with Reisz's classic documentary *We Are the Lambeth Boys*, which depicted the daily lives of young people in south London. The advent of the lightweight Nagra tape recorder the year before meant that Reisz could now shoot handheld and sync sound, and got long unscripted sequences of the boys talking and debating (although the still-noisy camera had to be blimped with a sleeping bag, 'a sacrifice of technical perfection in favour of spontaneity', as Reisz put it).[143]

THE ANGRY YOUNG MEN

The other signal event of 1956 that would have serious ramifications for British filmmaking was in fact a play: the opening of John Osborne's *Look Back in Anger*, which took place at the Royal Court Theatre on 8 May. Jimmy Porter's rejection of almost everything in British society led to the coining of the term 'angry young man' and things were never quite the same again. Osborne was one of a number of new writers who were emerging at around the same time as the idea of Free Cinema was forming in Lindsay Anderson's mind, including the likes of Kingsley Amis and the Movement poets.[144] But it was Osborne's play that effectively lit the blue touchpaper of cultural change, and the remaining years of the 50s and the early 60s saw a slew of new books published that were predominantly angry, disaffected, working class and Northern, such as Stan Barstow's *A Kind of Loving*, Alan Sillitoe's *Saturday Night and Sunday Morning* and the story *The Loneliness of the Long Distance Runner*, David Storey's *This Sporting Life*, John Braine's *Room at the Top* and Keith Waterhouse's *Billy Liar*.

When Osborne was approached about a possible film adaptation of *Look Back*, he insisted that the play's director, Tony Richardson, also direct the film. Richardson later noted that his 'prospects were negative. The British industry was smug, very closed and very opposed to new directors.'[145] The film finally happened – with Richardson directing – when they persuaded Richard Burton to play Jimmy Porter, a role taken by Kenneth Haigh in the stage version but who was felt to be less bankable than Burton. In order to protect the play, Richardson and Osborne formed a production company, Woodfall Films. But Woodfall did not exist solely to protect the artistic integrity of *Look Back*. As Tony Richardson recalled, 'The concept of Woodfall had not been just to showcase John's and my talents but to use what clout we developed to create opportunities for others to create their own movies.'[146] The company was not entirely independent: a key partner in the company was the unlikely figure of industry hustler, confirmed maverick – and future James Bond producer – Harry Saltzman. It may have seemed like a clash of cultures, but Woodfall was to produce some of the key works of the British New Wave.

'IN THE PRESENCE OF AN INNOVATION'

Woodfall didn't actually begin the British New Wave. That honour is usually given to Jack Clayton's *Room at the Top*, based on John Braine's novel. Film critics were not expecting something revolutionary from an old industry hand: they were looking in the direction of Lindsay Anderson and his Free Cinema circle. Indeed, prior to directing *Room at the Top*, Clayton had produced *Three Men in a Boat* (1956) and *Sailor Beware* (1956), 'which were not exactly portents of revolution'.[147] Clayton had come up through the ranks, beginning as a child actor and then switching to various assisting roles behind the camera at Denham Studios, run by Alexander Korda (a Hungarian émigré who had come to England from Hungary – see Chapter 6). Over the course of 20 years, Clayton went from tea-boy to assisting Korda as producer. Such a long apprenticeship was not unusual: speaking in a 1962 interview, Clayton declared that British cinema had 'suffered sadly from union restrictions on intake and from the lack of a proper film school: both made it very difficult to develop new talent'.[148]

Indeed, Clayton's transition to directing came about in a rather roundabout way. When Carol Reed's *A Kid for Two Farthings*, based on screenwriter Wolf Mankowitz's autobiographical novel of growing up in a Jewish neighbourhood in London's East End, was screened at Cannes in 1954, producer John Woolf 'got a little tipsy'[149] and promised actor David Kossoff (who played in the film) that if *A Kid* was a hit, he would fund a film of another Mankowitz script, *The Bespoke Overcoat*. Reed's film was indeed a success, and Woolf was good to his word. When looking for a director, Woolf knew that Clayton – whom he knew from Denham – was keen to get into directing,[150] and gave Clayton a call. As stage success helped launch the filmmaking careers of Tony Richardson and Karel Reisz (see below), so the ailing mainstream British film industry of the 1950s helped launch Clayton, who was to give it a rude awakening.

The Bespoke Overcoat was based on Gogol's short story, and starred Kossoff and Alfie Bass in the lead roles. In a departure from the original story, the whole film is framed as a flashback, beginning with the death of the clerk, Fender (Bass), the narrative then alternating between the memories of the tailor, Morry (Kossoff), who is making the new coat for Fender, and Fender's return as a ghost to claim the overcoat from his boss's warehouse in an act of supernatural revenge. An atmospheric, convincing and at times humorous portrayal of friendship (at one point, Morry asks Fender to prove that he really is a ghost by walking through a wall; Fender tells him that such a stunt would make him feel silly, announcing 'The old way's best. Through the door,' to which Morry replies, 'I even have to tell him how to be a ghost proper'), the film is also a testament to London's Jewish population. Clayton's film reminds us that the British New Wave was not just about angry young men – with whom Clayton did not identify – but also encompassed 'the humanity and poignancy of friendship... sympathy for the insulted and injured, and a compassion for the human situation.'[151] Shot quickly in a converted chapel in London, the film went on to win an Oscar for Best Short Film, a BAFTA, and a prize at Venice, and ran in London as a supporting film to Fellini's *La Strada*, prompting the *New Statesman* to trumpet, 'A good film at the Curzon, *La Strada*, has just been joined by a better one.'[152] (The pairing of Fellini's film with Clayton's is another example, if one were needed, of the way in which the various embryonic new waves of the 1950s tended to overlap in various ways, both in terms of public perception and the influence of one filmmaker upon another; the same would hold true well into the 1960s and beyond.)

Clayton followed his acclaimed short with his first feature, *Room at the Top* (1959), which effectively launched the British New Wave. Shot when Ealing Studios was ceasing feature film production (the BBC was to take it over), *Room at the Top* 'seemed symbolically to displace [the] Ealing tradition of gentility and restraint and raise the whole emotional temperature of British film'.[153] Joe Lampton (Laurence Harvey), the anti-authoritarian hero, arrives in the northern town of Warley to take up a new job in the Town Hall. An aggressively upwardly mobile character, Lampton lusts after both cars and women. He has affairs with Susan (Heather Sears), the daughter of a local dignitary, and Alice (Simone Signoret), an unhappily married older woman. Lampton has a huge chip on his shoulder, and is acutely conscious of his class. He hates being called 'Sergeant' by one of his colleagues, who is clearly middle-class and boasts a more impressive war record (the film is set in the late 1940s). When Lampton leaves Alice to go back to Susan, Alice gets drunk and dies behind the wheel of her car. A distraught – and drunk – Lampton receives a beating from a gang after making a move on one of their girlfriends. Joe is rescued by a work colleague and the film ends with his marrying Susan, although the wedding scene is highly ironic. Joe might have 'succeeded' in material terms, but the emotional cost has been disproportionately high. Lampton seems to acknowledge this tacitly: he tellingly pauses during the ceremony before uttering the words 'I will', as if he realises he has betrayed himself in the process of acquiring material wealth and social status.

For Clayton, the film was very much about the changed landscape of postwar Britain: 'It was about what happened to England when everybody came back from the war... Joe Lampton was a character who represented, to me, a new feeling that was universal in this country, as a result of people having been put through a very bad five years – and also having had the chance to look around.'[154] Such a view formed the bedrock of much of the new British cinema and, it could be argued, of most of the other European new waves as well.

The film was notable for its sexual frankness, and it received an X certificate. This was more a reflection of the implications of the dialogue rather than anything visual (there being no nudity in the film). It was also felt that a foreign actress would be advisable to play Alice, and the French Signoret was cast in the part, reinforcing the British stereotypical view of French women as sensuous temptresses. The scene in which Joe is beaten up was also strong for the time. And, contrary to standard practice, a great deal of the film was shot on location in Yorkshire, with Halifax standing in for the fictitious Warley.

The film was released in Britain in January 1959. Although it did not meet with universal acclaim, Alexander Walker felt that *Room at the Top* was the best British effort since *Brief Encounter*: 'so barren, timorous and blind have our studios been over a decade that it seems we are in the presence of an innovation.'[155] Dilys Powell, writing in *The Sunday Times*, commented that 'it gives one faith all over again in a renaissance of the British cinema'.[156] The film was screened at Cannes during the seminal 1959 festival, where it competed with *The 400 Blows* and *Hiroshima, Mon Amour*. Simone Signoret won the Best Actress award and, the following year, she also won an Oscar, becoming the first French actor to do so.

Although Clayton lost out to Truffaut, who won Best Director at Cannes that year, Truffaut praised Clayton's second feature, *The Innocents* (1961), calling it 'the best English film after Hitchcock goes [sic] to America'.[157] Based on Henry James's celebrated ghost story, *The Turn of the Screw*, the film was a surprise choice of subject matter. But, as Neil Sinyard notes, 'what [Clayton] was looking for... was something as unlike *Room at the Top* as possible. He had no desire to be typecast as the leader of the British cinema's 'new wave'.[158] This desire not to be typecast was in part a reaction to the publicity surrounding the French New Wave at Cannes; for Clayton, the important thing was not to be part of a new wave, but to find 'a subject one can believe in, love and actually feel... it must be valid for today: not the today of the newspaper stop press, which is usually dead by the time it is read, but the real today which, with different clothes, is true of yesterday and tomorrow. Finally the subject must try above all else to prise open the doors of convention and snap through as many archaic rules as possible.'[159] Clayton may not have been comfortable with being part of a new cinema but, in expressing such a credo, he was thoroughly 'new wave', and adhered to such beliefs for the rest of his career.

Despite its literary basis, *The Innocents* had autobiographical resonances for Clayton, who 'had never been to school. [Who] grew up not knowing his father, never settled in one place for long, in the company of pets and nannies.'[160] The ghostly mansion of the film echoed the houses of Clayton's childhood, 'being brought up in a house full of secrets and whispers... where to reveal the secret would produce horror'.[161] These links to his own experience shift *The Innocents* from being purely an exercise in genre to something that was auteurist, in line with the Free Cinema ideals that films should be 'statements [that] are entirely personal'.[162]

WOODFALL AND COMPANY

The link between the Angry Young Men and cinema was stressed in the 1957 book *Declaration*, edited by future publisher Tom Maschler. Featuring essays by John Osborne, Colin Wilson, Kenneth Tynan and Doris Lessing, the book was an anthology of manifestos that represented a 'certain pattern taking shape in British thought and literature'.[163] Lindsay Anderson contributed an article in which he asked 'What sort of cinema have we got in Britain?' He answered himself succinctly: 'First of all, it is necessary to point out that it is an *English* cinema (and Southern English at that), metropolitan in attitude, and entirely middle-class.'[164] Woodfall's early films were a response to this. Richardson believed that:

> The falseness, the stereotypedness, the staleness of British films
> is due to a refusal to approach a subject, the shooting of a scene,
> the use of a location, the design of sets, the casting of a small part,

in a fresh and new way. There is constantly a premium on 'this is the way it was done last time' rather than on 'this is the way it has never been done before'.[165]

Woodfall's first two films, *Look Back in Anger* (1959) and *The Entertainer* (1960), were adaptations of John Osborne's hit plays. Tony Richardson, whose sole film directing credit had been the documentary *Momma Don't Allow* (made with Karel Reisz in 1956), directed both plays and their big-screen incarnations. Big names were attached: *Look Back in Anger* starred Richard Burton as the archetypal angry young man, Jimmy Porter, while Laurence Olivier reprised his stage role as the seedy music-hall has-been, Archie Rice, in *The Entertainer*. In both cases, the films were fleshed out with location filming in East London, Morecambe and Bradford. This made the narratives less claustrophobic – both plays being set largely in Porter's and Rice's respective lodgings – and tried to refashion Osborne's theatrical techniques in terms that would work for the screen.

Many critics felt that the films did not quite repeat the success of their respective stage versions, neither doing particularly well at the box office. Burton was too old to play Jimmy Porter, critics (and Harry Saltzman) felt, while the figure of the angry young man was already, in 1959, 'a stock figure of our society' whose 'anger looks like petulance'.[166] Not only that, but Richardson's arguably excessive reliance on close-ups had the effect of over-emphasising Porter's rantings. Osborne felt that the film presented a 'softer-edged, more sympathetic portrait'[167] of Porter (but, despite his objections, he would continue to work with Richardson for the best part of another decade). However, David Robinson felt that the film was 'a breakthrough – to a much greater extent than *Room at the Top*', praising the film's mobile camera, which is 'never obtrusive', which has the effect of making us 'not so much aware of physical movement as of a turmoil and disturbance perfectly keyed to the action'.[168]

The Entertainer was arguably a better film, translating the play's Brechtian aspects – Rice as both embodiment of, and commentator on, the terminal decline of Britain – into a personal, northern social realism. Richardson chose Morecambe as his principal location, remembering it from 'dreary, horrifying wartime holidays' with his parents, 'hating the concrete pavements, the mean boarding-houses, the vulgarity of the restaurants and shows'.[169] The effective use of drab locations – theatres, streets, industrial waste ground – together with scenes that, in the play, were merely alluded to – Archie's affair with a beauty queen, his daughter Jean's art school days – contribute to the film's effective portrayal of a man whose best days are behind him, and who has nowhere else to go.

Making the film was not without its difficulties. *Look Back in Anger*'s middling box-office meant that Saltzman had to scrape financing together from various sources, including an early attempt at product placement, by approaching the brewers, Bass, whose ale forms a major part of Archie's diet in the stage version. Saltzman's idea was that Bass would fund the film if Olivier was seen to copiously consume their product in the screen version. To this end, 20-foot bottles of the beer – recalling the huge whisky bottle that looms expressionistically over David Farrar in Powell and Pressburger's *The Small Back Room* – were built in the hope that Bass would see their product in the test footage and invest. But, as Richardson noted in his memoirs, 'Larry was sliding towards becoming what today would be called unbankable,' and Bass declined to invest.

On the artistic front, Olivier and Richardson were opposites: as critic Alexander Walker noted, it was a case of the director's 'naturalistic preference' against his star's 'non-naturalistic technique'.[170] Richardson wrote that 'Larry couldn't understand my insistence on location shooting, on natural sound, on responding to light and shadows: the only scenes he was really happy with were those we shot in the studio'.[171] It was a simple case, in other words, of new wave versus old school, but Richardson's memoirs attest to the fact that Olivier was 'very loyal and accommodating'[172] and the balance of both tone and style they achieved in the film led to critical recognition. Penelope Huston, writing in *Sight and Sound*, declared that the film was 'a landmark in our cinema', but also noted that 'it was a brave film to make… anyone making this kind of film in Britain is on his own, in the sense that he has no screen tradition to guide him'.[173]

Richardson was, around the same time, developing projects for other directors. One of these was *Saturday Night and Sunday Morning*, based on Alan Sillitoe's autobiographical novel, directed by Karel Reisz. Using lightweight cameras and fast stock, Reisz and his DOP, Freddie Francis, were able to shoot much of the film in many of the actual locations in and around Nottingham that Sillitoe had lived and worked in. *Saturday Night* was Reisz's first feature, after several Free Cinema documentaries, including *Momma Don't Allow* (1956, co-directed with Richardson), the anti-nuclear *March to Aldermaston* (1959) and the seminal *We Are the Lambeth Boys* (also 1959), to which *Saturday Night and Sunday Morning* could be regarded as a thematic sequel of sorts.

Richardson, acting as producer, gave Reisz a free hand in making the film, not actually turning up on location until the last week of the shoot. As Reisz later recalled in an interview with critics John Tibbetts and Jim Welsh, Richardson '[would not] have had any desire to interfere... His attitude was "You have a go"'. Tibbetts replied that Richardson, true to the spirit of Free Cinema, was 'willing to let people "have a go"... and moreover, people who weren't really tested yet'. Reisz agreed, his answer neatly summing up the position of most of Woodfall's and the British New Wave's key personnel:

> Absolutely. I mean, a film like *A Taste of Honey* or a film like *Saturday Night and Sunday Morning* or *The Loneliness of the Long Distance Runner*, they were all made by writers who had never written, directors who had never directed, and actors who had never acted, and so on, all the way down the line. It was Tony's confidence and impresario genius which made it all possible.[174]

Richardson's faith in Reisz was well founded: *Saturday Night and Sunday Morning* was Woodfall's first commercial and critical success, and made a star of its then-unknown male lead, Albert Finney.

In many ways, *Saturday Night* was the archetypal Free Cinema/ Angry Young Man film. Finney plays Arthur Seaton, earning good money as a lathe operator in a factory, and spending his free time drinking, fighting and looking for girls. 'What I'm out for is a good time,' he announces. 'All the rest is propaganda.' The search for a good time includes having an affair with Brenda (Rachel Roberts), the wife of Jack (Bryan Pringle), his best friend. This results in an unwanted pregnancy, and also an X certificate for the film. The head of the British

Board of Film Censors, John Trevelyan, wrote to Saltzman criticising the script for its 'rather casual attitude to abortion'.[175] The film shows Brenda telling Arthur she wants to keep the baby, but later on Jack informs Arthur that he is 'taking care' of Brenda. It was precisely the ambivalence of this statement that Trevelyan objected to. Indeed, the film is decidedly ambivalent at its conclusion: Arthur is seen on a hillside above a new housing estate with his fiancée, Doreen (Shirley Anne Field), with whom he has been cheating on Brenda. A domestic future apparently awaits, but we do not see it. Will Arthur finally mend his ways and surrender to society, or opt out? We are left wondering as he and Doreen walk down the hill towards the estate.

A 'rather casual attitude to abortion' had been objected to on the grounds that *Saturday Night and Sunday Morning* was 'likely to be seen by a considerable number of young people... [therefore] social responsibility is called for'.[176] Likewise, the film's use of vernacular English met with opposition. Trevelyan let words like 'whore', 'bitch' and 'bastard' through, but drew a line at 'Christ' and 'bugger'. Such criticism was par for the course, and Woodfall developed a good working relationship with Trevelyan and the board of censors. In making films with contemporary relevance, the new wave filmmakers were offering audiences something that British audiences were not used to, having endured, throughout the previous decade, a 'cinéma du papa' of the decidedly British, stiff-upper-lipped variety. Trevelyan, to his credit, was aware of the need to reinvigorate the national cinema, and was not in principle opposed to challenging far reaching cinema screens. Indeed, he seems to have been in favour of anything that would contribute to a more sophisticated film culture in Britain. As Colin Gardner notes, 'Far from being a censorious watchdog, Trevelyan actually became an effective shaper of public taste.'[177]

Provided, of course, that the films stayed within certain limits. What was acceptable to the public was still constrained by notions of respectability that were rapidly becoming outdated. Despite wanting to encourage filmmakers, Trevelyan and his colleagues were in no way bohemian, as actor-turned-screenwriter-turned director Bryan Forbes recorded in his memoirs. Forbes was not part of the Woodfall group, but his early films, *The L-Shaped Room*, *Whistle Down the*

Wind and *Séance on a Wet Afternoon*, could all be considered new wave through their sympathetic treatment of northern, working-class characters, use of location shooting, and using books by new, young writers as source material.[178] Forbes's second feature, *The L-Shaped Room* – based on the novel by Lynne Reid Banks and originally intended by *Room at the Top* producer James Woolf to be a project for Jack Clayton – received a lengthy list of required changes from Trevelyan. The story follows the fortunes of Jane (Leslie Caron), a young unmarried woman who falls pregnant but has no wish to marry the baby's father, and ends up living in a boarding house – the L-shaped room of the title.

While acknowledging that the script is 'a fine piece of writing that should make a sincere and moving film',[179] he predictably balked at references to abortion, as well as the usual suspects like 'Christ', 'sod' and 'arse'. Also castigated were lines as memorable as 'That's the sort of thing that makes me want to fornicate right in the middle of Westminster Abbey during a Royal Wedding'.[180] 'Erotic visuals' were likewise discouraged: 'Care should be taken with the visuals of couples fondling one another... we would not want breast-rubbing or thigh-rubbing; nor would we want copulatory dancing', and neither did they want 'any censorable visuals especially in view of [Jane's] pregnant condition'.[181] Not only were direct references to fornication discouraged, but Trevelyan was not happy that John (Brock Peters) has heard his next-door neighbours fornicating: 'This kind of thing is going to need extreme care', and then, later in the same letter, 'I would prefer the removal of the emphasis on the fact that he has heard their making love.'[182] In the end, Forbes agreed to only six changes.

Tony Richardson was to explore similar ground in *A Taste of Honey* (1961). Like *The L-Shaped Room*, this film, based on the play by Shelagh Delaney, was about a young unmarried mother, Jo, played by Rita Tushingham. The father of Jo's baby is a black sailor, Jimmy (Paul Danquah), who returns to sea, leaving Jo alone with her alcoholic mother, Helen (Dora Bryan). Helen's behaviour forces Jo out, and she finds a flat of her own, befriending Geoffrey, a gay art student (Murray Melvin). Their friendship develops, Geoffrey even offering to marry her – more out of friendship than an attempt at making Jo 'respectable'.

(Given Geoffrey's sexuality, it is perhaps more the other way around.) With its questioning of race, class, gender and sexuality, *A Taste of Honey* proved to be as groundbreaking and successful a film as it had been a play, winning BAFTAs for Best Film, Best Screenplay, Best Actress (Bryan) and Best Newcomer (Tushingham). Tushingham also became the first Briton to win Best Actress at Cannes, while Murray Melvin picked up the award for Best Actor.

Issues of class and conformity dominated Richardson's return to the work of Alan Sillitoe with *The Loneliness of the Long Distance Runner* (1962). Tom Courtenay plays Colin Smith, a young, working-class offender doing time in a borstal called Ruxton Towers. His principal talent – apart from getting into trouble – is his ability as a distance runner, something that gets him noticed by Ruxton's upper-class Governor, played by Michael Redgrave. Colin soon becomes the Governor's favourite, being excused work in the machine shop in order to train. There is an upcoming cross-country race at which Ruxton's boys will compete against Ranley, a local public school, an event at which the Governor believes Colin's undoubted success will reflect well on Ruxton. By the time of the race, we have seen in flashback how Colin's father died after a long illness caused by many years of unhealthy working conditions in a factory, his mother's infidelity and the regime of beatings and deprivations endured by Colin's fellow inmates. On the day of the race, with victory assured, Colin stops dead in his tracks with the finish line in sight, allowing Ranley's best runner (James Fox) to win the race. The film ends with Colin once again in the machine shop, deprived of special treatment, but seemingly at peace.

Loneliness put Tom Courtenay's star firmly in the ascendant, and he was to rise to even greater heights the following year as the lead in John Schlesinger's *Billy Liar* (1963). Like most of the other British New Wave films, it had a literary source, in this case the 1959 novel by Keith Waterhouse, which in turn became a successful West End play, directed by Lindsay Anderson, the following year. The stage version starred Albert Finney as Billy, with Tom Courtenay first as his understudy and then taking over when Finney left to appear in the title role of John Osborne's *Luther* at the Royal Court (by which time, *Saturday Night and Sunday Morning* had made Finney a star).

John Schlesinger had, like other British New Wave directors, got into directing via documentaries, made either independently, for the BBC, or for companies sponsoring films. The Ford Motor Company had provided the money for Anderson's *Every Day Except Christmas* (1957) and Reisz's *We Are the Lambeth Boys* (1959), and British Transport stumped up the cash for Schlesinger's breakthrough film, *Terminus* (1961), a half-hour documentary about a day in the life of Waterloo Station. The film won a BAFTA for best short documentary and a Golden Lion at Venice. On the strength of this and other documentaries, Schlesinger directed *A Kind of Loving* (1962), based on Stan Barstow's 1960 novel of troubled love and domestic responsibilities in Manchester, and starring Alan Bates and June Ritchie. The film won the Golden Bear at the Berlin Film Festival, and cemented Bates's reputation as one of British cinema's rising stars.

Billy Liar was a very different film, highlighting again the British New Wave's ability to move away from the kitchen-sink-grim-up-North genre when the chance arose. Billy Fisher (Courtenay) is a working-class 19-year-old living with his parents and grandmother in the fictional Yorkshire town of Stradhoughton. Bored by working as a clerk for Shadrack & Duxbury, a firm of undertakers, Billy develops an active fantasy life in which he is variously the son of a retired naval captain, about to write scripts for a famous comedian, or ruling an imaginary country called Ambrosia. He manages to propose to two very different women, Rita (Gwendolyn Watts) and Barbara (Helen Fraser), neither of whom is suited for him. Only Liz (Julie Christie) understands his need for fantasy – she also despises the short-sighted, petty world of Stradhoughton – and offers him the chance of escape to London. Escape would indeed be good for Billy, as Rita and Barbara have found out about each other, Billy's theft of some mailroom cash from his employers has been discovered, and the comedian doesn't offer Billy any writing work. But with freedom beckoning, and Liz waiting for him on the train to London, Billy turns back and heads for home, once more the triumphant ruler of Ambrosia.

Billy's apparent refusal to break away seems at first to be more of a failure than Arthur's submission to married life at the end of *Saturday Night*. However, as B F Taylor has pointed out, the film has been dropping hints from early on that 'Billy's artistic aspirations will always leave him standing still... [they] will never generate sufficient momentum for his life to move forward the way that he would want it to'.[183] Doomed to stay in one place, Billy's decision to stay in Stradhoughton could be read as an act of British-stoicism-cum-Walter-Mitty-ish heroism. Director John Schlesinger certainly saw the film's ending that way: 'I didn't see it [Billy's inability to go to London with Liz] as weakness. Just because he couldn't face leaving home, I don't think that's necessarily weak. His decision to stay and live through his fantasy life was just as valid.'[184]

LINDSAY ANDERSON

An imaginative take on life in Britain also informed the work of the one figure who arguably started the British New Wave virtually single-handed, Lindsay Anderson. As we have already noted, Anderson was a virulent baiter of the old British cinema as much as Truffaut had been of the 'certain tendency' towards conservatism and a general life-denying dullness in the French cinema; Anderson was Free Cinema's 'publicist and priest' (to use Karel Reisz's phrase) and had already gained some success with short films. In addition to the Free Cinema classics, *O Dreamland* (1953) and *Every Day Except Christmas* (1957), Anderson won an Oscar for best short film with *Thursday's Children* (1954), a documentary about the Royal School for the Deaf in Margate, narrated by Richard Burton. But although Anderson 'had the makings of a good guerilla. He could travel light, go hungry, live frugally, above all shed blood with no regret if it served the cause',[185] his interest in British life was ambivalent, arguably much more so than that of Reisz and Richardson. Consider *O Dreamland*, shot at a fun fair near the Deaf School, for example: in addition to rollercoasters and slot machines, visitors witness 'famous executions', jukebox music blares relentlessly, overweight café customers stuff themselves with greasy food, the camera shows 'feet shuffling across ground fouled with litter... faces reacting to everything with the same almost catatonic lack of expression'.[186] But who is the recipient of Anderson's critical gaze? The masses who visit the fair? Or the owners, who herd them in and take their money? Or are the visitors complicit in the whole tawdry spectacle? As Gavin Lambert succinctly noted, 'If this is Dreamland, what kind of nightmare is everyday life?'

Perhaps not surprisingly, *This Sporting Life*, Anderson's debut feature, had ambitions beyond merely critiquing conditions for the working man in northern England. It was nearly a Woodfall Film. Anderson took the project to Tony Richardson, who liked the original novel by David Storey (published in 1960), but didn't think Anderson was the man to direct, thinking that he himself ought to be in the director's chair. Richardson made a bid for the rights, but lost out to Julian Wintle and Leslie Parkyn, who wanted Joseph Losey to direct. When Wintle fell out with Losey, he offered the project to Karel Reisz. Knowing of Anderson's interest, Reisz deferred and suggested to Wintle that Anderson should direct, with he himself producing (Reisz claiming that, at the time, he wanted to gain more experience as a producer).

Working with David Storey on the script, Anderson produced one of the key late films in the British New Wave. Richard Harris plays Frank Machin, a former coal miner who finds that he has a talent on the rugby pitch, where his natural aggression can find release. He is less successful in his private life, where he conducts an unfulfilling affair with his landlady, the doomed Mrs Hammond (Rachel Roberts). What differentiates *This Sporting Life* from earlier British New Wave fare is, Alexander Walker felt, 'in the introduction the audience gets to the interior landscape of the protagonist'. Anderson conveys Machin's inner state through a combination of flashbacks and subjective cutting. The use of flashbacks (a device also employed in the novel) drew comparisons with the work of Alain Resnais.[187] Unlike earlier British films whose narratives employed flashbacks (*Brief Encounter*, *Kind Hearts and Coronets*, *In Which We Serve*, for example), the cutting in *This Sporting Life* 'can be seen as a challenge since the flashbacks were used for breaking up linear narrative. The flashbacks were not logically connected to any particular point of view but were objective as well as subjective'.[188] Alexander Walker praised the film for its 'boldness of the subjective editing, evoking emotional states or implying events elliptically by direct cuts in time and space.'[189] However, Walker acknowledged that the film made demands on its viewers, commenting, 'The audience is made to work for the links and, if it grasps them at all, does so by instinct.'[190]

When the film opened in January 1963, critical reception was very positive, 'confirm[ing] Lindsay's reputation as the most artistically mature of the Free Cinema group'.[191] As Paul Ryan noted, what was perhaps the film's greatest strength 'was the complexity with which an adult relationship was portrayed... [the characters] confront us with the experience of their lives, and they demand that we respond from nothing less than our experience'.[192] Anderson himself dubbed the film as 'a film about all of us and our lives right now',[193] suggesting that he had found in interiority a way of taking Free Cinema from the relative objectivity of social realism to something closer to the work of Resnais and Godard, and one could argue that *This Sporting Life* brought a Continental, modernist sensibility to the British social realist field. As such, it stands apart from most of the Woodfall stable and looks ahead to Anderson's next films, *The White Bus* (1967) and *If...* (1968), which took their inspiration from Continental cinema – the Czech New Wave and the legendary French director, Jean Vigo, in particular.

'THE YEAR KITCHEN SINK WENT DOWN THE DRAIN'

Despite strong notices, *This Sporting Life* didn't fare well at the box office, either at home or abroad. Later that same year, Richardson and Woodfall enjoyed their biggest success yet with *Tom Jones* (1963), starring Albert Finney in the title role. The film was a cine-literate take on Henry Fielding's classic novel: it opened as a silent movie, only starting to use sound when one of the characters speaks; it breaks the fourth wall, as in the scene where Tom notices the camera and hangs his hat on it; characters also talk into camera, as if it were a confidante to the action. John Osborne's script was essentially another (disguised) attack on the British class system, with Finney as an eighteenth-century precursor to Jimmy Porter. In retaining the device of the omnipotent narrator from the novel, Richardson and Osborne were able to produce a film that was both self-reflexive and funny. It was hugely successful at the box office, and won four Oscars, including Best Film, Best Director and Best Screenplay.

But the tide had turned for the British New Wave. Alexander Walker noted that 1963 was 'the year "kitchen sink" went down the drain',[194] and most of the major players in the British New Wave either moved to America (*Tom Jones* was made with American money) or remained at home where they had to compete in an increasingly commercial, and international, cinema. The legacy of the British New Wave meant that British films 'could not easily return to the phoniness of earlier decades, presenting a cosily artificial image of Britain that bore little or no relation to the lives of the majority of its people'.[195]

Unlike France, British cinema was hampered by the absence of an effective culture of criticism. As B F Skinner noted, 'The act of interpretation in (British) cinema still arouses certain suspicions.'[196] Few critics would take criticism far enough to generate a real debate about the films and film culture. Films were still seen as entertainment, and the best that could be said about some of them was that they were 'interesting'. Critics were not up to the same level of creativity as filmmakers. As late as 1977, when the New Wave was long over, 'as far as film education went in [Britain], far more expeditions were being made to John Ford's Monument Valley... than Ealing Green'.[197]

What became dominant after 1963 was a different kind of phoniness, as embodied by the James Bond movies (the first, *Dr No*, was released in 1962). Although they can hardly be seen as 'new wave', their approach to the spy genre was novel, a comic-book reality that Hollywood immediately found appealing and, more importantly, profitable. Another key movie was Richard Lester's *A Hard Day's Night* (1964), capturing the Beatles in all their irreverent, Goons-esque glory. Lester admitted that the film had been highly influenced by the French New Wave, with jump-cuts and abrupt shifts of scene (including 'impossible' jumps, such as the group performing on a train, then, moments later, running outside it, trying to catch it up). It was released in the summer of 1964 worldwide, and became significantly one of the first widely distributed new wave films in the USA; it was through Lester and the Fab Four that the innovations of the French first found a mass audience in North America.

After 1963, many of the main names enjoyed – if that is the right word – sporadic careers. Lindsay Anderson made *If...* (1968), which won the Palme d'Or at Cannes in 1969 and was partially inspired by Vigo's *Zéro de Conduite* (and was itself an influence on Kubrick's *A Clockwork Orange*) and *O Lucky Man!* (1973). Jack Clayton went to Hollywood to direct *The Great Gatsby* (1974) and *Something Wicked This Way Comes* (1983), neither of which was particularly successful. He came back with two powerful late films, *The Lonely Passion of Judith Hearne* (1987) and *Memento Mori* (1992). Karel Reisz fared little better, his biggest success after *Saturday Night and Sunday Morning* coming 20 years later with his adaptation of John Fowles's *The French Lieutenant's Woman* (1981). John Schlesinger had a perhaps more successful career, taking advantage of the changes that were sweeping Hollywood in the late 1960s to make *Midnight Cowboy* (1969) and, as the New Hollywood was starting to evolve into something else, *Marathon Man* (1976).

Still, the British New Wave arguably had it better than the filmmakers who emerged in the late 1960s and early 1970s: Ken Loach and Alan Clarke, both of whom came up through TV; and a group of highly talented independent filmmakers, including Bill Douglas, Sally Potter, Peter Greenaway, Derek Jarman and Barney Platts-Mills. Despite getting small amounts of funding from the British Film Institute, the 1970s was a bleak decade for British film. One could be forgiven for thinking that the terms 'Britain' and 'cinema' were incompatible once more.[198]

SICK AND TIRED OF BAD FILMS: THE CZECH NEW WAVE

The state of Czechoslovakia came into being in 1918, making the country 20 years younger than the first films to be produced there.[199] It was not until 1934, however, that Czech cinema finally came to the attention of the film world, with the success of Gustav Machatý's *Ecstasy* (*Extase*) at the Venice Film Festival. Machatý had made a name for himself in Hollywood, working as an assistant to both Griffith and von Stroheim, before returning to Prague in the late 1920s. *Ecstasy* proved controversial, with its lyrical images of a nude Hedy Kiesler[200] bathing in a forest pool and, perhaps worse, its proto-feminist exploration of a woman's search for sexual satisfaction (the film showed Kiesler's character experiencing cinema's first onscreen orgasm). Although the film did good business, the Vatican condemned it and it also ran into trouble in the USA, where it was cut and then cut further once Kiesler had relocated to Hollywood and changed her name to Lamarr. In some ways, the situation served as a microcosm of what would eventually become the Czech New Wave: *Ecstasy* was a film with real characters who had real, human needs, and also had a sense of the poetry of both nature and the everyday, a film which found itself being buffeted around due to the politics of the time. The worsening political situation in the late 1930s had an effect on both the Czechs and Venice, with the former producing fewer films, while the latter was condemned for being a shop-window for Fascist propaganda.

The war itself did, strangely enough, bring good things to the Czech film industry. Barrandov studios outside Prague, built in 1933, was considerably expanded by the Nazis, who aimed to use it as a cheaper alternative to shooting films in the Fatherland. Shortly after the end of the war, laboratory and special effects facilities were added, making Barrandov one of the largest and best-equipped studios in Europe. 1946 also saw the foundation of a national film school, FAMU,[201] and the nationalisation of the industry. However, politics intervened once again in 1948 with the Communist takeover of the country – a democratic government having been elected in 1945 – and it would be a further ten years before the first omens of the Czech New Wave would be seen. Indeed, as Peter Hames has noted, 'Any sign of group identity [during the Stalin era] might have been interpreted as conspiracy.'[202]

The 1950s were not a total case of everyone staying at home and keeping their heads down: the puppet films of animator Jiří Trnka became successful both at home and abroad. Animation managed to slip under the Party's radar during these years largely due to the fact that the films were produced in studios usually deemed too small to be politically troublesome, and the films themselves often took themes from folklore or adapted fairytales, which were seen as 'safe' subjects. Indeed, when the Communists came to power, they saw Trnka's *The Czech Year* (*Spalicek*, 1947), his first feature, as a delightful children's film illustrating well-known Czech folktales and began to subsidise his work.[203] What the Party didn't seem to realise was that Trnka was making his films for adults, and that satire sometimes crept into his work. His last film, *The Hand* (*Ruka*, 1965), was a classic case in point. The hero, a puppet, is an artist whose work is controlled by an omnipresent hand (a live-action human hand) that only allows him to make works about the hand. The hand eventually causes the artist's death, and then arranges a full state funeral with all honours. The film was seen as a direct attack on totalitarianism and the cult of personality, and was eventually banned in 1970, ironically only months after Trnka's own death – and state funeral.

THE FIRST WAVE

While Trnka was working on one of his finest films, a version of *A Midsummer Night's Dream* (*Sen noci svatojánské*, completed in 1959), the immediate precursors to the Czech New Wave proper began to emerge. They are sometimes dubbed the First Wave, and included the first crop of important graduates from FAMU. Ján Kadár and Elmar Klos began working together as a writer/director team in 1952, with *Kidnapped* (*Únos*), a drama about an attempt by the CIA to hijack a Czech airliner. Despite its seemingly safe subject matter, the film was accused of 'bourgeois objectivism' and was only saved by the intervention of none other than Vsevolod Pudovkin. Their 1957 film, *House at the Terminus* (*Tam na konečné*), however, did seem to be making some serious criticisms of the socialist system. The film's heroine, Olina (Eva Očenášová), becomes pregnant, but her lover Karel wants her to have an abortion. She resists him and decides to have the child out of wedlock. The plot, simple as it is, plays out in a world of cynicism, despair and loneliness: when Olina tells her lover that a friend's husband has received an unjust prison sentence, Karel replies that the man will be forgotten about within the year. In the meantime, Olina's friend is being unfaithful with a young soldier. Elsewhere in the film, a grandmother dies a lonely death; an alcoholic remains in thrall to the bottle; Karel's cynicism remains unchanged. The importance of the film, as Peter Hames notes, 'lies in the fact that the loneliness, cynicism and compromise that it portrays were supposed to be either eliminated, or exceptional cases within a socialist society... One assumes that the Minister of Culture must have been looking the other way when this film was released.'[204]

The Party, however, certainly noticed Kadár and Klos's next film, *Three Wishes* (*Tři přání*, 1959). The film's hero is granted three wishes, and finds himself successful. However, he is left with the dilemma of whether or not to give up some of his success in order to help a friend who has lost his job due to being outspoken. The film was deemed critical of the Party, and discussions at the National Film Festival in Bánksa Bystrica in 1959 'condemned open expressions of revisionism'[205] and prohibited Kadár and Klos from making any more films for two years. Any films that were critical of the Party were also banned, which had the added effect of disabling 'any tendency to establish a united group'.[206]

By the time the party faithful had made their pronouncements at Bánksa Bystrica, however, several other notable films had already begun to emerge. In Ladislav Helge's *School for Fathers* (*Škola otců*, 1957), often seen as the first film of the First Wave, a schoolteacher attempts to mount an ideological stand but falls foul of the party; in 1959's *The Great Seclusion* (*Velká samota*), it was Helge himself who fell foul of the party. The film relates the attempts of Soucek, a provincial co-operative director, to turn things around in his village, but it is a battle he seems fated to lose. The original ending had Soucek turning to drink and denouncing the ideological cant he has hitherto been spouting. Helge was forced to substitute a new ending in which the farmers rally round their beleaguered director, suggesting that socialist agricultural policy will indeed win out and create a brighter future for all.

Desire (*Touha*, 1958), directed by Vojtěch Jasný, arguably 'the first filmmaker of importance to emerge from FAMU',[207] used a more lyrical approach to tell an apparently apolitical story. The film comprises four episodes, one for each season and the four stages of life. The first, fairytale-like part shows a boy on a farm in harmony with nature, a harmony enriched by the arrival of a baby sister; the young astronomer in part II can't seem to hold on to his demanding and ambitious girlfriend and seems to lose her altogether at the end when she gets onto a train; part III's female protagonist loses her best fields to a farming collective but, despite ill health, continues to work using a horse-drawn plough (with occasional help from a tractor driver); the final episode relates the story of an old woman living alone with just her dog for company in a mountain village, a solitary existence broken only by the surprise visit of Václav, one of her two sons. She makes him tea, he plays the piano, while the dog, pleased to see Václav, 'function[s] as a link with the times when the family was still together'.[208] After the old woman's death, the dog searches the house and village for her. The film concludes with Václav and his brother walking in an orchard, reminiscing, with the dog following them. Finally, Václav learns that his wife has given birth to a son, concluding the film on a note of 'honest pessimism': the cycle of the seasons, and of human life, the epiphanies are set against the loss of love, the end of innocence, and the realpolitik of collectivisation and the Party's empty rhetoric.

František Vláčil would also become known for a style that owed more to poetry than socialist realism. His debut feature, *The White Dove* (*Holubice*, 1960), tells the story of Susanne, a little girl living on a Baltic island who is waiting for the arrival of her homing pigeon. Unbeknownst to her, the pigeon has been shot down over Prague by a wheelchair-bound boy, Michal. The shooting is witnessed by Martin, an artist, who tries to get Michal to realise the significance of what he's done as he tries to help nurse the bird back to health. Dialogue is kept to a strict minimum,[209] with Vláčil instead employing striking imagery to tell the story: the empty beaches and clear waters of Susanne's island are contrasted with the Gothic spires, vertiginous alleyways and confined rooms of Michal's Prague. Michal himself could represent a country crippled by ideology, with the bird and Susanne representing Czechoslovakia before the Communists took over in 1948. But Vláčil was never one for ideology; *The White Dove* 'asserts simple humanist ideas [and strives] for poetic association rather than narrative context'.[210]

Such concerns were also evident in Vláčil's next film, *The Devil's Trap* (*Ďáblova past*, 1961). Set during the Counter Reformation, it tells the story of a simple miller whose knowledge of the natural world is taken by the Jesuits as proof that he is in league with the Devil. As Peter Hames observes, 'While the criticism of dogmatism clearly has an oblique reference to the present [the early 60s], the film is notable for its poetic power, the strength of its formal composition, the tenderness of its love scenes and a sense of history as present.'[211] Vláčil's next film would paint these themes on an epic canvas; but, by then, the New Wave proper had begun.

SICK AND TIRED OF BAD FILMS

1963 proved to be a watershed year for Czechoslovak cinema, as much as 1958/59 had been for the French and British. The feeling at home was that the national cinema was moribund and that there was a relatively urgent need to do something about it. As Miloš Forman remarked many times, they were simply sick and tired of bad films, and this, perhaps more than any ideological position, was one of the driving forces of the Czech New Wave. A renewal of Czech literature also stimulated them. As with the New Novel in France and the Angry Young Men in Britain, Czechoslovak cinematic culture had strong links with new writing. Writers such as Bohumil Hrabal, Arnošt Lustig, Václav Havel, Josef Škvorecký and Milan Kundera not only influenced the filmmakers of the new wave, but frequently collaborated with them.

In May, Jasný's charming but subversive fantasy, *Cassandra Cat* (*Až přijde kocour*, 1963), won the Special Jury Prize at Cannes, the first time a Czech film had enjoyed such international acclaim since the scandal surrounding Machatý's *Ecstasy* at Venice nearly 30 years before. Jasný's film is a classic example of the Czech fondness for surrealism and humour, and chronicles the strange goings-on at a provincial school. The children are encouraged to learn about society's faults while their teacher extols the virtues of friendship, honesty and fearlessness. The headmaster, however, doesn't approve of this liberalism, and even goes so far as saying 'fantasy does not exist!' after the children are told a fairy story about a cat with magic spectacles. Unfortunately for the headmaster, a circus then arrives in town, complete with a magician, a girl in a red catsuit, and her feline charge; the fairytale seems to have come to life. The cat's magic spectacles reveal the corruption and hypocrisy of the headmaster, forcing him to kidnap the cat in a last-ditch attempt to control the situation. It is only when the magician lures all the children away that the cat is safely returned.

The film is full of innovations, such as cinematographer Jaroslav Kučera's brilliant use of colour (through the cat's spectacles, the headmaster is seen to change colour, like a chameleon), rapid cutting and the use of split screens. It is not just the cat which stands for the liberating powers of the imagination: the film makes use of the children's paintings, and the players themselves are made up of members of the Black Theatre of Prague and the Theatre on the Balustrade, two celebrated ensembles.

As with Vláčil, Jasný steers away from direct subversion and party-baiting, preferring to cloak his aims in humour and good-natured farce and, in doing so, allies himself with the Czech tradition that stretches all the way back to Jaroslav Hašek and his great novel, *The Good Soldier Švejk*. He later commented, 'I don't care how socialist, or moralistic, or philosophical it sounds: I want to work toward people trying to be better, toward helping make things happen to help them become better.'[212]

Whilst Jasný enjoyed success in Cannes, there were even more remarkable developments back home. The feature debuts of Miloš Forman, Jaromil Jireš and Věra Chytilová all took place that year and, between the three of them, exemplify many of the main concerns and stylistic innovations that defined the Czech New Wave.

Forman, although he had graduated from FAMU as a screenwriter, was determined to become a director, and made *Audition* with a 16mm camera he had bought himself. Originally intended as a documentary, the film combined documentary footage of real auditions with an added fictional element, that of a shopgirl who defies her boss's orders by taking part in the audition. The film showed Forman's debt to both neorealism and *cinéma vérité*, and Forman later spoke of his desire to make films that were as 'close to reality as I could'. With pure documentary, however, he found that 'the camera's presence alters most situations... People become stilted, put on airs, wear masks, show off, get intimidated, so you cannot capture the everyday life by documenting it. You have to re-create it.' This process of re-creating reality necessarily involved narrative: 'I believe that we decipher the incoherent flow of life through stories. The stories may not add up to much, they may end abruptly or proceed according to mysterious logic, but my kind of film has to have them.'[213]

Although originally envisaged as a short film, *Audition* ended up running for three-quarters of an hour, traditionally an awkward length for theatrical distribution. After showing the film to producers at Barrandov, Forman was able to solve the problem by getting a second film commissioned: *If There Were No Music*, about a brass band competition in the provincial town of Kolín. As with *Audition*, Forman added a fictional strand – two of the bandsmen want time off rehearsals to go and watch a motorcycle race, end up losing their jobs and finally wind up playing for each other's band. It was sufficiently similar in style and content to the first film, and the two medium-length films were released as one feature-length film entitled *Talent Competition* (*Konkurs*, 1963). Although a little rough around the edges

– Forman called it 'the closest thing to a home movie that Barrandov has ever produced'[214] – *Talent Competition* nevertheless revealed Forman's humanism and his concern for the struggle of the individual against the group, and how these groups – in this case theatrical and musical – reflect society as a whole and act as microcosms of them.

By the time *Talent Competition* was released, Forman had shot his first feature film proper, *Black Peter* (*Černý Petr*, 1963, aka *Peter and Pavla*), which developed the director's wish to remain close to life while being faithful to its mysterious logic. The film follows the hapless Peter of the title as he starts a new job as a store detective in a supermarket, a job he is singularly unsuited for. He wrongly accuses one of his boss's friends of theft, and when he does happen upon a real thief – a little old lady – he lets her go. He is similarly unsuccessful in love and spends much of the film at loggerheads with his parents. 'You saw scenes like this in real life,' Forman later wrote, 'but never in the movies... This was precisely the point [of a film like *Black Peter*]... I had to collect the most "real"... snippets of life to make a deadly satire of it.'[215] The film received favourable notices at home and also won the main prize at the Locarno Film Festival.

A Blonde in Love (*Lásky jedné plavovlásky*, 1965, aka *Loves of a Blonde*), Forman's second feature, is a more polished, less satirical film. Andula (Hana Brejchová) works at a shoe factory in the provincial town of Zruč. The factory employs an all-female workforce, who live together in depressing dormitories. Feeling sorry for his lonely workers, the factory boss arranges a dance where the women can meet some off-duty soldiers. Unfortunately, they aren't the handsome young bucks the girls hoped for, but a motley assortment of overweight, balding middle-aged reservists. The film's dancehall sequence is a comic tour-de-force, as Andula tries to get the attention of Míla, the young pianist, whilst avoiding the attentions of one of the reservists. The pianist gives her his address in Prague, and the rest of the film concerns itself with Andula's attempts to meet him again in the city.[216]

Forman's third feature, *The Firemen's Ball* (*Hoří má panenko!*, 1967) returned to satire with such force that it was to prove Forman's last Czech film. Like *A Blonde in Love*, the film was taken directly from Forman's own experience, in this case of visiting a ball thrown by a provincial volunteer fire brigade when he found himself stuck on another screenplay. The film is a comedy of errors: raffle prizes go missing, the firemen organise a beauty contest at which they can show off their daughters, but, at the height of the celebrations, a fire breaks out elsewhere in the town. The rest of the film concerns itself with the, by now, drunk fire brigade's attempts to put the fire out and to draw their ball to some kind of close. The Party considered it an insult to the common man – the firemen are portrayed as corrupt and incompetent – but, like *A Blonde in Love*, it did well internationally and also got nominated for an Oscar.

Forman's Czech films can be seen as exemplifying the New Wave concern to use the everyday – to show normal people doing normal things – as a reaction against the bland, Party-approved socialist realist product they saw all around them. By creating films drawn from life, and even sometimes developing their scripts according to the abilities of the many non-actors who appear in them, Forman is arguably the Czech disciple of the Italian Ermanno Olmi, whose films he admired.

Lyricism of a different hue can be found in another of 1963's great débuts, Jaromil Jireš's *The Cry* (*Křik*). The story is simple enough: a young couple, Ivana and Slavek, are expecting their first child, and while he waits for news from the hospital, Slavek goes about his daily job as a TV repairman; various incidents in the couple's growing relationship are shown in flashback. This framework allows Jireš to examine the society the baby will be born into: Slavek's job means that he comes into contact with a wide range of people, including school teachers, a film critic (one of the film's in-jokes), and an attractive brunette. He is shown as bored and somewhat detached, nonplussed by party propaganda, whose major interaction with other people during the day is to intervene when a black man is attacked by a racist thug. At the end of the day, the call comes from the hospital that his wife has given birth to a boy. Not content with merely documenting this important moment in Slavek and Ivana's lives, Jireš also includes fantasy sequences. 'Historically, [*The Cry*] was at the forefront of the developments of the 1960s'[217] and was as conscious of form as anything made at the same time by the French New Wave. This alone was not enough to guarantee Jireš regular work, however, and it would be five years before he would be able to direct another feature.

Věra Chytilová's *Something Different* (*O něčem jiném*) was the other notable 1963 debut. While Forman's and Jireš's work exhibits lyrical humanism in varying degrees, *Something Different* was indeed just that. The film combines documentary footage of the gymnast Eva Bosáková with the fictional story of Věra, a housewife, the only direct connection between the two storylines being when Eva appears in a programme that Věra is watching on TV. Věra, trapped in a loveless marriage, conducts an affair, while Eva trains hard for the world championships. Věra's affair ultimately proves dissatisfying, while Eva triumphs in competition. Despite her win, Chytilová questions Eva's success: after all, she is still not free, being bound as she is by her ties to the national team and therefore the Party. What is ultimately important to Chytilová is not which of the two women is the happier, but to enquire into their respective roles without being overly judgemental.

After 1963, the floodgates opened and suddenly there were new Czech directors regularly springing up at film festivals all over the world. During the three years following the emergence of Forman, Jireš and Chytilová, over a dozen new filmmakers made startling debuts, including Jan Němec (*Diamonds of the Night/Démanty noci*, 1964), Evald Schorm (*Everyday Courage/Každý den odvahu*, 1964), Pavel Jurácek and Jan Schmidt (*Josef Kilián/Postava k podpírání*, 1964), Ivan Passer (*Intimate Lighting/Intimní osvětlení*, 1965), Hynek Bočan (*No Laughing Matter/Nikdo se nebude smát*, 1965), Antonín Máša (*Wandering/Bloudění*, 1965), Juraj Herz (*The Sign of Cancer/Znemení Raka*, 1966) and Jiří Menzel (*Closely Observed Trains/Ostře sledované vlaky*, 1966). Out of these filmmakers, it was arguably Němec, Passer and Menzel who were to join Forman, Chytilová and Jireš in making the biggest impact.

HOPELESS STRUGGLES, ETERNAL PROBLEMS

Jan Němec (b. 1936) can fairly claim to be the Czech New Wave's *enfant terrible*, although he originally intended to be a jazz musician. Němec decided instead to become a film director when his father pointed out to him that he might make more money in the film industry, but it would be inaccurate to say that Němec was motivated by fortune or fame. The themes of his Czech films are grounded in his observation that:

> There exists one everlasting conflict... the hopeless struggle between intelligence and stupidity, between the individual and the totality, and one eternal problem: the fundamental unwillingness of the people, or of humanity as a whole, to deal with problems which concern them.[218]

Němec's graduation film, *Sousto* (*A Loaf of Bread*, 1960), was an adaptation of Arnošt Lustig's story about two prisoners who steal a loaf of bread from a freight car guarded by the SS. The film won three international awards and helped Němec get his first feature off the ground. *Diamonds of the Night* (*Démanty noci*, 1964) was also based on a work by Lustig, *Darkness Casts No Shadow*, and tells the story of two Jewish boys who escape from a death train near the end of the war. They run through a forest, tired, exhausted, scared, and manage to beg some bread from a peasant woman. In the end, they encounter a group of old men who have gone out hunting rabbits, but now begin to hunt the two boys.

Němec, however, was not interested in producing a faithful adaptation of Lustig's work. Concerned with making the story as universal as possible, he made no reference to the year or country the story was taking place in, chose two actors who did not look particularly Jewish, stripped the dialogue down to the minimum – neither boy speaks during the film's first quarter-hour – and suggested their backstory with scenes that are too brief and non-dramatic to be called flashbacks in the traditional sense, but do a great deal to convey the boys' states of mind. Even when deep in the forest, Němec will suddenly show us one of the boys boarding a tram, or talking to a girl. Such a concern for the inner world of the characters places *Diamonds of the Night* on a par with Tarkovsky's *Ivan's Childhood*, which had been the toast of the Venice Festival two years earlier; Němec's film won the Grand Prix at Mannheim in 1964, and the Critic's Prize at Pesaro the following year.

Němec believed that stylisation, not realism, was the key to reaching an audience. His comments are worth quoting at length:

> It is necessary for the author to create in a film his own world, which is totally independent of reality... when we consider film, we may talk of very few authors who managed to create their own film world. We may certainly speak of Chaplin and Bresson, and Buñuel. Why do I consider it so important? If I were to aim in my films predominantly at an external similarity with the world, I would waste a lot of energy and divert the viewer's attention from the crux of the matter with which I am dealing. The viewer then necessarily asks, how life-like the work really is, whether it resembles life the way he experiences it, whether it duplicates it exactly, or only approximately. However, if it is evident from the very first shot, that external similarity is of no relevance, then the audience is forced to give up its favourite comparisons, and has to concentrate on the meaning and the author's intentions.[219]

Such an approach underlay Němec's next film, a nightmarish cross between Lewis Carroll and George Orwell. *The Party and the Guests* (*O slavnosti a hostech*, 1966; lit: 'About Celebrations') proved to be so controversial that it almost ended Němec's career on the spot; it is also one of the most celebrated of all Czech New Wave films, one that has not lost its power to unsettle and provoke. Its story is simple: a group of people are having a picnic in a forest when they are intercepted by a group of men led by the boyish Rudolph, who wears a tweed suit and plus fours. The group are then interrogated by Rudolph and his cronies, and are put in a 'cell' which is no more than a line drawn around them on the ground (recalling Buñuel's *The Exterminating Angel*, in which the petit bourgeois characters suddenly find themselves unable to leave the room they're in). An older man, the Host, then appears, apologising for the 'attack' – which was, he explains, merely a joke – and invites them all to a dinner party. A faint air of surrealism hangs over the proceedings: the tables – set with silverware and candelabra – are waited on by a host of serving staff but, as in dreams, this indoor scene has been transposed to the shore of a lake in the forest. The Host, a genial man, expresses concern for his guests' well-being and, during the meal, all of them confirm that they are happy and having a nice time. Except for one – a nameless character sometimes dubbed the Guest Who Refused to be Happy. He disappears, and the Host orders Rudolph – whom we now know to be his adoptive son – to head the search party. The film ends with the search party heading off deeper into the forest in search of the Guest Who Refused to be Happy, recalling the geriatric (but still dangerous) search party of *Diamonds of the Night*.

With the film finished, Němec found himself accused of criticising the Party, something he himself always denied. The writer Josef Škvorecký summarised the director's position: 'It is... a parable about the process which takes place in all modern societies – the adoption of a dominant ideology – and about the destruction of those who do not adopt it.'[220] As if expecting trouble, Němec shot the film quickly and almost everyone who appears in it were his friends or colleagues. (Jan Klusak, who plays Rudolph, was actually a composer, the Guest Who Refused to be Happy was played by Evald Schorm, a fellow New Wave director, while the bespectacled Škvorecký – who also worked as a film critic – is easy to spot amongst the guests.) 'People keep talking and talking [in the film] – yet the resulting mood of the film is a strange deafness, an appalling apathy, and a peculiar alienation.'[221] As if this wasn't bad enough, Ivan Vyskocil (the Host) looked vaguely like Lenin, which 'gave the scene a kind of flavour of impending horror'.[222] Although this was apparently accidental, the damage had been done. During a preview of the film, Škvorecký remembers, 'Mr President [Antonín Novotný] hit the ceiling, and stayed there throughout the screening.'[223]

It perhaps says something about the relative liberalism of Czechoslovakia in the mid-sixties that, despite the furore, Němec was able to continue making films. *Martyrs of Love* (*Mučedníci lásky*, 1966) comprised three stories about shy lovers, capturing 'daydreams, just as Buñuel once filmed dreams'.[224] As with his earlier films, Němec was mainly concerned with mood and poetic atmosphere. Škvorecký sees this as part of a Czech national tendency:

The particular emphasis on emotions and mood, and the lyrical approach make Němec's work an organic part of the great tradition of Czech art; if it were necessary to determine the Czech contribution to world art, its major offerings would be found in the realm of poetic and lyrical presentation of reality.[225]

If *The Party and the Guests* had seen Němec accused of subversion, now, with *Martyrs*, he was being charged with elitism. He responded by citing two of his heroes: 'The question is, whether a film is really a film – as Chaplin, Bresson, and others say – only if the auditorium is full.'[226] The implication being, of course, that a full auditorium does not mean that the film is worth seeing.

Němec was not alone in causing outrage and having charges of elitism levelled at him. Věra Chytilová's second feature, *Daisies* (*Sedmikrásky*, 1966), was a surreal – Dadaist might be a better word – assault on bourgeois values, to say nothing of conventional storytelling. Two bikini-clad young women, Marie I and Marie II (Ivana Karbanová and Jitka Cerhová), announce at the start of the film 'Everything is going bad', also noting that 'No one understands us'. They decide to go to 'someplace where something's going on', which sets up the film's very loose and free structure. The two Maries then engage in a series of games or happenings – shopping, lazing by an outdoor swimming pool, eating in a restaurant, play-fighting each other, getting drunk in a nightclub or antagonising men. They eventually decide 'We don't want to be bad' and set about trying to make amends by tidying up the banquet they've just trashed. This final scene ends by jump-cutting to shots of bombs going off, suggesting some kind of madcap apocalypse is occurring.

The film resists easy reading. Chytilová admitted in an interview[227] that *Daisies* was largely improvised, the only part of the script set in stone being the dialogue, from which they developed the Maries' adventures. At one point, the girls agree that they've 'gone bad', and that someone is going to have to pay for their outrageous behaviour. But Chytilová doesn't judge the Maries, she merely watches them run amok. With no conventional plot or character development, the film reflects the girls' antics with a restless, exuberant melting pot of stylistic devices: frequent drum-rolls recall a circus performance, while wooden creaks suggest that the two Maries are dolls (which they indeed claim to be at one point). Scenes are interrupted by bursts of music, or accompanied by the menacing ticking of an unseen clock. Sudden changes of location are frequent, such as the scene where Marie I slaps Marie II in their apartment, but Marie II is shown falling over in a field. Chytilová mixes her film stocks with equal relish, cutting from black and white to colour, and then filtering the colour, such as in the first restaurant scene. Time-lapse is used to great effect – the montage of train shots is one of the most visually arresting sequences in the entire film – and the film abounds with vivid colours; Ester Krumbachová's set designs are superbly captured by Jaroslav Kučera's cinematography.

COMEDIES ABOUT FUNERALS AND WAR

It was not all surrealism and subversion, however. Forman's scriptwriter Ivan Passer directed *Intimate Lighting* (*Intimní osvětlení*, 1965), a charming film about a city musician visiting his friend in the country, who teaches at a provincial school. *Intimate Lighting* could be described as 'a dramatic comedy in which nothing very much happens – many times over'.[228] Despite its apparent simplicity, the film has considerable power: Polish director Krzysztof Kieślowski was later to remark that it was 'one of the ten films that had most affected him'.[229] In common with the Georgian filmmaker, Otar Iosseliani, Passer is more interested in mood than plot and, as with Forman's *Audition* (which Passer co-wrote), concerns himself with characters for whom life has little meaning except through music. (Iosseliani was to tread similar ground in his 1975 film, *Pastorale*.)

Petr (Zdeněk Bezušek), together with his beautiful girlfriend, Štěpa (Věra Křesadlová), visit Petr's old friend, Bambas (Karel Blažek), for a weekend. The lives of the two men appear to have diverged sharply: Petr plays in an orchestra in Prague, while Bambas lives with his wife, children and wife's elderly parents, earning money by teaching music at the local school, where his administrative duties allow little or no time for him to actually play. As Petr finds out, Bambas's regular outlet for performing, and hearing the music of others, is at funerals, where he plays in a duo with his father-in-law (they need a little extra money to build an extension on the house, and get paid not in cash, but in bricks and tiles). Petr and Bambas discuss music and generally catch up, setting the world to rights in a late-night drinking session. With neither man in the first flush of youth, both Petr and Bambas are facing the death of their dreams and make a half-hearted attempt to make something of their lives by attempting a midnight flit from the house, vowing to play at funerals, as 'nobody wants to listen to concerts'. Come morning, they are back at Bambas's house.

Passer is after the simple mystery and poetry of everyday events: Štěpa tickling Petr with an ear of grass as Bambas chases the kids around the orchard; the discovery of the hen nesting in the garage, then Bambas running one over as the garage becomes inundated with the rest of the hens; the film then cuts with quiet humour and surrealism to a funeral procession, almost as if Passer is taking a few moments to mourn the demise of the hen. En route to the funeral, Bambas's father-in-law (the marvellous Jan Vostrčil, who also appeared as a hapless conductor of one of the amateur orchestras in *Talent Competition*) talks about how one sad song can go round the world, and that the car would run much better if it ran on tears. A man urinates against the cemetery wall to the strains of the funeral band's brass. Then more men emerge, not to piss, but because they have spotted a bikini-clad woman sunbathing in the long grass of the field next to the cemetery. Štěpa enters the church as a hymn is being sung, sunlight dappling the backs of the mourners' heads (beautifully shot by Miroslav Ondříček, who had to leave before production was over to shoot *The White Bus* for Lindsay Anderson; the film was finished by veteran cameraman Josef Střecha); no sooner has the music stopped than someone blows their nose; we then cut to Bambas, his trumpet to his ear, listening to the wind in the grass. Petr goes off himself to look at the woman in the bikini, who is now haymaking in the field. She looks into camera and we cut to an old woman dancing at the funeral reception, quiet poetic contrasting cuts from youth to age, from semi-clothed to clothed, from work to play, all the while serenaded by the brass band's sadly joyful/joyfully sad melody.

The link between youth and age, love and sadness, is reinforced when a drunk man at the funeral offers Bambas and his father a shot of the local liquor. They both refuse – they are still playing – and the man helps himself to both shots. Later, the man, now drunker than ever, approaches them again. Bambas asks him what he wants but, instead of replying, the man begins to sing a love song, at which most of the rest of the room join in. We cut to Štěpa in the car outside as the old women – just in from working in the fields – walk past the car, looking at her, both out of curiosity (she's the pretty young girl from the city) and sympathy (she won't be young and pretty forever, as their weather-worn faces attest). And yet, despite its sadness, *Intimate Lighting* is full of a quiet, stoical joy, of an acknowledgement that, regardless of one's circumstances – young, old, pretty or not – what matters is giving oneself over to the moment, of realising that day-to-day life is really a series of disappointments. Passer believed that everyday reality is a 'light sleep' from which we occasionally wake 'to realise what reality is really like'.[230] By the end of *Intimate Lighting*, Bambas and Petr, with their dreams of escape in tatters, have woken up. The film's lyrical sadness is retrospectively enhanced with the knowledge that Karel Blažek, who plays Bambas, died shortly after filming was completed. *Intimate Lighting* was to be his only film.

A similar 'happy sadness' infuses Jiří Menzel's *Closely Observed Trains* (*Ostře sledované vlaky*, 1966 – sometimes known as *Closely Watched Trains*). The film is in the tradition of good-natured subversion that goes back to Jaroslav Hašek's First World War novel *The Good Soldier Švejk*, in which the little-man anti-hero usually finds himself out of his depth but somehow manages to emerge as a hero. Menzel's film follows Miloš Hrma, who starts a new job as an apprentice dispatcher at a rural railway station. Miloš (played by Czech pop star Václav Neckář) wants both a successful career, and to lose his virginity to his girlfriend Máša (Jitka Bendová), a conductress on a local train.

After failing to consummate their relationship – he suffers from premature ejaculation – Miloš attempts suicide in a brothel, but is saved when a workman accidentally knocks his way into the room via a hole in the wall. He eventually manages to lose his virginity to a local resistance fighter, codenamed 'Viktoria Freie' ('Victory Freedom'), after the station guard, Hubička, shuts him in a room with her. (She knows about Miloš's 'problem'.)

The fact that the Second World War is going on in the background seems of little concern to Miloš and his colleagues, busy as they are with their various interests, making them all archetypal Hašekian figures. Station guard Hubička (Josef Somr) is obsessed with sex, but is far more experienced than Miloš. He seduces his 'cousin' on the stationmaster's prize Austrian sofa, which suffers a rip during the encounter. Later, Zdena (Jitka Zelenohorská), the young telegrapher, initiates a late-night encounter with Hubička in the office, which ends with him stamping her backside with an official station stamp. An official enquiry later gets underway into the misuse of both the sofa and the stamp.

The stationmaster himself (Vladimír Valenta) is a pigeon-fancier who greets Miloš with a bird on his head and covered in droppings. Nostalgic for the great days of the Austro-Hungarian empire, he grovels before the Countess. Living in an apartment at the station, he is privy to hearing Hubička entertaining young ladies in the office via a ventilator shaft, and rants about the moral decline of the age, predicting Armageddon. (He gets equally offended when the Countess tells him the altar in the local church will have to be rededicated as evidence has come to light that 'fornication' has happened behind it.) Everyone ignores the stationmaster's sermonising, most comically his wife, who asks him if his soup was salty enough, or whether he wants fried rabbit for dinner.

The only two main characters who seem to acknowledge that a war is actually going on are the Nazi controller, Zedníček (Vlastimil Brodský), and the resistance operative, Viktoria Freie (Nada Urbánková). In one of the film's most comically surreal moments, Zedníček arrives in an automobile adapted for use on railway lines, but the only problem is, it can't turn round, so when he leaves, he has to do so by reversing the way he came, seemingly unaware of the absurdity. Zedníček's arrival is one of the most Hašekian moments in the entire film: the stationmaster's new uniform isn't quite finished, and he has to meet his boss with one sleeve missing. Zedníček takes great pride in announcing tactical withdrawals in several key European theatres, claiming it is part of a great plan to trap the enemy. Further to the great plan, everyone has to sign a document acknowledging a harsh sentence for neglect of duty (they can be sentenced to ten years' imprisonment, or even life or death!); needless to say, virtually everyone is already guilty of neglect of duty, a vocation no one seems too keen to abandon. (Zedníček's claim that the Führer means well – surely the most knowingly ridiculous line in the entire Czech New Wave – falls on equally deaf ears.)

Viktoria Freie, by contrast, seems competent and effective. When Miloš and Hubička are recruited to the cause, they are asked to blow up a munitions train, the closely watched trains of the title. It is Viktoria who both delivers the bomb and, when she hears of Miloš's suicide attempt, seduces him on the stationmaster's sofa. (It gets torn again.) In a plot twist worthy of Hašek, Miloš becomes a resistance hero entirely by accident, as Hubička gets detained by the disciplinary enquiry into the case of the torn sofa and stamped bottom. Miloš has to come in and retrieve the bomb from a desk drawer while Zdena, the telegrapher, explains what happened. Hubička and Miloš exchange knowing glances, and Miloš leaves to bomb the train. A photograph of the girl's rear is shown to bemused officials, Zedníček concluding that, while no crime has been committed, such unauthorised use of the station stamp constitutes an abuse and disgrace of the German language. Meanwhile, Miloš successfully detonates his bomb, but manages to get himself killed in the process.

Closely Observed Trains remains Menzel's greatest film, continuing the grand tradition of *Švejk* in showing war as absurd and the enemy as human (Zedníček remains a sympathetic character throughout, despite being a Nazi functionary). It also has moments of dreamlike beauty, as when the Countess makes her first appearance, riding into the station over the railway lines on a white horse, or when the camera holds on smoke drifting up from a passing train at night, and ash falls from the smoke like snow. Menzel acknowledged the film's blend of happy and sad: 'We all know that life is cruel and sad,' he remarked in an interview. 'What's the point of demonstrating this in films? Let us show we're brave by laughing at life. And in that laughter let us not look for cynicism but reconciliation.'[231]

THE FIRST WAVE (II)

The filmmakers of the First Wave weren't idle during the mid-sixties as their younger colleagues began to enjoy success, and were to produce two of the most notable films of the period.

After being banned from making films for two years at the National Film Festival in Bánksa Bystrica in 1959, Jan Kadár and Elmar Klos returned with *Death is Called Engelchen* (*Smrt si říká Engelchen*, 1963), a film about the 1944 Slovakian uprising that employs a flashback structure reminiscent of Resnais' *Hiroshima mon amour* and Munk's *Passenger* to tell the story of a guerrilla (Jan Kačer), and his relationship with Marta, a woman who furnishes the partisans with information by working as an SS prostitute. When Kačer's character learns that Marta is still alive, he tracks her down. Marta rejects him on the grounds that he will never be able to forget what she did during the uprising.

Kadár and Klos's most famous film also dealt with wartime events in Slovakia. *A Shop on the High Street* (*Obchod na korze*, 1965, aka *The Shop on Main Street*) is the most celebrated Slovakian film to be made during the New Wave (it has been described as one of the first Czecho-Slovak co-productions[232]), and became the first Czechoslovak film to win the Best Foreign Film Oscar. *A Shop on the High Street* explored Slovak society's attitude toward the Nuremberg laws and the deportation of Slovakian Jews.

Set during 1942, when the Slovak government was actively collaborating with the Nazis, it tells the story of a carpenter, Tóno Brtko (Jozef Króner), who is asked by his brother-in-law, head of the local fascist militia, to become Aryan controller of a Jewish shop on the high street of their town. The owner of the shop, Mrs Lautmannová (Ida Kamińska), is an elderly and deaf Jewish woman who mistakes Tóno for an employee. Contrary to the belief that Jews hoard gold, Tóno finds that Mrs Lautmannová has no money whatsoever; the shop is full of old buttons and bits of lace, the bric-a-brac of a lifetime. She survives through the support of the local Jewish community. He can't bear to tell Mrs Lautmannová the reality of the situation, and plays along with her misunderstanding that he's her new assistant in the shop. When the deportations begin, Mrs Lautmannová gets accidentally left off the list. Tóno, fearing accusations of sheltering a Jew, unsuccessfully tries to persuade the old lady to voluntarily join the deportation. He pushes her into the cellar and, when the deportation trains have left, finds that she has died. In remorse, he hangs himself.

The subject of the film – the acceptance by normal Slovaks of Nazism and the deportations – is represented by Tóno's wife, who pressurises him into becoming Mrs Lautmannová's 'controller', and her brother, the commander of the local militia. Kadár and Klos handle this tragi-comically: in one scene, Tóno – dressed in a suit that belonged to Mrs Lautmannová's late husband – walks through the town with the despised brother-in-law. The brother-in-law smiles benevolently and gives the occasional Nazi salute; Tóno tries to do the same. His suit, however, makes him look like Charlie Chaplin, and his half-hearted attempts to give Nazi salutes immediately render the brother-in-law completely ridiculous (the scene would not look out of place in *The Great Dictator*). The militia constructs an illuminated pyramid, dubbed the 'Tower of Victory', which is completed as the deportations begin; it would be absurd in other circumstances; here it is both comic and sinister. Reconciliation is only possible, it seems, in dreams: in the concluding fantasy sequence, Tóno – dressed in the Chaplin suit – dances with Mrs Lautmannová as the town band play an upbeat tune.

František Vláčil's *Marketa Lazarová* (1967), set in mid-thirteenth century Bohemia, chronicles the bitter rivalry of two clans, the Kozlíks and the Lazars. The former are pagan, the latter, Christian, with one of the Lazar daughters, Marketa (Magda Vášáryová), being destined for a convent. The first half, entitled 'Straba', concentrates mainly on the antagonisms between the two families – violence and cruelty are commonplace – culminating in Marketa being kidnapped by the Kozlíks and raped by the film's ostensible hero, Mikoláš Kozlík (František Velecký). In the second part, 'Beránek Boži' (The Lamb of God), an itinerant monk, Bernard (Vladimír Menšík), is introduced, providing a comic element – he is accompanied everywhere by his pet lamb, until the Kozlíks eat it. But it is perhaps Marketa who is the real 'agnus Dei', not in any dogmatic fashion, but rather in the sense of simple, apostolic Christianity: her relationship with Mikoláš grows into one of love and acceptance and, after rejecting the church and being rejected in turn by her father, returns to Mikoláš in his final attempt to free Old Kozlík from prison.

Marketa Lazarová is far more unconventional than *The Devil's Trap*, Vláčil's earlier foray into period filmmaking. Vláčil stated that he wanted to treat mediaeval people as if they were his contemporaries – wanting to 'understand them, see through the eyes of their lives, their feelings, their desires'.[233] Perhaps its closest kin is Tarkovsky's *Andrei Rublev*, made at approximately the same time, which was equally concerned with viewing the past as 'realistically' as possible. Realism here should not be confused with documentary-style observation: Vláčil's camera is constantly tracking, frequently subjective; jolts in perspective and point of view, complete with unannounced flashbacks, visions and hallucinations 'are less a break with narrative convention than a renewal of possibilities'.[234]

Vláčil spent over two years shooting the film; props – weapons, tools, costumes – were made according to mediaeval methods, and the cast were encouraged to remain in character, living on location. Vláčil was aiming for psychological, not socialist, realism. The film's unconventional narrative also served to heighten the mediaeval aesthetic, being arranged as a series of tableaux connected by intertitles employing mediaeval phraseology, suggestive of chronicles of the time: 'How two Kozlík brothers hunted on the road', or 'How Lazar, rid of his worries/With his neighbour/(whom the captain hunts through the woods)/gives away his daughter without a dowry'. Some are almost poems in their own right: 'About the campaign/Which became a funeral/How the captain reflected/On the death of his aide/Who fell at the hands/Of the sons of Kozlík before Oboriste./He is buried at Rohacek.' The intertitles serve to fragment the narrative, impeding (forbidding, even) conventional plot development.

Fragmentation could be seen to be serving at least two purposes here: a response to the stylistic innovations of the time (Godard, Antonioni, Jancsó), but also to further Vláčil's desire to see the middle ages as if he were a contemporary, where the grand narrative of day-to-day survival is set against the localised narratives of storytelling, folklore and hearsay. This appears in the film through the use of voiceovers from an unseen narrator (who occasionally addresses characters, such as when we first encounter the monk, Bernard), and from various characters. Arguably the key voiceover in the film is provided by Kateřina, Old Kozlík's wife, who tells the story of Straba the werewolf, a figure who represents the violence and superstition of the time. As

Kateřina speaks, we see most of the film's characters, implying that all the men are linked to the wolf and its 'heritage of blood'; Mikoláš in particular is singled out as being 'not of the race of men'. (Ironic, given that he is one of the film's least bloodthirsty figures.) The film's visual motifs remind us we are in a violent, cruel world: images of wolves, ravens, deer, lamb, snakes, hunters and hawks recur throughout.

One aspect of the film that is not mediaeval is its rejection of Christianity – Marketa ultimately denounces the convent towards the end of the film, and goes to join Mikoláš as he attempts to free his father, Old Kozlík, from prison. She chooses physical love over spiritual love. Bernard the monk is not a holy fool, just a fool. Christianity could be seen as having parallels with communism – a repressing force whose doctrines are officially above reproach. Hostility to the church veiled hostility towards communism. As Vláčil commented, 'The similarity [between Christianity and communism] is striking... socialist thinking has... stopped developing, and turned into a religion... If you take a poke at them, you are a heretic. The historical material in my films occasionally makes me realise that it is a much better way to disclose contemporary problems.'[235]

1968 AND ALL THAT

By the time Soviet tanks rolled into Prague on 21 August 1968, ending the reforms of Dubček's Prague Spring, international interest in the Czech New Wave had peaked. The political clampdown had serious consequences for New Wave filmmakers: Forman and Passer emigrated to the United States as quickly as they could, while Chytilová and Němec found themselves unable to work, as did a number of First Wave directors, such as Vláčil. However, the Czech New Wave wasn't entirely over, as the period 1968–71 saw some of the most remarkable films of the entire period.

After clocking up more rejected scripts than any other director at the time, Jaromil Jireš finally returned with his second feature, *The Joke* (*Žert*, 1969), based on Milan Kundera's 1967 novel. The film follows the misfortunes of Ludvík Jahn (Josef Somr) after he gets into trouble at university for joking about Trotsky to Markéta, his politically committed girlfriend. (The film opens in the early 1950s.) His friend

Pavel turns against him, and is instrumental in getting Ludvík thrown out of both the university and the party. If that wasn't enough, Ludvík is sentenced to hard labour in the mines of Ostrava, followed by a period of military service. Ludvík returns after six years, and decides to get his revenge on Pavel by seducing his wife, Helena. Ludvík's plans soon come unstuck, however: Pavel, seemingly affected by 60s liberalism, is only too happy to be shot of Helena. Realising that Ludvík does not love her, Helena attempts suicide, but takes laxatives by mistake. (An ironic mistake, given that she makes her attempt in an outside toilet.)

As with The Cry, Jireš employs flashbacks to contrast the conformist 50s with the comparatively heady 60s, but does so in a way that directly links the two eras. After arranging to borrow a friend's flat for Helena's seduction, Ludvík wanders around town, recalling the tumultuous days of 1949 when May Day was also a day to celebrate the communist takeover. (There is a horrible, unintentional irony here: these scenes were shot during the Soviet invasion of August 1968.)[236] Jireš cuts this sequence in a way suggesting Ludvík can see the past happening right in front of him. Similarly, he has 'a conversation' with Markéta: she addresses her comments directly into camera, Ludvík 'responds' in voiceover. Later, Ludvík returns to his hotel room (in the present) and enters the meeting that expelled him from university (in the past). In what is perhaps the film's strongest use of this device, Ludvík, ever the ladies' man, follows a young woman into a building, only to find himself at a ceremony welcoming newborn babies into the world, in the hope that 'they be brought up to become the pride of the family'. This is intercut with his denunciation by Pavel and other students, and Pavel's recitation of the words of Czech journalist and war hero Julius Fučík, 'I had hoped to meet you [death] much later.' We cut to the children, and Pavel continues, intoning Fučík's desire to 'work and love and sing much longer'. In yet another of the film's ironies, Czech audiences would have known that Fučík was murdered by the Nazis. Comparing Nazism to communism was certainly an irony not lost on Prague Spring audiences. The Joke became Jireš's most successful film internationally, and remains one of the Czech New Wave's most outspoken attacks on Stalinism.

Jireš's next film could hardly have been more different. *Valerie and Her Week of Wonders* (*Valerie a týden divů*, 1970) was a dreamlike Gothic fantasy replete with vampires, witch-burning priests, dungeons and ambiguous carnival performers. Based on a novel by Vítězslav Nezval, the film was, despite first appearances, a fairly safe choice for Jireš and his co-writer Ester Krumbachová: Nezval was a leading member of the Czech Communist party whose reputation since his death in 1958 had remained high. Nezval was also one of the earliest Czech surrealists, and the film remains faithful to this aspect of the book. Ostensibly the fantasies of a 13-year-old girl in the week she starts to menstruate, the film's recurrent themes are sexuality and death, youth and age, control and liberation.

As a kind of Gothic *Daisies*, the film demands numerous viewings and suggests numerous interpretations. The main figures in the harlequinade are Valerie (Jaroslava Schallerová, who herself was 13 when the film was shot), her grandmother, a young man called Orlík, the priest (Jan Klusák, from *The Party and the Guests*) and the vampire-like figure of Tchoř. Most of these characters shift throughout the film: Orlík starts by seeming to be Valerie's boyfriend, but is later revealed as her brother. He may or may not be Tchoř's assistant, who himself fulfils the role of authority and, therefore, threat and repression (as a vampire, constable and preacher). Jireš leaves it open as to whether these threats are actual (socio-political forces) or psychological.

The plot, such as it is, revolves around a vague quest to establish the identity of Valerie's father – could it be Tchoř? When she finally meets her real father, he appears as a much younger man with red hair, but who then seems to change into Tchoř. There is also the possibility that Valerie has been 'sold' by her grandmother to Tchoř, who needs young blood to remain youthful. Jan Klusák's priest – who wouldn't look out of place in a film by Buñuel – also lusts after Valerie and, despite being hanged, returns from the dead to accuse Valerie of witchcraft. Although Valerie is tied to a stake in the town square, ready for burning, her magic earrings – one of the film's other recurrent devices – save her. The film ends with what appears to be a reconciliation, with all the main characters dancing and celebrating outdoors. The final image is of Valerie, asleep in her bed, which is no longer in her bedroom, but in the woods.

If *Valerie and Her Week of Wonders* can be seen as a portrait of a Czech town as much as of a young girl, liberated through dreams, Vojtěch Jasný's *All My Good Countrymen* (*Všichni dobří rodáci*, 1969) serves as its opposite. Focusing on a Moravian village during the period 1945–58, Jasný's film tells the story of seven friends who are affected in various ways by the introduction of agricultural collectivisation. František (Radoslav Brzobohatý) is a farmer who emerges in the film's second half as the hero – he resists Stalinism, endures imprisonment and stoically endures the incompetence of the collective. Očenáš (the great Vlastimil Brodský) is a church organist, choirmaster and music teacher who initially accepts the changes the Communists are imposing, but is later run out of the village by the mediocrities who confiscate his property in the name of the collective. Franta Lampa (Václav Babka) is a watchmaker nicknamed 'Lampa' because he collects lamps. Jožka Pyřk (Vladimír Mensík), meanwhile, is a ne'er do well whose history as a thief and former convict is softened by his lisp and hare-lip, making him not so much a threat to law and order as something of a village joke.

The film is, however, not realism in the strictest sense. Jasný based his script on stories his mother remembered – the village elders act as a kind of Greek chorus, giving the film a broader, deeper treatment of recent history. The political deterioration of the era is played out against a backdrop of local myth and hearthside tale; one character is referred to as the 'merry widow' who seems to have a fatal effect – literally – on her lovers and, at one point, Zášinek's dead wife – a Jew murdered by the Nazis – comes back to question him. Jaroslav Kučera's photography further emphasises the poetic and the eternal in the everyday: landscapes throughout the seasons punctuate the film, serving to remind of the eternal verities of nature against the gross stupidity and short-sightedness of human affairs. The film reminds us that the only certainties of life are birth, work, love and death. Jasný remarked in a 1967 interview that what he most of all wanted to do was 'to defend human dignity'.[237] In *All My Good Countrymen*, that dignity is constantly at the mercy of political realities.

The film concludes with an epilogue, set in 1968. Očenáš returns to the village and meets Marie, František's daughter, whom he taught and is now a musician herself. Before cycling off, he tells her somewhat sadly that everything has changed, a veiled reference to the Prague Spring. By the time of the film's February 1969 release, however, things had changed again, and not for the better; Očenáš's mournful air in the epilogue now seemed ironically justified.

All My Good Countrymen won Best Director and Special Jury prizes at Cannes in 1969, and Jasný served on the jury the following year. By then, things were looking bleak for Czech filmmakers. Josef Škvorecký noted that eight films were banned – including Evald Schorm's *Seventh Day, Eighth Night* (*Den sedmý, osmá noc*, 1969) and Menzel's *Skylarks on a String* (*Skřivánci na niti*, 1969) – and 12 or so films then in production were stopped.[238] Many new wave films were blacklisted in 1973, by which time most of the filmmakers had gone into exile, or were forced to produce 'safe' films: Vláčil, for instance, could only find work making children's films, while Menzel was forced to 'recant' his past 'sins' and was commissioned to produce *Who Looks for Gold?* (*Kdo hledá zlaté dno?*, 1974), a socialist-realist film about the building of a dam. It says something for the quality of post-1968 Czech cinema that 'the studio workers' nickname for this spectacle was *Two Million Dollars Worth of S__t*.'[239]

Among the blacklisted films of 1973, a handful of them, including *All My Good Countrymen*, *The Party and the Guests* and *The Firemen's Ball*, were 'banned forever'. By then, Jasný too was in exile, only allowed home on condition that he recanted *All My Good Countrymen*. He refused.[240]

IN THE SHADOW OF DUBIOUS THEORIES: THE OTHER EUROPE

HUNGARY

Cinema came to Hungary in 1896, and the country quickly established a thriving film industry. Like much of Europe, Hungary was to supply Hollywood with expatriate talent – perhaps the most successful of them being the director Mihály Kertész, who emigrated to America in 1926, changed his name to Michael Curtiz and went on to make *Casablanca*. But Hungarian filmmakers were not just interested in populist escapism: as John Cunningham has noted, 'Hungarians have a strong claim that they were the first in the world to take film seriously and discuss the medium as an art form.'[241] Béla Balázs, a young film and theatre critic, would go on to be one of the world's leading early film theoreticians, eventually publishing the influential book *The Art of Cinema* in 1945. Balázs's friend, the Marxist critic György Lukács, also wrote on film, and founded a film club with the philosopher Ernst Bloch to explore the 'latent artistic possibilities of the cinema'.[242] Another young Hungarian, a teenage journalist by the name of Sándor Korda, 'probably established the world's first regular film review column in a daily newspaper'.[243] Korda believed strongly in the importance of the director in filmmaking, foreshadowing the auteur theories of the French New Wave by 40 years.

Hungary, like the Soviet Union and Czechoslovakia, was to benefit from increasing liberalisation in the 1960s, which caused a seismic shift in its cinema. The revolution of 1956 had been crushed by Soviet troops and a puppet regime, headed by János Kádár, installed immediately after its fall. However, as John Cunningham has observed, 'The Hungarian state machine had neither the resources nor the political will to maintain a virtual state of war against almost its entire population'.[244] Dissidents were sent to camps or executed and then a turnaround began, with partial amnesties rehabilitating dissident individuals and organisations being declared in 1959 and 1960, with a full amnesty in 1963. Kádár implemented a number of economic, social and cultural reforms that proved initially fairly successful, famously announcing that 'He who is not against us is with us and welcomed by us'.[245]

For Hungarian filmmakers, this was to give them freedoms they had not enjoyed before. Since the Communist takeover of the country in 1949, film production had been centralised and controlled by the National Filmmaking Company and the News and Documentary Film Company. Those two studios were now (1962) split up, creating four new ones – Studios I–III, plus a fourth created out of the News and Documentary company and the old Hunnia studio (usually regarded as the first Hungarian film studio proper, founded in 1911). Studio heads were filmmakers themselves, not Party apparatchiks. Directors were normally attached to a studio, but had the option of submitting their scripts to other studios (as Cunningham notes, 'modelled to some extent on the Polish system'[246]). Scripts were approved by the studio heads in conjunction with the Ministry of Culture, but, once a film was shooting, there was no interference from the studio or the Party.

Subject matter, formerly restricted to traditional socialist realist fare – workers, factories and the like – was broadened with the relaxation of censorship laws, allowing filmmakers to tackle previously taboo subjects, including the 1956 revolution. Further innovation was encouraged at the Béla Balázs Studio, which grew out of post-revolutionary student filmmaker gatherings into a studio proper in 1960. Its remit was to make non-mainstream films and proved a fertile training ground for film graduates and newcomers. The studio even had its own cinema, where its work was regularly screened. Although mainstream filmmaking continued – and, indeed, thrived – throughout the 1960s, two major directors emerged whose names became a byword for the new Hungarian cinema: Miklós Jancsó and István Szabó.

Miklós Jancsó

Miklós Jancsó (b. 1921) began making documentaries and newsreels in the early 1950s, but did not get the chance to direct his first feature until 1959, when he made the now largely forgotten *The Bells Have Gone to Rome* (*A harangok Rómába mentek*). *Cantata* (*Oldás és kötes*, 1963) was a big improvement, filtering a socialist realist storyline through the modernist lens of Antonioni. (Jancsó has often said that *La Notte* was the biggest single influence on *Cantata*.) Ambrus, a young doctor played by the popular Hungarian actor Zoltán Latinovits, is plunged into a crisis when the wife of an old friend undergoes heart surgery. He returns to his home on the Hungarian Plain, where he sees old friends, but they don't offer much in the way of spiritual or intellectual sustenance. At one point, Ambrus gets down on all fours and eats with turkeys in the farmyard. Communism has let him down, it would seem, and so have the new freedoms.

Jancsó's next film was to be his international breakthrough. *My Way Home* (*Igy jöttem*, 1964) follows Joska (Jancsó regular András Kozák), a young Hungarian soldier who is attempting to return home at the end of the Second World War. He is captured several times by Russians, receives worse treatment at the hands of fellow Hungarians – who mistake him for a German – and ends up in the hands of the Russians again. He forms an unlikely friendship with his guard, Kolja, a Red Army soldier about his own age. As in *Cantata*, Jancsó never lets us close enough to the characters to be able to entirely predict what they will do; there is always a distance, stratas of story and elements of character withheld. When Kolya hands Joska his gun to shoot frogs, for instance, Joska turns the gun on his 'captor'. A few uneasy moments pass, and then the two men laugh, wrestling each other to the ground. Likewise, Jancsó is not interested in conventional plotting; Joska's fate is left open: at the end of the film, he is shown walking along a road that is identical to the scene at the beginning of the film.

The Round-Up (*Szegénylegények*, 1965) concerns itself with the aftermath of the 1848 revolution (a year of revolutions across Europe). Here Jancsó continues with his interest in history and the nature of political power. A group of outlaws, some of whom belonged to Sándor Rózsa's group, are being held in a compound on the Hungarian plain.

They are questioned by their captors, who are trying to find out if Rózsa, a notorious highwayman who fought on the side of the rebels, is among them. As with *My Way Home*, the viewer is given no clues as to how things will develop; the film's plot – such as it is – shifts several times, and the brutality of the guards and their superiors hints right at the beginning of the film that there is no way out for the prisoners. The miles of seemingly empty plain form a Kafkaesque prison from which it is impossible to escape.

Indeed, the start of the film suggests both the angle from which Jancsó is approaching history and his method of showing it: a voiceover informs us of the historical background whilst showing us documents from the time. However, the events of the film are not about 1848 itself, but a relatively minor episode that occurred sometime afterwards. As András Bálint Kovács has noted, 'The more the film emphasises its historicity, the more it becomes generalised.'[247] Jancsó is not interested in this one story *per se*, but in the very nature of political power in general: 'The events [of the plot] are only part of a *symbolic ritual* which, according to Jancsó, varies its form during history, but with its essence and results always remaining the same: oppression and humiliation.'[248]

The Round-Up reflects this 'symbolic ritual' in its camerawork. Jancsó extends the length of both takes and tracks, enabling the camera to circle and swoop around the characters as if it were another character, 'a threatening *deus ex machina*'.[249] Photographing in widescreen reduces the figures – both the prisoners and their uniformed captors – to abstraction (especially in the long shots). As in *My Way Home*, dialogue reveals little about the characters or the plot – it is just words spoken. Even when those words are specific, as in the introductory voiceover, they are revealing the unspoken: *The Round-Up* is not just about 1848; it is about 1956 (as no one at the time failed to realise); it is about the rituals of history and power, and they, Jancsó reminds us, are ongoing.

István Szabó

István Szabó (b. 1938) graduated from the Film Academy in 1961 with his diploma film *Concert* (*Koncert*, 1961), and then made two shorts at Béla Balázs Studio, *Variations Upon a Theme* (*Variációk egy témára*, 1963) and *You* (*Te*, 1963), which won Best Short Fiction Film at San Francisco. Traditional industry practice dictated that filmmakers had to serve a ten-year apprenticeship before they could graduate to features, but Szabó was able to direct his first feature film at the relatively young age of 25 due to the support of János Herskó, who was head of Béla Balázs Studio at the time. *The Age of Daydreaming* (*Álmodozások kora*, 1965) centres around a group of university students trying to embark on careers but coming up against bureaucracy and the conservatism and small-mindedness of the older generation. Although a lyrical film with obvious debts to the French New Wave – at one point a girl crosses the screen carrying a placard for *The 400 Blows* – the film is 'heavy with history',[250] a theme that would recur in Szabó's next film (and much of his subsequent work).

Father (*Apa*, 1966) tells the story of Takó, a boy whose father died when he was still a small child. Takó invents alternative histories for his father, as underground hero, great doctor, outdoorsman, statesman. Only later, when Takó falls in love with a Jewish girl and becomes involved in the events of 1956 does he realise the need to forge his own identity. The film is 'heavy with history' like its predecessor, in that Szabó is doing more than just telling a coming-of-age story: 'He is examining the relationship of man to his past. The boy, with no heritage that he knows of, feels the need to create a heroic one. His Jewish sweetheart, however, has a long and ancient history behind her, one that she says she would like to be free of, but cannot.'[251]

Although Szabó's own father was a doctor, he denied that the film was autobiographical. He saw the need for fathers – both real and imaginary, mythic – as a fundamental human need after the end of the Second World War, when so many actual fathers were dead. However, he recognised a downside to this, in that the need for a father figure could fuel personality cults. They could be benign – such as Roosevelt, news of whose death in 1945 appears in the film as newsreel footage – but more often than not they are dictators such as Stalin and his stooge, Mátyás Rákosi, who led Hungary in the postwar years up to 1956. Film for Szabó, as for Bertolucci, was a form of therapy, but for the Hungarian, it was very much public therapy. Szabó stated his mission succinctly: 'My task is not to amuse the viewer, but, on the contrary, to help, to act as therapy.'[252]

THE POLISH SCHOOL

Film clubs recur throughout the history of cinema, and of new waves in particular. Before the advent of DVD and Internet forums, they were the original meeting places of film enthusiasts where mainstream and non-mainstream fare would be screened far away from the tinsel and glamour of the early 'multiplexes' – the Odeons and Gaumonts – places where ideas could be swapped and, ultimately, from the 1950s on, ideas for new films could be born. Poland was no exception, and we can trace the history of the Polish New Wave – or Polish School, as it is more commonly known – back to a film club called START, which was established in the late 1930s 'by a group of neophyte directors', which was 'a kind of left-wing discussion club'.[253] The Second World War wiped out the Polish film industry – studios and laboratories were razed along with most of the rest of Warsaw – and filmmakers returning from the war, such as Aleksander Ford, were effectively starting again with a *tabula rasa*.

The Łódź Film School was set up in 1948 as part of the attempt to resurrect filmmaking in Poland. As in other Soviet Bloc countries, the state was in control of what got made, although it delegated a lot of responsibility to Ford and his colleagues, who 'hated the Polish films of the pre-war period'.[254] With no domestic films being made, they looked to foreign imports for inspiration, and none were more influential in Poland than the Italian neorealists, who were felt to be fellow travellers in describing the world of the impoverished, and a Europe in ruins; not just a case of 'Germany Year Zero', but of 'Poland Year Zero' as well. It was largely a combination of studying at film schools such as Łódź and the Kraków Film Institute, soaking up the neorealists and other foreign films screening at the film clubs, and working under Ford and his generation that revitalised Polish filmmaking and got the Polish School off the ground. Its first major director was Andrzej Wajda.

Andrzej Wajda

Andrzej Wajda (b. 1926) was a graduate from Łódź and afterwards worked as an assistant on Ford's *Five Boys from Barska Street* (*Piątka z ulicy Barskiej*, 1954). Ford's next project was due to be *A Generation* (*Pokolenie*), a film about an underground resistance group and based on the novel by Bohdan Czeszko, but Ford recommended Wajda instead. The project was approved, on the condition that Ford oversaw his protégé. Ford had his work cut out for him: 'They [the cast and crew] were all beginners,' Wajda recalled in 2002, 'from [Roman] Polanski the actor to [Jerzy] Lipman the cinematographer. It was fantastic, because we were the 'Generation' fascinated by cinema.'[255] The exteriors were shot on location in Warsaw and Łódź, with the interiors being done in a studio (lightweight sound equipment was still five or six years away at this point). The Party had been expecting 'a *lumpenproletariat* film [designed to] celebrate the tenth anniversary of the Polish People's Republic'.[256] What they got instead was a film that 'reeks of sadness'[257] in showing the doomed attempts of the young Communist underground members to defy the Nazi occupation. The film was first screened 'for the Politburo in 1954, in a heavily guarded resort house surrounded by barbed wire', the director remembers.[258] The Party hated the film, forcing Wajda to reshoot some scenes, but even so, reshooting did not turn the film into the propaganda vehicle they were hoping for. The film's release was delayed a year, by which time political events in Poland were about to turn in favour of Wajda and his 'generation'.

The pivotal event of 1956 was Nikita Khrushchev's speech denouncing Stalin, which led to a political thaw in the Soviet Union and also in certain parts of Eastern Europe. In Poland, 15,000 workers revolted in June, forcing the Party to install Władysław Gomułka as Party Secretary. Gomułka was a moderate who had been imprisoned during the Stalin years, and the early years of his term in office (which lasted until 1970) were crucial for Polish cinema in that they saw a relaxing of the censorship laws and a reorganisation of the studio system. The Unit system, which dated back to the 1930s but had been abandoned at the outbreak of war, was reintroduced. Units were essentially small filmmakers' co-operatives headed by a filmmaker who had either achieved a certain degree of success or whom the Ministry of Culture felt deserved a break.

With filmmakers now in charge of their own studios, and the relative lack of censorship, Wajda had less difficulty in getting his second film, *Kanal* (*Kanał*, 1957), up and running. It is certainly the sort of film that could never have been made prior to 1956, as it is not only set during the 1944 Warsaw Uprising; it is also based on a true story. A group of Home Army resistance fighters have been ordered to retreat from the Nazis through the sewers of Warsaw, only to become separated in the labyrinthine tunnels. The film steers clear of socialist realism: the opening voiceover announces that all the main characters have only hours to live, and the story that follows is as surreal as anything in Buñuel (whom Wajda regarded as his master). The pessimistic ending was seen by the authorities as being too anti-Soviet in that they do not come to the rescue of the Home Army, but this is merely reflecting what actually happened: the Soviets let the Poles die. Nevertheless, the authorities conceded that the film was original and powerful, and agreed to its being shown in Cannes the month after its Warsaw premiere. Cannes in those days was ruled by the kind of evening dress and rich dinner party sensibility so despised by Truffaut (who was to be banned from attending the festival the following year), and the irony of showing a film set in a sewer to people in evening dress was not lost on Wajda. Nevertheless, the film met with a positive response and was awarded the Special Jury Prize.

Ashes and Diamonds (*Popiół i diament*, 1958) formed the third part of Wajda's war trilogy, and made a star out of one of *A Generation*'s supporting actors, Zbigniew Cybulski. Cybulski plays Maciek, a young soldier in the right-wing Nationalist Army who is ordered, on the day the Germans surrender, to assassinate Szczuka, a newly arrived communist district secretary. He kills the wrong man, but is given a second chance. This time, he holes up in the same hotel as the district secretary, but things become complicated by his relationship with Krystyna, a barmaid (Ewa Krzyzewska). She represents the postwar world that will see the likes of Maciek redundant, and he is torn between her and carrying out his duty. The film made an immediate impact upon its release in 1958 and turned Cybulski into an icon.

Andrzej Munk

Andrzej Munk (1921–61) is arguably the most important Polish School filmmaker after Wajda. Like Wajda, he was concerned with the impact of history upon ordinary Poles and explored it in the five features he was able to complete before his untimely death in 1961 (he was killed in a car crash).

Man on the Tracks (*Człowiek na torze*, 1956) tells the story of Orzechowski, an elderly railway engineer who is struck and killed by a train in the first minutes of the film. What follows is a multiple-flashback investigation into his death – was it murder or suicide? – and also his life, revealing him to have been a not entirely sympathetic character, but one who is also a kind of folk hero, 'a spokesman for the superiority of practical experience over any idealism'.[259] In this sense he is a critic of the communist system; Munk gets out of being openly critical of the party by having Orzechowski killed in an apparent accident. On another level, the film is also a critique of the ordinary Pole as represented in popular culture, something Munk would address in his next feature.

Heroism (*Eroica*, 1958) deals with the Warsaw Uprising, but in a much more irreverent way than Wajda's *Kanal* (both *Man on the Tracks* and *Kanal* were written by Jerzy Stefan Stawinski). The first part, *Scherzo Alla Pollacca*, chronicles the misadventures of a character called Dzidzius (Babyface), who is more concerned with wine, women and song than the struggle to defeat the Nazis; he is, in effect, a sort of Polish Good Soldier Švejk. He is frequently shown looking in the opposite direction to other characters, or standing still while everyone else is in motion. In one of the film's most celebrated sequences, Dzidzius sits down to recover from enemy action by gulping from a bottle of wine, unaware that a German tank is approaching him from behind. In another sequence, he is charged with the mission of getting the Hungarians to come to the aid of the uprising. The film's second part, *Ostinato Lugubre*, takes place in a POW camp. One of the inmates, Zawistowski, attempts to escape from the camp. His fellow Poles aren't sure whether he actually got out, but they eventually become convinced that he succeeded; in reality, Zawistowski has been hiding in the attic of one of the other huts in the camp; he had not wanted to escape, merely to get away from the unbearable patriotism of his fellow countrymen.

Bad Luck (*Zezowate szczęście*, 1960) features another anti-hero, Jan Piszczyk (Bogumil Kobiela), who ricochets through history (the action takes place between 1930 and 1960) like some hapless pinball, switching sides whenever he deems it expedient to do so. Often he is simply in the wrong place at the wrong time: in one of the pre-war sequences, he is beaten up twice by the police, who mistake him first for a Jew and then for an anti-Semitic agitator. (He is neither.)

Munk's last film, *Passenger* (*Pasażerka*, 1963), is a very different piece of work. Although, like *Man on the Tracks* and *Bad Luck*, its narrative is structured around flashbacks, it is a subtler and darker film. Liza (Aleksandra Śląska), a former SS guard, is returning to Europe for the first time since the end of the war. She sees another woman on the liner whom she thinks may be Marta (Anna Ciepielewska), who had been a prisoner at Auschwitz. Liza admits to her husband that she was a guard at the camp, and recounts her relationship with Marta. Events are repeated twice, the second version suggesting that Liza has been lying to her husband, and possibly herself, as to what actually happened.

Passenger is stylistically innovative: Munk died while the film was still in production, so his collaborators, led by fellow director Witold Lesiewicz, decided to acknowledge this in the opening voiceover, using still photographs to cover the unshot present-day scenes. Only the past – Auschwitz – is seen in moving images, as if the past is still happening, being reinvented each time it is recounted. Such a device, borne of artistic necessity, also serves to heighten the themes of loss, regret and incompleteness integral to the film. As innovative as anything by Godard, Marker or Resnais, whose *Hiroshima mon amour* is perhaps its closest kin, *Passenger* is arguably greater than all of them: a key Holocaust film, and also one of the most challenging films about memory and representation, it also manages to create its own oneiric space in which all of these concerns intertwine, as if mid-twentieth-century history were a dream; or, perhaps more fittingly, a nightmare.

Roman Polanski

Roman Polanski (b. 1933) is arguably the most famous graduate of the Łódź Film School, and of the entire Polish School, although he only made one feature in Poland before emigrating. He began as a radio actor in Krakow after the war, while still at school. This led to stage work and a part in *Three Stories* (*Trzy opowieści*, 1953), a portmanteau feature by three students from Łódź. This in turn eventually resulted in a part in Wajda's *A Generation* (both were shot by Jerzy Lipman, whom Polanski had got to know during the shooting of *Three Stories*). Although Polanksi's role was minor, he hung around on set and acted as a runner on his days off, and was sufficiently inspired by Wajda's working methods to apply to Łódź himself. He got in and, after a few minor short films, made the award-winning *Two Men and a Wardrobe* (*Dwaj ludzie z szafa*, 1958), an absurdist, Beckett-like film that sees two men emerge from the Baltic carrying a wardrobe. They go into town, seeking accommodation and the attention of young women; they are not successful. A gang of thugs beats them up and breaks the mirror on the wardrobe's door. The two men return to the sea and disappear under the waves. The film won a prize at the Brussels World's Fair in 1958 and became the first short made at Łódź to be theatrically released in Poland. The film also came to the attention of Lindsay Anderson, who screened the film in London as part of the fourth Free Cinema programme, 'Polish Voices', in September 1958.

Polanksi's sole Polish feature is *Knife in the Water* (*Nóż w wodzie*, 1962). Andrzej Munk got him the chance to make the film, although it took several years to set up. (Munk was killed while Polanski was still shooting.) The film, a three-hander taking place on a yacht, is a fraught study of masculine rivalry and jealousy, revealing Polanski to be a master of action taking place in confined spaces. A rich couple, Andrzej (Leon Niemczyk) and Krystyna (Jolanta Umecka), take a young hitch-hiker with them for a day's sailing on their yacht. Tensions arise between Andrzej and the stranger (Zygmunt Malanowicz) and, when the hitch-hiker's prized knife is accidentally knocked into the water, a fight ensues between the two men, resulting in the hitch-hiker falling overboard. Believing him to have drowned, Andrzej swims to shore so he can call the police. But the stranger has not drowned, and gets back on the boat...

The film was not well received at home. As Polanksi's biographer Christopher Sandford remarked, 'The ministry apparatchiks objected to everything from the amount of cleavage to the deliberately ambiguous ending.'[260] *Youth Flag*, the official paper of the Young Communists, declared that 'the director has nothing of interest to say about contemporary man, and we don't identify with any of his characters'.[261] The Party may have objected to the film's themes (it is a film about the generational clash, amongst other things), its Freudian subtext (the knife), or its complete refusal to not mention the war (it was the first major Polish film since 1945 to do so). Polanski's crime, of course, was to not conform to the Party's idea of a filmmaker. And rather than having 'nothing of interest to say about contemporary man', Polanski has plenty to say about human nature: his trademark themes of the destructive nature of sexuality, voyeurism, and characters' propensities for games and rituals (both conscious and unconscious) are already present in this first feature, as well as surreal dark humour (Andrzej and the hitch-hiker engage in a li-lo inflation contest as a boxing match plays on the radio). *Knife in the Water* is a macabre game that ultimately opens the dark spaces in Andrzej and Krystyna's marriage. The final image is of their car on a country road, in the rain, going nowhere.

Knife's poor reception in Poland hastened Polanski's departure for the West. (He had already spent a period living in Paris – his birthplace – in 1960–61, where he made the short *The Fat and the Lean*.) In what would become a necessary tactic for survival, new wave directors – regardless of nationality – would sometimes be required to work abroad when work at home dried up for economic or political reasons. And *Knife in the Water* certainly fared better in the West than in the Soviet bloc: when the film premiered in the US in September 1963, it featured on the cover of *Time* magazine (the 20 September issue; a banner across the corner loudly proclaimed 'Cinema as an International Art'). Further acclaim followed in the shape of an Oscar nomination for Best Foreign Film (Polanski lost out to Fellini's *8½*).

Polanski's next three features were made in England. They bear some similarity to Antonioni's English-language films, the first of which,

Blow-Up, was made shortly after Polanski made his English-language debut with *Repulsion* (1965). Catherine Deneuve stars as Carol, a Belgian beautician working in London who shares a flat with her sister. When Helen, the sister, goes on holiday with her married lover, Carol is left alone and her already fragile mental state disintegrates. Set largely in the women's flat and seen almost entirely from Carol's point of view, *Repulsion* is an assault on domestic space, flatly contradicting communist propaganda suggesting that Polanski has 'nothing to say about contemporary man'. The film is markedly more Gothic than *Knife in the Water*, a portrait of swinging London through the eyes of foreigners, where everything in daily life is a threat to survival. The film's final image suggests the family is the breeding ground for madness: after Helen's lover, Michael (Ian Hendry), has carried the apparently comatose Carol out of the flat, the camera pans around the wreckage of the room to settle on a semi-obscured family photograph, showing the young Carol staring off into the distance with a glazed look in her eyes while her parents smile for the camera, unaware.

Cul-de-Sac (1966) reprises the central situation of *Knife in the Water*, where a couple's relationship is tried and tested through the arrival of a stranger. Once again, we are in Gothic territory: the couple, George (Donald Pleasance) and Teresa (Françoise Dorléac), live in a castle on the Northumbrian coast (actually Lindisfarne Castle, called Rob Roy in the film), and receive a visit from two small-time gangsters, Dickie (Lionel Stander) and Albie (Jack MacGowran), who arrive in a hijacked Morris 1100. Whatever job they have just bungled, they must call their boss, Mr Katelbach, in Mablethorpe, and Dickie's quest for a phone triggers the entire plot.

In lesser hands, this could have been a sitcom, but Polanski is intent on taking his characters into more grotesque situations. When Dickie arrives at the castle, an air of surrealism hangs over the place: Teresa's lover, Christopher, is first seen there walking on his hands and, a short while later, Teresa playfully mocks George, forcing him to put on one of her dresses and applying make-up to his face; George spends much of the film in drag. Transvestism here replaces the knife in Polanski's debut to undermine masculine roles. But it is not just George whose role is called into question: when visitors later arrive to congratulate George and Teresa on their wedding, Dickie is forced into assuming the role of 'James' the butler. By this time, domestic bliss has been completely shattered by Albie's death (from what we assume to be bullet wounds to the stomach) and night-time burial, with Dickie forcing George to dig the grave at gunpoint. In addition, George is completely unaware that Teresa is having an affair with Christopher, and his role as the 'man of the house' is finally destroyed at the end of the film, when Teresa goes off with Cecil, one of the visitors, who has returned to pick up his shotgun.

Cul-de-Sac could perhaps best be described as film noir meets Harold Pinter with a touch of the Theatre of the Absurd. Polanski's third British feature was absurd in a more direct way. *The Fearless Vampire Killers* (1967) was a parody of vampire films starring the great MacGowran as Professor Abronsius and Polanski himself as his assistant, Alfred. While little more than a colour, widescreen remake of *Carry on Screaming*, the film works as a kitsch piece of slapstick, complete with village idiots, lusty wenches and suave, Christopher Lee-type vampires. MacGowran's Abronsius is a gloriously silly creation who, at times, resembles nothing so much as a life-size Jiří Trnka puppet with his wild eyes and out-of-control hair. Abronsius's attempts to rid the world of vampires only, in the end, help spread them further.

Polanski wasn't finished with the horror genre: his next film would see him make the transition to Hollywood with the biggest success of his career, *Rosemary's Baby* (1968), starring Mia Farrow and John Cassavetes.

SOVIET THAW CINEMA:
IN THE SHADOW OF A DUBIOUS THEORY

1956 was a momentous year for Warsaw Pact countries. The 20th Party Congress in Moscow had seen Soviet Premier Nikita Khrushchev denounce Stalin, which led to the uprisings in Hungary and Poland. This in turn revitalised filmmaking in both of those countries, albeit indirectly. In the Soviet Union, the Khrushchev Thaw was immediately apparent in two films that re-established Russia as a filmmaking force: Mikhail Kalatozov's *The Cranes Are Flying* (*Letyat zhuravli*, 1957) won the Palme d'Or at Cannes, while *The Ballad of a Soldier* (*Ballada o soldate*, Grigori Chukrai, 1959) also received an enthusiastic reception in the West, winning the Special Jury Prize at Cannes in 1960. Sharing the concerns of many filmmakers across Europe – both in the east and the west – Kalatozov and Chukrai were concerned with representing the Second World War (or Great Patriotic War, as it was known in Russia) in a new light. Gone were the heroic figures of pre-war and Formalist cinema, the patriots and comrades fighting imperialism and the Chinese; they were replaced with more believable characters whom war-ravaged audiences could identify with. The big struggle for these characters was not victory, but survival.

New ways of representing war and history recur to startling effect in *Ivan's Childhood* (*Ivanovno Destsvo*, 1962), the first feature by Andrei Tarkovsky. As with the Czech and German New Waves, the Russian comprised two generations of filmmakers – Chukrai and Kalatozov being representative of the first wave, and slightly younger directors like Tarkovsky representing the second wave. Tarkovsky repeatedly said throughout his career that what interested him was 'man's inner world'; interior 'events' – dreams, memories, moods – were just as important, he argued, as external events: 'From these properties of memory a new working principle could be developed… the portrayal of the hero's individual personality … and the revelation of his interior world.'[262] Tarkovsky held that, through the careful selection of memories and dreams, he could create a world onscreen whose details 'seem to me most fully and exactly to express the elusive meaning of our existence'.[263]

It should come as no surprise to learn that *Ivan's Childhood* is a war film in which we see no fighting – the action of the film takes place in the lull between missions. To further distance the film from the standard war movie, *Ivan's Childhood* also begins and ends with dream sequences; Tarkovsky would become a master of the dream sequence, so much so that it is often difficult to differentiate dream from 'reality' in his films – but, to Tarkovsky, there was no essential difference. *Ivan's Childhood* is suffused with a lyrical sensibility; Tarkovsky's camera is just as interested in birchwoods and standing water as it is in soldiers marching to the front.

Such devices, along with the dreams, thwart the traditional tropes of war films. Further thwarting appears in the shape of Ivan himself, a 12-year-old boy who works as an army scout. Khrushchev objected to this portrayal, claiming the Soviets had never used children as scouts in the war (despite the fact that the film's source novel, *Ivan* by Vladimir Bogomolov, is based on the author's own experiences as a scout). Perhaps as a result, the film received only limited distribution in the USSR. By that time, however, the film had already won the Golden Lion at Venice and Tarkovsky was being fêted by the likes of Jean-Paul Sartre, who declared the film to be 'Socialist Surrealism' (although it wasn't either). Another of the film's admirers was Swedish director Ingmar Bergman, who wrote that discovering *Ivan's Childhood* was a 'miracle' and seems to have helped reinvigorate his own work (his 1966 film *Persona* has some distinctly Tarkovskian touches, for instance).

Another filmmaker closer to home was also stunned by *Ivan's Childhood*: the Armenian-Georgian director Sergei Parajanov (1924–90). Parajanov had studied under Dovzhenko at the Kiev Studios. (Dovzhenko survived the Stalinist Purges, but found his directing career thwarted; he ended up only able to get teaching work. Similarly, Dziga Vertov only found work in his later years editing run-of-the-mill, Party-approved documentaries.) Parajanov had a long-standing interest in folk-culture and fairy stories, which was apparent in his first feature *Andriesh* in 1955 (a remake of his graduation film, *A Moldavian Tale*, from 1951), and the later documentary, *Golden Hands* (*Zolotye ruki*, 1960). Parajanov went on to make several more documentaries and three features before seeing *Ivan's Childhood* changed everything. Parajanov declared all his films up to that point to have been 'garbage' (they are, in fact, far from that), and he went back to folklore for his next film, emboldened by Tarkovsky to find his own voice as one of cinema's great poets.

Shadows of our Forgotten Ancestors (*Tini zabutykh predkiv*, 1964) was an exhilarating take on Ukrainian folk culture, ostensibly recounting a Carpathian Romeo and Juliet story. Parajanov's heart lay in exploring what cinema could do, and he allows his camera to dive, swoop and track almost as if it is a dog let off the leash for the first time. There had been intimations of such a free camera before, as in the tracking shot around a room of soldiers listening to Beethoven's *Moonlight Sonata* in *Ukrainian Rhapsody* (*Ukrainskaya rapsodiya*, 1961), but in that film it feels as though Parajanov had managed to (or was forced to) keep a lid on such things; now, with *Shadows*, he had the confidence to give full rein to his *caméra-stylo*. Aside from the bravura camerawork, the film is notable for its art direction: as Josephine Woll notes, 'Physical ornament, dress, household art, music and religious rituals dominate the film.'[264] In addition, Parajanov got real Huzuls (Ukrainians living in the Carpathians, whose folk traditions the film employs) to participate in the film, both as actors and to ensure authenticity. 'Any trace of falsehood, any inaccuracy, stung them,' Parajanov said. 'They dressed themselves... they were offended when they saw an actress's manicured nails or an alien detail in the costume.'[265] *Shadows* is no mere 'costume drama' – what Parajanov was aiming for was a film of living, breathing folk tradition; its ethnographic realism, if we can call it that, ensured that the film steered clear of period kitsch, and effectively participated in the culture it was celebrating.

The film was well received at home, and was even distributed with its original Ukrainian soundtrack (the usual practice being to dub everything into Russian). Part of this approval was probably due to a perceived Soviet patriotism: the film was based on a novel by the Ukrainian writer Mykhailo Kotsiubynsky, and was made to celebrate the centenary of his birth. This is not to say that Parajanov's film was anything like Soviet Realism: the film was a paean to Huzul folk culture and wisdom, with its pagan spirits, sorcerers and reverence for nature – all anathema to a political system that valued atheism and materialism.

A reverence for paganism and the natural world is also evident in Tarkovsky's second feature, the mediaeval epic, *Andrei Rublev* (1966/69). Ostensibly a biography of the great fifteenth-century painter-monk, Andrei Rublev, Tarkovsky again avoids convention almost entirely, presenting Rublev's life in a series of eight[266] self-contained narratives that have seemingly little or no connection with each other. Events are sometimes seen from Rublev's point of view, while in other episodes – notably the celebrated final sequence of the casting of the great bell – he is merely an onlooker. Tarkovsky likewise makes no concessions in his depictions of the high and mighty: the Grand Duke is an appallingly cruel man who mutilates and murders on a whim; none of the other nobles in the film are sympathetic; only the pagans and the holy fool make the sign of the cross. The film was denounced for its realism and violence at home – the authorities felt that the film depicted Russians as barbarians – and was (mistakenly) seen as an allegory of Tarkovsky's own position as a persecuted artist by critics in the West.

While the Thaw brought in new sensibilities and new approaches to old stories and narrative forms, one thing it did not change was the way in which Soviet films were made: they were all still studio films, requiring approval by both the respective studio heads and also the Party. However, the Soviet system was – and this might seem strange to Westerners – pro-auteur: directors always had the right of final cut. If the resulting film was deemed un-Soviet – as with Tarkovsky's *Andrei Rublev* and Parajanov's *Sayat Nova* – then they were simply put on the shelf indefinitely. Tarkovsky campaigned for five years to get his film released; accolades at the 1969 Cannes Film Festival didn't help in this respect, as it meant that the authorities could not now bury the film, despite Brezhnev's declaration at the Moscow Film Festival in July 1969 that he never wanted the film to be screened in public again. The Soviet Premier was unaware that, due to a bureaucratic blunder that would not look out of place in Terry Gilliam's *Brazil*, the foreign rights to the film had already been sold, presumably by accident, to Hollywood giant Columbia. The film was finally released in Russia in 1971, and in the West two years later.

Parajanov was not so lucky: his film – a stylised film about the eighteenth-century Armenian poet Sayat Nova – was even more unconventional than *Andrei Rublev*, presenting the poet's life and times almost entirely in near-static *tableaux vivants*. What realism there was in *Shadows of our Forgotten Ancestors* was completely gone: this was clearly not realism of any sort, being about as far as you can get from the 'girl meets tractor' model so beloved of Soviet classicism. With its oblique narrative, tableaux style and sometimes pantomime acting, it was an intense, hallucinatory dream of a film, only speaking the language of poetry. Poetry was clearly not what the authorities wanted, and *Sayat Nova* was re-edited and released as *The Colour of Pomegranates* in 1969. None of Parajanov's other projects were greenlit by the studio, and in 1973 he was arrested on trumped-up charges that included homosexuality and the illegal trafficking of religious icons. He spent over four years in a labour camp.[267] It took an international campaign, headed by Tarkovsky, to get him released.

Soviet Thaw cinema was not all pagans and poets, however. Screenwriter Mikhail Papava commented, 'For a long time we were in the shadow of the dubious theory that you have to show life not as it really is, but as it should be.'[268] With the 'dubious theory' (socialist realism or classicism) discarded, Soviet filmmakers began to show life 'as it really is'. Marlen Khutsiev's *I Am Twenty* (*Mne dvadtsat let*, 1965) charts the friendship of three young men growing up in a Moscow suburb. Sergei (Valentin Popov) has just finished two years' military service, Slava (Stanislav Lyubshin) is struggling with marriage and parenthood, while Kolya (Nikolai Gubenko) determines to remain a free spirit. Indebted to the French New Wave, and Truffaut in particular, the characters attend parties, listen to jazz, fight with their spouses, hang out in the streets[269] and become increasingly disenchanted with the official pomp and circumstance of the Soviet regime. The regime took notice, and insisted the film be recut and retitled: the original title of *Ilyich's Gate* (the area of Moscow where the film is set) was dropped, and the film's running time was halved. (The original three-hour cut was finally screened in 1989.)

Elem Klimov's *Welcome, or No Trespassing* (*Dobro pozhalovat, ili postoronnim vkhod vospreshchen*, 1964) was set at a Young Pioneer's summer camp and satirised 'a great many Soviet pieties'.[270] With its many signs – 'Do not touch', 'Do not play in the river', 'No trespassing' – it was not hard to see what the camp and its deeply conservative director, Dynin (Evgeni Evstigneev), stood for. Klimov was convinced the film would be shut down, and tried as hard as possible to go over budget, his theory being that, if they spent enough money, the studio could not possibly pull the plug as that would automatically mean wasted funding. But the official summons to stop did eventually come, and Klimov dispatched screenwriter Semyon Lungin back to Moscow on the pretext that he would rewrite the script, while Klimov completed filming. The film was released in October 1964 and, despite official displeasure, proved a commercial success.

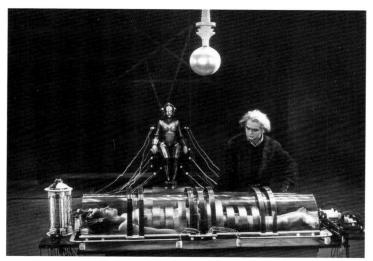

Fritz Lang's *Metropolis* (1927)

Andrzej Wajda's *Ashes and Diamonds* (1958)

François Truffaut's *The 400 Blows* (1959)

Jack Clayton's *Room at the Top* (1959)

Alain Resnais' *Hiroshima mon amour* (1959)

Federico Fellini's *La Dolce Vita* (1960)

Andrei Tarkovsky's *Ivan's Childhood* (1962)

Lindsay Anderson's *This Sporting Life* (1963)

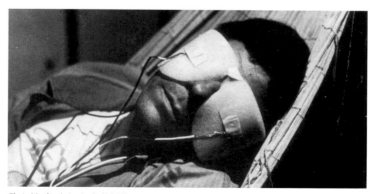

Chris Marker's *La Jetée* (1962)

Roman Polanski's *Knife in the Water* (1962)

Miloš Forman's *A Blonde in Love* (1965)

Věra Chytilová's *Daisies* (1966)

Alexander Kluge's *Yesterday Girl* (1966)

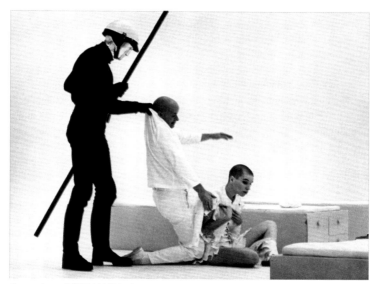

George Lucas' *THX 1138* (1971)

Pier Paolo Pasolini's *Salò, or the 120 Days of Sodom* (1975)

Francis Ford Coppola's *Apocalypse Now* (1979)

Rainer Werner Fassbinder's *Veronika Voss* (1982)

Larisa Shepitko (1938–79) was one of the few women directors in the Soviet New Wave. A graduate of VGIK, she made her diploma film, *Heat* (*Znoy*, 1963), in the Kirghizian steppe. The location was so hot the film stock melted, and Shepitko became so ill that she had to be carried to the location every day on a stretcher. *Heat* is 'a cruel film about hard work and human conflicts… without the usual propagandist highflown phrases of the official press and newsreels'.[271] Shepitko's first professional feature, *Wings* (*Krylya*, 1966), centres around Nadezhda Petrukhina (Maia Bulgakova), a former pilot who was decorated for her wartime service, but who now runs a vocational training college. She endures a strained relationship with her daughter, and remains unpopular among colleagues. Her only emotional contact seems to come once a year on Victory Day, when she meets her fellow veteran pilots. In her treatment of the war, Shepitko provides arguably the most radical aspect of the film: Petrukhina's war was not one of service to Mother Russia. Rather, she flew because she loved the challenge, the exhilaration. As Josephine Woll noted, 'Professional gratification, maternity, friendship – *Wings* undercut one truism after another.'[272] The film caused a minor scandal in the Soviet press, which objected to the portrayal of the strained relationship between Petrukhina and her daughter and her wartime experience. ('To show a war veteran in this way is to jeer at war heroes,' one commentator pronounced.[273]) Despite the outcry over the film, Bulgakova was voted actress of the year by film critics.

The Kirghizian steppe also provided the setting for Andrei Mikhalkov-Konchalovsky's debut feature, *The First Teacher* (*Pervyy uchitel*, 1965). The film tells the story of a young Bolshevik, Duyshen (Bolot Beyshenaliyev), who, after the end of the civil war in 1923, is sent to a village on the steppe to establish Soviet rule there. The locals react with incomprehension to 'So-cial-ism', as the children chant at one point, and Duyshen emerges as a singularly intransigent and unsympathetic character who does not understand village ways. Konchalovsky and his cameraman, Georgy Rerberg, wanted the film to look like a documentary, sometimes deliberately over- or under-exposing footage to make it look as though it was shot on the hoof.

Asya's Happiness (*Istoriya Asi Klyachinoy, kotoraya lyubila, da ne vyshla zamuzh*, 1966; lit: 'The Story of Asya Klyachinoy, Who Fell in Love But Never Married'), Konchalovsky's second feature, once again employed documentary techniques in its portrayal of village life, this time set in contemporary Russia. The minimal plot concerns a lame village girl, Asya (Iya Savvina), who falls pregnant, is abandoned by her lover, and later refuses an offer from another suitor to go and live with him in the city; she chooses to remain in the village, despite the hard life she has there. With only three professional actors in the film, *Asya's Happiness* 'is not a documentary embellishment into a feature film, but is an intrusion of cinema into real human life'.[274] The rest of the cast was made up of villagers themselves, and the entire film was shot on location. The film presents such an unflinchingly honest portrait of life in a contemporary Russian village that the completed film, despite a successful short run in cine-clubs, and despite being passed for release in March 1967, was then shelved for 20 years. Konchalovsky's 'crime' was to break from the collective farm-worker genre, showing an independent young woman determined to live by her own rules, not those of the village patriarchy or the state.

The Georgian Otar Iosseliani (b. 1934) suffered a similar fate. His diploma film, *April* (*Aprili*, 1961), a near wordless romance between 'She' (Guia Tchirakadze) and 'He' (Tania Tchantouria), was shelved indefinitely upon completion, on the usual grounds. Falling somewhat short of socialist realism, having more kinship with Buster Keaton or Jacques Tati, the film finally received a limited release in 1972. Disillusioned with the film industry, Iosseliani went to work on a fishing boat and, later, in a factory. He was finally able to make his feature debut with *Falling Leaves* (*Giorgobistve*, 1966), a comedy about Niko (Ramaz Giorgobiani), a young man who goes to work in a state-owned winery. Iosseliani wanted a documentary feel for *Falling Leaves* and, in order to get the most naturalistic performances possible, shot footage of the actors without them knowing the camera was rolling.[275] Having studied under Dovzhenko at film school, Iosseliani's films reflect something of the master's concern for natural rhythms and the apparent simplicity of (frequently) rural life. Iosseliani's films, including *There Once Lived a Songthrush* (*Iko shashvi mgalobeli*, 1970) and

Pastorale (*Pastorali*, 1975), are films that retain a documentary style, but celebrate mystery in the unlooked-for or unnoticeable. 'Only the most superficial, insensitive and formalistic critic could be so bogged down in documentary detail,' wrote Andrei Tarkovsky, 'as to miss the poetic vision which distinguishes Iosseliani's films... With Iosseliani, the poetic is embedded in what he loves, and not in something dreamt up to illustrate a quasi-romantic world-view.'[276]

THE GREEK NEW WAVE

Theo Angelopoulos

Greek cinema of the 1950s and 60s was dominated by comedy and melodrama, all of which were in competition with foreign imports from Hollywood, France and Italy. Arguably the most successful Greek filmmaker up to that point had been Michael Cacoyannis (1922–2011), whose early films such as *Stella* (1955), starring Melina Mercouri in her first lead role, were influenced by neorealism. Cacoyannis was also part of the studio system – his adaptation of Nikos Kazantzakis's novel *Zorba the Greek* (1964), starring Anthony Quinn and Alan Bates, was made for 20th Century Fox. But on the home front, as Andrew Horton has pointed out, 'cinema lagged behind the other arts in Greece'.[277] Political instability, lack of money and censorship played a part in this, making it difficult for Greek films to compete with Hollywood and other European countries. Perhaps the most important factor of all was 'a lack of interest in cinema on the part of the leading intellectuals, artists and writers'[278] who found song, poetry, prose and painting more suitable media.

By the mid-1960s, this was starting to change, and an initial new wave of Greek filmmakers began to emerge. However, the seizing of power in April 1967 by the fascist Junta of the Colonels put a stop to cultural renewal. As with Hungary and Poland, the initial clampdown led, in time, to a relaxation of censorship, allowing a second wave of filmmakers to emerge. Amongst their number was Theo Angelopoulos (1935–2012), arguably the most important figure of the Greek new wave, and his 1975 film *The Travelling Players* (*O Thiassos*) is one of the cornerstones of modern Greek cinema. Not only was the film made under the noses of the Colonels (he told the authorities he was making a film about the myth of Orestes), but it was technically challenging: at nearly four hours long and shot mainly in long takes with almost no close-ups, *The Travelling Players* 'is a work as unlike the world's dominant form of cinema – Hollywood – as could be imagined'.[279] The film was also a huge success, both in Greece and abroad, and established Angelopoulos as a major director.

Angelopoulos's cinema has parallels with those of Jancsó and Tarkovsky, in that it is long-take based. (There are only around 80 shots in *The Travelling Players*; if this was Hollywood, the number of takes for a film of that length would be in four figures.) He further challenges audiences with frequent use of Brechtian distancing devices. *The Travelling Players* begins with a shot of a closed theatrical curtain, from behind which one of the characters steps out to announce that the play *Golpho the Shepherdess* is about to begin. We then cut to the players arriving at the train station in the small town of Aegion in 1952, and the rest of the film cuts back and forth in time across the preceding 13 years – sometimes in the same take – to provide an overview of Greece during the tumultuous years of the Second World War and Civil War, as the players tour *Golpho* throughout Greece. Several times in the film, characters address the camera directly: Agamemnon's monologue on the train detailing his immigration to Greece from Asia Minor; Electra's description of the December 1944 Battle of Athens; and Pylades' description of the torture of political prisoners. Character names also act as additional Brechtian devices: aside from the Agamemnon, Electra and Pylades, the players also include an Orestes, a Clytemnestra, an Aegisthus and a Chrysothemis. The use of these names renders the characters effectively Everyman and Everywoman, whose stories of exile and suffering were shared by millions during the 13 years of the film's action.

But they also betray two other key aspects of Angelopoulos's cinema: his interest in history and myth. The use of names and themes from the literature of classical Greece set against the events of the mid-twentieth century remind us that history is ongoing, a constant homeward journey to Ithaca. (Indeed, Angelopoulos remarked in an interview that 'there really is nothing new. We are all just revisiting and reconsidering ideas that the ancients first treated.'[280]) The idea of life as endless journeying is suggested by Angelopoulos's never letting us know directly what era we are in: references to various political leaders appear on banners and slogans; elsewhere, the year or political climate is conveyed in songs sung by pro-government forces or EAM (the pro-Communist Greek Liberation Army) fighters, as well as the players themselves.

The choice of the nineteenth-century melodrama *Golpho* further blurs the boundary between history and myth, whose interplay is something that recurs throughout Angelopoulos's cinema. *Golpho* was also the first Greek feature film, made in 1912 by Kostas Bachatoris, 'a reminder that nostalgia for a Greece that never was cannot substitute for history'.[281] But Angelopoulos's players, being named after classical characters from Aeschylus's *Oresteia*, also operate in the liminal place where history, myth and fiction operate: 'The bloodletting [in Aeschylus] chronicles a national movement away from tyranny and private justice to one of democratic law.'[282] The actors therefore represent archetypes, both in the film and in the play-within-the-film, with 'none of them being deeper, better or more sophisticated'[283] than any other; the viewer does not necessarily have to know every nuance of Greek history and literature to appreciate the film. Angelopoulos's aim 'was to create a film that could meet the needs of different viewers'. The action of *The Travelling Players* is at once a chronicle, and also a hope expressed that democratic law, peace and stability would, indeed, one day return to Greece.

Costa-Gavras

Debate raged about how political issues could be best represented onscreen throughout the late 60s and into the 70s, the time the Greek New Wave was emerging. Angelopoulos (along with filmmakers such as Godard and Jancsó) could be said to represent one school of thought, in which 'radical content could only be faithfully served by a format that rejected the conventions of dominant media as resolutely as it rejected its ideology'.[284] Audiences – and working-class, less educated audiences in particular – should learn new ways of seeing, to regard form as being as important as content. An opposing camp wanted 'radical content wedded to popular formats, as this would provide access to the largest possible audience'.[285] Here, popular forms would serve the needs of radical content, 'purely entertainment genres, in effect, would be hijacked for political discourse'.[286] The work of Angelopoulos's contemporary, Costa-Gavras, is an exemplar of this second school of thought and practice.

Like Angelopoulos, Costa-Gavras (b. 1933) studied film at IDHEC in Paris, and made his first feature, *The Sleeping-Car Murders* (*Compartiment tueurs*, 1965), in France. The film was a routine thriller, but was important for establishing a working relationship with two actors who would feature in some of Costa-Gavras's major films, Yves Montand and Jean-Louis Trintignant. Costa-Gavras's third film, *Z* (1969), addressed the rule of the Colonels in Greece, although it was shot largely in Algiers, and in French. The film announces at the outset that 'Any similarity to living persons is deliberate'. The deliberate similarity is Yves Montand's character, based on the left-wing Greek politician Grigoris Lambrakis, who was assassinated in May 1963 by thugs in the pay of right-wing extremists.

The film follows Lambrakis's life fairly closely, showing the Deputy (Montand) being struck down in the street after giving an anti-nuclear speech at a political rally. Disbelieving the official government version of the deputy's death – that he was hit by a drunk driver – Jean-Louis Trintignant's magistrate begins to investigate the cover-up. He discovers a conspiracy, and seems to be on the verge of bringing those responsible in the government to justice. But, following rigged elections, the film ends with, not just a travesty of justice, but of democracy as well. There are news reports of the military seizing power; after detailing the regime's corruption, murders and lies, its absurdity is revealed by a long onscreen list of things it has banned, ranging from long hair and mini-skirts to Tolstoy, 'Russian-style toasts', The Beatles, Harold Pinter, learning Bulgarian, sociology, 'new mathematics', and, finally, even a letter of the alphabet: Z, meaning in Ancient Greek, 'he [Lambrakis] lives'.

Shot in a documentary style, Z has an urgency reminiscent of Gillo Pontecorvo's *The Battle of Algiers* (*La battaglia di Algeri*, 1966), perhaps the other most important political film of the era which, like Costa-Gavras's work, 'hijacks entertainment genres for political discourse'. *Z* reflects the tensions of its time, shot when the Colonels had been in power for a year, and when France was undergoing the near-revolutions of 1968. The film was hugely successful everywhere except Greece, where, perhaps not surprisingly, it was banned. Z won the Best Foreign Film Oscar, and was also nominated for Best Picture, becoming the first foreign-language film to be so honoured. But, as Roger Ebert pointed out when the film was released in the US, apart from being 'a brilliant suspense thriller',[287] the film's implications went far beyond Greece, whose fascist Junta was recognised by Washington: 'For Americans, it is about the My Lai massacre, the killing of Fred Hampton, the Bay of Pigs. It is no more about Greece than *The Battle of Algiers* was about Algeria. It is a film of our time.'[288]

The Colonels' regime was a wake-up call to young Greeks. As Angelopoulos said, 'I and many others sought the roots of the Junta through history, attitudes, social and political change.'[289] There was even a grim irony to the situation: 'In a way, the dictatorship was my source of inspiration. Had it not existed, I may have done very different films.'[290] Franco Solinas, who wrote *The Battle of Algiers*, echoed this comment when he said of Costa-Gavras's *State of Siege* (on which he was also screenwriter), 'The reason for the film's existence is imperialism, with its mechanism of repression, its murders, its tortures.'[291] The imperialism behind the Colonels' regime was ultimately American, which had been officially providing aid to Greece and Turkey since 1947. As Costa-Gavras explained: '[The US gives] a marvellous impression of nice people who work sincerely for Greece, who are there to help us, even to the point of saddling us with a dictatorship.'[292]

State of Siege (*État de siege*, 1972), set in an unnamed Latin American country, investigates another region on the verge of dictatorship. A guerrilla group kidnaps two men, one of whom is Philip Michael Santore (Yves Montand), an almost anonymous official from the US AID department (Agency for International Development). As Santore is interrogated, it becomes clear that the 'aid' he is providing to the government includes training the police to torture prisoners, supporting fascist groups and setting up death squads to eliminate political opponents. The group uncovers evidence that Santore has been providing such 'aid' in Latin America for most of the past decade, having previously been in Brazil and the Dominican Republic. An ultimatum is issued by the group in which they call for the release of all political prisoners. The government refuses.

As with *Z*, the film utilises the techniques and tropes of the political thriller – the investigative reporters, the Orwellian doublespeak of 'friendship', 'progress' and 'aid' in politicians' rhetoric and on various banners, placards and posters, the arrests of various members of the group and the countdown to the ultimatum – all shaped by the film's flashback structure. The kidnappings form the film's first important set-piece, with the guerrillas hijacking numerous cars and vans across the city. Some of their victims have been hijacked before, such as the taxi driver who tells them to beware of the dodgy second gear in his car. This blurring of boundaries between good and bad is reflected in the performances. As played by Montand, Santore is a largely sympathetic character, despite the atrocities he has been responsible for. Likewise, the group are a competent rabble, rebels with heart, who treat Santore with care, going to considerable lengths to get him treated for a bullet wound he accidentally receives during the kidnap.

Unlike *Z*, however, *State of Siege* was based on an original screenplay, the result of research conducted in the field by Gavras and his screenwriter, Franco Solinas. They spent several months in Uruguay, where the original events took place, interviewing National Liberation Movement rebels. Santore was based on Dan Mitrione, who was killed by the Uruguayan Tupamaros in August 1970. In the published screenplay, Gavras and Solinas were asked about what kind of man they thought Mitrione was. Solinas believed Mitrione to have been 'an American who really believes he is defending the "free world"', to which Gavras added, 'Mitrione is as sincere as the judges of the Catholic Church during the Inquisition.'[293] This is reflected in the film's superb score by Mikis Theodorakis (who also did the music for *Z*); the main theme is highly reminiscent of music from Westerns, suggesting the US government's attitude to Latin America is the same as their forebears' attitude to 'civilising' Native Americans and settling the Old West.

Gavras spoke of wanting people to ask questions after seeing the film. For him,

> Making a film is a political act. In my view, the cinema is a way of showing, exposing the political processes in our everyday life. In fact, a film is a political act as soon as one assumes a responsibility vis-à-vis a situation, a people, etc.[294]

The film portrays the 'aid' given by the US government as being solely for its own benefit, whose embassy is not just an embassy, but 'a centre of espionage, surveillance and political pressure'.[295] US aid also helps the oligarchy that runs the unnamed country the film takes place in. In another set piece, various members of the government arrive at an emergency meeting near the end of the film, and are shown getting out of their cars as one of the journalists identifies them in voiceover as all being either company directors and/or bankers in addition to holding political office. The guerrilla group fights 'for a different society, without exploitation, without private ownership of the means of production, without privileges – in short, a socialist society'.[296]

The chances for any change at all seem bleak as the film ends, with a new US AID official arriving. But reality caught up with *State of Siege* in a horrible irony. The film was shot in Chile because, as Gavras explained, 'It was absolutely necessary to shoot the film in Latin America, and Chile is the only country where there is freedom, almost complete freedom, without any problems of censorship or pre-censorship.'[297] This freedom was very short-lived indeed: within a year, the US-backed fascist dictatorship of General Pinochet had been installed, with the democratically elected president, Salvador Allende, perishing in the process.[298] The same year, a military dictatorship took over in Uruguay.

CINEMA OF TRUTH:
NEW WAVES IN DOCUMENTARY

THE FOUNDERS OF DOCUMENTARY

Cinema began with documentary: the workers leaving the factory, the train arriving at the station.[299] Audiences at the time, however, saw them as novelties, as did the filmmakers themselves (the Lumières famously remarked that cinema had no future). The first attempts to capture motion on film were therefore not seen as 'documents', and they were regarded as no different from the more fantastical films by filmmakers such as Georges Méliès and R W Paul. Ingmar Bergman would later observe that, when a film wasn't a document, it was a dream; early cinema audiences did not have (or perhaps even need) such critical distinctions, and the films they saw were often exhibited at fairgrounds. This in itself suggests two things: that films such as the Lumières' *Workers Leaving the Factory* were simultaneously documents (an everyday scene of people going home after work) *and* dreamlike (the novelty of movement and captured time); and that they also had mass appeal.

It is worth beginning this chapter with such reflections, as they go a little way to illustrating both the importance of documentaries, and the difficulty of defining what they actually are. Three figures are generally regarded as the founding figures of documentary, and all took different approaches to the form: the American Robert Flaherty made ethnographic documentaries that had a distinctly Romantic flavour; the Briton John Grierson believed that documentaries should be largely educational, whilst avoiding such a distasteful notion as 'art';

and, finally, the Russian Dziga Vertov believed that documentaries were 'life caught unawares' and that the camera possessed an insightful ability to capture what he dubbed 'kino pravda' – camera truth. All three made major contributions, and all three were partly right about what documentary could do; indeed, it was Grierson who coined the term, in a review of Flaherty's *Moana*.[300]

Nanook of the North (1922), Flaherty's film about an Inuit and his community, perfectly represents his strengths, which were, to his critics, his fatal weaknesses. Flaherty took a number of liberties in the name of poetic licence, the detractors point out: the hunt scenes were staged, Flaherty made Nanook and his people appear more backward, in terms of culture and their knowledge of Western society, than they actually were, and, to top it all, Nanook wasn't the central character's name (it was actually Allakariallak, which, admittedly, doesn't roll off the tongue as easily as Nanook). Flaherty responded by pointing out that he wanted to capture the 'former majesty and character of these people, while it is still possible – before the white man has destroyed not only their character, but the people as well'.[301] Further vindication came from Allakariallak and his people: they loved the film as it showed the world what their culture had been like, and would ensure that it was not lost forever.

Further Flaherty films followed the basic approach taken in *Nanook*: the director would be drawn to subjects he felt in some way close to, but this didn't stop him taking liberties if 'reality' stood in the way of a good story. In *Moana* (1926), shot in Samoa, he focused on the islanders' initiatic tattooing practices in order to give the film a dramatic structure, but completely ignored the Western colonial presence which had wrought so many changes detrimental to the islanders' culture. In *Man of Aran* (1934), Flaherty wanted to portray the islanders hunting basking sharks, the only trouble being they had forgotten how to; Flaherty taught them, in the process neglecting to mention that Aran's fish trade was almost entirely dependent upon the Irish mainland, and that absentee landlords had driven them from their traditional homes. *Louisiana Story* (1948) recounted the impact on Cajuns of oil drilling in their swamp. The film portrayed the oil rig as environmentally friendly; hardly surprising, as Flaherty's backer was John D Rockefeller's company, Standard Oil.

If Flaherty had been motivated by Romanticism and the idea of the noble savage, then John Grierson came to documentary motivated by a desire to educate society. Inspired by Flaherty's work, Grierson would actually only personally direct one film, *Drifters* (1928), a film about herring fishing in the North Sea, before finding his real vocation as a producer, lobbyist and teacher. Education and political engagement were very much in the air at the time: the BBC had been founded in 1927 with a remit to educate the British public, whilst *Drifters* was first screened at the British premiere of *Battleship Potemkin*. While admiring Eisenstein, Grierson was concerned that, unless the British public were educated via documentaries, communism could easily take firm root in Britain.[302] Hired by the Empire Marketing Board to make films that promoted trade in Britain and her empire, he became the political opposite of Vertov on his agit-train. However, although he thought the Russian's films were too 'tricksy', some of Grierson's statements are ironically close to Vertov's position, as they both believed passionately in the power of documentaries to effect social change. Grierson saw the documentary filmmaker's job as the 'business of ordering most present chaos' in order to make films that are, and make a statement of being, 'honest and lucid and deeply felt and which fulfils the best ends of citizenship'.[303] Elsewhere he admitted that 'the documentary was not basically a film idea at all [but] a need for public education' also noting that, 'You can be totalitarian for evil and you can be totalitarian for good.'[304] Most famously, he declared that documentary is 'the creative treatment of actuality'.[305]

Grierson's totalitarianism was recalled in 1975 by director Basil Wright, who remarked that Grierson was 'murderous' to work for, never missing the daily screening of rushes[306] of whatever film was currently in production. If he disapproved, 'he didn't say anything and just spat on the floor. You knew you had to go back and shoot absolutely everything over again. If he just cursed you, you only had to re-shoot some of it.'[307] *Industrial Britain* (1931) was directed by Flaherty, who came to blows with Grierson over the portrayal of Britain's nostalgia for her past. Despite being told not to romanticise, Flaherty did just that and was removed from the film. Another of Grierson's alumni to fall into disfavour was Humphrey Jennings, whose films Grierson regarded as elitist and patronising. Even when Jennings had become the star of the British documentary movement, with films such as *Listen to Britain* (1942), *Fires Were Started* (1943) and *A Diary for Timothy* (1945), Grierson was still suspicious of Jennings's poetic cinema, although he did commission Jennings's last film, *Family Portrait* (1950), made for the Festival of Britain. (Jennings, it has to be said, regarded most of the GPO Film Unit as Grierson's 'little boys' and regarded Griersonian notions of 'realism' and 'pure documentary' as 'systems of self advertisement'.[308])

Despite the rigours of working for Grierson, his teams of filmmakers produced some seminal work, first for the EMB, and then the GPO Film Unit, to which Grierson moved in 1933. *Housing Problems*, made in 1935 by Harry Watt and Grierson's sister Ruby, highlighted the need for better inner-city housing, and let slum dwellers speak for themselves. *Night Mail* (1936), directed by Wright and Harry Watt, followed the progress of a letter through the postal system, and featured a celebrated narration by W H Auden and music by Benjamin Britten. Despite an innate, patrician conservatism in many of the films – this was 1930s Britain, after all – the work done in the golden age of British documentary, the years spanning 1930 to 1950, is amongst Britain's most significant contributions to world cinema, and the man behind it all was John Grierson. In addition to his work as a producer, he worked as an educator, founding film schools (such as the one at Newport in South Wales) and was instrumental in setting up the National Film Board of Canada. In his later years he became a well-known TV personality, dying in 1972. The shadow he cast was a long one indeed.

We have already touched upon the work of Dziga Vertov, whose documentary maxim had been 'life caught unawares' ('off-guard' might in fact be a more accurate translation). Whether he would have liked to have been grouped with Flaherty and Grierson as part of a sort of holy trinity of early documentarists is a moot point; all three were enormously influential in the form, and it was against – or sometimes in tandem with – their visions that the new waves in documentary would kick.

But they were not the only members of the 'old guard' of documentary: the propaganda film genre, for instance, had many talented filmmakers working within it: Jennings is a prime example, although it's often difficult to think of some of his films as propaganda, so much do they transcend the genre. The same could be said for Dutch film-maker Joris Ivens, whose *The Spanish Earth* – narrated by Ernest Hemingway – took the Republican side in the Spanish Civil War. On the opposite side of the political divide, Leni Riefenstahl's *Triumph of the Will* (1935) was a Wagnerian piece of Nazi propaganda whose cameras track around the massed crowds at the 1934 Nuremberg Rally.

Public information films formed another strand of the genre's fabric: in Britain, housewives were told, via newsreel films, how to bake bread, make the most of their spare time, etc; in the USA, audiences were warned of the dangers of drug use in the alarmist – and unintentionally hilarious – *Reefer Madness* (Louis J Gasnier, 1936).

While Flaherty's work could be described as ethnographic, he did not invent the genre. *Torres Strait*, filmed during the 1898 Cambridge University expedition, and depicting the lives of the islanders of the Torres Strait, is among the earliest films that could be described in this way, while Flaherty's immediate precursor is arguably Edward S Curtis, whose *In the Land of the Headhunters* (1914) showed the rites – recreated for the film – of the native American Kwakiutl people.

There was also an avant-garde tradition in documentary, which included the city symphony film, already noted, and also works such as Benjamin Christensen's *Haxan* (*Witchcraft Through the Ages*, 1922), a drama-documentary about mediaeval witchcraft that controversially included scenes of nudity and fairly gruesome (for the time) violence, and Luis Buñuel's *Las Hurdes: Tierra sin Pan* (*Land Without Bread*, 1932), a travelogue around one of rural Spain's poorest regions, whose images of poverty are accompanied by a neutral voiceover intended, in typically Buñuelian fashion, to provoke outrage. Like *Haxan*, it was banned.[309]

CINÉMA VÉRITÉ

Cinéma vérité was a term coined by the French anthropologist and eth-nographical filmmaker Jean Rouch (1917–2004). The phrase, meaning 'cinema of truth', intentionally echoed Vertov's 'kino pravda', the main difference between the two approaches being in the visibility of the filmmaker. In Vertov, the filmmaker is very much alive and noticeably up to his tricks; in Rouch, he retreats – a filmic equivalent, perhaps, of Barthes' 'death of the author', an idea which was gaining credence around the time *cinéma vérité* appeared, circa 1960. But *cinéma vérité* was not formed in response to developments in critical theory – although Rouch may well have been aware of them – but in response to debates raging within anthropology at the time relating to notions of objectivity and impartiality. *Cinéma vérité* is the first real 'new wave' in documentary since the time of Vertov, and arguably the most influential.

Rouch was very much influenced by Flaherty, admiring his empathy for his subjects, and by Vertov, for his insistence on life being caught 'unawares' and then being shaped by the filmmaker to conform to a larger vision. His passion for film was enhanced – as with so many other postwar Parisian cinéphiles – by frequent visits to the Cinémathèque. He started making films in 1947, with *Au pays des mages noirs* (*In the Land of the Black Magi*), a film depicting a Songhay possession dance in Niger.[310] Going against the grain of normal documentary practice, he shot much of the film with a handheld camera, due to the fortuitous loss of his tripod in the first week (it fell into a river). Despite this accidental innovation, the film was re-edited by the producer against Rouch's wishes, with 'tropical muzak' being added, in addition to a voiceover that was essentially colonial in its viewpoint. (Rouch was finally able to record a new narration in 1991.) *Les maîtres fous* (*The Mad Masters*, 1955) was Rouch's first important film, winning a prize at the Venice Film Festival. This time, the setting is Ghana, and the film follows a ritual in which migrant workers entered trances and took on personas that mimicked – often parodying – colonial officials. For much of the film, Rouch lets the ceremony unfold with minimal directorial intervention, other than a little narration. Rouch concludes that the ritual allows the participants a temporary release from their life under colonialism, as well as being an expression of their attitude towards it.

Rouch's technique began to evolve. *Jaguar* (1955) and *Moi, un noir* (*Me, A Black Man*, 1958) employed semi-fictional techniques, reflecting Rouch's belief that there was no real difference between 'documentary' and 'drama':

> There is almost no boundary between documentary film and films
> of fiction. The cinema, the art of the double, is already the transition
> from the real world to the imaginary world, and ethnography, the
> science of the thought systems of others, is a permanent crossing
> point from one conceptual universe to another.[311]

This approach continued in films such as *The Lion Hunters* (1965),
which was structured like a child's bedtime story in order to retain the
mythical qualities of the hunt, as experienced by the hunters. Taking
his cue from Flaherty, who had involved the Inuit in the production of
Nanook, Rouch began to think of his work as 'shared anthropology', in
which he took an active role in the events he was filming, and often got
the subjects of his films to watch the rushes or early edits so that he
could incorporate their suggestions into the finished films. By working
in this way, Rouch made hazy the boundary between documentary and
fiction, filmmaker and subject, going against the traditional, Griersonian
model of filmmaker and subject always being separate.

Although much of Rouch's work was made in Africa, it was a film
shot in Paris that is arguably his masterpiece. *Chronique d'un été*
(*Chronicle of a Summer*, 1960), made with the sociologist Edgar Morin,
follows a group of young, politically aware Parisians over the course of
one summer. In keeping with Rouch's idea of 'shared anthropology',
the group comments on the film as it goes along, interview each other
and also passersby in the street. It also revealed to Rouch that, when
people are being filmed, they behave differently, recalling the discovery
in Quantum physics that the observer changes the experiment. For
Rouch, this was not a problem, as he felt he had got around it by
getting the subjects to have a say in the making of the film and, in
some cases, to actually shoot parts of it themselves (as happened in
Moi, un noir). But it also showed him that people could, even if they
were playing for the camera, say some very revealing things:

> Contrary to what one might think, when people are being recorded,
> the reactions that they have are always infinitely more sincere
> than those they have when they are not being recorded. The fact
> of being recorded gives these people a public... they begin to try
> to think – perhaps for the first time sincerely – about their own

problems, about who they are and then they begin to express what they have within themselves. These moments are very short, and one must know how to take advantage of them. That's the art of making a film like *Chronique d'un été*.[312]

Rouch also believed that *cinéma vérité* films should have a point of view, which brings them close to the concept of the essay film (which we shall discuss shortly). When asked if *cinéma vérité* laid claims to objectivity – one of the chief concerns of the new wave documentarists – Rouch replied:

That's false. Essentially you have to make a choice: if I look at you, I look here and not there; what's behind me is perhaps more important because of the woman making noise, and perhaps my attention will be drawn to her, and from the moment that I've chosen to look in one direction or another, I've made a choice – which is a subjective process. All editing is subjective.[313]

Such notions, as we will see, set Rouch and his continental contemporaries apart from their American and Canadian counterparts, who employed a much stricter methodology, reflected in the name they chose for themselves: Direct Cinema.

DIRECT CINEMA

The origins of Direct Cinema can be traced back to Quebec in the late 1950s, and can be seen as a reaction against British influence in Francophone Canada, and also certain tendencies within films made by the National Film Board of Canada, which Grierson had helped set up. (Grierson later denied this, and tried to take credit for Direct Cinema, claiming it was merely aping the practices of the GPO Film Unit.)

Although Direct Cinema and *cinéma vérité* are often seen as the same movement, differences did exist, and they are significant. Unlike Rouch, the adherents of Direct Cinema in general did not believe in point of view, or voiceover. They felt that it was enough to show something happening and to follow the characters (in Britain, this movement became known as 'observational documentary', which is perhaps a more apt name). That is not to say the two movements remained apart: Rouch hired Québécois filmmaker and cinematographer Michel Brault to shoot *Chronique*, as Brault had developed lightweight equipment which was, at that time, unavailable in France; and in 1963 the two sides met in Lyon to discuss their respective approaches at a conference organised by Radio Television Française. To their practitioners, the new forms of documentary were a freeing of the form from Griersonian control; other filmmakers such as Joris Ivens were suspicious: whose truth were the new forms depicting? The new lightweight cameras might have the advantages of portability and sync sound, but they ran the risk 'of skimming reality instead of penetrating it'.[314]

If *cinéma vérité*, at least in the hands of Rouch, was ethnographic, Direct Cinema was concerned with social and political issues within the filmmaker's own culture. In the United States, Direct Cinema was more focused on exposing the abuses of the system: racism, political machinations, unions and institutions all came under the gaze of its practitioners. Politicians were portrayed in Robert Drew's *Primary* (1960), which followed the Wisconsin primary in the presidential election between John F Kennedy and Hubert Humphrey. Drew, a photojournalist for *Time-Life*, used a lightweight camera and new sound equipment that allowed – like the new Nagras – for sync sound to be recorded by handheld cameras, increasing the crew's mobility. Drew and his team followed Kennedy and Humphrey as they campaigned and debated, and portrayed the US election process with an immediacy that had not been possible before. *Time-Life*, which backed the film, balked at the end result, announcing that the film 'looked like rushes' and withdrew its commitment to broadcast it.

Drew decided to continue on his own. *Adventures on a New Frontier* (1961) and *Crisis: Behind a Presidential Commitment* (1963) continued the focus on politics, showing President Kennedy at work. Drew and his team were allowed to film inside the Oval office, the first time documentary filmmakers had been allowed to do so. Not only did these films have a seismic effect on American television and documentary practice, they also spawned films by other members of Drew's team. Drew's production company, Drew Associates, also included D A Pennebaker, Albert and David Maysles and Richard

Leacock, all of whom would go on to become some of the most celebrated names in Direct Cinema over the ensuing decade.

Leacock can claim direct artistic descent from Flaherty, being one of the cinematographers on *Louisiana Story*. Leacock later recalled one day they were scheduled to shoot a Cajun boy and his pet raccoon. En route to the location, however, Flaherty spotted a spider web, and spent the day filming that instead. It was a pivotal moment for Leacock, something he later dubbed 'the most difficult discipline', that is, 'never to stop looking, never to stop responding to the world around one'.[315] Leacock made films for public television and also the US Information Service that showed 'a growing aversion to voiceover narration'.[316] For Leacock, this was an essential part of filmmaking; subjects revealed themselves unconsciously. 'It is when I'm not being told something... this is when it gets exciting for me... The minute I sense I'm being told the answer, I tend to start rejecting it.'[317]

Leacock formed a production company with Pennebaker after leaving Drew Associates. Leacock-Pennebaker produced some of the seminal Direct Cinema films of the period, including *Don't Look Back* (1967), which followed Bob Dylan on his 1965 tour of the UK. Dylan performs, travels between venues, parties in hotel rooms with his entourage and is interviewed. In one celebrated sequence, Dylan demolishes a middle-aged reporter with his trademark quick-fire wit. Critics have argued that, although the film claims to 'give you the feeling of being there' – as Richard Leacock might put it – this press conference scene actually betrays Pennebaker's view of the media as much as Dylan's. Such accusations of bias would consistently be levelled at Direct Cinema.[318]

Musicians would continue to feature in Direct Cinema films. The Maysles' *Gimme Shelter* (1970) followed the Rolling Stones on their 1969 tour of the States, including the fateful concert at Altamont, in which Hell's Angels, hired as security, stabbed an audience member to death. Americana of a different sort would form the subject matter of the two films for which the Maysles are perhaps best known, *Salesman* (1968) and *Grey Gardens* (1975). The former follows the trials and tribulations of a group of door-to-door Bible salesmen, focusing on the Irish-American Paul Brennan. From the wintery Midwest to balmy Florida, Brennan struggles to make sales, frequently singing *Fiddler on the Roof*'s 'If I Were a Rich Man'. His boss, an overweight, sexist conservative, hectors Brennan and his colleagues to increase their profits but seemingly to no avail. Brennan complains towards the end of the film, 'I can't see any deals here'; *Salesman* is a portrait of the failure of the American Dream straight out of Arthur Miller. *Grey Gardens* depicts failure of a different sort, its subjects being Edith Bouvier Beale, and her daughter, Little Edie, two of the more eccentric members of the Kennedy clan. They live in Grey Gardens, a ramshackle mansion in the Hamptons, so ramshackle, in fact, that the local authorities want to evict them from it because it's a health hazard. Only intervention from Jackie Kennedy herself – related in a montage of press clippings – saves the Beales from losing their home.

Direct Cinema also turned its gaze on the other end of the social spectrum. Barbara Kopple served her apprenticeship with the Maysles, finally making the transition to director in 1971, when she co-directed the trenchant anti-Vietnam film, *Winter Soldier*. But her masterpiece is *Harlan County, USA* (1976). The film depicted a bitter industrial dispute in Kentucky between miners and Duke Power Company, the company which owned the mine. Kopple and her crew followed the miners and their families through a difficult year: strikebreakers hired by Duke took to brandishing guns, Kopple was physically attacked while shooting and received death threats, and one young miner was killed. This final outrage was the event that made strikers and management finally sit down and negotiate. When finally completed, the film won an Oscar for best documentary feature.

Perhaps Direct Cinema's most significant practitioner, though, was Frederick Wiseman (b. 1930). Wiseman's films concentrate on institutions – hospitals, prisons, schools, military bases – 'through which society propagates itself, or which cushion – and therefore reflect – its tensions'.[319] He produced Shirley Clarke's *The Cool World* (1964 – see Chapter 8) before making his directorial debut with *Titicut Follies* (1967), shot inside the State Prison for the Criminally Insane in Bridgewater, Massachusetts. Showing the patients distressed, confused and ranting was not a good advertisement for the Commonwealth of Massachusetts, and the film was withheld from distribution for many years. Wiseman received funding from the burgeoning source of public television, which was to be a long-term supporter of his work. The films he made over the next few years remain amongst his best known: *High School* (1968), *Law and Order* (1969), *Hospital* (1970), *Basic Training* (1971), *Essene* (1972), and *Primate* (1974).

As Erik Barnouw has noted, Wiseman's films were 'destroyers of stereotypes… Issues were always shown to be more complicated – and more fascinating – than dogma was inclined to make them.'[320] And, despite their apparent objectivity, they are tightly edited. Wiseman might be off-camera in the films, but his presence is subtly revealed in the cutting. Wiseman generally does not have a single protagonist in his films: instead the various institutions are shown in what he termed a 'mosaic' structure, in which each sequence focused on one or two individuals, before moving on to other characters. The films are, ultimately, a form of fiction, or 'reality fictions' as he has termed them.[321]

THE ESSAY FILM

The French New Wave, while being associated with *cinéma vérité*, can also make a claim to championing another new wave in documentary, that of the essay film, which was pioneered by filmmakers such as Chris Marker. The essay film could be described as essentially a documentary with a point of view so pronounced that its bias is an integral part of its narrative. Defining it in these terms, films such as *Titicut Follies* and *Harlan County, USA* could be regarded as essays. However, the essay film as a form could be stretched much further and, in the hands of filmmakers like Marker, went into places that no film ever had before.

The genre had its precursors: the city symphonies of the 1920s are essentially essayistic, as are the films of Humphrey Jennings (to say nothing of his Nazi 'rival', Leni Riefenstahl). Rouch and Wiseman could be regarded as essayists of a sort, as could the political investigations of Emile de Antonio. *Point of Order* (1963) comprised footage shot at the 1954 congressional investigations into Senator Joseph McCarthy, while *Rush to Judgment* (1967) examined the Warren Commission's findings on the Kennedy assassination. By using newsreel footage and new interviews, de Antonio manages to be critical of the US political system without resorting to hectoring narration. This is achieved simply: by interviewing people who were not called to testify before the Warren Commission, and whose eyewitness statements flatly contradict the official lone gunman theory the Commission wanted to disseminate. Intertitles, too, are used to sobering effect, quoting sections of the Commission's report as if it were Holy Writ; in this context, the written word is synonymous with untruth, the onscreen titles conveying the implied threat of a regime intent on making the world believe its own version of what happened in Dallas on 22 November 1963.

In the Year of the Pig (1969) tackled Vietnam and furthers a technique de Antonio dubbed 'radical scavenging' – using found footage that proved too controversial for its original purposes. Here he combines newsreel, interviews, scenes of Vietnamese life and military parades – all originally shot for television – to produce a kaleidoscopic, Vertov-esque pronouncement on the evils of the war. (Surprisingly, the film was nominated for the Best Documentary Oscar. It didn't win.) *Millhouse: A White Comedy* (1971), another product of radical scavenging, attacked Nixon, while *Underground* (1976) daringly interviewed members of the radical group The Weather Underground, at a time when the FBI was hunting for them. de Antonio was subpoenaed, but refused to hand the film over or reveal where the Weathermen were hiding.

Radical politics also informed the essay films of Jean-Luc Godard, who abandoned conventional feature films during 1967–68 and became a committed Maoist; in 1972, he declared, 'I think of myself as an essayist.'[322] He formed a collective, the Dziga Vertov Group, with Jean-Pierre Gorin (b. 1943), and they produced a series of films between 1968 and 1972 that aspired to the agit-prop passion of Dziga Vertov himself. In common with de Antonio's work, the films 'radically scavenge', using found footage, interviews, stills, intertitles and voiceover to attack the bourgeoisie, repression, capitalism, the political establishment and even 'the bourgeois concept of representation'.[323]

Godard and Gorin's attack on representation famously included the long tracking shots of *Weekend* (1967) and *British Sounds* (1969), and even the use of blank frames that recall the textless pages of *Tristram Shandy*. *One Plus One* (1968) intersperses the Rolling Stones recording 'Sympathy for the Devil' with tableaux scenes illustrating Maoist thought, while *Pravda* (1969) examines post-invasion Czechoslovakia. The film is dominated by a narration from two characters called Vladimir (Lenin) and Rosa (Luxembourg). Ordinary Czechs come in for as much flak as the invading Soviets, and Godard famously encounters Vera Chytilová, whom he criticises for speaking like 'Arthur Penn and Antonioni'. He proclaimed 'Chytilová = Zanuck and Paramount'.[324] Smug and utterly humourless, it shows Godard's work of this period to be 'impossible to consume as entertainment or as engaged documentary, the films carry the modernist project to an abrasive extreme'.[325] Like much of the Dziga Vertov Group's films, it has not aged well, and the best one can say of the pro-Maoist stance is that it is of its time; seen now, it comes across as ludicrous, if not downright repugnant. Had Godard become a Taoist in 1966, not a Maoist, he might have made better films.

However, despite their manifold failings, the Dziga Vertov films epitomise Godard's first concerted attempts to make not *political films*, but to *make films politically*. He is thus opposed to filmmakers like Costa-Gavras, who wanted to make political films using mainstream narrative techniques. All one has to do is watch Costa-Gavras's Czech film, *The Confession* (1970), and the vast difference between the two approaches is painfully apparent. However, both are necessary. One could argue that Godard was thinking of the filmmaker when stating that films needed to be made politically, while Costa-Gavras was thinking of the audience, of getting the message out. It is an irony, though, that most of the Dziga Vertov Group's films were funded by decidedly non-revolutionary sources (such as TV stations), and that their best film is arguably the drama, *Tout Va Bien* (1972), about a factory strike, starring Jane Fonda and Yves Montand.

Chris Marker

Chris Marker (1921–2012) was one of the key proponents of the essay film, but he was as much a poet, philosopher and photographer as he was a politician. Marker took the documentary and did something highly personal and idiosyncratic with the form. His films 'reassess what the term "documentary" means'. Indeed, Marker only used the term 'because nobody has come up with anything better'.[326] As Kevin Macdonald and Mark Cousins remarked, 'Watching a Marker film is like being engaged in a passionate, fascinating, if at times puzzling, conversation.'[327]

Marker was active in founding ciné-clubs in Paris after the Second World War, and came to filmmaking from a background as a writer. (Like Eric Rohmer, he also wrote fiction, publishing a novel in the 1940s – translated into English as *The Forthright Spirit*.) Marker was also active in the cultural and educational organisations Travail et Culture and Peuple et Culture, the latter sponsoring Marker's first completed film, *Olympia 52* (1952), a portrait of the 1952 Helsinki Olympics. Another cultural body, Amitiés Franco-Chinoises, helped Marker get to Peking to shoot *Dimanche à Pékin* (1956), the first of his essays on time and memory, concerns that resurfaced in one of his most celebrated works, *La Jetée* (1962).

Ethnographic and anthropological themes were to run through much of Marker's work. He collaborated with Alain Resnais on *Statues Also Die* (*Les Statues meurent aussi*, 1953), which examined the effects of colonialism on African art. The film proposed that statues, ritual masks and fetish objects lose their original purpose when they become part of Western museum collections; the societies that used the artefacts are no longer able to, and the objects effectively 'die'. The film's anti-colonial stance did not sit well with French censors, and it was not until 1968 that it was shown in its full version.

Letter from Siberia (*Lettre de Sibérie*, 1958) is Marker's most important early work. In it, an unnamed narrator tells us he is writing to us 'from a distant land'. The film is an idiosyncratic 'report... that bypass[es] the fixed problems that are supposed to beset our view'[328] of Siberia. The film is playfully discursive, beginning with shots of the steppe and a birch grove and then panning to a team of men erecting telegraph wires. A new city is shown, but then we are back in the 'stone age forest', among the birches. The narrator relates a Siberian proverb that attributes the planting of the forest to the Devil, and claims that the forest is as big as the United States. 'But maybe the

Devil made the United States too.' A Siberian graveyard provokes the narrator into wanting to revive the dead with a breath, and then they could continue their lives, 'leading their herds to milder pastures'. Folk melodies lilt on the soundtrack, the voices of women and girls. Cattle appear, right out of Dovzhenko, who are in turn undercut by ducks 'on naval manoeuvres'. The film then unexpectedly introduces animated mammoths, a half-sung ditty informing us how 'the mammoths of old Siberia dreamt of a holiday in Iberia'. (Later in the film, there is a mock television advert praising reindeer, while another describes an 'imaginary winter'.)

The playfulness becomes more leavened in a central section. We cut to the city of Yakutsk, where a bus drives by; a construction crew levels the surface of the road; a man looks into the camera. The narrator wonders who these images will satisfy, and the same sequence repeats three times. In the first version, Yakutsk is described as a progressive Soviet city in which people are optimistic about the future, the road crew happily making Yakutsk a better place to live; the man walking by is 'a picturesque denizen of the Arctic reaches'. In the second version, Yakutsk is dark and evil, the passerby a 'sinister Asiatic', the road crew working with primitive equipment. The third version describes the city more objectively, saying that the bus is less crowded than its London or New York counterparts, that the passerby has an eye infection, and that the road crew are working hard to improve the appearance of a city that could certainly use it.

Le Joli Mai (1963; lit: 'The Beautiful/Joyous May') stands comparison with Rouch's *Chronicle of a Summer* in that both films study the lives and opinions of Parisians. But Marker did not follow Rouch's practice of inviting his films' subjects to be effectively their co-authors (he would do that a few years later, in his work with the SLON group) and instead investigates the lives and thoughts of Parisians with 'the flavour of a stranger's view'.[329] The first part, 'Prière sur la Tour Eiffel', situates Parisians in the shadow of French history, as epitomised by the shadow of the Tower falling across the city, and the narrator (Yves Montand) quoting Jean Giraudoux (one of Marker's favourite authors). Marker questions various people – a shop owner, an inventor, stock exchange workers, a young married couple – about happiness, hopes, ambitions and whether they think of anything outside their own immediate concerns, such as other people or current affairs.

The second part of the film, 'Le Retour de Fantomâs', broadens the canvas to focus more on the time the film was shot, May 1962. Over shots of Montmartre cemetery, the narrator informs us the legendary villain, Fantomâs, has left his lair among the tombs to cast his shadow over Paris, recalling the criminal web of Lang's Dr Mabuse. Shots follow of riots, tanks in the streets, broken windows, a burnt-out car. People are questioned about Algeria, and the use of torture by French forces against suspected Algerian insurgents. Women questioned about the trial of a right-wing general who tried to overthrow De Gaulle say they don't feel personally concerned. A priest who converted to communism says he doesn't have time to think about the existence of God. A young student from Dahomey talks about his experiences of racism in France, and a young Algerian says his future lies in Algeria. Unlike the other interviewees, he is encouraged to think about his own happiness.

The film ends with time-lapse shots of traffic buzzing around the Arc de Triomphe. Montand tells us how much rain fell in Paris in May 1962; how much food was eaten; how much wine was drunk. We then cut to a shot of the hexagonal monolith of the Petite Roquette women's prison, hearing the voices of the inmates, who admit that the other women make their life unbearable. Montand ruminates further that the prisoners would be amazed by some of the people in the film, 'because they carry a prison around inside themselves'.[330] Over shots of pensive – and, frankly, unhappy-looking – Parisians, Montand wonders if they are 'harbouring somewhere that voice which says: as long as misery exists, you are not rich; as long as distress exists, you are not happy; as long as prisons exist, you are not free.'[331]

Marker followed *Le Joli Mai* with the film that has become his most well known, *La Jetée* (1963; lit: 'The Pier'). Issues of happiness and freedom recur here, too, but in a different context. Made up almost entirely of still photographs, *La Jetée* is a science-fiction film ostensibly about the aftermath of World War III. Survivors live in the tunnels beneath the Palais de Chaillot, where prisoners are experimented on. With the planet uninhabitable, the doctors perfect a technique to send people back in time – the only way to ensure humanity's survival. One prisoner (Davos Hanich) has a very vivid memory of a woman (Hélène Chatelain) standing at the end of the viewing platform (the jetée, or pier, of the title) at Orly Airport. He is sent back and, little by little, begins a relationship with her. The scientists in the tunnel, however, have other plans for him...

Despite running only 29 minutes, *La Jetée* is a film with numerous strata of meaning. It is as much about the past as it is about the future: the shots of a ruined Paris are clearly scenes of urban devastation from the Second World War; the tunnels of Chaillot were used during the war by the French resistance; the doctors whisper in German, suggesting Nazi camp experimentation; and one of the final images recalls Robert Capa's famous photograph of the death of a soldier in the Spanish Civil War. The tunnels also suggest the present, calling to mind the torture meted out by the French to Algerian FLN fighters, and the whole film is overshadowed by the possibility of a real Third World War, in the shape of the Cuban Missile Crisis.

But *La Jetée* offers antidotes: memory (represented in the film by images and the act of looking) and the possibility of love. The history of cinema is a ghostly presence: Chaillot was for many years also the home of the French Cinémathèque, and the head doctor is played by Jacques Ledoux, then head of the Belgian Cinémathèque. History itself is represented by the scene in the Natural History Museum; and, finally, there's hope in the scene where the sleeping woman opens her eyes – the only piece of moving footage in the film.

As Sarah Cooper notes, 'The world of images becomes the protagonist's reality. Although he is said on several occasions to be uncertain whether what he sees is remembered, created or dreamt, all of these possibilities exist.'[332] The theme of images, memory and reality recur in Marker's work, and the narrator's comments early on in *La Jetée* could equally serve to describe, not only Marker's oeuvre, but also his aesthetic and working practice: 'This was the aim of the experiments: to send emissaries into time, to summon past and future to rescue the present.' Once we, like Marker, have summoned past and future through images, we are able to 'wake up in another time [and] be born again, as an adult'. It is through looking, and remembering, that we are able to appreciate 'this timeless world which amazes [us] with its riches'.

Werner Herzog

Although he established himself as a director of feature films (see Chapter 9), much of Werner Herzog's work falls within the essay category. Indeed, these films are referred to as 'documentaries', with deliberate inverted commas around the term, by Paul Cronin.[333] The distinction between fact and fiction in Herzog is a slim one, as he admits in an interview:

> The word 'documentary' should be handled with care because we seem to have a very precise definition of what that word means... this is only due to our need to easily categorise films and the lack of a more appropriate concept for a whole range of cinema... For me, the boundary between fiction and 'documentary' does not exist; they are all just films.[334]

This is an almost direct echo of Chris Marker's words that 'documentary' is a term used because no one has thought of a more appropriate one.

Herzog's 'documentaries' grew out of two fairly straightforward films, *The Flying Doctors of East Africa* (*Die fliegenden Artze von Ostafrika*, 1969) and *Handicapped Future* (*Behinderte Zukunft*, 1971). Herzog dubs these films *Gebrauschfilm*, or 'films of practical use' (akin to the British public information film, or the American public service announcement). The earlier film documents the flying doctor services of Kenya and Tanzania; perhaps its most Herzogian motifs are the ideas of flight and attempting to bring the trappings of Western civilisation (in the form of medicine) to inaccessible parts of Africa.

But while in Africa in late 1968, Herzog began shooting one of his most acclaimed films, *Fata Morgana* (1970). The film is a quest to film mirages, and is an early example of Herzog's wish to film 'embarrassed landscapes', or landscapes that have been defiled by human presence. Herzog has also described *Fata Morgana* as a science-fiction film about the end of colonialism. But this is not an anthropological treatment of colonialism and imperialism: shots of abandoned factories, endless dunes, planes flying overhead, oil refineries and depots, dead animals, wandering children, seemingly crazed natives and equally odd German expatriates populate the spaces of the film. They are not contextualised, but are put into a mythological perspective through the inclusion in the narration of the Mayan sacred text, the Popol Vuh (read by film historian Lotte Eisner), together with Judeo-Christian material, and further lines added by Herzog himself.

As with Chris Marker, the voiceover complicates our understanding of the image by taking us away from the visible and specific to the unseen and unexpected universal. As Amos Vogel noted, 'Here, working solely with the materials of reality, Herzog, in a cosmic pun on *cinéma vérité*, recovered the metaphysical beneath the visible.'[335] In *Fata Morgana*, as in much of Herzog's work, landscape is not only a state of soul, but also a state of civilisation. Man has abused and then abandoned the landscape, which has become too hostile for all but the most recalcitrant, stubborn or insane.

Handicapped Future was intended to show 'The Situation of Physically Handicapped Children in the Federal Republic of Germany', as the subtitle puts it. Most of them are suffering from thalidomide. The children and their parents are asked about life with disabilities; the children's able-bodied peers are asked whether they think the children are in any way different to them; teachers show us art made by the children. There is also a narrator (not Herzog, for one of the few times in his oeuvre) who explains that the children face a bleak future, a far remove from California, where we meet a wheelchair-using German academic who leads a relatively independent life (he even drives his own specially adapted car). Further forward thinking comes from little Dagmar's mother, who tells Herzog she gets Dagmar and her brother – also physically disabled – to help around the house, 'otherwise they would be apathy in a wheelchair'. And, in one of the film's few 'Herzogian' scenes, a group of teenage boys talk about their plan to film themselves shoplifting in order to provoke a response from the able-bodied. Despite being quite affecting, the film is stylistically unremarkable.

However, during shooting, Herzog and his cinematographer, Jörg Schmidt-Reitwein, met Fini Straubinger, a 56-year-old deaf-blind woman. Herzog decided to film her. From only three hours of footage, he and his editor, Beate Mainka-Jellinghaus, created *Land of Silence and Darkness* (*Land des Schweigens und der Dunkelheit*, 1971), a radically different film from *Handicapped Future*. Fini's narration begins the film. She tells us she can see 'a road going across the bare fields and clouds are flying overhead'. We then cut to two roads meeting on what appears to be heathland under a dramatic sky. The image flickers; it could be a shot from an expressionist film. The title appears, followed by a subtitle: 'From the life of the deaf-blind Fini Straubinger.' Fini then tells us about how she remembers watching a ski-jumping competition as a child, 'before I was like this'. Cut to ski-jumpers. And then an intertitle: 'I always jump when I'm touched. Years go by in waiting.'

This is a stylised, memorable opening for a documentary. It is also completely fictitious: Herzog has put words into Fini Straubinger's mouth, and given her a false childhood memory. Likewise, the film's other two intertitles – 'When you let go of my hand, it is as if we were a thousand miles apart' and the closing 'If a world war broke out now, I wouldn't even notice' – are also written by Herzog. 'This is something I wrote that I felt encapsulated, in only a few words, how someone like her might experience the world,' Herzog remarked in an interview, adding that such fabrication was justifiable on the grounds that they were 'great image[s] to represent Fini's own inner state of mind and solitude'.[336] He stressed that 'no scenes were shot contrary to Fini's wishes and she did not mind speaking the lines I had written for her. The wonderful thing about her was that she never argued about it; she immediately understood and squeezed my hand.'[337] Herzog arguably gets away with his fictional touches because they are relatively slight – the film is 'from the life', as the subtitle puts it, rather than 'the life'. More importantly, *Land of Silence and Darkness* is a film of considerable empathy. Herzog has spoken many times of his admiration for Fini Straubinger, whose loneliness is at the heart of the film, a 'loneliness... taken to unimaginable limits'; despite – or maybe because of – this, Herzog speaks of Fini as having a 'radical dignity'.[338]

Fini's loneliness, however, recedes as the film progresses. After describing a visit to the zoo, going up in a plane for the first time and then having a birthday party, we see Fini at a speech given by the

West German president, Gustav Heinemann, in which he calls for the disabled to be integrated into society. We learn that Fini became deaf-blind as the result of falling downstairs as a girl, and now works for the League of the Blind in Bavaria, visiting other deaf-blind and listening to their needs.

It is here that the film goes even further towards the 'unimaginable limits' of loneliness, in the figure of Else Fährer, who was only able to communicate with her mother, but, since her mother's death, has remained completely isolated from the world. She seems to be aware of Fini's presence, but remains uncommunicative. Vladimir Kokol, deaf-blind since birth, has never learned to communicate or even walk, and spends much of the time blowing raspberries and hitting himself in the face with a ball. Finally, Fini meets Heinrich Fleischmann, who lives in an old people's home with his mother, despite the fact that Heinrich is only 51. The narrator tells us that Heinrich was 'so neglected by his family that he forgot how to speak and write… rejected by human society, he sought company with animals. He lived with the cows in a stable for a long time.' In the film's final moments, Heinrich is seen running his hands around a tree in the home's garden.

In *Handicapped Future*, Heinrich's plight may have been explored more – why is he in an old people's home, not a proper facility for the deaf-blind? Ditto Else. But Herzog does not want to put these figures into a sociological context. Herzog refuses 'to have the handicapped, the blind or the sick become subsumed under the discourse of institutionalised medicine, charitable religion or the welfare worker, before they have a chance to appear first and foremost as human beings'.[339] Herzog's empathy for Fini and all the other characters in the film takes it beyond both documentary and fiction: it is nothing less than a report from another plane of existence.

The Great Ecstasy of Woodcarver Steiner (*Die Grosse Ekstase des Bildschnitzers Steiner,* 1974) also strives to represent unusual levels of experience, in this case that of the champion ski-jumper, Walter Steiner. The film documents Steiner over a few months in 1973–74 as he effortlessly outclasses the competition: at Oberstdorf, he 'flies too far' to be world champion, while at Planica he jumps at only half-strength but still manages an enormous jump – 'the distance markers won't go that far' – which is eventually measured at 169 metres, a ramp record. Even when he has a bad landing, resulting in medical attention, he goes even further, and is told 'you have exceeded all expectations – will you still jump?' Steiner still manages to win the competition, despite voluntarily imposing a handicap on himself by starting further down the slope.

Steiner has much in common with Herzog's fictional heroes, Aguirre and Fitzcarraldo (see Chapter 9), in that he attempts the impossible – in this case, to fly. Herzog does little to impose himself on Steiner, except to get him to tell a story about how, as a boy, he had to kill a tame raven. The film ends with an onscreen statement about freedom and solitude that appears to be by Steiner, but is actually a doctored (by Herzog) quote from Robert Walser. Such doctoring was justifiable, Herzog argued, as, 'Through invention, through imagination, through fabrication, I become more truthful than the little bureaucrats.' The 'little bureaucrats' were the practitioners of *cinéma vérité*, a movement Herzog held some animosity towards. What Herzog attempts to do in his documentaries is go beyond the truth of the merely seen, to show a wider reality beyond it, something he dubbed 'ecstatic truth'. 'I know that by making a clear distinction between "fact" and "truth" in my films, I am able to penetrate into a deeper stratum of truth most films do not even notice.'[340]

FILMS THE COLOUR OF BLOOD:
THE NEW HOLLYWOOD

ARTISTS, HIPSTERS & BEATNIKS

A seismic disturbance in American filmmaking, one that would in time be felt in Hollywood and beyond, began one cold day in New York in February 1957, when a young actor and screenwriter by the name of John Cassavetes started shooting his first feature, *Shadows*. He planned to finance the film himself, with money earned from his acting work. He was not the first American filmmaker to fund his work this way: Orson Welles had been working like this ever since his departure from Hollywood in 1948, shooting as and when he could in Europe and North Africa.[341] Welles became an icon for filmmakers, both in North America and also Europe (the French New Wave revered him, with Truffaut's alter ego in *Day for Night* having a recurring dream in which he steals lobby cards for *Citizen Kane* from his local theatre).

Independent filmmaking in the States prior to 1957 had been largely the province of avant-garde filmmakers, animators and artists – figures such as Maya Deren, Jonas Mekas, Kenneth Anger, James and John Whitney and Harry Smith, who had been working outside the system since the 1940s. Films like Deren's *Meshes of the Afternoon* (1943), the Whitneys' *Five Film Exercises* (1945), and Anger's *Fireworks* (1947) became underground classics. (Fittingly, the first use of the term 'underground film' also dates from 1957, when critic Manny Farber used it in an essay.[342]) Most of these films were either self-funded or occasionally made for non-profit organisations. As in Europe, independent film culture in postwar America flourished at galleries, such as the San Francisco Museum of Art, and in the form of film clubs.

The largest and most celebrated film club was New York's Cinema 16, set up in 1947 by cineastes Amos and Marcia Vogel, who had been inspired by Deren's pioneering method of renting theatres herself in order to exhibit her work. In addition to showing work by American filmmakers, the Vogels also screened films by filmmakers from Europe and the Far East, including Roman Polanski, Jacques Rivette, Alain Resnais and Japanese New Wave master Nagisa Oshima. The club ran until 1963, when financial pressures forced the Vogels to shut up shop. (However, later the same year, Amos carried on the good work by founding the New York Film Festival with critic Richard Roud.)

The idea for Cassavetes' *Shadows* came from an acting workshop the director was teaching in January 1957. A month later he started shooting, using equipment loaned to him by fellow New Yorker Shirley Clarke. Cassavetes and his team developed their characters through improvisation, a method entirely in keeping with the Greenwich Village/ Beatnik milieu the film tales place in. Ben (Ben Carruthers) and his sister Lelia (Lelia Goldoni) live 'just beyond the bright lights of Broadway' as Cassavetes described it. Their older brother Hugh is a struggling musician. The film follows their daily round through Manhattan's hipster scene as they attempt to make something of their lives. Cassavetes drew on his own experience of being a struggling actor in the New York of the early 1950s to infuse the film with depth. *Shadows* has its sympathies firmly with the Beatniks and dropouts of New York, speaking about them in a tone they would understand, giving the film some similarity with documentary filmmakers like Jean Rouch.

Cassavetes made *Shadows* on fiercely independent terms. As the film features a number of African-American characters and inter-racial relationships – a subject deeply off-limits to mainstream filmmakers – the NAACP (the National Association for the Advancement of Colored People, an influential civil rights lobby) offered funding. Fearing he would lose control of the film, Cassavetes turned them down. It was not an easy shoot: Cassavetes ended up scrapping much of what he shot in the first eight weeks, as he felt the actors had not found their characters fully and still appeared slightly stiff on camera. (A truthful performance for Cassavetes was more important than beautiful compositions or perfect lighting, and he developed a reputation as an actor's director.) A cut running 78 minutes was completed and screened in November 1958 at the Paris Theatre in New York. The audience response was negative – Jonas Mekas and future director Henry Jaglom[343] were among the very few to offer Cassavetes any encouragement – and Cassavetes reshot approximately half the film. A second version of *Shadows* was screened at Cinema 16 a year later, and it won the Critics' Prize at the Venice Film Festival the year after. Although the film only received a very limited theatrical release in the States in 1961, a few eminent critics did get to see it, and Leonard Maltin later hailed *Shadows* as 'a watershed in the birth of American independent cinema'.

Sadly, the same can't be said for *A Child is Waiting* (1963), an unhappy Hollywood experience for Cassavetes. Unlike *Shadows*, *A Child is Waiting* suffered from clashes between Cassavetes and producer Stanley Kramer. Cassavetes was called in after Jack Clayton, the film's original director, withdrew from the project, and Cassavetes brought with him improvisational techniques that neither Kramer nor the two stars, Burt Lancaster and Judy Garland, were used to. The film's subject matter – a school for mentally ill children – appealed to both Kramer and Cassavetes. Many of the children in the film suffered from mental health issues in real life, and their scenes were improvised, something which suited Cassavetes' working methods to a tee. Where Cassavetes and Kramer fell out was over the sentimental storyline involving the main child, Reuben, and his relationships with his teacher (Garland) and his father. Eventually Kramer fired Cassavetes and recut the film.

The problems *A Child is Waiting* suffered from were essentially due to a clash of cultures, the old way of Hollywood against the new way of the independents. As the film's editor, Gene Fowler, Jr, recalled, 'It was a fight of technique. Stanley is a more traditional picture-maker, and Cassavetes was, I guess, called Nouvelle Vague. He was trying some things, which frankly I disagreed with, and I thought he was hurting the picture by blunting the so-called message with technique.'[344] Cassavetes felt the problem essentially boiled down to differing views of how to treat mentally ill children, with Kramer's recut suggesting that 'retarded children belong in institutions and the picture I shot said retarded children are better in their own way than supposedly healthy adults'.[345] Despite some good notices, Cassavetes disowned the film, and it would be five years before he was able to complete another one.

Faces (1968) was a middle-class reincarnation of *Shadows*, portraying a disintegrating marriage in high-contrast black and white. The two films have much in common in terms of how they were made. Like *Shadows*, *Faces* was self-funded and also distributed by Cassavetes. The film was shot and edited at Cassavetes' own home, but spent considerable time in postproduction due to problems with the sound. (The film was actually shot in 1965.) With its handheld camerawork and largely improvised script, *Faces* confirmed the promise Cassavetes had shown in his debut, and its 'home-movie' method of production was to be the *modus operandi* by which Cassavetes would make most of his subsequent films as director. Because he was distributing the films himself, they necessarily had small releases, but Cassavetes' groundbreaking methods of production and distribution made him a hero to many: for Martin Scorsese, 'Cassavetes... made it possible for me to think I could actually make a movie.'[346]

Hipsters, dropouts, artists and Beatniks would play a large part in the birth of new forms of cinema in the US. Photographer Robert Frank made *Pull My Daisy* (first screened on the same bill as the second version of Cassavetes' *Shadows*) in 1959 with Beat icons Jack Kerouac and Allen Ginsberg, and would go on to make a number of documentaries in the Direct Cinema school. Shirley Clarke, who had provided Cassavetes with the camera on which he shot *Shadows*, was one of the founders in 1961 of the Filmmakers' Co-Operative in New York City, along with Jonas Mekas, Stan Brakhage and others. Their manifesto, for what it termed 'a new American cinema', announced, 'We don't want rosy films... we want them the colour of blood'.

The year following the founding of the Co-Op, Clarke made her debut feature. *The Connection* (1962) concerned itself with the drug scene depicted a few years later by The Velvet Underground in songs like 'Waiting for the Man' and 'Heroin'. Indeed, Clarke's film is actually about 'waiting for the man' – the dealer or 'connection' of the title. Six jazz musicians wait in a room for their dealer to turn up. The film has a mockumentary element, in that one character is a young filmmaker intent on filming the deal and the men taking their drugs. The filmmaker, evidently a graduate of the Method school, decides to partake himself. Like *Shadows* and *Pull My Daisy*, but entirely unlike Otto Preminger's Frank-Sinatra-with-a-drug-problem vehicle, *The Man with the Golden Arm* (1954), *The Connection* comes from the world it depicts.

The Cool World (1964), Clarke's second feature, was also a film from the streets, offering a sympathetic portrayal of black gang culture. The film was significant for being shot on location in Harlem and featured real gang members. Based on the novel of the same name by Warren Miller, the film, like *The Connection*, has a documentary feel to it, and was the first film to be produced by Frederick Wiseman, who would go on to become one of the greatest figures in Direct Cinema (see Chapter 7).

Clarke herself had started in documentaries, and she managed to straddle the worlds of independent and mainstream film, much like Cassavetes, who worked in Hollywood as an actor – most famously in Robert Aldrich's *The Dirty Dozen* (1967) and Polanski's *Rosemary's Baby* (1968). Clarke was nominated for an Oscar with her film *Skyscraper* (1960), and won the award for *Robert Frost: A Lover's Quarrel with the World* (1963), a documentary about the poet. *Portrait of Jason* (1967) was a character study of a very different individual, a black rent boy.

B-MOVIES ATTACK HOLLYWOOD

As John Cassavetes continued to work as an actor in Hollywood, and as a director outside of it, other changes were afoot in American film. They came from a world far removed from the East Coast art scene: the world of the drive-in and the B-movie. It is ironic that B-movies should have proved such fertile ground for a renewal of cinema: the French New Wave was obsessed with them – Godard famously dedicated *Breathless* to Monogram Pictures, a by-then defunct B-movie studio – and they were to prove almost equally important for American filmmakers. While film clubs proved a fertile incubation ground for artists and film enthusiasts, Roger Corman found his audience at drive-ins, and the mid-60s were their heyday. Corman had a captive audience – captive in their cars and wanting to see movies that went with cruising, hanging out, films for the young. Date movies. Daft movies. Disposable cinema.

Corman's methods were similar to Cassavetes': shoot quickly, shoot cheaply and use whatever was available by way of location and props. Corman frequently used film students on his shoots; they were cheap to hire and, in turn, learned valuable lessons working for Corman – Francis Ford Coppola made his feature debut with *Dementia 13* (1963) under Corman's aegis, and Corman inspired the young Coppola to pursue his dream of running his own studio, free from Hollywood interference. Peter Bogdanovich made his first feature for Corman, Martin Scorsese his second, and the early careers of actors such as Jack Nicholson and Peter Fonda were given a huge boost by Corman's films.

Corman was savvy about the emerging youth market and catered to an audience that was not being served by conventional Hollywood fare. The studio system was coming close to collapse, a situation not helped by a series of expensive disasters such as *Cleopatra* (1963), which nearly bankrupted 20th Century Fox. While Rome burned, Corman fiddled happily away, producing exploitation pictures by the dozen: a series of Poe adaptations, surf movies, sci-fi films, monster movies, racing movies. 1966/67 saw Corman release a spate of films that were harbingers of things to come: *The Wild Angels* (1966), a Hell's Angels film starring Peter Fonda, *The Trip* (1967) – starring Fonda again, and written by Jack Nicholson – about a TV commercials director who turns on, tunes in and drops out. The writer Joan Didion noticed a change in the air around this time, later commenting that she went to see *The Wild Angels* because, 'There on the screen was some news I was not getting from the *New York Times*. I began to think I was seeing ideograms of the future.'[347]

The 'news' included one of 1967's biggest films, Arthur Penn's *Bonnie and Clyde*. In celebrating the notorious gangsters Clyde Barrow and Bonnie Parker, Penn and his co-writers David Newman and Robert Benton were paying homage to Godard and *Breathless*, and also acknowledging the debt they owed the French New Wave in general. Early versions of the script were sent to Truffaut – whom Benton and Newman had originally wanted to direct – and Truffaut replied with detailed notes on ways to improve it. As Newman noted, there were no screenwriting manuals available to budding filmmakers in those days; they just wrote the kind of film they wanted to go and see. Truffaut passed the project on to Godard; in the end, both went on to make other films instead (*Fahrenheit 451* and *Alphaville* respectively), although Truffaut effectively got the project going by giving the script to Warren Beatty in Paris in 1965. The debt owed by the *nouvelle vague* to B-movies was about to be repaid.

Bonnie and Clyde nailed its 'us against them' colours firmly to the mast. Like Corman's work, it was a film that unashamedly appealed to younger audiences, who were in tune with its anti-authoritarian sympathies. There was no moralising about crime being bad: it was simply what Barrow and Parker did as a lifestyle choice. As Peter Biskind aptly phrased it, *Bonnie and Clyde* 'says "fuck you" not only to a generation of Americans who were on the wrong side of the generation gap, the wrong side of the war in Vietnam, but also a generation of Motion Picture Academy members that had hoped to go quietly, with dignity. *Bonnie and Clyde* made that impossible, brutally showing them out the door.'[348]

A confused Warner Brothers released the film on the art-house circuit, hoping they didn't have a turkey on their hands. As with Corman aiming for the drive-ins, this was precisely where the audience was, and the film became a huge hit. It was nominated for the Best Picture Oscar, alongside another watershed film, Mike Nichols' *The Graduate* (1967), starring Dustin Hoffman. The increasing liberalisation of censorship laws allowed Nichols and his team to invest the film with a new level of frankness in its story of Benjamin Braddock's seduction by cinema's most famous older woman, Mrs Robinson (Anne Bancroft). 1967 was the year Hollywood's defences were breached.

'THIS USED TO BE A HELL OF A GOOD COUNTRY'

The cultural and political tumult of 1960s America saw the escalation of the Vietnam war, racial tensions and assassinations. The generational shift represented by *Bonnie and Clyde* was also a real shift in Hollywood. As Peter Biskind noted, 'The studios were still in the rigor-mortis-like grip of the generation that had invented the movies.'[349] In 1965, Adolph Zukor was still on the board at Paramount, despite being 92; Jack Warner continued to run Warner Brothers at 73; at Fox, the 63-year-old Darryl F Zanuck was still very much in charge. Columbia was run by 60-year-old Abe Schneider. His three sons, Stanley, Harold and Bert, all worked at Columbia in various capacities, until Bert formed a production company of his own and produced a film that would be an even bigger hit than *Bonnie and Clyde*.

Bert Schneider's partner in Raybert Productions was Bob Rafelson; when colleague Steve Blauner joined them, the company became BBS Productions. Fresh from the success of their Beatles-inspired TV show *The Monkees*, Raybert/BBS were to make some of the most iconic films of the period, none more so than Dennis Hopper's countercultural landmark, *Easy Rider* (1969).

Hopper's film re-imagined the Western as a road movie chronicling two Hell's Angels, Wyatt (Peter Fonda) and Billy (Dennis Hopper) as they bike through the American South and Southwest. The two characters were named after Wyatt Earp and Billy the Kid. Contrasting hippie ideals with redneck Hicksville, the film's attitudes are famously summed up by its soundtrack, including Steppenwolf's 'Born to be Wild', The Byrds' 'Wasn't Born to Follow', and Roger McGuinn's version of Bob Dylan's 'It's Alright Ma (I'm Only Bleeding)'. The heart of the film is arguably the campfire scene, in which Jack Nicholson's character, the drunken lawyer Hanson, laments: 'This used to be a hell of a good country. I can't understand what's gone wrong with it.' Fonda's Wyatt (aka Captain America), realising the hippie dream of freedom is illusory, simply states, 'We blew it.' That all three main characters are killed randomly by rednecks suggests their failure is not entirely their own fault; a way out from the old order is necessary, but no one seems to know what it is.[350]

BBS continued to examine American failure in *Five Easy Pieces* (Bob Rafelson, 1970), another road movie with Jack Nicholson, in which his character, classical pianist turned oilfield worker Bobby Dupea, drives from Los Angeles to Seattle with his waitress girlfriend, Rayette (Karen Black), to be reconciled with his ailing father. 'A small, personal film, European in sensibility, character- rather than plot-driven,'[351] it is a film that examines the gap between generations and the blue and white collar worlds, whose motto could be the line from Thom Gunn's poem 'On the Move (Man You Gotta Go)': 'One is always nearer by not keeping still.' Nicholson's work on *Five Easy Pieces* – the title refers to five supposedly easy piano pieces that Bobby's sister Partita plays – earned him an Oscar nomination for Best Actor; Karen Black likewise for her performance as the white-trash Rayette.

The Last Picture Show (1971), directed by Corman graduate Peter Bogdanovich, was one of BBS's finest films, a critical success that received eight Oscar nominations and won two. Bogdanovich, a film journalist for *Esquire*, had been offered a job on Corman's Peter Fonda biker film, *The Wild Angels*. Corman had then offered him a chance to direct; *Targets* (1968), starring Boris Karloff, had been the result, which had then come to Bert Schneider's attention. Schneider gave Bogdanovich the chance to spread his wings with *The Last Picture Show*. Based on Larry McMurtry's novel, the film is an elegaic coming-of-age story set in a small Texas town in the early 1950s, hauntingly shot in black and white by Robert Surtees. The film featured Timothy Bottoms and Jeff Bridges, both in love with the same girl – Cybill Shepherd in her first acting role. Shepherd's Jacy is no innocent, using several men for sex, and discarding them when she loses interest. Indeed, the film is notable not just for Shepherd, but for a number of other strong parts for women, including Cloris Leachman as Ruth, who won an Oscar for her role, and Ellen Burstyn as Lois, Jacy's mother.

The plot is a tangle of affections and shattered dreams: Bottoms' character Sonny has an affair with an older woman, Ruth; Duane (Bridges) chases Jacy, who then dumps him; Sam the Lion (Ben Johnson – the film's other Oscar winner) dies, leaving Sonny his pool hall in his will. One of his other businesses, the local cinema, falters after his death and the film ends with a watershed in Sonny's life: Duane leaves for Korea (a thinly veiled stand-in for Vietnam, as it was in Robert Altman's *M*A*S*H*, made the year before), and the cinema closes down. Its final bill shows Howard Hawks's *Red River*, a homage to a director who had long been championed by the French

New Wave. The final shot of the film, main street empty and the cinema closed for good, is, as Peter Biskind rightly observed, 'as powerful an image of loss and alienation as anything in Antonioni'.[352]

FRANCIS FORD COPPOLA & AMERICAN ZOETROPE

Despite the success of the BBS filmmakers, the single most important Corman protégé was probably Francis Ford Coppola. Coppola began working for him while still a student at UCLA, recutting a Russian sci-fi movie and turning it into something Corman could farm out to the drive-ins: a monster movie. Coppola quickly became, as biographer Peter Cowie put it, 'Corman's Man Friday, serving as script doctor, production assistant, second-unit director, and even sound recordist'.[353] Shooting a film called *The Young Racers* in Ireland, Coppola pitched an idea to Corman. Corman agreed, with the proviso that the man in Coppola's story became a woman (clothes had to be taken off), and that he would shoot it with Corman's cast and crew. The resulting film, *Dementia 13* (1963), a horror movie, provided Coppola with valuable experience and confidence. Its theme of family conflict would reappear in later, and much more famous, productions.

The same year that Coppola shot *Dementia 13*, he won the Samuel Goldwyn Writing Award for an original screenplay. Although the film was never made, it brought Coppola to the attention of an emerging studio called Seven Arts. Like Corman, they were willing to offer new talent a chance, and they offered Coppola regular writing work. He adapted Carson McCullers' *Reflections in a Golden Eye* for them (although the film, finally shot in 1967 by John Huston, used a different script), and Tennessee Williams' *This Property is Condemned* (made in 1966 by Sydney Pollack, starring Natalie Wood and Robert Redford). He also received credit alongside Gore Vidal on the all-star war movie *Is Paris Burning?* (René Clément, 1966).

Ultimately frustrated with the writing jobs Seven Arts was giving him, Coppola decided to take the plunge and make his first feature film. *You're a Big Boy Now* (1967) was made as his Masters' thesis for UCLA, and was started 'on hope and credit'.[354] It was the first time Coppola used his own credit cards to make a film; it would not be the last. Coppola had offered the project to Corman but, when Seven

Arts found out Coppola had written the script during days off from *Is Paris Burning?*, they insisted the film be produced under their aegis. *You're a Big Boy Now* is a coming-of-age story influenced by Richard Lester's *A Hard Day's Night* and *The Knack*, as well as the French New Wave. Bernard (Peter Kastner) is told by his father (Rip Torn) to 'grow up', and he spends much of the film doing just that. Bernard works at the New York Public Library, and rollerskates between bookshelves. Although Amy (Karen Black in her first film role) is interested in him, Bernard pursues the unattainable Barbara Darling (Elizabeth Hartman), a go-go dancer who has a grudge against men ever since she was assaulted by a one-legged albino hypnotherapist, whose wooden leg she keeps as a souvenir. Bernard's landlady, the superbly named Miss Thing (Julie Harris), keeps cockerels on the stairs to act as an early warning system for any illicit goings-on in Bernard's room, and spies on him. The film is cut from the same cloth as *The Graduate* and, like its more famous cousin, features a pop score, in this case by the Lovin' Spoonful. But Coppola's film was released nine months before *The Graduate*, making it the first film to feature a soundtrack by a group. (*The Graduate*, of course, rocketed Simon & Garfunkel to superstardom.)

Coppola was then given the chance to make *Finian's Rainbow*, a rather ill-advised piece of Oirishry starring Fred Astaire as an Irishman, Petula Clark as his daughter and Tommy Steele as a leprechaun. But, as with Stanley Kubrick making *Spartacus* in order to get out of his contract with Kirk Douglas, so Coppola dutifully worked for Warners (who had, by then, been taken over by Seven Arts) largely in order to gain independence. *Finian* allowed Coppola sufficient clout to make a bid for freedom and, during its shooting, he also became good friends with a USC film graduate who had won a student scholarship to Warners, George Lucas. Like Coppola, Lucas yearned for freedom from the studios, 'see[ing] Hollywood through the eyes of a Calvinist – moviemakers operate under the shadow of original sin'.[355]

The Rain People (1969) was Coppola's first attempt at an independent, personal film. Shirley Knight stars as Natalie, a newly pregnant Long Island housewife who walks out on her marriage and embarks on a cross-country voyage of self-discovery. En route, she picks up a hitch-hiker, Jimmy 'Killer' Kilgannon (James Caan), a brain-damaged ex-footballer, and toys with the possibility of a relationship with Gordon (Robert Duvall), a traffic cop who books her for speeding. Although the characters and dialogue were finalised before shooting began, the locations were not, and the film was shot on the road across 18 states, with Coppola and his crew living and working out of a convoy of station wagons. (The film was even edited in one.) Locations were added as and when circumstance dictated: when Coppola and his team arrived in Chattanooga, Tennessee, they discovered that an Armed Forces Day parade was about to take place, and so included it in the scene they were to shoot that day. But even that improvisation led to another: Coppola was ill with flu and had to make continual visits to the nearest bathroom – in this case, in the local Greyhound Station. He spent so much time there that he decided to use it as a location for another scene.

Although a small-scale film, *The Rain People* proved to Coppola that films could be made cheaply outside the system, and was a significant stepping stone on the way to establishing his own studio. It also developed one of his main themes – familial conflict – and was, in its own modest way, every bit as dark in its view of America as *The Godfather*. It was also significant for the simple fact that the central character is a woman.

Coppola's plans for an independent studio came to fruition after *The Rain People*'s release. Inspired by the use on that film of a disused grain warehouse in Ogallala, Nebraska, as a makeshift soundstage, Coppola leased a warehouse at 827 Folsom Street in downtown San Francisco in November 1969, and installed the equipment he had used on *The Rain People*. Several projects got off the ground quite quickly with money from Warner-Seven Arts. As George Lucas recalled, 'Francis saw Zoetrope as a sort of alternative *Easy Rider* studio where he could do the same thing: get a lot of young talent for nothing, make these movies, hope that one of them would be a hit, and eventually build a studio that way.'[356] Lucas was convinced that, 'Nobody's *ever* going to let anybody make a movie. You have to go out and do it. And those who can figure out how to do it – do it. And nothing can stop them.'[357] This was Zoetrope's philosophy, by which the 'original sin' of Hollywood could be redeemed.

Amongst Zoetrope's inaugural slate of projects were Coppola's *The Conversation*, a thriller about a bugging expert, and John Milius was hired to write a screenplay about the Vietnam war entitled *Apocalypse Now*, which took a decade to reach the screen. By the time it did so, Milius's gung-ho green berets and John Wayne politics had been superseded by Coppola's reworking of the script as a phantasmagorical adaptation of Joseph Conrad's *Heart of Darkness*. Zoetrope's other major project was George Lucas's first feature, *THX 1138* (1971).

Even more uncompromising than *Apocalypse Now* would turn out to be, *THX* was dystopian science fiction that showed a futuristic population living a life of orderly sedation; emotions are forbidden; deviance is punishable by death. Citizens are watched constantly from an Orwellian Mission Control, and make regular use of confessional booths, where they admit their wrongdoings to a deity called OMM 0000 (represented by a painting of Christ by Hans Memling). The film is dominated by voices from Mission Control, and OMM's HAL-like pronouncements: 'For more enjoyment and greater efficiency, consumption is being standardised', 'If you feel you are not properly sedated, call...', 'Are you now, or have you ever been...', 'Work hard, increase production, prevent accidents, and be happy', 'Let us be thankful we have commerce. Buy now. Buy more now. Buy, and be happy.' Told in a narrative as disjointed as THX's drug-addled consciousness, the film is dominated by the colour white – walls and uniforms – and close-ups of the shaven-headed citizens, part-way between Dreyer's *Passion of Joan of Arc* and Todd Browning's *Freaks*. When THX 1138 (Robert Duvall) has sex with his roommate, LUH 3417 (Maggie McOmie), and stops medicating himself, punishment isn't long in arriving...

Coppola took *THX 1138* to Warner-Seven Arts in May 1970. The day became known as Black Thursday. They hated Lucas's film so much that they cited a clause in Coppola's contract: if they deemed a film to be unsuitable for release, he had to buy back the picture from them. Suddenly Coppola was on the verge of bankruptcy, and Zoetrope was effectively dead in the water after a matter of months. Although *THX* would get a limited release nearly a year later, only slightly cut, Coppola was now desperately in need of work. Luckily, fate intervened in the shape of another studio picture: Paramount needed a director for a film about the Mafia and Coppola, being of Italian extraction, was deemed suitable. The film would restore his fortunes, and get the Zoetrope dream back on track.

The Godfather was a three-hour adaptation of Mario Puzo's bestselling 1969 novel about the mob. The words 'Mafia' and 'Cosa Nostra' were conspicuous by their absence, a largely successful attempt to placate the Italian-American lobby, who feared the film would depict the entire community in an unsavoury light. They need not have worried. Coppola was at first reluctant to sign as director, thinking the project was 'a hunk of trash' and protesting 'I want to do art films'.[358] George Lucas reminded Coppola that, since Black Thursday, they were broke; Coppola agreed to direct the film. Once he had begun to work with Puzo on the script, Coppola discerned the art within the 'trash', and saw a way of taking the film above and beyond the normal constraints of the gangster genre. He became fastidious on set, insisting on multiple retakes, coming to blows on more than one occasion with Gordon Willis, his brilliant cinematographer. Coppola stuck by his casting of Al Pacino when Paramount wanted to recast him, a move supported by the film's star, Marlon Brando. Emphasising character over violence, *The Godfather* became, in Coppola's hands, an epic study of the family, the temple-like darkness of Don Corleone's inner sanctum at its heart, where the lines between blood relation and business associate are blurred.

Despite going behind schedule and over budget, *The Godfather* was a runaway success as soon as it opened in March 1972, receiving highly favourable notices and quickly becoming one of the most successful films of all time, establishing itself as a cultural landmark. The film's success allowed Coppola to play mogul once more – up to a point – and he helped George Lucas get his next film, *American Graffiti*, off the ground, resurrected *The Conversation* and signed to do a *Godfather* sequel. Continuing his screenwriting career – he had won an Oscar for *Patton* (Franklin J Schaffner, 1970; actually written in 1966) – Coppola penned an adaptation of *The Great Gatsby*, directed by Jack Clayton.

Coppola also became involved in The Directors' Company, a partnership with William Friedkin and Peter Bogdanovich, both of whom were riding high at that time due to their respective successes with *The French Connection* and *The Last Picture Show*; financial backing came from Paramount. The concept behind the company was to capitalise on the auteur status of all three men, getting them to each direct three films over the next six years, as well as executive producing a fourth. It was arguably the high-water mark of the director as auteur in the US, and Coppola had great plans for The Directors' Company: 'Part of my desire to get involved with them is revenge,' Coppola explained in an interview in 1972. 'Part of me really wants to take control and own a piece of that film business, for lots of vindictive, Mafia-like reasons – because I'm so mad at Warner Brothers [for Black Thursday].' However, there was one caveat: 'I know that I can't do it alone... What if we [Coppola, Friedkin and Bogdanovich] get together? We could really take over the business. In a company like that, for six years' work, you could make $20 million, and then spend the rest of your life making little movies that don't have to make money.'[359]

Coppola produced *The Conversation* for The Directors' Company. A long-cherished project – Coppola had been working on the idea since the mid-60s – it would be, like *The Rain People*, another small, personal movie. The story of surveillance expert Harry Caul (Gene Hackman), 'the best bugger on the West Coast', the film did for sound what Antonioni's *Blow-Up* had done for images (the latter being released in the US in 1967, the year Coppola started developing the idea for his film). *The Conversation*'s theme of paranoia at the possibility of faceless government agencies and nameless corporations spying on citizens was unwittingly prescient: the film was released in March 1974, just as the Watergate crisis was about to force US President Richard Nixon to resign.

The Conversation was a critical success; it received good notices and won the top prize at Cannes. But it was a commercial flop, being out of theatres by the time Nixon finally resigned in August. The film's poor box office did not impress William Friedkin, who, fresh from the success of *The French Connection* and *The Exorcist*, had yet to make a film for The Directors' Company. Peter Bogdanovich, meanwhile, made *Paper Moon* for them. The film – a Depression-era caper about a con man (Ryan O'Neal) and the orphan who becomes his sidekick (played by O'Neal's nine-year-old daughter, Tatum) – had been a sizeable hit, but Bogdanovich had followed it up with a poorly received adaptation of Henry James's *Daisy Miller* (1974). Friedkin made nothing for The Directors' Company, which died a quiet death shortly after.

Meanwhile, as Coppola was shooting *The Conversation*, George Lucas was working on *American Graffiti* (1973). Set over one summer night in 1962, the film focuses on four friends, whose lives will diverge forever by the end of the night. After the cold and bleak *THX*, Lucas deliberately made an upbeat film for people of his own generation, whose age-group was fast becoming one of the main demographics of cinema audiences. Nostalgia was also big business, as Peter Bogdanovich had found with *The Last Picture Show* and *Paper Moon*. The early 70s were marked by what Drew Casper has defined as 'confusion, impotence and cynicism'.[360] It was an era of Vietnam, Watergate, the increasing influence of corporate interests on government, economic slowdown, the oil crisis, and a 'media [that] was biased and exploitative, rendering it difficult, well-nigh impossible to see the difference between fact and fabrication'.[361] Faced with a country in the doldrums, audiences found the appeal of a kitsch past appealing, whether mediated through films, music, television or the theatre. 'Whether charming or parodic, the product was meant to connect the young and/or reconnect the not-so-young with a simpler, happier time, taking their minds off the unpleasant present.'[362]

American Graffiti caught this zeitgeist and became the most profitable film ever made in Hollywood up to that time (for every $1 Universal invested, they got more than $50 back). Its box office and critical success gave Lucas the power to move ever further away from Hollywood and work on his own terms. Coppola was not directly involved with the financing, much to his chagrin: as Lucas recalled, 'If he had just financed the film himself, he would have made 30 million dollars on the deal.'[363]

However, Coppola himself enjoyed further success the following year with *The Godfather Part II* (1974), an even more ambitious film than the original, and one that scored significant Oscar success, becoming the first sequel to win the Best Picture award; it also netted Coppola Best Director. Suitably bolstered, Coppola gambled everything he had on his next film, which would be part made with his own money, with United Artists being co-producer. It was still very much a case of playing by Hollywood's rules in order to ultimately be free of them.

Originally conceived by George Lucas and John Milius,[364] *Apocalypse Now* (1979) became one of the defining films of the New Hollywood. It was shot under famously difficult circumstances: made on location in the Philippines, the film suffered typhoons, military coups, problems with the script (the ending in particular), and problems with the stars. Coppola started shooting with Harvey Keitel, but fired him after a month of shooting. Marlon Brando arrived on set so overweight he had to be shot in shadow for most of his scenes, and Keitel's replacement, Martin Sheen, suffered a heart attack. Coppola himself thought he might die, so immense did the film's problems seem. When editing finally began in 1977, Walter Murch, Lisa Fruchtman and Gerald B Greenberg had over a million feet of film to work with.

What makes *Apocalypse Now* remarkable is its revisionism. Revisionist approaches to genre and form were two defining characteristics of New Hollywood – and, indeed, of most New Wave cinemas. There was a concern to rework traditional narrative structures, to breathe new life into tired forms. In *Apocalypse Now*, the heart of US imperialism is laid bare with hell-bent singlemindedness, a heart that is truly one of darkness and madness. No one is innocent; everyone seems tainted by madness and moral corruption on an almost Old Testament scale. About to be sent on his mission, Willard (Martin Sheen) believes instead he is about to be arrested, and tiredly mutters, 'What are the charges?' He is told he has to 'terminate with extreme prejudice' an American officer named Colonel Kurtz (Brando), who has committed the ultimate sin of going native.

The implication of Kurtz's defection is that he shows up the Americans for what they are: when Willard does finally encounter him in his compound, Kurtz ruminates on the horrors and hypocrisies of war: 'We train young men to drop fire on people, yet their commanding officers won't let them write "fuck" on their airplanes, because it's obscene.' By then, we have witnessed one of the most operatically deranged moments in cinema: Lt Col Kilgore (Robert Duvall) bombing villages as his helicopters blast out Wagner's *Ride of the Valkyries*, prompting Willard to muse, 'If that's how Kilgore fought the war, I was beginning to wonder what they had against Kurtz.' Later in the film – further upriver towards Kurtz, at the Do-Lung Bridge – Willard encounters fighting. When he asks a soldier, 'Who's the commanding officer here?' he is met with the chilling reply, 'Ain't you?'

'A REAL GEE-WHIZ MOVIE'

After *American Graffiti*, Lucas continued with his project of independence. He determined that his follow-up would be a film for an even younger audience, 'a real gee-whiz movie',[365] a film set 'in a galaxy far away, a long time ago'. 'There's a whole generation growing up without any kind of fairytales,' said Lucas at the time. 'And kids need fairytales – it's an important thing for society to have for kids.'[366] Lucas began reading books about fairytales and myths, classics such as Bruno Bettelheim's *The Uses of Enchantment* and Joseph Campbell's *The Hero with a Thousand Faces*, noting the reasons why certain types of story always seemed to work. These all fed into *The Adventures of Luke Starkiller*, as early drafts of *Star Wars* were known.

Lucas read Carlos Castaneda's *Tales of Power*, fascinated by its mysticism, and devoured science fiction of all kinds, from Edgar Rice Burroughs' Martian books, to the space opera of E E 'Doc' Smith, to contemporary books like Frank Herbert's *Dune*. Old movie serials he had seen as a boy also influenced the idea, Buck Rogers and Flash Gordon in particular; the original 1936 *Flash Gordon* series and the novel *The Lion Men of Mongo* were favourites. Westerns and films about the Knights of the Round Table became part of the mix. For the battles between spaceships, Lucas watched World War II newsreels, as well as films like *The Blue Max* (John Guillermin, 1966) and *The Battle of Britain* (Guy Hamilton, 1969) for their aerial combat scenes. Even *THX 1138* provided material: that film's shell-dwellers became the Jawas of *Star Wars*, while OMM was reworked as The Force.

There were other, more technical reasons for *Star Wars*' importance. The first was its reinvention of special effects. Lucas was a fan of *2001: A Space Odyssey*'s special effects and hired John Dykstra, who had been Douglas Trumbull's assistant on Kubrick's film. Dykstra's operation became a new division of Lucas's company, Lucasfilm, and soon became a revolutionising force in the world of special effects: Industrial Light and Magic. The company had humble beginnings, being based in a disused warehouse in Van Nuys. Unlike Kubrick, Lucas did not have the budget to shoot spaceships gracefully circling for minutes on end, so most of the special-effects shots in *Star Wars* were very short, by reason of necessity.

The other side to *Star Wars* is arguably the defining moment between the New Hollywood and What Came After. In order to safeguard his financial interests, Lucas wanted control of the merchandising; Lucas's wife called the film a 'tinker-toy movie'. They got the merchandising rights for a song; although merchandising had been around for decades, it was not looked on as a significant part of a film's marketing. When *Star Wars* became a phenomenon on its release in 1977, quickly becoming the biggest film of all time in terms of box-office receipts, the success of the ubiquitous Luke Skywalker dolls, Darth Vader capes and toy light sabres woke Hollywood up to New Ways to Make Money.

Inadvertently, Lucas had let a rather large cat out of the bag. The second *Star Wars* film, *The Empire Strikes* Back (Irvin Kershner, 1980), has the distinction of being the most successful independent film of all time, and Lucas was announcing around that time that he had had it with Hollywood, and wanted nothing more than to make small experimental films up in Marin County. Yet the *Star Wars* franchise helped commodify films to a degree they never had been before. A film would no longer be just a film: there would be the games, the toys, the pop-up books to take into consideration. The film would be merely part of the overall package of safe, saccharine entertainment. It was quite an irony for a filmmaker so implacably opposed to Hollywood.

As Marlon Brando's Kurtz lies dying in *Apocalypse Now*, his final, whispered words could well be a wry comment on the wrong turn merchandising represented, signalling the end of the New Hollywood: 'The horror, the horror.'

MARTIN SCORSESE

Martin Scorsese wanted to be a priest. Growing up in an Italian-American household in New York City, he attended seminary school but was kicked out after a year when two new discoveries replaced his nascent religious fervour – girls and rock'n'roll. Scorsese's other great passion was the movies and, not having good enough grades to attend the Jesuit University at Fordham, he enrolled on New York University's film course in 1960.

NYU was one of the best film schools in the country (along with UCLA and USC), and Scorsese – an archetypal movie fanatic – thrived under the legendary professor Haig Manoogian. The fearsome, fast-talking Armenian-American 'didn't actually lecture', Scorsese's biographer, Vincent LoBrutto, wrote. 'He delivered a cinematic homily in Old Testament tradition.'[367] Manoogian would 'hit you with a lecture for one-and-a-half hours, and then show a film', Scorsese recalled.[368] Despite his habit of kicking students off the course at the drop of a hat, Manoogian was an inspiring teacher: 'He had this almost religious zeal, so that if you had an idea, before you knew it you were out on the streets and in the middle of filming!'[369] Manoogian – an evangelist for auteur theory – urged his students to find a personal vision, to make their films a reflection of their lives. 'Film what you know' was his impassioned instruction. Scorsese made two award-winning shorts while at NYU, *What's a Nice Girl Like You Doing in a Place Like This?* (1963) and *It's Not Just You, Murray!* (1964). The latter, about a small-time Italian-American crook, would serve as a blueprint for a territory Scorsese would make a unique contribution to in ground-breaking films like *Mean Streets* (1973) and *Raging Bull* (1980).

Religious zeal of an Old Testament nature would be an apt way to describe Scorsese's cinephilia. The New York Film Festival began in 1963, halfway through his time at NYU, which proved an essential part of Scorsese's film education. Not only did the festival expose him to the French New Wave, Bergman, Fellini, Antonioni and others, but, as NYU was located in Greenwich Village, Scorsese was also in the epicentre of underground filmmaking. It was a vibrant period for film writing, too: Jonas Mekas was writing a weekly column for the *Village Voice* and Andrew Sarris was promoting auteur theory in *Film Culture* magazine.

After graduation, Scorsese began his first feature, *Who's That Knocking at My Door* (1967), as an NYU graduate project. It would occupy him for four years, due to the piecemeal nature of production, resulting in three versions of the film. His original idea had been to make a trilogy about the Italian-American experience, 'a search for a messiah in the Lower East Side'.[370] The films, inspired by Fellini's *I Vitelloni* and Bertolucci's *Before the Revolution*, were to have been called *Jerusalem, Jerusalem, The Season of the Witch* and *Bring on the Dancing Girls*. In the end, the latter idea was the one Scorsese actually shot, on 35mm, and on a $6,000 loan his father provided. The film was shot largely at weekends in conditions that Scorsese's biographer, Vincent LoBrutto, dubbed 'oppressive':[371] the camera, a bulky Mitchell, was so big and the locations – usually apartments belonging to friends and family – were so small that there was no room to move the camera, and not much space for the actors to work, either. Despite the guerilla nature of the production, Scorsese storyboarded the entire film on the basis that 'paper is cheaper than film'.[372]

The first version of *Who's That Knocking, Bring on the Dancing Girls* (1965), depicted a group of friends hanging out, 'just sitting or driving around... on another [level] it was about sexual hang-ups and the Church'.[373] Harvey Keitel played JR, Scorsese's alter ego (even going so far as to adopt Scorsese's mannerisms in some scenes). Although not properly finished, the film was screened. However, it was not a success. The film 'just confounded everyone' and 'was universally hated'.[374] Critic Richard Roud, then programming the New York Film Festival, saw *Dancing Girls* and advised Scorsese that he was 'living aesthetically beyond [his] means'.[375] The NYFF rejected the film.

That might have been the end of the saga but, the following year, Manoogian and Joseph Weill, an NYU student who was also a lawyer and the publisher of *Cahiers du Cinema in English*,[376] raised another $37,000 to continue the project. At this point, the character of The Girl was developed further, with Zina Bethune – then a reasonably bankable name due to appearing in the CBS TV series *The Nurses* – replacing the original actress. These new scenes were shot on a 16mm Éclair, a camera small and light enough to move freely, unlike the Mitchell. This second version was retitled *I Call First* and was unveiled at the 1967 Chicago Film Festival, where it was praised by Roger Ebert, who hailed the film as '[bringing] together two opposing worlds of American cinema',[377] that of mainstream filmmaking, as represented by Elia Kazan's *On the Waterfront*, and independent and underground cinema, citing Jonas Mekas and Shirley Clarke, and Cassavetes' *Shadows*. Ebert described the film as 'a great moment in American movies', a film that was 'among the most evocative descriptions of American life I have ever seen'.[378] Scorsese himself, well aware of the film's limitations, was more modest, simply claiming that 'it was the first film to show what Italian-Americans really were like and that was what was good about it'.[379]

Distributor Joseph Brenner saw the film and agreed to release it, provided Scorsese added a sex scene. Brenner had a background in exploitation films, but wanted to branch out into the new market of art movies; Brian De Palma's *Greetings* and John Cassavetes' *Faces* were two of the more prominent independent films of the period, and Brenner wanted a piece of the market, whose largest demographic was young people. Scorsese complied. He was in Amsterdam at the time, eking out a living making commercials,[380] and flew a visibly older Harvey Keitel over to shoot the scene with Anne Colette, thus making the scene an 'accidental tribute to Godard',[381] as she had appeared in Godard's short *Tous les Garçons S'appellant Patrick*. Scorsese had further problems in that he couldn't afford all the music he wanted. Although there was enough money to use The Doors' 'The End' in the sex scene, Scorsese had to make do with alternatives for most of the other music cues.

The film finally emerged as *Who's That Knocking at My Door* (a title chosen by Brenner, from one of the songs that did make it into the final version), in 1969. The following year, it had a short run in Los Angeles, under yet another title, *JR*, where Roger Corman saw it and offered Scorsese the chance to direct *Boxcar Bertha*, an exploitation film set during the Depression, in the style of *Bonnie and Clyde*. Corman gave Scorsese a relatively free hand on the film, with the proviso that the script had nudity and violence every 15 pages. The film taught Scorsese how to shoot quickly and to a producer's demands. In Scorsese's hands, the crime drama became a religious allegory, with Bertha (Barbara Hershey) as Mary Magdalene to Big Bill Shelley's (David Carradine) Christ. Shelley, a union activist, ends up being crucified to a boxcar for defending railroad workers' rights.

Scorsese had had a peripatetic career after the release of *Who's That Knocking*. He had returned to NYU as an instructor, and worked as an editor on various music documentaries, among them Michael Wadleigh's *Woodstock* (1970; Wadleigh had shot the 16mm sections of *Who's That Knocking*). Scorsese had also met one of his heroes, John Cassavetes, who had offered the younger filmmaker encouragement after a screening of *Who's That Knocking*. The two men remained friends and, at a particularly low financial point, Cassavetes offered Scorsese the job of sound editor on the film he was then making, *Minnie and Moskowitz*. Cassavetes thought *Boxcar Bertha* was not the sort of film Scorsese should be making. 'Do you realise you just spent a year of your life making shit?' Cassavetes is alleged to have said.[382] 'Any director in Hollywood could have made that, and you're better than them, you have something honest to say.' That 'something honest' turned out to be *The Season of the Witch*, the script Scorsese resurrected after his meeting with Cassavetes. Or, as it was now known, *Mean Streets*.

Mean Streets begins where *Who's That Knocking at My Door* left off: in church. Or, rather, the earlier film ended with JR going to confessional; the new one began with a voiceover, spoken by Scorsese himself: 'You don't make up for your sins in church – you do it in the streets – you do it at home – the rest is bullshit and you know it.' We then cut to Charlie (Harvey Keitel) waking, as if he had just dreamt the voiceover. He spends the film learning the truth his conscience imparted. He is torn between his conscience and his duty to family, friends, and mob associates. These aren't the big guns of *The Godfather*; these are street corner wise guys and hustlers: bar owner Tony (David Proval), entrepreneur-cum-loanshark Michael (Richard Romanus) and small-time gambler and all-round loose cannon Johnny Boy (Robert De Niro). Charlie is also torn between his relationship with Johnny Boy's cousin, Teresa (Amy Robinson), whose epilepsy causes her to be ostracised from the family, and his attraction to Diane (Jeannie Bell), who works as a stripper in Tony's bar; that's not so much the problem as the fact that she's black. Charlie dreams of running his own restaurant and having Diane work there. If *The Godfather* was an opera, this was a home movie, with a jukebox soundtrack.

Mean Streets abounds with energy, the film driven by pounding music. The film's tutelary deities are Samuel Fuller and Michael Powell, who influenced Scorsese's mobile camera and the choice of often garish colours (such as the dominant, brooding red of Tony's bar). The tracking shots, like Johnny Boy's celebrated entrance into Tony's place as the Rolling Stones' 'Jumping Jack Flash' plays on the soundtrack, are inspired by what Fuller termed 'emotional violence': 'The tracking implies more violence than there really is... giving you a sense of being swept up in the fury and the anger.'[383] Again, with the colour palette and use of sound, Scorsese transforms realism – or early-70s-style neorealism – into expressionism by saturating colours and slowing down natural sound, and by having the voiceover-of-conscience comment on characters so that we're inside Charlie's head, experiencing the world as he sees it. ('The pain in hell has two sides. The kind you can touch with your hand. The kind you can feel in your heart... the worst of the two is the spiritual.')

There is a more directly personal quality in *Mean Streets*, Haig Manoogian's 'film what you know' philosophy in action. Charlie's inner turmoil can be read as Scorsese's own, as the director explained:

> My voice is intercut with Harvey's throughout the film, and for me that was a way of trying to come to terms with myself, to redeem myself. It's very easy to discipline oneself to go to Mass on Sunday mornings. That's not redemption for me: it's how you live, how you deal with other people, whether it be in the street, at home or in the office.[384]

This sense of spiritual anguish, noticeably lacking in most other American films from the period, be they new wave or old guard, gives *Mean Streets* a distinctive pedigree, marking it out as being part of a tradition of spiritual cinema that includes Carl Dreyer's *Day of Wrath* and Robert Bresson's *Diary of a Country Priest*.

There is a lighter side to the film. The opening titles play over home movies, some of which is actual Scorsese family footage, intercut with new material shot for the film. The sequence acknowledges and honours family and memory (two poles that define 8mm). As Scorsese remarked, '*Mean Streets* was an attempt to put myself and my friends on the screen, to show how we lived, what life was like in Little Italy. It was really an anthropological or sociological tract.'[385] The sequence also glorifies the medium itself – we see the frame, the scratchy white leader, the jumpy print, the visible splicing. (Truffaut did the same thing in *Day for Night* – made the same year – in which he shows the film's optical soundtrack onscreen.) These scenes of Little Italy life play over the Ronettes' hit 'Be My Baby'. This is the music Scorsese grew up listening to, so much so that the songs define an era, a specific neighbourhood for him, whose precise meaning may not be apparent to the viewer (in the sense that they were not party to Scorsese's actual life), but which conveys sufficient emotional power for the scenes to work. 'For me,' Scorsese admitted, 'the whole movie was "Jumping Jack Flash" and "Be My Baby".'[386]

The film screened at the New York Film Festival in 1973 and was a huge critical success, launching Scorsese's career – and also that of Robert De Niro. They would enjoy a fruitful working relationship: *Taxi Driver* (1976) and *Raging Bull* (1980), in particular, would become classics, and Scorsese and De Niro the best actor/director double-act this side of Werner Herzog and Klaus Kinski. For long-time Scorsese supporter Roger Ebert, *Mean Streets* was 'an astonishingly influential film... one of the source points of modern movies'.[387] And John Cassavetes, who was one of the first people to see the rough cut, loved it. He advised Scorsese to stick to his principles, to keep it personal: 'Don't cut it whatever you do.' Scorsese, perhaps recalling the unnecessary sex scene he had been forced into including in *Who's That Knocking at My Door*, reminded Cassavetes of a bedroom scene in the *Mean Streets* edit. 'Oh yeah,' Cassavetes replied, 'you could cut that.'[388]

NEW FORMS OF FREEDOM:
THE NEW GERMAN CINEMA

West Germany in the 1950s was dominated by the Allied occupying forces and the Marshall Plan. Politically, it was felt that West Germans needed to be 're-educated' and 'de-Nazified', and American films were seen as a good way to disseminate US notions of freedom, democracy and enterprise. Spyros Skouras, head of Twentieth Century Fox, felt that both American (and, of course, Fox) films were a useful way of 'indoctrinating people into the free way of life and instil[ling] in them a desire for freedom... We as an industry can play an infinitely important part in the world-wide ideological struggle for the minds of men, and confound the Communist propagandists.'[389] The result of this Cold War-mongering was one of the worst national cinemas in the world, a cinema of 'highly provincial, escapist [films] largely unsuitable for the export market'.[390]

There were no import quotas in Germany, as in other European countries, so Germany was flooded with Hollywood product. The great powerhouse of UFA was dismantled, and only small production companies – who would not threaten the US monopoly – were allowed to remain. As a result, German films of the 1950s were often *Heimatfilm* (tales of simple rural life), adventure films based on popular German novels, historical films set in Austria or romantic comedies. 'Thus, by the end of the 1950s the Allies' pursuit of their own political and economic interests had played a significant role in rendering West German cinema artistically impoverished and economically vulnerable.'[391]

Things were not aided by the fact that, by 1960, 40 per cent of the West German film industry was run by former Nazis. Also, from 1955, quality ratings were awarded, helping determine what films got made. These committees were staffed by government people, by whom the 'events of the 1930s and 1940s [were] either ignored or treated as something remote, regrettable and faintly unmentionable, like halitosis or prostitution in Paraguay'.[392] As Thomas Elsaesser notes, 'Instead of quality and experiment, [West German film policy] encouraged mediocrity and conformism, and the official list of "valuable" films for the 1950s reads more like a roll call of the world's worst movies than a guide to a nation's film culture.'[393]

This feeling that the country was producing drivel on an industrial scale was borne out by the lobbying of parliament in the late 1950s, as it became apparent that, without state intervention, the industry would die. This was followed by two stinging rebukes from the industry itself: in 1959, the Venice Film Festival rejected *all* the West German entries, while, two years later, the Berlin Festival did not award the Federal Prize (for films from the Federal Republic, i.e. West Germany) as it was felt there was no film good enough to win. Television was also playing a part in the decline of filmmaking, and film-going, in the Federal Republic: the peak year for movie-going had been 1956, when 900 million tickets were sold; over the next few years, as TV sets entered more homes, this number fell dramatically. By 1960, cinemas were closing at the rate of one a day.

THE OBERHAUSEN MANIFESTO

The rallying cry for change – the one that, in the end, made all the difference – was first heard at the Oberhausen Short Film Festival in February 1962, where 26 filmmakers, led by Alexander Kluge, signed what became known as the Oberhausen Manifesto. It was the West German equivalent of the essays Truffaut and his colleagues had written for *Cahiers du cinéma* just a few years earlier. The declaration read:

> The future of the German cinema lies with those who have demonstrated that they speak the new language of cinema...

This new cinema requires new forms of freedom: freedom from the conventions and habits of the established industry; freedom from the interference by commercial partners, and finally freedom from the tutelage of other interest groups.

We have concrete plans for the artistic, structured, and economic realisation of the new German cinema.

We are collectively prepared to take the economic risks.

The old cinema is dead. We believe in the new.

Amongst the signatories were Edgar Reitz, Alexander Kluge, and several other names who would go on to become some of the key figures in what would become known internationally as the New German Cinema, but was known domestically as either *Das Neue Kino* (the New Cinema) or *das junger kino* (the young cinema). With the critical position outlined at Oberhausen, filmmakers in West Germany now had the vision to lay to rest the 'old cinema'. A matter of weeks later, in April, the government announced plans to launch a new scheme to provide grants for feature films, scripts and script outlines.

THE FIRST WAVE: THE KURATORIUM YEARS

Setting up the scheme took much longer than planned, and it was not until October 1965 that the *Kuratorium junger Deutscher Film* (Board of Young German Film) was launched. The Kuratorium featured a board made up of film critics and journalists to award grants which were repayable upon the release of each film; production was centred around Munich, which rapidly established itself as the filmmaking capital of the Federal Republic (although production was also occurring in some of the other major cities, such as West Berlin and Cologne). The new filmmakers were generally born around the end of World War II and, due to the funding strictures of the Kuratorium, their films were 'based on an artisanal mode of production which allowed a high degree of experimentation and close collaborations'.[394] This combination of experimentation and collaboration would produce some of the most important European films of the 1970s. The first successes occurred, however, during 1966–67.

Within two years, the Kuratorium had produced 25 films, including Kluge's *Yesterday Girl* (*Abschied von gestern*, lit: 'Taking Leave of Yesterday', 1966), plus another three films by Oberhausen signatories: Hans Jürgen Pohland (*Cat and Mouse/Katz und maus*, 1966), Edgar Reitz (*Mealtimes/Mahlzeiten*, 1966) and Haro Senft (*The Gentle Course/Der sanfte Lauf*, 1967). The big three European film festivals lauded this new cinema, with *Yesterday Girl* winning eight awards at the 1966 Venice festival, including the Silver Lion, the first time a German film had won anything at Venice since the war. The following year, Reitz's *Mealtimes* won the Best First Film award. At Berlin, Peter Schamoni's *Closed Season for Foxes* (*Schonzeit für füchse*, 1966) picked up the Silver Bear, while three films that had managed to get made without Kuratorium help – Volker Schlöndorff's *Young Törless* (*Der junge Törless*, 1966), Jean-Marie Straub and Danièle Huillet's *Not Reconciled* (*Nicht versöhnt*, 1965) and Ulrich Schamoni's *It* (*Es*, 1966) – were all well received at Cannes. 'The press was unbelievably positive,' Edgar Reitz remembers. 'And when the first films came out, there was a degree of public interest which has never been matched since. Films like *Yesterday Girl*, or my own *Mealtimes*, attracted audiences of over a million.'[395]

As the French New Wave had suffered from something of a backlash in the early 60s, so the New German Cinema suddenly found itself threatened by the old guard, which started lobbying for changes. This took the form of a new committee, the Film Development Body (FFA), set up in order to revitalise what was euphemistically known as the 'commercial sector' – in other words precisely those films the Oberhausen signatories railed against. The FFA ruled that first-time directors who got money from the Kuratorium were ineligible for further funding, as the money they administered – garnered from a levy on every cinema ticket sold in the Federal Republic – was based on the success of the filmmaker's previous film. Most of the first batch of Kuratorium films had done well, but not well enough to pay back their loans; suddenly new filmmakers found that they could only get funding if they already had a track record: the classic filmmakers' catch–22. The advent of the FFA not only threatened the nascent New German Cinema, it also signally failed to revive the 'commercial sector' in encouraging the production of bland product. The drivel had returned.

Television came to the rescue. The major broadcasters ARD and ZDF didn't produce much of their own content, but were willing to commission production companies and regional broadcasters, some of which became highly involved in feature production, such as the Cologne-based WDR. From 1974, further legislation meant that films were guaranteed a cinema release before being broadcast on TV and, as the 1970s wore on, broadcasters began to assume an ever-greater role in production. Indeed, some of the greatest films of the New German Cinema were, strictly speaking, 'television films' – albeit ones that enjoyed theatrical releases – such as Fassbinder's *Berlin Alexanderplatz* (1980) and the era's swansong, Reitz's *Heimat* (1984). Regional funding was introduced in 1977, with Berlin leading the way; over the next four years, Bavaria, Hamburg, and North Rhine-Westphalia followed suit. The Bavarian scheme was largely based on economic criteria, while the others were based on cultural stipulations and were mainly administered by filmmakers. The spirit of the Kuratorium had somehow survived.

The collaborative spirit encouraged by the Kuratorium also emerged in the sphere of distribution. By the early 1970s, with TV money only just starting to make a difference, filmmakers themselves, perhaps unwilling to entirely trust the television companies any more than the Kuratorium, began to handle their own distribution. As the 1970s dawned, all commercial distributors were still US-controlled, thereby not guaranteeing that New German Cinema films would find an audience. From April 1970, cinemas were offered subsidies to show a 'suitable quota' of 'good' German films; in December 1976, awards began to be given to distributors for releasing 'quality' films (i.e. not American).

THE SECOND WAVE: THE FILMVERLAG YEARS

Despite the subsidies, filmmakers frequently resorted to their own methods to get their work shown and, of necessity, became their own distributors. Perhaps the most important company to thus emerge was the Filmverlag der Autoren (Film Publishing House of the Auteurs), hurriedly set up in April 1971 by Wim Wenders, Thomas Schamoni and Rainer Werner Fassbinder's business partner Michael Fengler, amongst others, as a production company, but which soon became focused on distribution. Over the course of the next few years it became a major player in this field, handling the films of numerous key players in the New German Cinema, including Wenders, Herzog, Fassbinder, Schlöndorff, von Trotta and Sanders-Brahms.

The 1971 Cannes Film Festival was arguably another pivotal moment for the New German Cinema, but one that, after the relative false starts of 1962 and 1965–67, did actually help set events in motion that would bring the new films to an international audience. The festival wanted four New German films for the Director's Fortnight sidebar, including Herzog's *Fata Morgana* (1970) and Fassbinder's *Pioneers in Ingolstadt* (*Pioniere in Ingolstadt*, 1971). Critic Richard Roud saw the Fassbinder, and booked it on the spot for the upcoming New York Film Festival, which marked Fassbinder's introduction to US audiences. Simultaneously, the Goethe Institute – a body whose remit was and remains to promote German art and culture abroad – booked the four films for international screenings. With the support of other eminent critics (such as the *New York Times*' Vincent Canby), the New German Cinema began to get noticed.

The films that were being noticed fell into a number of loose categories, in terms of theme and subject matter. As Julia Knight notes,[396] they revolved around topics that were both politically and culturally important, which she dubs 'Counter-Myths of German Identity':

The *Gastarbeiter* film: films that dealt with the subject of *gastarbeiters*, or guest workers. As a part of postwar reconstruction, the FDR received a large number of guest workers from countries such as Turkey, producing an understandable tension in a country that was infamous for its earlier intolerance of foreign nationals. Notable films in this category include Fassbinder's *Katzelmacher* (lit: 'Cock-Artist', 1969) and *Fear Eats the Soul* (*Angst essen seele auf*, 1973), and Helma Sanders-Brahms' *Shirin's Wedding* (*Shirin's Hochzeit*, 1975).[397]

Terrorism and politics: West Germany in the 1970s was haunted by the spectre of domestic terrorism. The Red Army Faction (aka the Baader-Meinhof gang) began an arson campaign in 1968, burning down department stores as a protest against what they saw as an unacceptable level of Americanisation in West Germany. Their activities escalated to include bombings, hijackings and murder, culminating in the crisis of 1977, in which the industrialist (and former Nazi) Hanns-Martin Schleyer was kidnapped. The terrorists' demands were not met and, as a result, the RAF hijacked a plane. This was followed by the 'suicides' of Andreas Baader and two other leading terrorists, which in turn precipitated the murder of Schleyer. A portmanteau feature, *Germany in Autumn* (*Deutschland im Herbst*, 1978), co-directed by Fassbinder, Kluge, Reitz and Schlöndorff, amongst others, was one of the notable responses to the situation. Terrorism also features in Margarethe von Trotta's first three features, *The Lost Honour of Katharina Blum* (*Die Verlorene Ehre der Katharina Blum*, 1975, co-directed with Volker Schlöndorff), *The Second Awakening of Christa Klages* (*Das Zweite Erwachen der Christa Klages*, 1977) and *The German Sisters/Marianne and Juliane* (*Die Bleierne Zeit*, 1981), while Fassbinder returned to the theme in *The Third Generation* (*Die dritte Generation*, 1979).

Nazis and German history: Terrorism was not the only ghost haunting the West Germany of the 1970s. The legacy of Hitler and the Nazis was still a hugely contentious and controversial area, with many former Nazis (Schleyer and his ilk) still at large. Hans-Jürgen Syberberg's seven-hour *Hitler – A Film from Germany* (*Hitler – Ein film aus Deutschland*, 1977) is arguably the greatest – and most controversial – cinematic response to this issue, known in German as *Vergangenheitsbewältigung* (coming to terms with the past). Aspects of West Germany's recent past are also explored in Fassbinder's *The Marriage of Maria Braun* (*Die Ehe der Maria Braun*, 1979), Kluge's *The Patriot* (*Die Patriotin*, 1979), Sanders-Brahms' *Germany, Pale Mother* (*Deutschland, bleiche Mutter*, 1980), Reitz's *Heimat* (1984) and Schlöndorff's *The Tin Drum* (*Die Blechtrommel*, 1979).

American cultural imperialism: The Marshall Plan saw West Germany subject to a concerted and wide-ranging campaign of Americanisation in the years following 1945. This prompted various cinematic responses, from Fassbinder's *Love is Colder Than Death* (*Liebe ist kälter als der Tod*, 1969), *Gods of the Plague* (*Götter der*

Pest, 1970) and *The American Soldier* (*Der amerikanische Soldat,* 1970), to Wenders' *Kings of the Road* (*Im Lauf der Zeit,* 1976), *The American Friend* (*Der amerikanische Freund,* 1977), and Herzog's *Stroszek* (1977).

Feminism: The emergence of the women's movement in the late 1960s was reflected in a number of New German films. Most of the notable initial films in this area were made by already established male directors, such as Fassbinder's *The Bitter Tears of Petra von Kant* (*Die bitteren Tränen der Petra von Kant,* 1972) and Kluge's *Occasional Work of a Female Slave* (*Gelegenheitsarbeit einer Sklavin,* 1972). However, as the 1970s wore on, films made by women began to appear, including Helke Sanders' *The All-Round Reduced Personality – Redupers* (*Die allseitig reduzierte Persönlichkeit,* 1977), Jutta Brückner's *A Thoroughly Demoralised Girl* (*Ein ganz und gar verwahrlostes Mädchen,* 1977) and *Years of Hunger* (*Hungerjahre,* 1980), Doris Dörrie's *Come Rain or Shine* (*Ob's stürmt oder schneit,* 1977), Elfi Mikesch's *I Often Think About Hawaii* (*Ich denke oft an Hawaii,* 1978), Jeanine Meerapfel's *Malou* (1980) and Claudia von Alemann *Blind Spot/The Trip to Lyon* (*Die Reise Nach Lyon,* 1980). Producers such as Regina Ziegler, Clara Burckner and Renee Gundelach offered support to female directors, and were active lobbyists. In addition, women filmmakers formed a powerful union, the Verband der Filmarbeiterinnen (the Union of Women Film Workers). By 1980, West Germany 'possess[ed] proportionally more women filmmakers than any other film producing country'.[398] And the most successful West German film of the 1980s was directed by a woman, Doris Dörrie's *Men* (*Männer,* 1985).

Domestic audiences remained small, largely due to the fact that films had to have an American-controlled distributor to ensure success. As funding later in the 1970s became increasingly conservative, a number of directors began to look abroad to make films (Wenders, Schlöndorff and Wolfgang Petersen went to the USA, Herzog went to Australia). Nevertheless, New German Cinema had gained an international reputation by 1978, with a number of films doing well internationally, including Schlöndorff and von Trotta's *The Lost Honour of Katharina Blum,* Wenders' *Kings of the Road,* von

Trotta's *The Second Awakening of Christa Klages*, Syberberg's *Hitler – A Film from Germany*, Herzog's *Nosferatu, the Vampyre* (*Nosferatu – Phantom der Nacht*, 1979), Fassbinder's *The Marriage of Maria Braun* (*Die Ehe der Maria Braun*, 1979) and Schlöndorff's *The Tin Drum* (*Die Blechtrommel*, 1979), winner of the Academy Award for Best Foreign Film; Schlöndorff also shared the main prize at Cannes that year with Coppola's *Apocalypse Now*. It had been a long journey indeed from the New German Cinema's first success, Alexander Kluge's *Yesterday Girl*.

ALEXANDER KLUGE

If any one filmmaker can be called the father of New German Cinema, it is Alexander Kluge (b. 1932). While training as a lawyer in Frankfurt, he met the philosopher Theodor Adorno, and, through Adorno, Fritz Lang, for whom he worked as an assistant on *The Tiger of Eschnapur* (*Der Tiger von Eschnapur*, 1959), the first of Lang's two films that make up his 'Indian Epic'. Kluge began making films in 1960, with *Brutality in Stone* (*Brutalität in Stein*), a short study of Nazi architecture. In 1962, he published a volume of short stories, *Lebenslauf* (translated into English as *Case Histories*). The following year, he set up the Federal Republic's first film school, the Institut für Filmgestaltung (Institute for Film Design) with fellow Oberhausen signatories Edgar Reitz and Detten Schleiermacher.

An articulate theorist, Kluge's ideas were shaped by Marxist and Brechtian thought. In the Brechtian model, there are two kinds of realism – one that merely confirms (and therefore affirms) outward reality, such as traditional Hollywood narratives or Griersonian documentaries – while the other is subversive and critical, 'seeking out the truth beneath the deceptive surface of things.'[399] As John Sandford notes, commercial cinema, with its emphasis on the first kind of realism, treats its audiences like Pavlovian dogs: 'Money, time and their own experience are taken from them,'[400] while the second form of realism is 'closely associated for Kluge with protest, for it involves an active confrontation with the world rather than passive receptivity.'[401] Cinema is for Kluge as theatre was for Brecht, a means to raising an audience's awareness, 'to provoke and question rather than soothe and confirm.'[402] Film must engage the senses, for it is only through them that the imagination can be activated, and that, for Kluge, was the key. Then cinema becomes not a monologue, but a dialogue, with the audience essentially becoming a co-author of the film, bringing their own ideas, experiences, streams of consciousness and daydreams into the act of both reading and constructing the narrative they are watching.

Yesterday Girl is based on a story from *Case Histories*. Alexandra Kluge, the director's sister, plays Anita G, a young Jewish woman who comes to West Germany from the East to make a new life for herself. (Anita was based on a real woman Kluge had heard about.) In a picaresque and impressionistic narrative, the film follows Anita through a series of dead-end jobs, an attempt at further education, a few attempts to steal, and a series of unhappy affairs that end with her becoming pregnant by a government official. Not able to support herself financially, she turns herself over to the police, and the baby is born in prison.

Kluge employs an arsenal of Brechtian techniques in *Yesterday Girl*. After a pre-credits shot of Alexandra Kluge that feels more like footage of her rehearsing her lines, we are dropped straight into the narrative (Anita in court for a minor theft) and are given no time to orientate ourselves. Kluge avoids conventional coverage (establishing shots, shot-reverse shot for conversations) and gives us no idea of timespan (what is a flashback? what is the present?). Scenes are frequently short, the cutting rapid. Time-lapse sequences erupt without warning; sometimes the camera prowls slowly; sometimes the sound drains away to silence.

The fragmentary narrative makes frequent leaps over what, in a conventional film, might be major plot strands (has Anita had an affair with her boss?). Fantasy sequences (the animated toy soldiers, Anita running from authority figures) add more by way of sheer verve than narrative sense. Intertitles punctuate the film. Some comment on action almost unnecessarily – 'One day in the manager's absence, Anita is fired' – while others are abstract: 'Will yesterday come tomorrow?', 'Truth is killed when it really appears', 'I know a miracle will happen one day'. Characters address the camera, either to comment on Anita's situation (the pious office woman), explain their job (the language record boss) or talk about their wartime experiences (the hotelier). Kluge further distances the audience from traditional identification with character and action through the use of seemingly inappropriate music: light and airy pieces play over sombre visuals.

Yesterday Girl received a divided response upon release. Many critics found the film difficult – hardly surprising given that the viewer has to be active in constructing meaning and narrative throughout the entire film; given the fast pace, it is an almost impossible task on first viewing. But *Yesterday Girl* won the Golden Lion at Venice, and Alexandra Kluge was also named best actress, making it the first postwar German film to win an award at a film festival; a far cry from Venice in 1959, where *all* the West German entries had been rejected.

JEAN-MARIE STRAUB & DANIÈLE HUILLET

Jean-Marie Straub and Danièle Huillet provided the first wave of New German Cinema with even more formal rigour and innovation than Kluge. They were also its unofficial international arm: both were born in France but moved to Munich in 1958 so that Straub could avoid being conscripted into the Algerian War. Straub had run a film club in Metz (his hometown) between 1950 and 1954, and worked in Paris as an assistant to Gance, Renoir, Astruc, Rivette and Bresson, his hero. Straub deeply admired Bresson's *Les Dames du Bois de Boulogne*, which he described as 'mystical', and much of his and Huillet's work could be seen as having a Bressonian influence. The Straubs took from Bresson a preference for deadpan acting, an insistence on live (rather than post-synched) sound, the use of a largely static camera, and a total refusal to make concessions. Their style was also informed by German Marxism, and the idea of a return to zero: 'The work we have to do is to make films which radically eliminate art, so that there is no equivocation.'[403] They saw themselves as outside the system, regarding the whole idea of a subsidised film industry with suspicion, and did not sign the Oberhausen Manifesto.

Unable to find funding for a long-cherished film about Bach, the Straubs turned to making a film of Heinrich Böll's novel *Billiards at Half-Past Nine*. They spent two years looking for a producer, without success. In the end, they were able to raise the finance – independently – to shoot a film based on a story by Böll, which became the basis of their first short film, *Machorka-Muff* (1963). Böll's satire on West German 'restoration' or *Vergangenheitsbewältigung* (coming to terms with the past) concerns his eponymous hero (whose name roughly means 'tobacco fug'), a colonel who receives a promotion, marries his aristocratic mistress and manages to clear the name of a leading Nazi. Rather than flesh it out to a fully fledged black comedy on the fascism they detected lingering in postwar Germany, the Straubs pared the narrative down until it became a quasi-documentary that refused to pander to anyone's expectations of what a short film should be. It angered critics on both the Right – who saw it as an attack on the values of the Federal Republic – and the Left, who felt that it didn't go far enough. The film was initially rejected by Oberhausen, but the Straubs lobbied, and the selection committee relented. The struggle to get the film made, and the hostility it aroused amongst critics, in many ways exemplified the solitary path the filmmakers would take in their subsequent career.

While their maiden film only found a small band of supporters – including the composer Karl-Heinz Stockhausen, and Jacques Rivette, who wrote a positive review for *Cahiers du cinéma* – the Straubs managed to realise a film of *Billiards*, now retitled *Not Reconciled*, adding a subtitle from Brecht's *St Joan of the Stockyards: Only Violence Helps Where Violence Reigns* (*Nicht versöhnt, oder Es hilft nur Gewalt, wo Gewalt herrscht*, 1965). Once again preoccupied with the role of history, the action of the film takes place on a single day in 1958, and centres around the figure of Robert Fähmel, a man who remains conscious of the crimes of history, who is 'not reconciled' to what has gone before. As if to remind us that the past is still very much continuing under another guise in the present, the film switches without warning between 1958 and scenes from the past (1910, 1914, 1934, the War). It is the arrival of an old school friend, Schrella, that prompts Fähmel into recalling their days during the 1930s when they were involved in an attempt to kill a Nazi. Schrella's arrival also reminds Fähmel's father Heinrich of his youth in which he served during the Great War, and of his marriage to Fähmel's mother,

Johanna, who was later committed to an asylum after two of her children died in the war (she had earlier caused a scandal by calling the Kaiser a fool). Returning to the present at the end of the film, Johanna is let out of her sanatorium to attend Heinrich's 80th birthday party. Across the street, a parade of war veterans is taking place, amongst those attending being former Nazis from the film's 1930s scenes. She is dissuaded from shooting one of them, but instead shoots a minister in the current government, on the basis that 'he is the killer-to-be of your grandson'. Hitler might be dead, but his ghost still inhabits the corridors of power in Bonn. Johanna is taken away, and the birthday party takes place without her. It transpires that the minister was not fatally wounded, and the film ends with Heinrich hoping that the minister will never lose the look of surprise on his face at the moment he was shot.

Not Reconciled makes absolutely no compromises. It is frequently very difficult to tell what is going on; the Straubs – showing a debt to Bresson – de-dramatise things, with the actors uttering their words in a monotone and the camera frequently holding on empty frames once the characters have disappeared out of shot. Scenes are also very short, pared down not just to the bone, but the marrow. The film was shown out of Competition at the Berlin Film Festival in July 1965, where it met with an 'unbelievably hostile reaction [that made] the reception of *L'Avventura* at Cannes seem like a triumph by comparison'.[404] In after-film discussions, it became apparent that many in the audience hated the time shifts and the non-naturalistic way in which the actors (non-professionals all) delivered their dialogue. Amongst the slew of bad press after the premiere, the best of them was: 'The worst film since 1895.'

Not Reconciled did, however, do well abroad, where it won prizes at both the New York and London Film Festivals, and also had a champion in the shape of Jean-Luc Godard, who helped pay for a screening in Cannes the following May, where it had a much better reception than in Berlin. Godard (together with Truffaut and others) also helped secure finance for the Bach film, now entitled *The Chronicle of Anna Magdalena Bach* (*Chronik der Anna Magdalena Bach*, 1968). Some of the funding came from the Kuratorium, despite seemingly endless bureaucratic problems. Straub came to feel that the obstructions were deliberate, as they were making 'yet another film about the unresolved German past'.[405] As Straub commented:

> It was of course idealist in the bad sense [to try and work with the subsidy system] because I didn't know the power relations yet that operated in film production and distribution. [We thought], if they try so hard to stop us making this film, then we just have to make it... It is obvious, a film made outside the system will never get inside. The system takes revenge.[406]

But the system in this instance was not able to take much, if any, revenge: the film was the Straubs' biggest success in commercial terms. Covering the latter part of the composer's life, the *Chronicle* was based on around 20 original sources (letters by Bach himself, and the few authentic words by his wife). The film was shot for very little money, in black and white (they had wanted colour), in the autumn of 1967. The main element in the film was the music, for which they hired the best musicians they could find. In keeping with their aesthetic, the music was played live on camera and on period instruments, and it is the music that informs and shapes the film.

On one level, it is a love story. It begins with the marriage of Bach to Anna Magdalena, and then relates their life together, told in Anna's words without sentiment or inflection. They are rarely shown together; their intimacy is only physically expressed in a brief caress. As Straub has suggested, the film is also a documentary about Gustav Leonhardt, who plays Bach. In contrast to the traditional costume drama, no attempt was made to make Leonhardt look like Bach – he is in fact much thinner than Bach appears in the surviving portraits – and he does not wear make up. He is merely an actor reciting lines – 'quoting', as Brecht would say – and playing music. The documentary element, however, reveals a paradox: in reality, Anna did not write a journal, and the various sources the script was based on were written by either Bach himself, or other family members. So is the film drama, or a documentary or a drama-documentary? One final element to the film is its political dimension. The film's various devices, such as adherence to actual sources, inexpressive acting and live performance, take it firmly out of convention; the audience then have the time to contemplate what exactly Bach's role is, if we take him to be a cipher in a larger whole. For the Straubs, he represents a part of German culture buried under the horrors of the twentieth century, but he is not the sort of ostrich-with-its-head-in-the-sand German that Machorka-Muff is: instead, Bach represents not just the artist striving to work in the face of an uninterested or hostile public – and thereby standing for the Straubs themselves – but also the thinker, the reformer, who seeks to enlighten society and cast off the shackles of patronage and power.

Ultimately, *The Chronicle of Anna Magdalena Bach* is a means by which Germans can come to terms with their own history, and 'until they are able to lucidly accept both the good and the bad in their history,' Straub remarked, 'they will never achieve any sense of wholeness, of health.'[407]

RAINER WERNER FASSBINDER

If any one filmmaker is synonymous with the New German Cinema, it is Rainer Werner Fassbinder (1945–82). He may not have been an Oberhausen signatory – he didn't make his first short film until 1965 – but he was to become, by the mid-1970s, the most famous German filmmaker since the days of Murnau and Lang. It was a controversial career in which he incurred the wrath of both left and right, the feminist lobby and the gay community. It was also legendarily prolific: between 1969 and his death in 1982, Fassbinder directed over 40 films, a significant number of which were landmarks in the New German Cinema.

One of the results of the Oberhausen Manifesto had been the opening, in 1966, of film schools in West Berlin and Munich. Fassbinder applied to Berlin, but was turned down. His first two shorts – funded by a wealthy boyfriend – were both rejected by Oberhausen. Undeterred, he struggled to get work as an actor, and joined a Munich theatre group called the Action Theatre. He gradually took over the group, which began to enjoy success under his direction. After the demise of the Action Theatre in 1968 (one of the more deranged members of the Baader-Meinhof gang burnt the theatre down), Fassbinder formed a new company, the Antitheater, which became the repertory company that would also appear in his first films.

Fassbinder later spoke of his early theatre work. 'I wanted to make films from the start, but it was much easier to begin in the theatre,' he explained. 'And it has paid off: when I did start making films, my previous work in the theatre made it much easier.'[408] Not having been to film school, Fassbinder resolved to gain experience as a filmmaker by appearing as an actor in films by other directors, and also working in a variety of crew positions. In addition to his own early shorts, Fassbinder also appeared in Straub and Huillet's *The Bridegroom, the Actress and the Pimp* (*Der Bräutigam, die Komödiantin und der Zuhälter*, 1968), which had its basis in an Action Theatre production that Straub and Huillet – then living in Munich – also directed.

Fassbinder's first feature was triggered by an acting job. While playing the title role in Volker Schlöndorff's adaptation of Brecht's *Baal* (1969), Fassbinder met Ulli Lommel, then an up-and-coming male lead. He offered Lommel a role in a feature he was making, and Lommel accepted; Fassbinder then wrote the script, and founded a production company, Antitheater-X Film. *Love is Colder Than Death* (*Liebe ist Kälter als der Tod*, 1969), starring Lommel, was independently funded, mainly from an angel investor living in Munich, Hannah Axmann von Rezzori, wife of the writer Gregor von Rezzori, and, more importantly from Fassbinder's point of view, an heiress to the Bosch fortune. Hannah paid for most of the film, and even appeared as an actress in several of Fassbinder's later productions.

Love is Colder Than Death inaugurated a remarkable cycle of 11 feature films, all made in little more than 18 months, between April 1969 and November 1970, in what could be termed Fassbinder's 'first period'. Fassbinder's debut feature is a deconstruction of the gangster genre, dedicated to Straub, Eric Rohmer and Claude Chabrol (and also to two characters from Damiano Damiani's allegorical spaghetti western, *A Bullet for the General*, played by Gian Maria Volonté and Klaus Kinski). Aside from Lommel, the cast included actors from the Antitheater group, including Hanna Schygulla, who would go on to become one of Fassbinder's – and the New German Cinema's – biggest stars. The film was a highly stylised take on gangster movies 'filtered through postwar Hollywood films and ten years of the French cinema's New Wave', as Fassbinder biographers Robert Katz and Peter Berling described it, that had also 'been personalised by [Fassbinder's] boyhood on the streets'. The story of Franz (played by Fassbinder), a gangster who wants to play by his own rules – Lommel was given the other main part of Bruno, the gangster sent to kill Franz – the film is a static, theatrical performance, effectively deconstructing the genre. As long-time Fassbinder critic Christian Braad Thomsen put it, 'The plot is only suggested, in fragments whose possible inter-relationship often has to be guessed by the viewer.'[409] For Fassbinder, the film was a film about 'poor souls... who didn't know what to do with themselves, who were simply set down, as they are, and who weren't given a chance.'[410]

Fassbinder carried his 'static' style through into his second feature, *Katzelmacher* (1969), shot in August for even less money and on an even tighter schedule than his debut. Based on one of Fassbinder's own plays staged the year before, the film 'portrays the life of a group of young people after work and demonstrates that in an unfree society even so-called free time cannot be free'.[411] The arrival of Jorgos, a Greek *gastarbeiter* (played by Fassbinder), introduces a note of tension and threat into the group, and the men turn on him. Well received on its premiere at the Mannheim Film Festival in October 1969, *Katzelmacher* had a cinema release the following month, making it Fassbinder's first film to hit the cinema circuit (*Love is Colder Than Death* didn't get a cinema release until January 1970). Although *Katzelmacher* didn't do much business at the box office, the film earned over a million marks in prizes and state subsidies. Quite an achievement for a film that was shot in nine days and cost only 80,000 DM to produce.

By the time *Katzelmacher* was wowing the critics in Mannheim, Fassbinder was shooting his third feature in six months, *Gods of the Plague* (*Götter der Pest*, 1969), another crime drama. The genre appealed to Fassbinder. Not only had he seen countless Hollywood noirs in Munich's fleapits, but he felt the crime movie was a way of investigating contemporary social and political concerns: 'The gangster environment is a bourgeois setting turned on its head, so to speak. My gangsters do the same things that capitalists do, except they do them as criminals. The gangster's goals are just as bourgeois as the capitalist's.'[412] As soon as he had finished *Gods*, Fassbinder went straight into production on another film, *Why Does Herr R Run Amok?* (*Warum läuft Herr R Amok?*, 1969), a very different treatment of petit bourgeois values. Herr R (Kurt Raab) is a middle-class man who cracks under pressure and kills his family before committing suicide.

Fassbinder put his ability to work quickly down to being 'extremely sure of [him]self'.[413] Most of the films were shot very quickly, often taking only 10–20 days. Some of them – such as *Katzelmacher*, *The American Soldier*, and *Pioneers in Ingolstadt* – had already been produced on stage. Aside from punishing, round-the-clock schedules – 'We hated days off and simply abolished Sundays', as Kurt Raab later remembered[414] – Fassbinder's prodigious work rate was aided by working with the same troupe of actors and technicians, some of whom Fassbinder lived with in a commune on the outskirts of Munich where, according to Raab, 'Fassbinder behaved like Louis XIV.'[415] Initially, this was the Antitheater group, but the company would evolve over time as people either fell from favour or new talent caught Fassbinder's eye. Aside from Ulli Lommel and Hanna Schygulla, Lilo Pempeit, Lilith Ungerer, Irm Hermann, Ingrid Caven, Harry Baer, Günther Kaufmann, Kurt Raab, Margit Carstensen, Margarethe von Trotta, Brigitte Mira, El Hedi ben Salem, Volker Spengler, Gottfried John, Günther Lamprecht and Barbara Sukowa all appeared in numerous films. The repertory company extended to crew members also: editors Thea Eymèsz and Julianne Lorenz; cinematographers Dietrich Lohmann, Michael Ballhaus and, later, Xaver Schwarzenberger; and composer Peer Raben. All worked repeatedly on Fassbinder productions. Some, such as Kurt Raab and Harry Baer, worked on both sides of the camera. The repertory company was not particular to Fassbinder and his circle, however: as Julia Knight has noted, it tended to be a feature of New German Cinema for purely practical reasons. The Kuratorium could only offer a maximum loan of 300,000 DM, meaning that budgets were considerably lower than their equivalents in France or Italy, where budgets might be ten times higher.[416]

After the intensity of the 1969–70 period, Fassbinder only shot one film in 1971, but this would mark a turning point, the onset of his 'second period'. Feeling that the films made under the Antitheater-X banner had run their course, he dissolved the company and founded a new production outfit, Tango Film, and became a partner in the Filmverlag der Autoren. More importantly, he discovered the work of Douglas Sirk. Sirk's great melodramas – including *All That Heaven Allows*, *Magnificent Obsession*, *Imitation of Life*, *Written on the Wind* – made Fassbinder realise he could continue to explore the complex world of human emotions, but do so in a way that would reach a wider audience. Fassbinder spoke of his admiration for Hollywood films, how directors working there had the strength to be simple 'without the complications of the art film'.[417] Elaborating on his admiration for the older filmmaker, Fassbinder remarked, 'My encounter with Sirk removed the fear I had of "selling out"... Sirk gave me the courage to make films for the public. Before that I believed that serious work meant shunning the Hollywood model. Hollywood movies, which do in fact emulate precise models, seemed quite stupid to me.'[418]

As Christian Braad Thomsen noted, Fassbinder 'wanted to make a kind of German Hollywood, a cinema "that is as wonderful and as generally accessible as Hollywood, but at the same time not so false".'[419] Unlike the 1969–70 films, with their tableaux staging, static cameras and Brechtian distance, the new period would be characterised by an increasingly Baroque camera. Fassbinder became fascinated with showing people against, or through, windows, bars, any form of lattice pattern that would suggest imprisonment. Rather than being either static or performing simple movements, the camera – especially in the hands of the great Michael Ballhaus – became mobile, a prowling presence that constantly produces a tension, suggesting a balancing act between possible escape or further, more permanent imprisonment.

The first films of the 'Sirk era' became two of his most acclaimed works, *The Merchant of the Four Seasons* (*Der Händler der vier Jahreszeiten*, 1971) and *The Bitter Tears of Petra von Kant* (*Die Bitteren Tränen der Petra von Kant*, 1972). *Merchant* tells the story of Hans Epp (Hans Hirschmüller), a struggling fruit seller. Unhappily married and increasingly unsuccessful in business, Hans spends a great deal of time in the pub. After being laid low by a heart attack, however, his luck begins to change. As his business becomes more successful, the more he resents his increasingly middle-class lifestyle; it does not end happily.

If the films of the 1969–70 cycle can be seen to deal 'with washouts of radical attempts to live free', as Robert Katz and Peter Berling put it,[420] films that essentially admit that 1968 had failed and they were now living in post-revolutionary times, then *Merchant* can be seen as Fassbinder's first major attempt to inhabit the world of the lower middle class, to see it from the inside (rather than the alienated outside of a film like *Why Does Herr R Run Amok?*). The world he finds is one of repression and control, and the film forms part of what has been termed Fassbinder's 'victim cycle', where a well-meaning central character is destroyed by a system they either cannot articulate or understand. As Ronald Hayman noted, 'In many of Fassbinder's films the most sympathetic characters are the least articulate, and the most memorable sequences are those which depend on his sympathetic understanding of feelings which cannot be articulated.'[421] Hans's inarticulateness manifests in his final drinking binge, Herr R's by his murder-suicide. The link between characters like Hans Epp, Herr R and Petra, is the theme 'that his principal characters are victims of bourgeois society and not really rebels at all'.[422]

As Fassbinder's second period developed, he would continue to explore the machinations of oppression. *The Bitter Tears of Petra von Kant* (1972) focuses on a lesbian relationship scarred by manipulation and jealousy. Based on one of the plays Fassbinder wrote in his 1971 hiatus from filmmaking,[423] it centres on the relationship between Petra von Kant (Margit Carstensen), a successful fashion designer, her slave-like assistant, Marlene (Irm Hermann), and the object of Petra's affection, Karin (Hanna Schygulla). Set entirely in Petra's flat, the film was shot in ten days, and was based on an actual gay relationship – in this case, Fassbinder's love for one of his leading men. It was not the first time he had used autobiographical elements for a film: *Beware of a Holy Whore* (*Warnung vor einer Heiligen Nutte*, 1970) was based on the shooting of *Whity* (also 1970). For Fassbinder, cinema was as personal as it was political; in Fassbinder's work, the two are frequently meshed together.

Fear Eats the Soul (*Angst essen Seele auf*, 1974), a love story inspired by Sirk's *All That Heaven Allows*, is about an odd couple: Emmi, a middle-aged cleaning lady (Brigitte Mira), and Ali, a Moroccan *gastarbeiter* (El Hedi ben Salem). As their relationship blossoms, so the couple become steadily ostracised, and Emmi is tested by Ali's levels of commitment. If *Petra von Kant* could be seen as a film about the innate relationship between emotion and its exploitation – a recurring theme – then *Fear Eats the Soul* is a film about the pressures that come to bear on emotions at the margins of society. Emmi is thought of as eccentric, a marginal figure who becomes even more so as her relationship with Ali progresses. Ultimately gentler than *Merchant* and *Petra*, *Fear Eats the Soul* reveals what is perhaps the heart of Fassbinder's cinema: as Andrew J Mitchell has noted, 'Fassbinder's films are films of tenderness... [he depicts] a world of characters living out the most fragile and delicate relationships, causing each other pain, providing each other succour.'[424]

Despite – or maybe because of – the influence of Sirk, Fassbinder worked in a wide variety of styles. Having cut his teeth in crime dramas, with forays into the avant-garde (*The Coffee House* [*Das Kaffeehaus*], 1970) and the western (*Whity*, 1970), Fassbinder now, with an eye on mass audiences, expanded into television, with a mini-series centred on a tool factory, *Eight Hours Are Not a Day* (*Acht Stunden sind kein Tag*, 1972). The series was cancelled after five of the planned eight episodes were made when Fassbinder let it be known that he wanted 'to make things dangerous to the so-called ruling class'.[425] He came under fire from the left as well, for not portraying the factory workers as good Marxists fighting the class struggle.

The mini-series was followed by, amongst others, Fassbinder's take on the serial killer film, *Bremen Freedom* (*Bremer Freiheit*, 1972); science fiction – *World on a Wire* (*Welt am Draht*, 1973); adaptations of classics – *Nora Helmer* (1973, based on Ibsen's *A Doll's House*); costume drama – *Effi Briest* (1974); semi-autobiographical drama – *I Only Want You to Love Me* (*Ich will doch nur, daß ihr mich liebt*, 1976); and screwball comedy – *Satan's Brew* (*Satansbraten*, 1976). Never one to shy away from controversy, Fassbinder's portrayal of the gay community in *Fox and his Friends* (*Faustrecht der Freiheit*,

1974) angered critics who felt the film was too negative. Fassbinder countered that all aspects of society are repressive, and the gay community could be just as oppressive and manipulative as that of the straight bourgeoisie, as he had already shown in *Petra von Kant*. 'The theme's remained the same,' Fassbinder explained in a 1977 interview, 'and always will remain the same: the manipulability, the exploitability of feelings within the system that we live in, and that at least one generation or more after us will certainly have to live in.'[426]

Fassbinder's final period covered the last five years of his life, and saw him working with international stars – Dirk Bogarde in 1977's *Despair*, scripted by Tom Stoppard from Nabokov's novel; Jeanne Moreau and Franco Nero in 1982's *Querelle*, based on the novel by Jean Genet. But he remained controversial: *Mother Küsters' Trip to Heaven* (*Mutter Küsters' Fahrt zum Himmel*, 1975) premiered at the Berlin Film Festival where it '[drew] bile and fire from the left'.[427] The film charts the fallout from a murder-suicide. The husband of Mother Küsters (Brigitte Mira) kills his boss and then himself; seeking to clear her husband's name, Mother Küsters is exploited by the media, her family and various left-wing factions. With its title ironically alluding to Phil Jutzi's Brecht-inspired film *Mother Krause's Trip to Happiness* (*Mutter Krausens Fahrt ins Glück*, 1929), Mother Küsters is one of Fassbinder's great victims, a figure who has no one she can trust, and in turn 'falls victim to various parasitical ideologies'.[428] But rather than seek political solutions to Germany's crises of the 1970s, *Mother Küsters* is 'an antipolitical film, which indicts the inhuman element in all ideologies'.[429]

Germany in Autumn (*Deutschland im Herbst*, 1978) was a portmanteau feature made as a response to the West German terrorist crisis of 1977. Fassbinder knew Andreas Baader and some of the other Red Army Faction members (indeed, they had burnt down his theatre in 1968), but always kept his distance, despite covertly approving of their aims, if not their methods. Fassbinder's episode in *Germany in Autumn* was a rare foray into documentary and, as with *Mother Küsters*, seems to acknowledge a failure to find political solutions. Fassbinder shows himself arguing with his mother and lover about the terrorist crisis. He goads his mother into making reactionary statements, and verbally attacks his boyfriend. Fassbinder comes over, as Kristin Thompson and David Bordwell put it, 'as [a] confused and dispirited participant'[430] in the crisis.

Terrorism reappeared in *The Third Generation* (*Die Dritte Generation*, 1979), which has big business – Eddie Constantine's computer impresario – financing left-wing terrorists as a way of maintaining the status quo. Returning to gay themes, *In a Year with 13 Moons* (*In einem Jahr mit 13 Monden*, 1978) showed the last five days in the life of a transsexual who is rejected by his/her lovers and friends, and features a towering performance by Volker Spengler in the lead.

Perhaps Fassbinder's greatest films of his final period were those dealing with German history from the 1930s to the present, in particular the BRD Trilogy and *Berlin Alexanderplatz*. The trilogy comprises *The Marriage of Maria Braun* (*Die Ehe der Maria Braun*, 1979), *Lola* (1981) and *Veronika Voss* (*Die Sehnsucht der Veronika Voss*, 1982). The three films all deal with postwar German history as seen through the eyes of three women, respectively played by Hanna Schygulla, Barbara Sukowa and Rosel Zech. Whereas his earlier 'women's films' – *The Bitter Tears of Petra von Kant*, *Effi Briest*, *Martha*, *Nora Helmer* – had drawn flak from some quarters of the feminist movement for daring to criticise their heroines as much as the patriarchy that imprisoned them, the BRD Trilogy portrays its women as complex, resourceful characters. That does not guarantee them happiness, of course: Veronika Voss, an actress whose career is on the wane,[431] is also a drug addict, while Maria Braun and Lola are ruthless in their quest for survival and personal gain.

Berlin Alexanderplatz (1980) is a 15-hour adaptation of Alfred Döblin's 1929 novel made for television. The book had long obsessed Fassbinder, and its central character, Franz Biberkopf (played by Günter Lamprecht in the film), was almost the director's alter ego. The film is at once an epic homage to a favourite novel, a political credo and a study in psychological autobiography. Set in the Berlin of the 1920s, the film follows the childlike Franz as he is released from prison and attempts to make his way in the world. Trying to forge a new life, Franz works various odd jobs, falling in with a small-time gangster, Reinhold (Gottfried John), with whom he has an intense friendship. Franz drifts towards the underworld, becoming a pimp. Then, after suffering a breakdown, he gets work as a park attendant, defeated by the capitalist system he did not want to be a part of. But the system is about to undergo a change: the Weimar era is all but over, and the 'unlimited reign of crime' of the Nazis about to begin.

Franz's struggle to live life on his own terms epitomises Fassbinder's core philosophy, summed up eloquently in an interview from 1975:

> My films are often criticised for being pessimistic. In my opinion there are enough reasons to be pessimistic, but, in fact, I don't see my films like that. They developed out of the position that the revolution should take place not on the screen, but in life itself, and when I show things going wrong, I do it to make people aware that this is what happens unless they change their lives. If, in a film that ends pessimistically, it's possible to make clear to people why it happens like that, then the effect of the film is not finally pessimistic. I never try to reproduce reality, my aim is to make mechanism transparent, to make it obvious to people that they must change their reality.[432]

WERNER HERZOG

Werner Herzog (b. 1942) was not an Oberhausen signatory, and funded his first short films by working as a welder. He did, however, benefit from the changes in production Oberhausen helped initiate. In 1963, he won the 10,000 DM Carl Mayer Screenwriting Prize (named after the writer of *Dr Caligari*) and if any one filmmaker can claim direct descent from the Expressionists, it is Herzog. His films explore (exalt, even) dreams, visions and madness, and question reality, sanity and civilisation. In Herzog's hands, these concepts are shown to be false, or at least highly dubious. Those who are somehow set apart from society – through madness, physical disability (or its inverse – physical ability as a strongman, a champion athlete, etc) or isolation – are the ones who are privileged with insights into the human condition that the ordinary herd are not party to. Sceptical of 1968, Herzog's films were instead philosophical and poetic statements on man's place in the universe, filtered through a sensibility harking back to Burke, Kant and the Romantics. Conscious of film's origins in Victorian sideshows, he was hostile to theory, claiming 'film is not the art of scholars, but of illiterates'. He also lamented the fact that 'we live in a society that has no adequate images anymore, and, if we do not find adequate images and an adequate language for our civilisation with which to express them, we will die out like the dinosaurs'.[433]

His first feature, *Signs of Life* (*Lebenszeichen*, 1968), was funded by the Mayer Prize and a further subsidy, granted in 1966. The film was shot on the Greek island of Kos, but Herzog and his crew were forced to decamp to Crete when the Colonels seized power. Set during World War II, the film depicts the descent into madness of Stroszek (Peter Brogle), a soldier who remains stationed on the island. The film is, in many ways, a feature-length version of his short film *The Unprecedented Defence of the Fortress Deutschkreuz* (*Die beispiellose Verteidigung der Festung Deutschkreuz*, 1966), which told the absurd story of four men guarding a derelict Austrian castle from imaginary attackers as they gradually lose their sanity. With *Signs of Life*, Herzog had no intention of making a 'realistic' film; he wanted to make a more existential point about the absurdity of war. In one of the film's most famous sequences, Stroszek mounts a futile attack on the nearby town with fireworks. Herzog felt that 'he is reacting in an almost necessary way, meeting violence with violence, absurdity with absurdity'.[434] Another sequence shows a landscape replete with hundreds of windmills, which are never explained: do they represent Stroszek's mind? Or nature mocking him? As with there being a thin line in Herzog's documentaries between 'fact' and 'truth', so in his dramas is there an equally thin line between 'external' and 'internal' – landscapes more often than not represent the soul or mind of the characters.

By the time of Herzog's second feature-length drama, *Even Dwarfs Started Small* (*Auch Zwerge Haben Klein Angefangen*, 1970), he had established a working pattern that he would repeat throughout his career. Common practice dictated that filmmakers cut their teeth with short films and documentaries, before moving on to features. Herzog ignored this, moving from feature-length dramas back to shorts, and from documentaries back to dramas. Immediately after *Signs of Life*, for instance, he made the short *Precautions Against Fanatics* (1969), and then made two documentaries, *The Flying Doctors of East Africa* (1969) and *Fata Morgana* (1970), before returning to feature-length drama with *Dwarfs*. And, immediately after that film, he went back to documentary with *Handicapped Future and Land of Silence and Darkness* (discussed in Chapter 7). As we have seen, there is a considerable overlap between Herzog's documentaries and his fiction films, so much so that one is tempted to put both categories in inverted commas (especially the so-called documentaries).

Even Dwarfs Started Small is the film that really set Herzog apart from his contemporaries. Set in a reform institution, it tells the story of a revolt by the inmates. What marks the film out is the cast: they are all dwarves, recalling not only Expressionism, but Todd Browning's *Freaks* (1932). It is the darkest of comedies, a black farce about both the nobility of, and necessity for, revolt. As with *Signs of Life*, the revolt goes nowhere, and a sense of gleeful nihilism pervades the film as the dwarves destroy the institution. The film was felt to be mocking the revolutions of 1968, and Herzog found himself facing accusations of fascism, to say nothing of charges of exploiting (or even mocking) the diminutive cast. The dwarves are a symbol of a world out of proportion. 'The dwarfs in the film are not freaks,' Herzog said in an interview, '*we* are the dwarfs... Just look around us: the worlds of commerce and consumer goods have become such monstrosities these days... if the film is saying anything, it is that it is not the midgets who are monstrous, it is us and the society we have created for ourselves.'[435]

Aguirre, The Wrath of God (*Aguirre, Der Zorn Gottes*, 1972) was Herzog's international breakthrough, and marks his first collaboration with the legendarily volatile actor Klaus Kinski. After the problems with *Even Dwarfs Started Small* – Herzog had had to release the film himself in West Germany – he wanted his next project to be commercial. Like many West German films of the period, it was part-financed by television money, in this case Hessischer Rundfunk (Hessian Broadcasting), as well as money from his producer brother, Lucki Stipetič. The film was inspired by a letter the Spanish Conquistador Lope de Aguirre had written to Philip II of Spain, in which Aguirre strips Philip of all his rights and proclaims himself emperor of El Dorado and

New Spain. Herzog claimed the letter interested him 'because of its language, its defiant tone and its absolute madness'.[436] As with his two previous feature-length dramas, Aguirre's rebellion is one that is doomed to fail: 'Aguirre fascinated me because he was the first person who dared defy the Spanish crown and declare the independence of a South American nation. At the same time he was completely mad, rebelling not only against political power but against nature itself.'[437]

Aguirre was the first of Herzog's jungle films, and remains his most famous. The shoot also experienced problems, although crises on location became something of a Herzog trademark. Some of Herzog's problems may have been purely down to lack of resources: the film was shot in Peru, with a crew of less than ten; they only had one camera. The budget was a mere $370,000, a third of which was Kinski's fee. Kinski and Herzog fell out, to the extent that Herzog resorted to death threats to get his leading man to stay.[438] To add to Herzog's problems, halfway through the shoot, it looked as though everything they had shot up to that point had been lost in transit to the lab (which was in Mexico). 'It was a barefoot film,' Herzog recalled, 'a child of poverty.'[439]

Klaus Kinski was the perfect choice for the mad Conquistador, whose attempt to find El Dorado leads his party over the mountains and deep into the jungle. Aguirre 'dares to defy nature to such an extent that nature inevitably takes its revenge on him',[440] and the jungle comes to reflect his state of mind; things warp and surprise. Herzog's own view was that 'it is as if the audience is being taken directly into the interior of things'.[441] At one point, Aguirre and his party come upon a boat in a tree – a sign that the world has turned upside down, a theme popularised by Northern Renaissance painters such as Pieter Bruegel.[442] The film gradually becomes more surreal, where 'logic plays no part in this; grandiose stylisations have taken over.'[443] Much of the latter part of the film could be an hallucination – even the deaths do not seem real. Characters fade away, leaving only Aguirre's obsession and defiance.

In its use of landscape, *Aguirre*'s blood relative is not *Signs of Life*, but *Fata Morgana*. Herzog drew a line between his own use of landscape, and that of Hollywood:

In my films landscapes are never just picturesque or scenic backdrops as they often are in Hollywood films... The jungle is really all about our dreams, our deepest emotions, our nightmares. It is not just a location, it is a state of mind... it is a vital part of the characters' inner landscapes.[444]

The Enigma of Kaspar Hauser (*Jeder für sich und Gott gegen alle*, 1974; lit: 'Every Man for Himself and God Against All') continued both Herzog's project to find the 'radical dignity' of the downcast and excluded (as he had done in *Land of Silence and Darkness*), and also fed the myth of Herzog as megalomaniac, the auteur who would stop at nothing to reveal 'ecstatic truth' on screen. The film is nominally based on the story of the teenage foundling, Kaspar Hauser, who appeared from nowhere in the town square in Nuremberg one day in 1828. Like *Aguirre* and *Signs of Life*, the film is not historically accurate: Kasper was thought to be about 16 years old, but the actor Herzog chose to play him, Bruno S, was 42 when the film was made. Herzog discovered Bruno, a street musician, after seeing the documentary *Bruno the Black: One Day a Hunter Blew His Horn* (*Bruno der Schwarze – Es blies ein Jäger wohl in sein Horn*, Lutz Eisholz, 1970). Bruno was the son of a prostitute who beat him so severely as a child that he went deaf for a while. He had been in and out of institutions for most of his life. Herzog elicited a remarkable performance from Bruno; it is one of his most sympathetic treatments of an outsider in all his work, and certainly bears comparison with Fini Straubinger, the heroine of *Land of Silence and Darkness*.

Like its predecessors, *Kaspar Hauser* has a philosophical bedrock, although here the tone is less extreme than *Aguirre*. There is no rebellion, merely incomprehension – both from Kaspar and the town worthies who try to 'civilise' him. As such, the film takes an almost anthropological look at German culture, although this could stand for the West as a whole. Kaspar's line, 'It seems to me that my coming into this world was a terrible fall', is one of the few historically accurate lines of dialogue in the film, and manages to comment on the straitjacket of so-called 'civilised' society, as well as being a Gnostic comment on the human condition. Kaspar, like all of Herzog's protagonists, is forever on the outside. When a doctor announces that an aberration has been found in Kaspar's brain, it seems to satisfy the townsfolk; the enigma of Kaspar Hauser has finally been solved. But as Herzog remarked, 'These people are blind to the fact that the aberration is in their own bourgeois society.'[445]

An aberrant society was the focus of Herzog's next feature, *Heart of Glass* (*Herz Aus Glas*, 1976). Set in eighteenth-century Bavaria, the film recounts the disaster that befalls a small town whose prosperity is based on the famed ruby glass made at the local glassworks. When the master glassblower dies, the secret is lost, and no one is able to replicate it. At the same time, Hias, a local prophet (Josef Bierbichler) warns of the destruction of the factory and the end of the world. The film is Herzog's most Bavarian: Hias was based on a real peasant seer, Mühlhiasl of Apoig, and was shot close to where the director grew up. Most famously, almost the entire cast acted under hypnosis, with the exception of Bierbichler and the glassblowers. The usual charges of exploitation and megalomania were levelled, but Herzog insisted the hypnosis was 'for reasons of stylisation not manipulation'.[446]

Such stylisation marks the film out as a grandchild of Expressionism, whose most famous character, Dr Caligari, was a hypnotist. Caligari's familiar, the somnambulist Cesare (Conrad Veidt), is able to predict the future from his catatonic state; here, the townspeople, in their inability to make any more of the ruby glass, are sleepwalking to their doom. The film is a portrayal of collective madness, a town living a communal lucid nightmare. The misted forests and mountains add to this sense of a shared dream – it is one of Herzog's most beautiful films – but whose dream does the landscape represent? Likewise the extraordinary apocalypse sequence, shot at Skellig Michael off the coast of Ireland. They could be the dreams of Hias, the prophet, but there is a sense in which they could be *our* dreams, as viewers, as well. Herzog is keenly aware of this aspect of film: '[The films are] not only my dreams. My belief is that these dreams are yours as well... the distinction between me and you is that I can articulate them. And it is my duty. Because this might be the inner chronicle of what we are, and we have to articulate ourselves. Otherwise we would be cows in a field.'[447] *Heart of Glass* is an articulation of such a dream, the strange, slow-motion performances a paradoxical embodiment of collective insanity – in that the characters go to their doom, almost willingly – and also of waking up to the truth, or 'ecstatic truth' as Herzog is wont to call it. A final key component of Herzog's Bavarian gnosis: 'I wanted to provoke poetic language out of people who had never before been in touch with poetry.'[448]

Herzog's last two films of the 1970s, *Nosferatu, the Vampyre* and *Woyzeck*,[449] based on Murnau's 1922 film and Georg Büchner's 1836 play respectively, look back beyond German history's own collective insanity, and the 'unlimited reign of crime' (from *Dr Mabuse*), to connect with what he saw as the best of German culture and film. Herzog spoke of these films as his contribution to 'the final chapter of the vital process of "re-legitimisation" of German culture that had been going on for some years'.[450] For some filmmakers, such as Hans-Jürgen Syberberg (see *Suggestions for Further Viewing* at the end of this book), this was a direct confrontation with Nazism, in the form of *Hitler – A Film from Germany* (1977), but, for Herzog, it meant first and foremost a reconnection with Weimar cinema – the era of Caligari and Mabuse, of Murnau and Lang.

The New German Cinema was a generation of orphans 'with no one around who could give us points of reference... [as] with a few exceptions... there had been no "legitimate" German cinema since 30 January 1933, the day Hitler came to power'.[451] It was vital for Herzog to make a direct connection, something his friendship with the eminent critic Lotte Eisner seems to have fulfilled:

> Lotte Eisner [gave] us her blessing. She was the missing link, our collective conscience, a fugitive from Nazism, and for many years the single living person in the world who knew everyone in cinema from its first hour on... So she alone had the authority, insight and the personality to declare us legitimate, and it was vitally important when she insisted that what my generation was doing in Germany was as legitimate as the film culture that Murnau, Lang and the other Weimar filmmakers had created all those years previously.[452]

Nosferatu, the Vampyre (*Nosferatu – Phantom der Nacht*, 1979) was therefore both a culturally charged remake and conscious homage to F W Murnau's 1922 silent classic. In his second collaboration with

Herzog, Klaus Kinski brings more humanism and sympathy to the role of the Count than Max Schreck, who played the vampire in the original. Herzog stayed closed to Murnau where he felt it appropriate, but was not averse to making changes – most notably the ending, when Van Helsing is arrested for the Count's murder, and the infected Jonathan escapes. He rides off with the words 'I have much to do', implying the vampire plague will spread across the world.[453]

'Many of my generation shared a similar attitude to Murnau and his contemporaries: cinema as legitimate culture,' Herzog stated. 'When I had finished *Nosferatu* I remember thinking, "Now I am connected, I have reached the other side of the river at last."'[454]

THE HAMBURG DECLARATION

Cannes, 1979. Francis Ford Coppola finally unveiled *Apocalypse Now*, and Volker Schlöndorff *The Tin Drum* (*Die Blechtrommel*). The films shared the festival's top prize, the Palme d'Or, and Schlöndorff would go on to win the Academy Award for Best Foreign Language Film. With the international success of Fassbinder's *The Marriage of Maria Braun* – first screened at the Berlin Film Festival earlier that year – 1979 was arguably the high-water mark of the New German Cinema.

The filmmakers themselves sensed that they were at a defining moment and, at the Hamburg Film Festival that year, issued a 'sequel' to the Oberhausen Manifesto of 17 years earlier, the Hamburg Declaration. As James Franklin commented, '[If] the Oberhausen manifesto had been a statement of things to come, the Hamburg declaration is more a statement of things that are.'[455] The declaration noted that 'Our strength is diversity', while insisting on solidarity: 'We will not let ourselves be divided – neither feature films from documentaries, nor filmmakers who have already made films from the new generation.' When Oberhausen had been signed, the appeal had been to the government for state subsidies. The 1970s had seen West German films steadily financed by television money, a fact Hamburg acknowledged by issuing a challenge to TV commissioning editors: 'Fantasy cannot be administered. Commissioners cannot determine what a productive film should do. The German film... can no longer be diverted by commissions, institutions, and interest groups.' Finally, the filmmakers declared, 'We have proven our professionalism. We can therefore no longer consider ourselves apprentices. We have learned that only the audience can be our ally: those are the people who work, who have wishes, dreams, and interests: those are people who go to the movies and people who do not go to the movies and even people who can imagine a totally different kind of film. We have to keep moving.'[456]

EPILOGUE: DOGME, DIGITAL AND THE DEATH OF NEW WAVES

Cannes, 1998. Forty years since François Truffaut had been banned from the festival, and 39 since he had pulled off the cinematic equivalent of the Entry into Jerusalem with *The 400 Blows*. 1998 would be another watershed; perhaps not as iconic as the *annus mirabilis* of 1959, but perhaps as *mirabilis* as cinema was likely to get in a postmodern, materialistic and thoroughly cynical world. Two Danish films screened in Competition that year: Thomas Vinterberg's *Festen* (*The Celebration*) and Lars von Trier's *The Idiots* (*Idioterne*), the first films made under the banner of Dogme95, which proclaimed itself to be a new movement. Some dismissed it as the latest joke from the notorious trickster von Trier, who himself would later match Truffaut's feat of getting himself banned from Cannes for some light-hearted remarks about Hitler. Certainly, *The Idiots* could be regarded as a 'serious joke' – a joke some people didn't get at all. Others took Dogme more seriously. Perhaps there was more to Dogme than mere publicity?

To judge by *Festen* and *The Idiots*, Dogme certainly seemed to have something going for it, with Vinterberg's film winning Cannes' Jury Prize. Dogme95 had been launched by von Trier in 1995 in a scatter of leaflets thrown from a balcony in a Paris cinema. What attracted attention at Cannes was the fact that both were shot on consumer-level digital video cameras (DV itself then being a new format, replacing the earlier Hi-8), and both adhered to the so-called 'Vow of Chastity', a document Dogme directors had to declare allegiance to before being allowed to make a film under the banner. The 'vow' is:

1. Filming must be done on location. Props and sets must not be brought in. If a particular prop is necessary for the story, a location must be chosen where this prop is to be found.

2. The sound must never be produced apart from the images or vice versa. Music must not be used unless it occurs within the scene being filmed, i.e. diegetic.

3. The camera must be a hand-held camera. Any movement or immobility attainable in the hand is permitted. The film must not take place where the camera is standing; filming must take place where the action takes place.

4. The film must be in colour. Special lighting is not acceptable (if there is too little light for exposure the scene must be cut or a single lamp be attached to the camera.)

5. Optical work and filters are forbidden.

6. The film must not contain superficial action (murders, weapons, etc, must not occur.)

7. Temporal and geographical alienation are forbidden (that is to say that the film takes place here and now).

8. Genre movies are not acceptable.

9. The film format must be Academy 35mm.

10. The director must not be credited.

What this actually resulted in was a vaguely social realist/neo-neorealist movement. Certainly, *Festen* and *The Idiots* were doing nothing that had not been done before. Vinterberg's film centred around a family patriarch's 60th birthday, at which some highly uncomfortable secrets emerge, while von Trier's film has something of Godard's *La Chinoise* (1967) about it, in that it concerns a group of people out to push the bounds – or buttons – of respectable society. In Godard's film, it was through allegiance to political radicalism but, in the politically different climate of the 1990s, von Trier chose to have his characters testing polite society by publicly imitating people with mental illnesses (dubbed 'spassing').

Technically, both looked not entirely professional. Vinterberg's film becomes grainier and grainer as the night comes on and, at one point, he shoots with the camera attached to a broomstick. Von Trier deliberately kept shots that showed other camera operators straying into frame, a directorial equivalent of 'spassing'. And both filmmakers confessed they had broken certain vows: Vinterberg by using a filter on a window (and some felt that using a broom as a makeshift jib was, strictly speaking, in contravention of the Vow), while von Trier blotted his copybook by using music. It was tongue-in-cheek; no one could accuse the Brothers, as the Dogme directors dubbed themselves, of being entirely serious. Yet Dogme is a good example of how far cinema has come since the glory days of new waves, if we can call them that, came to an end.

I have chosen 1979 to end this survey; it is a somewhat arbitrary cut-off point, the year the New German Cinema reached its apogee, with *The Tin Drum* triumphing at Cannes along with *Apocalypse Now.* Other new waves had, by then, wilted. No one spoke of the French New Wave as an active force, although all its main practitioners were still at large and producing good work. The Hungarian New Wave was no longer being spoken of either, although a new Hungarian Wave, the Budapest School, had emerged by the mid-to-late 70s, from whence emerged its most famous alumnus, Béla Tarr, who shot his first feature, *Family Nest* (*Családi tüzfészek*), in 1977.

It is perhaps fitting that, with the slippery concept of new wave, school or even Brotherhood in the Dogme style, Tarr became known in the West for films that did not adhere to the Budapest School's version of neorealism – films like *Damnation* (*Kárhozat*, 1988) and *Sátántangó* (Lit: 'Satan's Tango', 1994). He was influenced by Cassavetes early on – something the Budapest School approved of – but then developed a long-take, metaphysical style reminiscent of Tarkovsky, Angelopoulos and Jancsó, with a sardonic black humour that would not have looked out of place in the work of Samuel Beckett. (Tarr himself claimed Fassbinder as his biggest influence.)

The example of Béla Tarr is instructive: so often, filmmakers are not really part of a wave or group, but are great individualists. Into this group we could induct the extraordinary Kurdish filmmaker Yílmaz Güney (1937–84). Described as 'something like Clint Eastwood,

James Dean, and Che Guevara combined',[457] he rose to fame in 1960s Turkey as an actor in action pictures, before turning to directing. His films, such as *Umut* (*Hope,* 1970), owe much to neorealism, but being a left-wing Kurd in Turkey was enough to get him noticed and, ultimately, into trouble. Remarkably, he directed some of his most notable films, by proxy, from prison, such as *Yol* (*The Way,* 1982). He escaped and made his final film, *The Wall* (*Duvar,* 1983), in France.

The Polish School, like the Hungarian New Wave, was, by the late 70s, also a thing of the past. It was superseded by the Cinema of Moral Concern (or Moral Anxiety), which gave new life to the work of Andrzej Wajda (*Man of Marble* [*Czlowiek z marmuru*] from 1977, *Man of Iron* [*Czlowiek z zelaza*] from 1981), as well as introducing the world to the films of Krzysztof Kieślowski, Krzysztof Zanussi and Agnieszka Holland. And the British New Wave had, in 1963, the year of its greatest success – Tony Richardson's *Tom Jones* winning at the Oscars – 'gone down the drain', to quote Alexander Walker. But the end of a new wave can also have interesting and entirely unforeseen offshoots: in its death throes, British cinema produced two monumentally influential films, Terence Young's *Dr No* (1962) and Richard Lester's *A Hard Day's Night* (1964).

Since 1979, there have, of course, been a number of significant new waves. The Chinese Fifth Generation came to the attention of Western critics in the mid-80s, and filmmakers such as Chen Kaige and Zhang Yimou became international stars with films like *Yellow Earth* (*Huang tu di,* 1984) and *Red Sorghum* (*Hong gao liang,* 1987). The Fifth Generation, although a diverse group, were linked in that they were seen to be reacting against the dogmatism and socialist classicism, Chinese-style, of the Cultural Revolution. Two further Chinese-speaking territories, Hong Kong and Taiwan, also saw new waves emerging in the work of filmmakers such as Edward Yang, Hou Hsiao-Hsien, John Woo and Wong Kar-wai.

Further west, the Iranian New Wave enjoyed rejuvenation, partially as a result of the so-called Digital Revolution. The Dogme brothers had, by using cheap cameras, shown what could be possible on a very low budget and with consumer-level equipment. For middle-class filmmakers in Denmark, this was partially a pose but for filmmakers in Iran, oppressed initially by the regime of the Shah, and then by the Islamic Revolution, using small cameras and cheap tape stock was a liberation. As long as their films adhered to the Morality Code imposed by the Revolutionaries – oddly reminiscent of the Hays Code of 1940s Hollywood, with its restrictions on explicitly violent and sexual images – digital cameras meant filmmakers were relatively free to shoot what they liked. Some thrived on this: Abbas Kiarostami's *Ten* (*Dah*, 2002) took place entirely in a taxi, and was shot on a digital palmcorder mounted on the dashboard.[458]

LETZTE WORTE

Most new waves – however many filmmakers comprise them – adhere to the loose ground rules laid down at the start of this book: they will be united by new technology, a shared ideology, be working under politically auspicious conditions, have access to new sources of funding, and/or new opportunities for exhibition or distribution.

Perhaps the one thing that unites all the filmmakers in this book is an ethical conviction that self-expression is necessary for cinema and its audiences. This expression takes many forms, but often as not seeks to give a voice to those who cannot speak – for cultural or political reasons – or whose lives are not represented on screen. It is a cinema that provokes, questions, celebrates; that experiments with new forms of storytelling; that wants to be a trickster; that wants us to look again at the world.

The growth of digital cinema, in terms of production, postproduction and exhibition, has caused perhaps the biggest worldwide revolution in filmmaking since the French New Wave. But the basic challenge of making committed cinema – whether one is committing to politics or poetry – remains the same. It has been, and always will be, difficult to make films, whatever the circumstances the filmmaker finds themselves in. It comes down again and again to a good story, a strong form, a vision and, as George Lucas said, the willingness to just 'do it'.

The future of independent cinema, whatever it may be, will be defined by new technologies of production, exhibition, distribution and delivery as their foremost components. This will apply whether the cinemas or waves in question are party political or, if I can hazard a guess, humanitarian-political. The problems faced by Godard, Marker et al in the 1960s are still the same – perhaps worse, even – but the methods for dealing with them may well be found in alternative, web-based methods of financing such as crowd funding. The Party may be dead; the People are not.

The same goes for new waves themselves. Always a concept that was open to ridicule or controversy at the time – such as the claim made by Truffaut in 1959 that the French New Wave 'was all a fiction, made up [by] those outside'[459] – there will probably not be any new waves now to speak of. The cultural and critical landscapes have changed: as Mark Betz notes, '"Art cinema" is no longer a phrase with the same institutional currency that it once enjoyed some 20 years ago, when it served to demarcate a coherent body of contemporary film practice. "World cinema" is now the moniker of choice, albeit one with a more encompassing range of stylistic possibilities.'[460] Cinema itself also has less cultural importance than it once did: when Visconti died in 1976, thousands attended his funeral; the streets of Rome were gridlocked with mourners.

Perhaps, therefore, individual filmmakers, working alone or in groups, united or at least linked by the Internet, smartphones or some piece of digital telepathy yet to be dreamed of, will be the way forward. (If there is a 'forward' – and, indeed, a cinema – to speak of. Perhaps those concepts themselves are now out of date. Who knows?)

But future new waves, world cinemas or independent filmmakers – whatever their circumstances – would do well to heed Dziga Vertov's advice. Vertov reminds us that, essentially, making a film carries with it an ethical responsibility, perhaps akin to the idea of bearing witness, as espoused by the Quakers. A responsibility that, if the filmmaker is serious, cannot be ignored:

> Our eyes see very little and very badly – so people dreamed up the microscope to let them see invisible phenomena; they invented the telescope... now they have perfected the cinecamera to penetrate more deeply into the visible world, to explore and record visual phenomena so that what is happening now, which will have to be taken account of in the future, is not forgotten.[461]

SUGGESTIONS FOR FURTHER VIEWING

Given that DVD labels come and go, and also due to the number of films mentioned in this book, I have decided against DVD/Blu-Ray recommendations. Rather, the following suggestions fill in a few gaps, either because they were omitted from earlier chapters for reasons of length, or because they fell outside of my self-imposed 1959–79 window. As with the rest of this book, the list is entirely my own, and no doubt I have missed out films that really ought to be mentioned. But such is the nature of cinema. Or memory.

PIONEERS

Restorations and rereleases are the watchwords here, the various filmmakers themselves not having sat in a director's chair of late. Perhaps the most notable discovery is what is thought to be a near-complete version of Fritz Lang's *Metropolis*, uncovered in Buenos Aires in 2008.

FRENCH NEW WAVE

The Zanzibar Group, briefly active in the late 60s, embodied the spirit of the key year of 1968. Their most well-known ex-member is Philippe Garrel. See Sally Shafto's *Zanzibar: The Zanzibar Films and the Dandies of May 1968* (Paris: Classiques de l'Avant-Garde, Éditions Paris Expérimental, 2007).

And, of course, there was a French New New Wave in the 1980s, a label given to filmmakers such as Luc Besson, Jean-Jacques Beineix and Leos Carax. The 'movement' is sometimes dubbed the *Cinéma du look* due to the films' glossy production values.

Chantal Akerman could be said to be one of Agnès Varda's heirs, being the most important woman director to have emerged in Francophone cinema in the 1970s. (Akerman is Belgian.) Her most well-known film is *Jeanne Dielman, 23 quai du Commerce, 1080 Bruxelles* (1975), a study of a Belgian housewife who works as a prostitute.

Claire Denis is probably the most important French woman director to have emerged since the 1980s, making her debut in 1988 with *Chocolat (Chocolate)*.

ITALY

Gillo Pontecorvo's *The Battle of Algiers (La battaglia di Algeri*, 1966) is one of the most important Italian films of the 1960s. Indebted to neorealism, the film's devoutly anti-imperialist stance has proved extremely durable and influential.

Speaking of neorealism, Ermanno Olmi deserves a mention. Olmi is best known for his Cannes prizewinner, *The Tree of Wooden Clogs (L'Albero degli zoccoli*, 1978), a meditative three-hour portrait of Lombard rural life in the late nineteenth century.

The Taviani Brothers have their neorealist moments, but were also influenced by Brecht, Pasolini and Godard; their most celebrated film is *Padre Padrone (Father and Master*, 1977), another Cannes triumph.

Lina Wertmüller emerged in the early 70s as the most significant Italian woman director. She worked as Fellini's assistant on *8½* and became the first woman to be nominated for the Best Director Oscar for *Seven Beauties (Pasqualino Settebellezze*, 1975).

BRITISH NEW WAVE

The 1970s were a particularly grim period for British films. The major figure by far was Bill Douglas, whose trilogy of autobiographical films (*My Childhood, My Ain Folk* and *My Way Home*, 1972–78) about growing up in a poverty-stricken mining village outside Edinburgh were recognised as classics of poetic cinema. Sadly, Britain hasn't produced many since. Douglas died in 1991, only able to produce one further film, the neglected masterpiece *Comrades* (1987), the story of the Tolpuddle martyrs. The film is an impassioned plea for workers' rights, but is never party political. Its theme of unity and love put it far above that, almost on a par with the work of Carl Dreyer. (It also contains loving homages to early and pre-cinema.)

CZECH NEW WAVE

Jan Švankmajer, animator and surrealist, directed classics such as *Jabberwocky* (*Žvahlav aneb šatičky slaměného Huberta*, 1971). His darkly surreal work often combines live action, puppets and stop-motion. (In a similar vein, the Polish animator Walerian Borowczyk made films such as *Renaissance* [1963] and *Les Jeux des anges* [*Game of Angels*, 1964] before going over to largely live-action films from the late 60s on.)

Juraj Jakubisko has been hailed as the most important Slovak director of the Czechoslovak New Wave. *Birds, Orphans and Fools* (*Vtáčkovia, siroty a blázni*, 1969), banned for 20 years, is his most well-known film.

THE POLISH SCHOOL

Jerzy Kawalerowicz (1922–2007) made the remarkable *Mother Joan of the Angels* (*Matka Joanna od Aniołów*, 1961); like Ken Russell's *The Devils* (1971), the film was inspired by the case of the seventeenth-century priest, Urbain Grandier.

Wojciech Has (1925–2000) had a surrealist tint to his work. Among his notable films are *The Saragossa Manuscript* (*Rękopis znaleziony w Saragossie*, 1964), an adaptation of Jan Potocki's novel, and *The Hour-Glass Sanatorium* (*Sanatorium pod klepsydrą*, 1973), based on the stories of Bruno Schulz.

Tadeusz Konwicki (b. 1926) has been active for decades as a writer. Among his films are *Winter Twilight* (*Zimowy zmierzch*, 1957), Venice prize-winner *The Last Day of Summer* (*Ostatni dzień lata*, 1958) and *All Souls' Day* (*Zaduszki*, 1961).

As mentioned, the heirs to the Polish School were the filmmakers of the Cinema of Moral Concern/Moral Anxiety. Emerging in the 1970s, this group aimed to examine Polish history from a moral perspective in the bleak, post-Gomulka years of the 1970s and 1980s. Among its most notable proponents were Krzysztof Zanussi, Agnieszka Holland and Krzysztof Kieślowski.

HUNGARY

Károly Makk's *Love* (*Szerelem*, 1971) won the Jury Prize at Cannes, and is notable for being the first Hungarian film to acknowledge the tyranny of the Hungarian regime during Stalin's final years.

Márta Mészáros was the first woman to ever direct a feature film in Hungary, *The Girl* (*Eltavozott nap*, 1968). She remains best known for her much later *Diary for My Children* (*Napló gyermekeimnek*, 1984).

YUGOSLAVIAN *NOVI FILM*

The former Yugoslavia, like the former Czechoslovakia, was one of the more liberal of the Soviet Bloc countries, although this was mainly due to the country's leader, Marshall Tito, 'forever cocking a courteous snook at Moscow',[462] rather than any deliberate policy. However, a revised film law (1962) gave the republics greater autonomy, and this resulted in the high-water mark of what became known as *Novi film*, or New Film. Dušan Makavejev was the major figure. Active in ciné-clubs in the 1950s, Makavejev's interest in cinema was further bolstered by Henri Langlois, who visited the Belgrade Film Archive in 1954, bringing films with him 'by diplomatic bag', as Makavejev later recalled.[463] Influenced by Brecht and Godard, Makavejev was not afraid to ruffle the feathers of the Tito regime, whose Marxism he felt was 'fifty per cent Groucho, fifty per cent Karl'.[464] He was also a 'radical scavenger' (to use Emile de Antonio's phrase), and much of his most well-known film, *WR: Mysteries of the Organism* (*WR: Misterije organizma*, 1971), is made up of found footage. The film intercuts between a fictional story about the seduction of a Soviet ice-skater by a Yugoslavian woman who believes 'communism without free love is a wake in a graveyard', and an investigation into the life and works of psychoanalyst Wilhelm Reich. This aspect of the film has been memorably dubbed 'Direct Cinema footage of current erotic practices in the United States'.[465] Its frank approach to sexuality – and ribald anti-party humour – led to Makavejev being banned from his homeland for nearly two decades.

SPAIN

Tyranny in Europe was not restricted to the Soviet Bloc. Spain suffered for decades under the Franco regime, which ended with the Generalísimo's death in 1975. The greatest Spanish film of the 70s is generally regarded as Víctor Erice's *The Spirit of the Beehive* (*El espíritu de la colmena*, 1973), one of the best films about childhood ever made (as well as being a great homage to James Whale's version of *Frankenstein*). A poet on a par with Tarkovsky, Erice has to date made only two further features, *The South* (*El Sur*, 1983) and *The Quince Tree Sun* (*El Sol del Membrillo*, 1992). For more on Erice, see *The Cinema of Víctor Erice: An Open Window*, edited by Linda C Ehrlich (Lanham, MD: The Scarecrow Press, 2007).

The most important figure to emerge in the Spanish cinema of the 1960s was probably Carlos Saura, who exposed the reality of Madrid's slums in *The Delinquents* (*Los golfos*, 1960). His international breakthrough came with *The Hunt* (*La Caza*, 1966), a psychological thriller about three Spanish Civil War veterans on a rabbit hunt, 'a dramatic and jagged-edged assault on the legacy of Fascism'.[466]

DOCUMENTARY

Cinéma vérité: Louis Malle's *Phantom India* (1968) initially ran six hours, but was later edited down for television. The *Calcutta* episode was the most widely distributed. Overwhelmed by India, Malle captured the subcontinent as a vast pageant, full of love and beauty, but not shirking from horror. Malle included passages of narration, but this was far from the quiet polemic of Jean Rouch: 'Far from drawing conclusions, Malle's comments expressed his inability to reach any.'[467]

Direct Cinema: Michel Brault, who shot *Chronique d'un Été* for Jean Rouch and Edgar Morin, made the seminal *Les Raquetteurs* (*The Snowshoers*, 1958) with Gilles Groulx for the National Film Board of Canada after its move to Montreal in 1956. The film portrayed rural Quebecois at a snowshoe convention and, partially in contravention of the 'rules', was not shot with synchronous sound. This drawback didn't stop it becoming one of the landmark Direct Cinema films.

Another Canadian film, Allan King's *Warrendale* (1967), shot in a school for 'troubled young people', is a more benign cousin of Wiseman's *Titicut Follies*, made the same year.

Essay Film: Marcel Ophüls' *The Sorrow and the Pity* (*Le chagrin et la pitié*, 1969) is an epic investigation into collaboration with the Nazis in Vichy France. Telling truths some French would rather forget, the film was banned there until 1981. Ophüls returned to the subject of the war a number of times, perhaps most famously in *Hôtel Terminus: The Life and Times of Klaus Barbie* (*Hôtel Terminus: Klaus Barbie, sa vie et son temps*, 1989), which won the Academy Award for Best Documentary Feature.

And while we're mentioning the war, Claude Lanzmann's nine-hour Holocaust essay *Shoah* (1985) is required viewing. A decade earlier, BBS had scored one of their last triumphs with the Oscar-winning Vietnam documentary, *Hearts and Minds* (Peter Davis, 1974).

NEW HOLLYWOOD

'The thirteen years between *Bonnie and Clyde* in 1967 and *Heaven's Gate* in 1980,' Peter Biskind wrote, 'marked the last time it was really exciting to make movies in Hollywood, the last time people could be consistently proud of the pictures they made, the last time the community as a whole encouraged good work, the last time there was an audience that could sustain it.'[468] This period, roughly half the period of this book's concern, contains an embarrassment of riches, so it is impossible to list all the essential films here.

One great, unsung auteur from this period is Hal Ashby, remembered (if remembered at all) for the Warren Beatty vehicle *Shampoo* (1975) and *Being There* (1979), Peter Sellers' last great film. He also made *The Last Detail* (1973), starring Jack Nicholson, and one of the first anti-Vietnam films, *Coming Home* (1978), starring Jon Voight and Jane Fonda, both of whom won Academy Awards for their performances. Ashby's best film is arguably *Harold and Maude* (1971), the archetypal oddball romance, in this case between the death-obsessed teenager, Harold (Bud Cort), and the 79-year-old Maude (Ruth Gordon).

No Wave

Growing out of the New York independent filmmaking scene, No Wave emerged in the mid-70s, at the same time as punk. There was always a strong link between the two movements, and No Wave began with two no-budget documentaries shot at CBGBs, Amos Poe and Ivan Král's *The Blank Generation* (1975) and *Night Lunch* (1975). Both films documented performances by emerging punk legends such as The Ramones, Patti Smith, Blondie, Talking Heads, Television and Richard Hell.

Poe decided to launch a do-it-yourself film movement via ads in *The Village Voice*, and shot *Unmade Beds* (1976), a homage to Godard's *Breathless*. Painter Duncan Hannah got his first acting role, starring as Rico, a photographer who thinks he's a gangster; Debbie Harry played his girlfriend. Hannah was surprised that the *New York Times* reviewed the film 'like it was a real movie... [and] Godard saw it and, like, took it seriously.'[469]

Like punk, attitude mattered more than technical perfection. 'I didn't give a shit,' Poe later said.[470] 'The whole No-Wave movement was something like Rube Goldberg, like Godard, with a Warhol approach, making the mistakes work. The polished professional is boring compared to the insane amateur.' Poe followed up *Unmade Beds* with *The Foreigner*, shot for $5,000. None of it was spent on the audio. Much as Godard had, Poe took his inspiration from B-movies, this time doing an idiosyncratic take on the spy genre. But the spirit of the 60s remained with him: in 1984, Poe made his first feature on 35mm, *Alphabet City*, which he described as 'the *Battle of Algiers* in the Lower East Side'.[471]

Following in Poe's wake were the likes of Eric Mitchell, Beth and Scott B, Jim Jarmusch, Abel Ferrara, Lizzie Borden, Richard Kern, and Nick Zedd, among others. Musical influences aside, they too drew inspiration from the French New Wave, B-movies, the avant-garde, exploitation and even porn (so-called Cinema of Transgression). If they couldn't stretch to *The Foreigner*'s budget, then they shot on Super-8, sound Super-8 having been introduced in 1974 (producing audio of a quality 'raw, like an answering machine at best'[472]). See Clayton Patterson's *Captured: A Lower East Side Film and Video History* (New

York: Seven Stories Press, 2005). *No Wave* by Marc Masters (London: Black Dog Publishing 2007) is an illustrated history of the whole No Wave scene, including musicians, artists and poets alongside the filmmakers. For actor/painter Duncan Hannah's reminiscences about the making of *Unmade Beds* and *The Foreigner*, see Legs McNeil and Gillian McCain's *Please Kill Me: The Uncensored Oral History of Punk* (London: Abacus, 1997), pp 378–9 and 381–3.

NEW GERMAN CINEMA

Wim Wenders (b. 1945) was, along with Fassbinder and Herzog, one of the most prominent West German filmmakers of the 1970s. His ambivalence about America and its corrosive influence on Germany manifests in much of his work. His breakthrough film, *The Goalkeeper's Fear of the Penalty* (*Die Angst des Tormanns beim Elfmeter*, 1971), is a deconstructed noir. This was followed by a trilogy of films in that quintessentially American genre, the road movie: *Alice in the Cities* (*Alice in den Städten*, 1974), *Wrong Move* (*Falsche Bewegung*, 1975, based on Goethe's *Wilhelm Meister's Apprenticeship*) and *Kings of the Road* (*Im Lauf der Zeit*, 1976; lit: 'In the Course of Time'). *The American Friend* (*Der amerikanische Freund*, 1977), a masterly adaptation of *Ripley's Game* by Patricia Highsmith, starred Dennis Hopper and Bruno Ganz. Wenders' style is one of detachment and quietude. Showing a typical new wave fascination with Hollywood auteurs, the film featured Nicholas Ray in a small role. Wenders collaborated with Ray, by then seriously ill, on *Lightning Over Water* (1980), which turned out to be Ray's final film as a director.

Hans-Jürgen Syberberg (b. 1935) saw cinema as a form of *gesamtkunstwerk*, a synthesis of all the arts, in the way that Wagner regarded opera. (Michael Powell also saw cinema in broadly similar terms.) Famous for his seven-hour *Hitler – A Film From Germany* (1977), distributed in the US by Francis Ford Coppola under the title *Our Hitler*, he remained an outspoken critic of the New German Cinema and Germany itself: 'I have nothing more in common with these people. Why should I, and what use or pleasure is it to anyone? We are living in a dead country.'[473] *Hitler* was well regarded in France and England, but, perhaps predictably, not in Germany.

The Hitler film was not, in fact, Syberberg's first foray into *Vergangenheitsbewältigung*. It forms the final part of his 'German Trilogy', on which his reputation rests. The earlier instalments are *Ludwig: Requiem for a Virgin King* (*Ludwig – Requiem für einen jungfräulichen könig*, 1972), which was unavoidably compared to Visconti's *Ludwig*, made the same year, and *Karl May* (1974), a film about Germany's most popular nineteenth-century novelist. Its cast members were associated with the Nazi era, such as Helmut Käutner (May) and Kristina Söderbaum (first wife Emma), as Syberberg wanted to 'emphasise the continuity of 19th century romantic idealism, the Nazi perversion of that idealism, and implicitly the unavoidable cultural schizophrenia of modern West Germany.'[474]

Controversy also courted *The Confessions of Winifred Wagner* (*Winifred Wagner und die Geschichte des Hauses Wahnfried von 1914–1975*; lit: 'Winifred Wagner and the History of the House of Wahnfried from 1914–1975', 1975), a five-hour documentary about Winifred Wagner, who married one of Richard Wagner's sons and directed the Bayreuth festival from 1930. Wagner revealed that the family had had close ties to Hitler, but later claimed that some interviews were recorded without her knowledge. The Wagner family accused Syberberg of exploiting a vulnerable old woman, despite the fact that the 'vulnerable old woman' in question was an unrepentant Nazi.

Of the other New German filmmakers, Werner Herzog continued his quest for 'adequate images', which resulted in the spectacular *Fitzcarraldo* (1982), which saw Klaus Kinski drag a steamship over a mountain in South America. 'It's a metaphor for something,' Herzog later admitted, 'but I don't know what.' Herzog went on to make some of his best work in the 1990s and 2000s (*Lessons of Darkness*, 1992; *Bells from the Deep*, 1994: *Little Dieter Needs to Fly*, 1997; *Pilgrimage*, 2001; *Grizzly Man*, 2005; *Cave of Forgotten Dreams*, 2010). He received an Oscar nomination for *Encounters at the End of the World* (2007). He is now arguably better known than the generation of filmmakers whence he came.

Jean-Marie Straub and Danièle Huillet continued unabated until Huillet's death in October 2006. The Venice Film Festival showed their final film that year, *Quei loro incontri* (*The Meeting*, 2006, based on Cesare Pavese's *Dialoghi con Leucò*), but they did not attend. Straub issued the following statement to explain why:

> Besides [Danièle Huillet's illness] I wouldn't be able to be festive in a festival where there are so many public and private police looking for a terrorist — *I* am the terrorist, and I tell you, paraphrasing Franco Fortini: so long as there's American imperialistic capitalism, there'll never be enough terrorists in the world.[475]

Edgar Reitz's *Heimat* (1984) is well worth repeated viewing. It stands as the unofficial end of the New German Cinema, on a par with Fassbinder's *Berlin Alexanderplatz*.

Speaking of RWF, his death in June 1982 is another putative end point for the New German Cinema. Contrary to tabloid rumour, Fassbinder did not die of suicide or a drug overdose; he was the victim of a stroke.[476]

CHILDREN OF THE SUN-TRIBE: THE JAPANESE NEW WAVE

The Japanese New Wave has the distinction of being one of the few new waves to be actually created by a studio system, rather than emerging in opposition to it. Aware of an expanding youth market in the mid-1950s, studios such as Nikkatsu and Toei catered to it by producing thrillers, rock and roll movies and swordfight films, collectively known as *taiyozuko*, or 'sun-tribe' films.[477] By the end of the decade, cinema attendance had grown to a postwar high. The success of the *taiyozuko* films and the emergence of the French New Wave prompted Japan's most hidebound studio, Shochiku, to promote a young assistant director, Nagisa Oshima (1932–2013), to director, with the intention of launching the *Nuberu bagu*, or Japanese New Wave. Although they merely hoped to regain ground lost to other studios, and recoup money incurred from a few mainstream flops, they had instead opened a Pandora's box. As Kristin Thompson and David Bordwell noted, the Japanese New Wave 'went further than even their German contemporaries in showing that authoritarian forces continued to rule their country long after democracy had supposedly come'.[478]

Oshima proved to be a prolific and controversial filmmaker. Beginning as an assistant director at Shochiku, he started writing film journalism as opinionated as anything written by Truffaut, attacking what he saw as conservative traditions within Japanese cinema and society. Oshima saw reality as constantly changing, and called for films that would be 'weapons used to change reality, [films that] must always follow through with their objective of revolutionising consciousness'.[479] *Cruel Story of Youth* (*Seishun zankoku monogatari*, 1960), Oshima's second feature and first major film, was certainly in the revolutionary camp. The story of a schoolgirl and her criminal boyfriend (who initiates their relationship by raping her), it must 'scarcely have been recognisable as Japanese to western connoisseurs of Akira Kurosawa, Kenji Mizoguchi and Yasujiro Ozu'.[480] With its Pop-Art colours and decentred framing, *Cruel Story* depicts a Japan populated by the self-centred, violent and cynical. *Night and Fog in Japan* (*Nihon no yoru to kiri*, 1960) quickly followed. Stylistically more challenging than its predecessors, the film used tableaux staging and a rigorous flashback structure to conduct a post-mortem on the failures of the Japanese left at the time of the renewal of the US-Japanese security pact in 1959, uncannily pre-empting by nearly a decade the fall-out from May 1968.

Shochiku felt the film was too controversial and pulled it from cinemas after only a week. Oshima, furious, left to form his own production company. The Japanese film industry at the time was a closed-shop; it was virtually impossible to work outside it. By becoming independent, Oshima was following a trail blazed in France by Jean-Pierre Melville and Agnès Varda. Other Japanese New Wave directors would follow suit, starting by working for the studios, and then jumping ship after a couple of films, leaving the studios to think of new ways to increase revenue (such as *yakuza* films and 'pink' films – erotica). The New Wave was greatly helped by the Art Theatre Guild (ATG), a company set up in 1962 to distribute foreign films in their own chain of cinemas. In 1964, the ATG began offering funding and distribution to independent filmmakers, thus offering a lifeline to directors like Oshima working outside the system.

Throughout the sixties, Oshima continued to explore both cinematic form, refusing to be tied down to any one style, and attacking what he saw as the militaristic and imperialistic elements of Japanese society, both past and present. Among his many films of the period are *The Catch* (*Shiiku*, 1961), the first of Oshima's collaborations with the novelist Kenzaburo Oe, *Pleasures of the Flesh* (*Etsuraku*, 1965), *Violence at Noon* (*Hakuchu no torima*, 1966), *A Treatise on Japanese Bawdy Songs* (*Nihon shunka-kô*, 1967), *Japanese Summer: Double Suicide* (*Muri shinjû: Nihon no natsu*, 1967), *Diary of a Shinjuku Thief* (*Shinjuku dorobô nikki*, 1968), *Death by Hanging* (*Koshikei*, 1968) and *Boy* (*Shonen*, 1969). In his radicalism (politically, stylistically) and prolificacy, Oshima resembles Godard, with whose works he was familiar, or Fassbinder.

Shohei Imamura (1926–2006) started out as an assistant to Yasujiro Ozu, working with the master on *Early Summer* (*Bakushu*, 1951), *The Flavour of Green Tea over Rice* (*Ochazuke no aji*, 1952) and *Tokyo Story* (*Tokyo monogatari*, 1953). However, the films Imamura would go on to make were as far removed from Ozu as possible. Working his way up through the ranks at Nikkatsu Studios, Imamura made his debut as a director with *Stolen Desire* (*Nusumareta yokujo*, 1958), about a troupe of travelling actors. The film, a bawdy comedy, has more in common with Fellini's *Nights of Cabiria* than Angelopoulos's *Travelling Players*, and revealed Imamura's interest in what he termed 'the relationship of the lower part of the human body and the lower part of the social structure on which the reality of daily Japanese life obstinately supports itself'.[481]

Pigs and Battleships (*Buta to gunkan*, 1961) was Imamura's breakthrough. Savagely satiric, the film follows the fortunes of a yakuza gang that raises pigs on a rubbish dump outside a US naval base. Imamura depicts a Japan of 'petty racketeers, prostitutes and mothers anxious to sell off their daughters to GIs'.[482] The film caused concern at the studio, as did Imamura's follow-ups, *The Insect Woman* (*Nippon konchuki*, 1963) and *Intentions of Murder* (*Akai satsui*, 1964). The films continued Imamura's project of showing the lives of people living at the margins of Japanese society. Both films feature strong female characters, very much going against the way women had been depicted by earlier filmmakers such as Mizoguchi, Naruse or Imamura's own mentor, Ozu. Similarly, Imamura favoured a documentary realist style, a far cry from Ozu's low-level, locked-off camera.

Leaving Nikkatsu, Imamura set up his own production company, and shot *The Pornographer* (*Erogotoshi-tachi yori: Jinruigaku nyûmon*, 1966), a black comedy about a middle-class man who embarks on a career as a blue movie producer, believing himself to be rendering Japanese society a service. The film is ironically subtitled 'An Introduction to Anthropology'. *A Man Vanishes* (*Ningen johatsu*, 1967) furthers Imamura's 'anthropological' studies. Mixing documentary and fiction, Imamura investigates the life of a man who has disappeared. We are never sure of what we are seeing – is it documentary or drama? At the film's end, the various interviewees gather in a restaurant to discuss what may have happened to their absent colleague. Suddenly, the roof and walls of the room pull away to reveal that we are in fact in a film studio after all. And yet the film manages to retain its documentary credentials; Imamura is telling us that film – and possibly Japanese society as a whole – is real and fake at the same time.

Imamura would later become one of the very few filmmakers to win the Palme d'Or at Cannes twice, for *The Ballad of Narayama* (*Narayama-bushi ko*, 1983) and *The Eel* (*Unagi*, 1997).

Other notable Japanese New Wave directors include Hiroshi Teshigahara (1927– 2001). The son of an ikebana master, Teshigahara later took over his father's school and became an ikebana master himself. His films are more allegorical and absurdist than realist: *Woman of the Dunes* (*Suna no onna*, 1964) is the story of a scientist trapped with a mysterious young woman in the giant sandpit where she lives.

Yoshishige Yoshida (b. 1933) became a director at Shochiku after Oshima's departure, making *Akitsu Springs* (*Akitsu onsen*, 1962), a film in the spirit of Resnais and Antonioni. He later went overtly Godardian in *Eros Plus Massacre* (*Eros purasu gyakusatsu*, 1969), a deconstruction – amongst other things – of the samurai film.

Masahiro Shinoda (b. 1931), on the other hand, made films whose visual sensibilities harked back to Japanese films from the 1930s. Like Imamura, he worked as an assistant to Ozu, but, unlike Imamura, made films that clearly show the influence of the older filmmaker, as well as Mizoguchi, Shinoda's idol. Shinoda adopted a revisionist position, however, to examine Japanese society. Shinoda's key films include *Assassination* (*Ansatsu*, 1964), *With Beauty and Sorrow* (*Utsukushisa to kanashimi to*, 1965), based on Yasunari Kawabata's novel, and *Double Suicide* (*Shinju: Ten no amijima*, 1969).

AUSTRALIA AND NEW ZEALAND

The Australian New Wave has the distinction of being the only new wave to be launched (somewhat inadvertently, it has to be said) by the great British filmmaker Michael Powell. Unable to find work after the scandalous fall-out from *Peeping Tom* (1960), Powell made *They're a Weird Mob* (1966) and *The Age of Consent* (1969) in Australia, and the success of both films caused a shift in attitudes to the possibility that Australia might be able to sustain a homegrown film industry of her own. Prior to this time, Australia was largely considered a cinematic backwater that received occasional visits from the outside world, such as Stanley Kramer's *On the Beach* (1959) and Fred Zinnemann's *The Sundowners* (1960), both of which were shot in Australia with Hollywood stars. Tony Richardson followed Powell Down Under, shooting *Ned Kelly* (1970), starring Mick Jagger as the eponymous bushranger-turned-outlaw. A year later, Canadian Ted Kotcheff made *Wake in Fright* (1971) and Nicolas Roeg *Walkabout* (1971), cementing Michael Powell's pioneering efforts.

Things began to change: starting in 1970, government subsidies were made available, followed by the establishment of several bodies designed to foster indigenous production: the Australian Film Development Corporation, the Experimental Film Fund and the Film and Television School. Within ten years, the new Australian cinema had made some of the most notable English-language films of the 1970s. Filmmakers such as Bruce Beresford, Peter Weir, Fred Schepisi, Paul Cox, Gillian Armstrong, Philip Noyce and George Miller were responsible for such films as *The Cars that Ate Paris* (Weir, 1974), *Picnic at Hanging Rock* (Weir, 1975), *The Last Wave* (Weir, 1977), *The Getting of Wisdom* (Beresford, 1977), *The Chant of Jimmie Blacksmith* (Schepisi, 1978), *Mad Max* (Miller, 1978), *Newsfront* (Noyce, 1978), *My Brilliant Career* (Armstrong, 1979), *Breaker Morant* (Beresford, 1980), *Gallipoli* (Weir, 1981), *Road Warrior* (Miller, 1981), *The Year of Living Dangerously* (Weir, 1982) and *Man of Flowers* (Cox, 1983).

This selection represents some of the most original and incisive films of the 1970s. Not only were Australian filmmakers working, rather than visiting Hollywood glitterati, but the subjects themselves were very much new wave in their thinking, among them revisionist takes on history (*Breaker Morant, Gallipoli*), Aboriginal issues (*The Last Wave, The Chant of Jimmie Blacksmith*), and cult weirdness (*The Cars that Ate Paris, Mad Max, Man of Flowers*).

New Zealand's film industry was given a shot in the arm by the creation of the New Zealand Film Commission in 1978. Vincent Ward's Tarkovskian *Vigil* (1984) became the first New Zealand film to be screened at Cannes. Ward's follow-up, *The Navigator: A Medieval Odyssey* (1988), perhaps owing more to Herzog than Tarkovsky, likewise received international attention. Jane Campion's *Sweetie* (1989) was made in Australia, before she returned home to make *An Angel at My Table* (1990), both films dealing with mental illness, before completing the Cannes prize-winner *The Piano* (1993).

BRAZILIAN CINEMA NOVO AND THIRD CINEMA

Brazil's cinema in the early 1950s was moribund, dominated by American-style films made by production companies such as Vera Cruz, the MGM of São Paolo. The bankruptcy of Vera Cruz prompted some filmmakers to produce their work independently, under the influence of Italian neorealism. Nelson Pereira dos Santos was the most important figure, whose *Rio 40 Graus* (*Rio 40 Degrees*, 1955) signalled a sea-change in Brazilian cinema. Following various characters – boys from the *favela*, a con-artist, a landowner, a footballer, a pregnant working-class woman – the film showed their lives in Rio without glamour. So much so, in fact, that the film was censored in its entirety, but the ensuing controversy meant that it was finally released in 1956. The debate about the film's Rossellini-like take on Rio was symptomatic of the cultural and political changes Brazil was going through in the late 50s, and it was in this climate of renewed optimism that Cinema Novo – new cinema – appeared.

'Cinema Novo has no birthdate,' wrote one of its practitioners, Carlos Diegues,[483] and 'was created by no one in particular', although it was certainly getting going by 1961. Like dos Santos, whom they revered, Cinema Novo filmmakers aimed to rejuvenate Brazilian cinema with films that were at once critical of the status quo and formally innovative; they saw themselves as 'part of a larger process transforming Brazilian society'.[484] Aside from Diegues, Cinema Novo included filmmakers such as Joaquim Pedro de Andrade, Arnaldo Jabo and Ruy Guerra (who also appeared as an actor in Herzog's *Aguirre, The Wrath of God*). They were active theoreticians as well as filmmakers who 'saw filmmaking as political praxis, a contribution to the struggle against neo-colonialism'.[485] Important early films include *Cinco Vezes Favela* (*Favela Five Times*, 1961, a portmanteau feature), *Ganga Zumba* (1963, Carlos Diegues), Ruy Guerra's *The Hustlers* (*Os Cafajestes*, 1962) and *The Guns* (*Os Fuzis*, 1964), and dos Santos's *Barren Lives* (*Vidas Secas*, 1963). These films were dominated by themes of poverty, violence, hunger, alienation and exploitation, 'sad, ugly films, screaming, desperate films where reason does not always prevail.'[486]

So wrote the filmmaker most associated with Cinema Novo, Glauber Rocha (1939–81), in his seminal essay, 'An Aesthetic of Hunger' (1965). Rocha started as a journalist in his native Bahia, becoming culturally and politically active. Journalism led to filmmaking; he was Bahia's 'Young Turk', as impassioned as Truffaut or Godard had been in Paris at *Cahiers*. Rocha remained an active polemicist throughout his life, and the 'Aesthetic of Hunger' came to stand for both his own thought, and that of Cinema Novo as a whole. He saw hunger, a product of colonialism, as Brazil's national shame; Europeans 'cannot truly comprehend the misery of the Latin American'.[487] And the natural response of the starving was to make the coloniser aware of the colonised through violence. Only then 'does the coloniser understand... the strength of the culture he exploits. As long as they do not take up arms, the colonised remain slaves.'[488]

Rocha made his first short film in 1959 with money he'd earned from journalism. *Barravento* (1962), his first feature, was set in a Bahian fishing village and dealt with the locals' adherence to the Candomblé religion, seen by Firmino, the protagonist, as a tool of political and social oppression. It is arguably the most neorealist of Rocha's films, a spiritual descendant of Visconti's *La Terra Trema*.

Black God, White Devil (Deus e o Diabo na Terra do Sol, 1964; lit: 'God and the Devil in the Land of the Sun'), set in the 1940s, is the story of a cowherd, Manoel, who becomes a follower of a wandering 'saint' after killing a landowner in an argument. The saint prophesies the overthrow of the established order and the arrival of paradise in the form of an island. Manoel later joins the gang of the cangaceiro Corisco, who in a sense is even madder than the saint. With its themes of struggle and the liberation of the exploited from religious and political oppression, it resembles Pasolini (another great polemicist), with its focus on folk customs and visionaries, it recalls Rouch and anticipates Herzog. With its casual violence and general air of derangement, it has the sensibility of a spaghetti western (especially in its second half).

Land in Anguish (Terra em transe, 1967; aka Earth Entranced), set in a country called El Dorado (the mythical island of Black God?), is a study of political reforms and the inevitable betrayals of the poor and the idealistic. The film's stylistic bravura pell-mell reflects the real political turmoil in Brazil: a military coup in 1964 had ousted the liberal regime of João Goulart. This forced Rocha into an ever more radical position: he is the figure to whom we owe the term 'guerrilla filmmaking', from his essay 'The Tricontinental Filmmaker', published in Cahiers du cinéma in 1967, a time when it carried considerably more political weight than it does now.[489] Other Cinema Novo filmmakers went the other way, trying to appeal to wider audiences with films like Leon Hirszman's Garota de Ipanema (The Girl from Ipanema, 1967); it was as if they were going from Godard to Costa-Gavras (with Godard never being entirely absent).

By the time Rocha made his third feature, Brazil had suffered an even more reactionary coup. Antonio das Mortes (O Dragão da Maldade contra o Santo Guerreiro, 1969; lit: 'The Dragon of Evil against the Holy Warrior') is a sequel to Black God, taking up the story of the eponymous gunslinger who kills the bandit Corisco. In the earlier film, he had been working for the church and landowners. Given another job by them, he becomes a turncoat, siding with the poor and oppressed. The film was even more of a Brechtian spaghetti western than Black God, and won Rocha the Best Director prize at

Cannes in 1969 (when Lindsay Anderson's *If...* and Tarkovsky's *Andrei Rublev* also screened).

Yet another coup, in 1971, forced Rocha into exile. (Ruy Guerra and Carlos Diegues left, too.) By then, Cinema Novo had split into factions – 'cannibal-tropicalism', which used bad taste, allegory and kitsch, and *Udigrudi* (meaning 'underground') or Novo Cinema Novo, which wanted to get back to the 'aesthetic of hunger'. Meanwhile, the government had set up a body called Embrafilme, to help Brazilian film production and distribution. As Cinema Novo became increasingly irrelevant, Embrafilme was happily green-lighting 'erotic comedies' like *Um Soutien Para Papai* (*A Bra for Daddy*), the average military junta always finding sexism, hypocrisy and male chauvinism preferable to social change.[490]

In exile, Rocha made films in Europe and Africa, where he can be seen as helping forge the kind of cinema he had envisaged in 'The Tricontinental Filmmaker'. This has been dubbed Third Cinema, designating films from the Third World (what would nowadays be euphemistically called 'developing countries'; developing, that is, into Western capitalist economies). Third Cinema addresses issues of colonialism and imperialism, made by those colonised. Amongst their number, we could cite Chilean filmmaker Raul Ruiz, African filmmaker Ousmane Sembene and Cuban filmmaker Tomás Gutiérrez Alea. Alea is emblematic of Third Cinema, in that Cuba had been the subject of films from both sides of the Iron Curtain, such as Chris Marker's *¡Cuba Sí!* (1961) and Mikhail Kalatozov's *I Am Cuba* (*Soy Cuba*, 1964), before Alea rose to prominence with *Memories of Underdevelopment* (*Memorias del subdesarrollo*, 1968), which, unlike the earlier films, casts a cynical eye over Castro's Cuba.

In a sense all new waves were responses to imperialism – the imperialism of the classical Hollywood narrative. Like 'new wave', 'third cinema' is now a slightly outmoded name, with 'world cinema' usurping both; the issues remain. For more on Third Cinema, see Pines and Willemen, *Questions of Third Cinema* (London: British Film Institute, 1989) and Wayne, *Political Film: The Dialectics of Third Cinema* (London and Sterling, VA: Pluto Press, 2001).

SATYAJIT RAY AND PARALLEL CINEMA

Sometimes seen as a pioneering figure of Third Cinema, Bengali director Satyajit Ray (1921–92) was the first major filmmaker to emerge from the Subcontinent. Influenced by the neorealists and Renoir (whom Ray met in 1949 during the shooting of Renoir's *The River*), Ray made his first film, *Pather Panchali*, independently between 1952 and 1954. Telling the story of Apu, a boy growing up in poverty in 1920s Bengal, the film was a critical success at the 1956 Cannes Film Festival, enabling Ray to make two further Apu films, *Aparajito* (1956) and *The World of Apu* (1959). Going against the grain of mainstream Bengali cinema, Ray's films are marked by their humanism, a debt to both Renoir and the poet Rabindranath Tagore, and their lyrical sensibility. Ray's later films addressed a variety of issues: the aristocracy (*The Music Room*, 1958), the plight of women (*Mahanagar*, 1963, and *Charulata*, 1964), and corruption (*The Middleman*, 1975), in addition to comedies, films for children, historical epics, ghost stories and documentaries. Ray was also the consummate auteur, not only directing his films, but often also writing, editing and shooting them, in addition to working as his own composer, casting director, costume designer and publicist. Despite being perceived as arthouse, Ray's films often did well with Bengali audiences, which found in his work a refreshing directness and beauty.

Ray's work can also be seen as a forerunner of, and major influence on, Parallel Cinema, a government-sponsored new wave based in Mumbai (or Bombay, as it was then), that began to emerge in the late 1960s. Parallel Cinema encouraged low-budget films that, like Ray's work, ran counter to the mass-market trends of Bollywood. Again, like Ray and so many other new waves in other countries, the filmmakers of the Parallel Cinema offered new ways of looking at India, new ways of thinking about old problems. Key films include Mrinal Sen's *Bhuvan Shome* (1969), Basu Chatterji's *The Whole Sky* (*Sara Akash*, 1969), Mani Kaul's *A Day's Bread* (*Uski Roti*, 1969), Kumar Shahani's *The Mirror of Illusion* (*Maya Darpan*, 1972) and Ritwik Ghatak's *Reason, Argument and Tale* (*Jukti Takko Aar Gappo*, 1974). These are films that deal with India's colonial past and tumultuous present, combining

European influences (Brecht, Bresson, Godard) with Indian ones (mythology, music, politics, cultural traditions).

CINEMA MOTEFÄVET: NEW IRANIAN CINEMA

Mention has been made earlier of the putative distinctions between 'new wave' and 'world cinema'. The Iranian New Wave, or *Cinema motefävet*, qualifies as both. (That is, if terms are important; more important, I would suggest, are the films themselves.) The founding texts of the Iranian New Wave were films such as Dariush Mehrjui's *The Cow* (*Gav*, 1969), Masoud Kimiai's *Qeysar* (1969), and Naser Taghvai's *Tranquillity in the Presence of Others* (*Aramesh dar Hozur Deegaran*, 1970). Influenced by neorealism, these films studied the lives of ordinary Iranians and culture, going so far on occasion as to criticise the regime, such as Bahman Farmanara's *Tall Shadows of the Wind* (*Sayehaye bolande bad*, 1978). Although the Shah's regime was initially wary, these films proved popular with domestic audiences and even did well internationally sometimes (*The Cow* was smuggled out of Iran for its screening at the 1971 Venice Festival, where it won the International Critics' Award). Small government subsidies became available to showcase the new films, which were usually screened at the Tehran Film Festival, the country's shop-window for its industry.

The Islamic Revolution of 1979 could have wiped the New Wave off the map altogether, were it not for the fact that the Ayatollah apparently approved of *The Cow*. In addition, the regime realised – as regimes usually do – that cinema could be used to support their aims, and set up the Farabi Cinema Foundation to provide financial support for first-time directors. Nonetheless, censorship – in the form of so-called 'Modesty Laws' – remained: violence, nudity, sex, and anything suspected of being influenced by the West, were taboo. There was an outright ban on American films. Filmmakers were forced to work around these restrictions, often opting to make films about children, who were seen to be apolitical, and representative of a hopeful future. (Films about children had also been made under the Shah.) And, with the country at war with Iraq for most of the 1980s, hope was a valuable, if scarce, commodity. But these privations and restrictions were ultimately to raise Iranian cinema from a minor 1970s new wave to a major contributor to world cinema in the 1990s. As Hamid Dabashi noted, 'In the case of Iranian cinema it was the trauma of a bloody revolution and a devastating war that ultimately coagulated a national cinema.'[491]

Arguably the two most prominent filmmakers to emerge from Iran's second (i.e. post-revolution) wave were Abbas Kiarostami and Mohsen Makhmalbaf, although both directors had already been working for some time. Kiarostami (b. 1940) made his first shorts for the Centre for the Intellectual Development of Children and Young Adults, an organisation he was attached to until 1992. His early films were either dramas featuring children as protagonists (such as his first short, *Bread and Alley* [*Nan va kuche*, 1970], about a boy returning home from the baker's with bread, only to find himself confronted by a barking dog in an alleyway), or were documentaries addressing educational issues (*Tribute to the Teachers* [*Bozorgdasht-e moallem*, 1977], *Painting* [*Rang-zani*, 1977]). Kiarostami's first feature, *The Traveller* (*Mosafer*, 1974), chronicled the attempts of a schoolboy trying to get to Tehran to see a football match against his parents' wishes.

Kiarostami came to international attention with *Where is the Friend's House?* (1987), a typically understated film about a boy trying to return his friend's homework that does for school assignments what De Sica did for bicycles.[492] After shooting, the area where the film was made was hit by an earthquake, and Kiarostami travelled there to find out if any of the cast had been affected. This in turn became the story of *And Life Goes On* (aka *Life and Nothing More/ Zendegi va digar hich*, 1992), in which an actor plays the part of Kiarostami, taking the film away from neorealism into something more self-consciously metatextual. A third film, *Through the Olive Trees* (*Zir-e derakhtan-e zeytun*, 1994), focused on the shooting of *And Life Goes On*, again using actors, turning the three films into the filmic equivalent of a Russian doll. Such a blurring of boundaries between 'fact' and 'fiction', and Kiarostami's belief that a film should be left 'incomplete', requiring the audience to be active in resolving the story, led Jean-Luc Godard to declare, 'Film begins with D W Griffith and ends with Abbas Kiarostami.'[493]

The Koker trilogy, as it became known (named after the village where *Friend's House* was shot) was not Kiarostami's sole venture into the borderlands of fact and fiction. *Close-Up* (*Namay-e nazdik*,

1990) retold the true story of a man found guilty of impersonating Kiarostami's colleague, Mohsen Makhmalbaf, and featured the actual people playing themselves (including Makhmalbaf).

Unlike Kiarostami, Mohsen Makhmalbaf (b. 1957) had been working since the early 1980s, and was the first major figure of post-revolutionary Iranian cinema. *Boycott* (*Bycote*, 1985) is an apparently autobiographical account of a man sentenced to death in pre-revolutionary Iran for his Communist sympathies. *The Cyclist* (*Bicycle-ran*, 1987), focuses on an Afghan refugee who attempts to raise money for his wife's operation by riding his bicycle in a circle for seven days and nights while local gangsters take bets on his chances of succeeding. Later films, such as *Actor* (*Honarpisheh*, 1993) and *A Moment of Innocence* (*Nun va Goldoon*, 1997), follow Kiarostami's work by blurring the boundaries between fact and fiction; the latter film also entrenched Makhmalbaf as a staunch critic of the regime in Tehran, a position he has continued to hold.

Makhmalbaf's daughter Samira (b. 1980) and wife Marzieh Meshkini (b. 1969) are also notable filmmakers. Samira's *The Apple* (*Sib*, 1997) and Marzieh's *The Day I Became a Woman* (*Roozi ke zan shodam*, 2000) are both fiercely critical of Iran, while at the same time celebrating the quiet heroism of ordinary people in extraordinary circumstances.

THE TRUTH OF THE STREET, THE TRUTH OF THE EARTH

Glauber Rocha died in 1981, at the age of 42. Although revered in Brazil, his work – and that of Cinema Novo as a whole – seems to be in eclipse elsewhere. The same could be true for a number of the films and filmmakers in this book, in fact – Fassbinder, for example. Jancsó, too, seems to be a filmmaker referred to almost exclusively in the past tense.

Bernardo Bertolucci, who remembered Glauber Rocha as 'extraordinary', complained: 'It's very sad to realise now, when you speak to young people, that nobody has heard his name.'[494] Martin Scorsese, one of cinema's great evangelists and caretakers, echoes this. He met Rocha after a screening of *Antonio das Mortes* in New York in the early 1970s. Being struck by its sympathy for the plight of the poor, he said:

I responded to the film emotionally... I responded to the truth of the street, the truth of the earth... *Antonio das Mortes* makes it very clear, there's the haves and the have-nots... [and] people who have not will be heard from, and I think this is something that there will be a day of reckoning, and I think this film shows that, and I think all of Cinema Novo I think at that time was expressing that. The whole world was going that way, and it is that way now too.[495]

What Scorsese is talking about here seems analogous to the spirit exemplified by Dogme95: in the 60s and 70s, there was commitment, both to political and artistic goals. We had films that expressed that. Now we have filmmakers (and much of the arts as a whole) hiding behind the concept of 'irony' – von Trier and his mates being prime examples – which is another way of saying no one has the courage or the nous to commit to anything other than self-promotion and a belief (however unexpressed) in the status quo. Can any of us imagine, in the twenty-first century, that, when a director dies, their funeral procession will cause gridlock – as Visconti's did in Rome in 1976? We are all hollow men in comparison, and we have the cinema to prove it. I wish this were not so. The filmmakers I have written about in this book have long been heroes of mine – all of them, literally – and I don't mind admitting that. What we sorely need now are new filmmaking heroes; the greats have long gone; it is time for new greatness, new mould breakers and risk takers who will not play anyone's corporate or political game. New visionaries, new politicians, new poets. This is the kind of cinema envisioned by Fassbinder and Glauber Rocha, by Formalists and neorealists, by Young Turks and Left Bank activists, by fugitive poets in Hungary and the Czech Republic, by lone auteurs in Turkish and Soviet prison cells, by Pinewood dissidents and Angry Young Men, by women on barricades and demonstrations, by punks on the streets of the Lower East Side.

The deaths of Fassbinder and Rocha mark the end of new waves proper and, since then, we have been living in a ghost world of echoes and shadow, an increasingly virtual existence without much in the way of coherent visions or purpose. The world, and cinema, has splintered into a hall of mirrors, playing into the hands of classical narratives and the political, economic and cultural structures that support them. What we need to break those mirrors and structures is, as Martin Scorsese correctly identifies, a 'day of reckoning'.

So, until that day comes, I would like to end with Glauber Rocha's own words from the 'Aesthetic of Hunger'. I hope they are words that will inspire anyone who has read this book who wishes to broaden the scope of their film viewing, or anyone who hopes to make a film of their own. (And, if you are going to make a film of your own, just remember: the future of filmmaking may depend on you. Or it may not. But good luck just the same. Cause trouble. Touch hearts and minds. Fassbinder and Rocha would expect nothing less.)

Cinema Novo is a phenomenon of new peoples everywhere and not a privilege of Brazil. Wherever one finds filmmakers prepared to film the truth and oppose the hypocrisy and repression of intellectual censorship there is the spirit of Cinema Novo; wherever filmmakers... place their cameras and their profession in the service of the great causes of our time there is the spirit of Cinema Novo.[496]

Amen.

SELECT BIBLIOGRAPHY

GENERAL

Linda Badley, R Barton Palmer & Steven Jay Schneider (eds), *Traditions in World Cinema* (Edinburgh: Edinburgh University Press, 2006)

Mark Cousins, *The Story of Film* (London: Pavilion Books, 2004)

Peter Cowie, *Revolution!: The Explosion of World Cinema in the 60s* (London: Faber and Faber, 2004)

Rosalind Galt and Karl Schoonover (eds), *Global Art Cinema* (Oxford: Oxford University Press, 2010)

Aristides Gazetas, *An Introduction to World Cinema* (Jefferson, NC: McFarland & Company, 2008)

Mark Kermode, *The Good, the Bad and the Multiplex: What's Wrong with Modern Movies?* (London: Random House, 2011)

Geoffrey Nowell-Smith (ed), *The Oxford History of World Cinema* (Oxford: Oxford University Press, 1997)

_____, *Making Waves: New Cinemas of the 1960s* (London and New York: Continuum, 2008)

James Phillips (ed), *Cinematic Thinking: Philosophical Approaches to the New Cinema* (Stanford, CA: Stanford University Press, 2008)

Kristin Thompson and David Bordwell, *Film History: An Introduction* (New York: McGraw-Hill, 1994; second edition, 2003)

David Thomson, *The New Biographical Dictionary of Film* (New York: Knopf, 2004)

Amos Vogel, *Film as a Subversive Art* (London: Weidenfeld & Nicolson, 1974)

GERMAN EXPRESSIONISM

Lotte Eisner, *Murnau* (London: Secker & Warburg, 1973)

_____, *The Haunted Screen: Expressionism in the German Cinema and the Influence of Max Reinhardt* (Stanford, CA: University of California Press, 1974)

_____, *Fritz Lang* (Boston: Da Capo Press, 1986)

Thomas Elsaesser, *Weimar Cinema and After: Germany's Historical Imaginary* (London: Routledge, 2000)

Siegfried Kracauer, *From Caligari to Hitler: A Psychological History of the German Film* (Princeton, NJ: Princeton University Press, 2004)

S S Prawer, *Caligari's Children: The Film as Tale of Terror* (Oxford: Oxford University Press, 1980)

Eric Rentschler (ed), *The Films of G W Pabst: An Extraterritorial Cinema* (New Brunswick, NJ: Rutgers University Press, 1990)

Dietrich Scheunemann, *Expressionist Film: New Perspectives* (New York: Camden House, 2006)

RUSSIAN/SOVIET CINEMA

David Bordwell, *The Cinema of Eisenstein* (London: Routledge, 2005)

Ian Christie & Richard Taylor (eds), *Eisenstein Rediscovered* (London: Routledge, 1993)

Alexander Dovzhenko, *Poet as Filmmaker: Selected Writings* (Cambridge, MA: MIT Press, 1973)

Sergei Eisenstein, *Film Form* (New York: Harcourt Publishers, 1969)

_____, *The Film Sense* (New York: Harcourt Publishers, 1969)

_____, *Notes of a Film Director* (Amsterdam: Fredonia Books, 2003)

David C Gillespie, *Early Soviet Cinema: Innovation, Ideology and Propaganda* (London: Wallflower Press, 2000)

Lev Kuleshov, *Kuleshov on Film: Writings by Lev Kuleshov* (Stanford: University of California Press, 1992)

George O Liber, *Alexander Dovzhenko: A Life in Soviet Film* (London: British Film Institute, 2000)

Mike O'Mahony, *Sergei Eisenstein* (London: Reaktion Books, 2008)

Vsevolod Pudovkin, *Pudovkin on Film* (Calcutta: Seagull Books, 1990)

_____, *Selected Essays* (Calcutta: Seagull Books, 2006)

_____, *Film Technique and Film Acting – The Cinema Writings of V I Pudovkin* (Read Books, 2007)

Amy Sargeant, *Vsevolod Pudovkin: Classic Films of the Soviet Avant-garde* (London: I B Tauris, 2001)

Richard Taylor (ed), *The Eisenstein Reader* (London: British Film Institute, 1998)

Richard Taylor & Ian Christie (eds), *The Film Factory: Russian and Soviet Cinema in Documents, 1896–1939* (London: Routledge, 2004)

_____, *Inside the Film Factory: New Approaches to Russian and Soviet Cinema* (London: Routledge, 2004)

Emma Widdis, *Alexander Medvedkin* (London: I B Tauris, 2005)

NEOREALISM

Roy Armes, Patterns of Realism: A Study of Italian Neo-Realist Cinema (London: Tantivy Press, 1971)

Peter Bondanella, *The Films of Roberto Rossellini* (Cambridge: Cambridge University Press, 1993

_____, *Italian Cinema: From Neorealism to the Present* (New York: Continuum, 2001)

David Overbey (ed), *Springtime in Italy: A Reader in Neorealism* (North Haven, CT: Archon Books, 1978)

Vincent Rocchio, *Cinema of Anxiety: A Psychoanalysis of Italian Neorealism* (Austin: University of Texas Press, 2000)

Laura E Ruberto & Kristi M Wilson (eds), *Italian Neorealism and Global Cinema* (Detroit: Wayne State University Press, 2007)

Mark Shiel, *Italian Neorealism: Rebuilding the Cinematic City* (London: Wallflower Press, 2005)

Christopher Wagstaff, *Italian Neorealist Cinema: An Aesthetic Approach* (Toronto: University of Toronto Press, 2007)

FRENCH NEW WAVE

Richard Abel, *French Film Theory and Criticism: A History/Anthology, 1907–39* (2 vols) (Princeton, NJ: Princeton University Press, 1988)

Don Allen, *Finally Truffaut*, (London: Secker & Warburg, 1985)

Roy Armes, *The Films of Alain Robbe-Grillet* (Amsterdam: John Benjamins, 1981)

Guy Austin, *Claude Chabrol* (Manchester: Manchester University Press, 1999)

André Bazin, *What is Cinema?* (2 Vols) (Stanford: University of California Press, 2004)

Ronald Bergan (ed), *François Truffaut: Interviews* (Jackson, MS: University Press of Mississippi, 2008)

Bert Cardullo (ed), *Interviews with Eric Rohmer* (Gosport: Chaplin Books, 2012)

Anthony N Fragola and Roch C Smith, *The Erotic Dream Machine: Interviews with Alain Robbe-Grillet on His Films* (Carbondale, IL: Southern Illinois University Press, 1992)

Jean-Luc Godard, *Godard on Godard* (London: Secker & Warburg, 1972)

Peter Graham & Ginette Vincendeau (eds), *The French New Wave: Critical Landmarks* (London: British Film Institute, 2009)

Naomi Greene, *The French New Wave: A New Look* (London: Wallflower Press, 2007)

Fiona Handyside (ed), *Eric Rohmer: Interviews* (Jackson, MS: University Press of Mississippi, 2013)

Annette Insdorf, *François Truffaut* (Cambridge: Cambridge University Press, 1995)

Jacob Leigh, *The Cinema of Eric Rohmer: Irony, Imagination, and the Social World* (New York and London: Continuum, 2012)

Catherine Lupton, *Chris Marker: Memories of the Future* (London: Reaktion Books, 2004)

Michel Marie, *The French New Wave: An Artistic School* (Oxford: Blackwell, 2003)

James Monaco, *The New Wave: Truffaut, Godard, Chabrol, Rohmer, Rivette: 30th Anniversary Edition* (Sag Harbor, NY: Harbor Electronic Publishing 2004)

Richard Neupert, *A History of the French New Wave* (Madison, WI: University of Wisconsin Press, 2003)

John Phillips, *Alain Robbe-Grillet* (Manchester: Manchester University Press, 2011)

Eric Rohmer, *Six Moral Tales* (London: Lorrimer Publishing, 1980)

Jonathan Rosenbaum (ed), *Rivette: Texts and Interviews* (London: British Film Institute, 1977)

P E Salles-Gomez, *Jean Vigo* (London: Faber and Faber, 1998)

Alison Smith, *Agnès Varda* (Manchester: Manchester University Press, 1998)

David Sterritt (ed), *Jean-Luc Godard: Interviews* (Jackson, MS: University Press of Mississippi, 1998)

_____, *The Films of Jean-Luc Godard: Seeing the Invisible* (Cambridge: Cambridge University Press, 1999)

Michael Temple, *Jean Vigo* (Manchester: Manchester University Press, 2011)

François Truffaut, *The Films in My Life* (Boston: Da Capo Press, 1994)

_____, *Hitchcock* (London: Paladin Books, 1986)

_____, *Letters* (London: Faber and Faber, 1990)

William F Van Wert, *The Film Career of Alain Robbe-Grillet*, (Boston: G K Hall & Co, 1977)

Chris Wiegand, *French New Wave* (Harpenden: Pocket Essentials, 2007)

Alan Williams, *Republic of Images: A History of French Filmmaking* (Cambridge, MA: Harvard University Press, 1992)

Emma Wilson, *Alain Resnais* (Manchester: Manchester University Press, 2006)

ITALIAN CINEMA

Michelangelo Antonioni, *That Bowling Alley on the Tiber* (New York: Oxford University Press, 1986)

Peter Bondanella, *The Cinema of Federico Fellini* (Princeton, NJ: Princeton University Press, 1992)

_____, *Italian Cinema: From Neorealism to the Present* (London: Continuum, 2001)

_____, *The Films of Federico Fellini*, (Cambridge: Cambridge University Press, 2002)

_____, *A History of Italian Cinema* (London: Continuum, 2009)

Peter Brunette, *The Films of Michelangelo Antonioni* (Cambridge: Cambridge University Press, 1998)

Robin Buss, *Italian Films* (London: Batsford, 1989)

Seymour Chatman, *Antonioni, or The Surface of the World* (Berkeley: University of California Press, 1985)

Costanzo Costantini (ed), *Fellini on Fellini* (London: Faber & Faber, 1995)

Federico Fellini, *Comments on Film*, (Fresno, CA: California State University Press, 1988)

_____, *The Book of Dreams* (New York: Rizzoli, 2008).

Naomi Greene, *Pier Paolo Pasolini: Cinema as Heresy* (Princeton, NJ: Princeton University Press, 1990)

Anna Keel and Christian Strich (eds), *Fellini on Fellini* (Boston: Da Capo Press, 1996)

Tullio Kezich, *Fellini: His Life and Work* (London: Faber and Faber, 2006)

Pier Paolo Pasolini, *Heretical Empiricism* (Washington DC: New Academia Publishing, 2005)

_____, *The Ragazzi* (Manchester: Carcanet Press, 2007)

_____, *A Violent Life* (Manchester: Carcanet Press, 2007)

Sam Rohdie, *Antonioni* (London: British Film Institute, 1990)

Patrick Rumble, *Allegories of Contamination: Pier Paolo Pasolini's 'Trilogy of Life'* (Toronto: University of Toronto Press, 1996)

Laurence Schifano, *Luchino Visconti: The Flames of Passion* (London: Collins, 1990)

Gaia Servadio, *Luchino Visconti: A Biography* (London: Weidenfeld & Nicolson, 1981)

Geoffrey Nowell-Smith, *Luchino Visconti* (London: BFI Publishing, 2003)

Geoffrey Nowell-Smith, James Hay and Gianni Volpi (eds), *The Companion to Italian Cinema* (London: Cassell/BFI, 1996)

Monica Stirling, *A Screen of Time: A Study of Luchino Visconti* (New York: Harcourt Brace Jovanovich, 1979)

John Caldwell-Stubbs, *Fellini as Auteur: Seven Aspects of his Films* (Carbondale, IL: Southern Illinois University Press, 2006)

Carlo Testa (ed), *Poet of Civic Courage: The Films of Francesco Rosi* (Trowbridge: Flicks Books, 1996)

Claretta Micheletti Tonetti, *Luchino Visconti* (London: Columbus Books, 1987)

_____, *Bernardo Bertolucci: The Cinema of Ambiguity* (Boston: Twayne Publishers, 1995)

Wim Wenders, *My Time with Antonioni* (London: Faber and Faber, 2000)

Mary P Wood, *Italian Cinema* (London: Berg Publishers, 2005)

BRITISH NEW WAVE

Lindsay Anderson, *Never Apologise: The Collected Writings*, Paul Ryan (ed), (London: Plexus Publishing, 2004)

_____, *The Diaries*, Paul Sutton (ed), (London: Methuen, 2004)

Ian Buruma, *Conversations with John Schlesinger* (New York: Random House, 2006)

Bryan Forbes, *A Divided Life: Memoirs* (London: William Heinemann, 1992)

Colin Gardner, *Karel Reisz* (Manchester: Manchester University Press, 2006)

Erik Hedling, *Lindsay Anderson: Maverick Film Maker* (London: Cassell, 1998)

Gavin Lambert, *Mainly About Lindsay Anderson – A Memoir* (London: Faber and Faber, 2000)

Samantha Lay, *British Social Realism: From Documentary to Brit Grit* (London: Wallflower Press, 2002)

Tony Richardson, *Long Distance Runner: A Memoir* (London: Faber & Faber, 1993)

David Sherwin, *Going Mad in Hollywood: And Life with Lindsay Anderson* (Harmondsworth: Penguin, 1997)

Neil Sinyard, *Jack Clayton* (Manchester: Manchester University Press, 2000)

B F Taylor, *The British New Wave: A Certain Tendency?* (Manchester: Manchester University Press, 2006)

Alexander Walker, *Hollywood, England: The British Film Industry in the Sixties* (London: Michael Joseph, 1974)

James M Welsh and John C Tibbetts, *The Cinema of Tony Richardson: Essays and Interviews* (Albany, NY: State University Press of New York, 1999)

CZECH NEW WAVE

Peter Hames, *The Czechoslovak New Wave* (London: Wallflower Press, 2005)

_____, *Czech and Slovak Cinema: Theme and Tradition* (Edinburgh: Edinburgh University Press, 2009)

Robert Buchar, *Czech New Wave Filmmakers in Interviews* (Jefferson, NC: McFarland & Co, 2003)

Antonín J Liehm, *Closely Watched Films: The Czechoslovak Experience* (White Plains, NY: International Arts and Sciences Press, 1974)

Josef Škvorecký, *All the Bright Young Men and Women: A Personal History of the Czech Cinema* (Toronto: Peter Martin Associates, 1971)

Miloš Forman and Jan Novák, *Turnaround: A Memoir* (London: Faber and Faber, 1994)

EASTERN EUROPE

Paul Coates, *The Story of the Lost Reflection: The Alienation of the Image in Western and Polish Cinema* (London: Verso, 1985)

John Cunningham, *Hungarian Cinema: From Coffee House to Multiplex* (London: Wallflower Press, 2004)

Peter Hames (ed), *The Cinema of Central Europe* (London: Wallflower Press, 2004)

Dina Iordanova, *Cinema of Flames: Balkan Film, Culture and the Media* (London: British Film Institute, 2001)

_____, *Cinema of the Other Europe: Industry and Artistry of the East Central European Film* (London: Wallflower Press, 2003)

Sean Martin, *Andrei Tarkovsky* (Harpenden: Kamera Books, 2011)

Ewa Mazierska, *Roman Polanski: The Cinema of a Cultural Traveller* (London: I B Tauris, 2007)

James Morrison, *Roman Polanski* (Urbana and Chicago: University of Illinois Press, 2007)

John Orr & Elżbieta Ostrowska (eds), *The Cinema of Roman Polanski: Dark Spaces of the World* (London: Wallflower Press, 2006)

Graham Petrie, *History Must Answer to Man: The Contemporary Hungarian Cinema* (Budapest: Corvina Books, 1978)

Roman Polanski, *Roman by Polanski* (London: Heinemann, 1984)

Christopher Sandford, *Polanski* (London: Century, 2007)

Andrei Tarkovsky, *Sculpting in Time* (London: The Bodley Head, 1986)

Jeanne Vronskaya, *Young Soviet Filmmakers* (London: Allen & Unwin, 1972)

Andrzej Wajda, *Double Vision: My Life in Film* (London: Faber and Faber, 1990)

Josephine Woll, *Real Images: Soviet Cinema and the Thaw* (London: I B Tauris, 2000)

GREEK & BALKAN CINEMA

Costa-Gavras, Franco Solinas et al (screenplay translated by Brooke Leveque; documents translated by Raymond Rosenthal), *State of Siege* (London: Plexus Publishing, 1973)

Andrew Horton (ed), *Theo Angelopoulos: The Last Modernist* (Trowbridge: Flicks Books, 1997)

_____, *The Films of Theo Angelopoulos: A Cinema of Contemplation* (Princeton: Princeton University Press, 1997)

Lorraine Mortimer, *Terror and Joy: The Films of Dušan Makavejev* (Minneapolis, MN: University of Minnesota Press, 2009)

Michael J Stoil, *Balkan Cinema: Evolution after the Revolution* (Ann Arbor, MI: UMI Research Press, 1982)

DOCUMENTARY

Patricia Aufderheide, *Documentary Film: A Very Short Introduction* (New York: Oxford University Press, 2008)

Erik Barnouw, *Documentary: A History of the Non-Fiction Film* (New York: Oxford University Press, 1993)

Keith Beattie, *Humphrey Jennings* (Manchester: Manchester University Press, 2010)

Sarah Cooper, *Chris Marker* (Manchester: Manchester University Press, 2008)

Timothy Corrigan, *The Essay Film: From Montaigne, After Marker* (Oxford: Oxford University Press, 2011)

Forsyth Hardy (ed), *Grierson on Documentary* (London: Faber and Faber, 1979)

Randolph Lewis, *Emile de Antonio: Radical Filmmaker in Cold War America* (Madison, WI and London: University of Wisconsin Press, 2000)

Philip C Logan, *Humphrey Jennings and British Documentary Film: A Reassessment* (Farnham: Ashgate, 2011)

Kevin Macdonald & Mark Cousins, *Imagining Reality: The Faber Book of the Documentary* (London: Faber and Faber, 1997)

Laura Rascaroli, *The Personal Camera: Subjective Cinema and the Essay Film* (London: Wallflower Press, 2009)

Charles Warren (ed), *Beyond Document: Essays on Nonfiction Film* (Hanover, NH: University Press of New England, 1996)

AMERICAN CINEMA

Christopher Beach, *The Films of Hal Ashby* (Detroit: Wayne State University Press, 2009)

Peter Biskind, *Easy Riders, Raging Bulls: How the Sex 'n' Drugs 'n' Rock 'n' Roll Generation Saved Hollywood* (London: Bloomsbury, 2001)

Ray Carney (ed), *Cassavetes on Cassavetes* (London: Faber and Faber, 2001)

_____, *Shadows* (London: British Film Institute, 2001)

Drew Casper, *Hollywood Film 1963–1976: Years of Revolution and Reaction* (Malden, MA and Oxford: Wiley-Blackwell, 2011)

Ian Christie & David Thompson, *Scorsese on Scorsese* (London: Faber & Faber, 2003)

Peter Cowie, *Coppola* (London: Faber & Faber, 1989)

Nick Dawson, *Being Hal Ashby: Life of a Hollywood Rebel* (Lexington, KY: University Press of Kentucky, 2009)

_____ (ed), *Hal Ashby: Interviews* (Jackson, MS: University Press of Mississippi, 2010)

Marshall Fine, *Accidental Genius: How John Cassavetes Invented American Independent Film* (New York: Miramax Books, 2005)

Mark Harris, *Scenes from a Revolution: The Birth of the New Hollywood* (Edinburgh: Canongate, 2009)

Sally Kline (ed), *George Lucas Interviews* (Jackson, MS: University Press of Mississippi, 1999)

Vincent LoBrutto, *Martin Scorsese: A Biography* (Westport, CT: Praeger, 2008)

Gene D Phillips & Rodney Hill, *Francis Ford Coppola: Interviews* (Jackson, MS: University Press of Mississippi, 2004)

Dale Pollock, *Skywalking: The Life and Films of George Lucas* (London: Elm Tree Books, 1983)

Michael Pye & Linda Myles, *The Movie Brats: How the Film Generation Took Over Hollywood* (New York: Holt, Rhinehart & Winston, 1979)

Michael Schumacher, *Francis Ford Coppola: A Filmmaker's Life* (London: Bloomsbury, 1999)

P Adams Sitney, *Visionary Film: The American Avant-Garde 1943–1978* (New York: Oxford University Press, 1979)

NEW GERMAN CINEMA

Ursula Böser, *The Art of Seeing, the Art of Listening: The Politics of Representation in the Work of Jean-Marie Straub and Danièle Huillet* (New York: Peter Lang, 2004)

Barton Byg, *Landscapes of Resistance: The German Films of Danièle Huillet and Jean-Marie Straub* (Berkeley: University of California Press, 1995)

Paul Coates, *The Gorgon's Gaze: German Cinema, Expressionism, and the Image of Horror* (Cambridge: Cambridge University Press, 1991)

Timothy Corrigan (ed.), *The Films of Werner Herzog: Between Mirage and History* (London: Routledge, 1986)

_____, *New German Film: The Displaced Image* (Bloomington, IN: Indiana University Press, 1994)

Paul Cronin (ed), *Herzog on Herzog* (London: Faber and Faber, 2002)

Thomas Elsaesser, *New German Cinema: A History* (Basingstoke: Macmillan, 1989)

_____, *Fassbinder's Germany: History, Identity, Subject* (Amsterdam: Amsterdam University Press, 1996)

Rainer Werner Fassbinder, *Plays* (New York: Performing Arts Journals, 1987)

_____, *The Anarchy of the Imagination: Interviews, Essays, Notes* (Baltimore, MD: Johns Hopkins University Press, 1992)

James Franklin, *New German Cinema: From Oberhausen to Hamburg* (Boston: Twayne, 1983)

Alan Greenberg, *Every Night the Trees Disappear: Werner Herzog and the Making of Heart of Glass* (Chicago: Chicago Review Press, 2012)

Ronald Hayman, *Fassbinder: Film Maker* (London: Weidenfeld & Nicolson, 1984)

Werner Herzog, *Of Walking in Ice* (New York: Tanam Press, 1980)

_____, *Screenplays* (New York: Tanam Press, 1980)

Robert Katz & Peter Berling, *Love is Colder Than Death: The Life and Times of Rainer Werner Fassbinder* (London: Paladin Books, 1989)

Julia Knight, *New German Cinema: Images of a Generation* (London: Wallflower Press, 2004)

_____, *Women and the New German Cinema* (London: Verso, 1992)

Juliane Lorenz, *Rainer Werner Fassbinder* (New York: Abrams, 1997)

_____ (ed), *Chaos as Usual: Conversations about Rainer Werner Fassbinder* (Milwaukee, WI: Applause Theatre Books, 1998)

Peter C Lutze, *Alexander Kluge: The Last Modernist* (Detroit: Wayne State University Press, 1998)

Solveig Olsen, *Hans Jürgen Syberberg and His Film of Wagner's Parsifal* (Lanham, MD: University Press of America, 2006)

Rachel Palfreyman, *Edgar Reitz's Heimat* (London: Peter Lang, 2000)

Brad Prager, *The Cinema of Werner Herzog: Aesthetic Ecstasy and Truth* (London: Wallflower Press, 2007)

_____ (ed), *A Companion to Werner Herzog* (Oxford: Wiley-Blackwell, 2012)

Tony Rayns (ed), *Fassbinder* (revised and expanded edition; London: British Film Instiute, 1980)

Eric Rentschler (ed), *West German Filmmakers on Film: Visions & Voices* (New York: Holmes & Meier, 1987)

Richard Roud, *Jean-Marie Straub* (London: Secker and Warburg, 1971)

John Sandford, *The New German Cinema*, (London: Eyre Methuen, 1981)

John Sandford, Susan Sontag, Betsy Erkkila & Hans-Jürgen Syberberg, *Syberberg: A Filmmaker from Germany* (London: British Film Institute, 1992)

Hans-Jürgen Syberberg, with a preface by Susan Sontag, *Hitler: A Film from Germany*, (Manchester: Carcanet Press, 1982)

Christian Braad Thomsen, *Fassbinder: The Life and Work of a Provocative Genius* (London: Faber and Faber, 1999)

DOGME

Stig Bjorkman, *Trier on von Trier* (London: Faber and Faber, 2004)

Mette Hjort and Scott MacKenzie (eds), *Purity and Provocation: Dogma 95* (London: British Film Institute, 2003)

Richard Kelly, *The Name of this Book is Dogme95* (London: Faber and Faber, 2000)

Jan Lumholdt, *Lars von Trier: Interviews* (Jackson, MS: University Press of Mississippi, 2003)

John Rockwell, *The Idiots* (London: British Film Institute, 2003)

Shari Roman, *Digital Babylon: Hollywood, Indiewood and Dogme 95* (Los Angeles: Lone Eagle Publishing, 2001)

Jack Stevenson, *Dogme Uncut: Lars von Trier. Thomas Vinterberg, and the Gang that Took on Hollywood* (Solana Beach, CA: Santa Monica Press, 2004)

_____, *Lars von Trier* (London: British Film Institute, 2002)

IRANIAN CINEMA

Hamid Dabashi, *Close Up: Iranian Cinema, Past, Present and Future* (London: Verso, 2001)

_____, *Makhmalbaf at Large: The Making of a Rebel Filmmaker* (London: I B Tauris, 2008)

_____, *Conversations with Mohsen Makhmalbaf* (Calcutta: Seagull Books, 2010)

Farhang Erfani, *Iranian Cinema and Philosophy: Shooting Truth* (New York: Palgrave Macmillan, 2012)

Alberto Elena, *The Cinema of Abbas Kiarostami* (London: Saqi Books, 2005)

Lloyd Ridgeon, *Makhmalbaf's Broken Mirror: The Socio-political Significance of Modern Iranian Cinema* (Durham: University of Durham, Centre for Middle Eastern and Islamic Studies, 2000)

Richard Tapper, *The New Iranian Cinema: Politics, Representation and Identity* (London: I B Tauris, 2002)

AFRICAN CINEMA

Roy Armes, *African Filmmaking: North and South of the Sahara* (Edinburgh: Edinburgh University Press, 2006)

_____, *Third World Filmmaking and the West* (Berkeley: University of California Press, 1987)

Lizbeth Malkmus & Roy Armes, *Arab and African Filmmaking* (London: Zed Books, 1991)

David Murphy & Patrick Williams, *Postcolonial African Cinema: Ten Directors* (Manchester: Manchester University Press, 2007)

JAPANESE & ASIAN CINEMA

Chris Berry and Feii Lu (eds), *Island on the Edge: Taiwan New Cinema and After* (Hong Kong: Hong Kong University Press, 2005)

Audie Bock, *Japanese Film Directors* (Tokyo and New York: Kodansha International, 1985)

David Bordwell, *Planet Hong Kong: Popular Cinema and the Art of Entertainment* (Cambridge, MA: Harvard University Press, 2000)

Bert Cardullo (ed), *Satyajit Ray: Interviews* (Jackson, MS: University Press of Mississippi, 2007)

_____, *Out of Asia: The Films of Akira Kurosawa, Satyajit Ray, Abbas Kiarostami, and Zhang Yimou; Essays and Interviews* (Newcastle: Cambridge Scholars Publishing, 2008)

David Carter, *East Asian Cinema* (Harpenden: Kamera Books, 2007)

Pak Tong Cheuk, *Hong Kong New Wave Cinema (1978–2000)* (Bristol: Intellect Books, 2008)

David Desser, *Eros Plus Massacre: An Introduction to the Japanese New Wave Cinema* (Bloomington, IN: Indiana University Press, 1988)

K Moti Gokulsing and Wimal Dissanayake (eds), *Routledge Handbook of Indian Cinemas* (London: Routledge, 2013)

Guo-Juin Hong, *Taiwan Cinema: A Contested Nation on Screen* (New York: Palgrave Macmillan, 2011)

Anthony Leong, *Korean Cinema: The New Hong Kong* (Bloomington, IN: Trafford Publishing, 2003)

Nagisa Oshima, *Cinema, Censorship, and the State: The Writings of Nagisa Oshima, 1956–1978*, Annette Michelson (ed), (Cambridge, MA and London: MIT Press, 1992)

Satyajit Ray, *My Years with Apu* (London: Faber & Faber, 1997)

Donald Richie, *Japanese Cinema: Film Style and National Character* (London: Secker and Warburg, 1972)

_____, *Japanese Cinema: An Introduction* (Oxford, New York and Hong Kong: Oxford University Press, 1990)

Jerome Silbergeld, *China Into Film: Frames of Reference in Contemporary Chinese Cinema* (London: Reaktion Books, 1999)

Isolde Standish, *A New History of Japanese Cinema: A Century of Narrative Film* (New York: Continuum, 2005)

Julian Stringer & Chi-Yun Shin (eds), *New Korean Cinema* (Edinburgh: Edinburgh University Press, 2005)

Stephen Teo, *Hong Kong Cinema: The Extra Dimensions* (London: British Film Institute, 1997)

AUSTRALIA/NEW ZEALAND

Ian Conrich and Stuart Murray (eds), *New Zealand Filmmakers* (Detroit: Wayne State University Press, 2007)

Brian McFarlane, *Australian Cinema 1970–1985* (London: Secker & Warburg, 1987)

Tom O'Regan, *Australian National Cinema* (London: Routledge, 1996)

CINEMA NOVO/LATIN AMERICAN CINEMA/THIRD CINEMA

Julianne Burton, *The New Latin American Cinema: An Annotated Bibliography 1960–1980* (New York: Smyrna Press, 1983)

Michael Chanan, *Cuban Cinema* (Minneapolis, MN: University of Minnesota Press, 2004)

Coco Fusco (ed), *Reviewing Histories: Selections from New Latin American Cinema* (Buffalo, NY: Hallwalls Contemporary Arts Center 1987)

Anthony Guneratine & Wimal Dissanayake (eds), *Rethinking Third Cinema* (London and New York: Routledge, 2003)

Burnes Saint Patrick Hollyman (ed), *Glauber Rocha and the Cinema Novo in Brazil: A Study of His Films and Critical Writings* (London: Taylor & Francis, 1982)

Randal Johnson & Robert Stam (eds), *Brazilian Cinema* (New York: Columbia University Press 1982; Expanded edition 1995)

Michael T Martin (ed), *New Latin American Cinema Vol 1: Theory, Practices, and Transcontinental Articulations* (Detroit: Wayne State University Press, 1997)

_____, *New Latin American Cinema Vol 2: Studies of National Cinemas* (Detroit: Wayne State University Press, 1997)

Lúcia Nagib, *Brazil on Screen: Cinema Novo, New Cinema, Utopia* (London: I B Tauris, 2007)

Other Cinema (ed), *The Other Cinema Film Catalogue* (London: The Other Cinema/ BFI, 1975)

Jim Pines & Paul Willemen (eds), *Questions of Third Cinema* (London: British Film Insitute, 1989)

Mike Wayne, *Political Film: The Dialectics of Third Cinema* (London and Sterling, VA: Pluto Press, 2001)

NOTES

Epigraphs: Rivette: Unifrance press release, June 1970, quoted in James Monaco, *The New Wave*, p 313; Tarr: Interview from http://home.earthlink.net/~steevee/bela. html, accessed 28/11/07; Godard: cited by J Hoberman, 'Tout va Bien Revisited' (2005), http://www.criterion.com/current/posts/356-tout-va-bien-revisited, accessed 23/11/12; Vertov: http://sensesofcinema.com/2003/great-directors/vertov/, accessed 23/11/12.

1   For instance, George Lucas's *The Empire Strikes Back*, which most would regard as a Hollywood studio film, is actually an independent, i.e. a film that did not get made through a studio.

2   For more on the technical innovations of the late 50s, see Cowie, pp 55–58.

3   J P Telotte, 'German Expressionism: A Cinematic/Cultural Problem', *Traditions in World Cinema*, p 15.

4   Other influences included the 19th century Romantics, and German folklore.

5   Lotte Eisner, *The Haunted Screen*, p 129.

6   In other (written) versions of the legend, the creature is disabled by the removal of a letter from its forehead, changing *EMETH* (truth) into *METH* (death).

7   After three films in Hollywood – *Sunrise*, the now-lost *Four Devils* and *City Girl* – Murnau yearned for independence, and to this end went into partnership with Robert Flaherty, making *Tabu* (1931) with him in the South Pacific. For more on Flaherty, see Chapter 7.

8   As an indicator of how fluid some of Eisenstein's concepts were, this can also be seen as an example of intellectual montage.

9   Yuri Tsvian, 'Russian Symbolist Culture and *October*', in Ian Christie and Richard Taylor, *Eisenstein Rediscovered*, pp 97–98. Of course, the feeling that the peacock could not possibly equal *just* vanity could be a classic case of overenthusiastic scholars misinterpreting a misinterpretation.

10   A number of people who had taken part in the revolution were conscripted to appear in *October* as extras. One of them remarked that the actual revolution had done less damage to the Winter Palace than Eisenstein's filmed reconstruction.

11   An extraordinary thing to say, we might think from this distance in time, yet there was an odd admiration by the Soviets for America during the 1920s. The Selznick quote is from Helen Grace, 'Battleship Potemkin', from http://www. sensesofcinema.com/contents/cteq/00/4/potemkin.html, accessed 27/11/07.

12 The term 'socialist classicism' is perhaps more accurate, as the staple narratives of this period had little to do with the everyday experience of the ordinary people. Indeed, socialist realism has been summed up as 'girl meets tractor'.

13 Mark Shiel, *Italian Neorealism: Rebuilding the Cinematic City*, p 54. Church and state are rarely shown in a flattering light in neorealist films, with the possible exception of the monastery episode in Rossellini's *Paisan*.

14 Welles, interviewed in 1960. Cited in http://www.asharperfocus.com/shoeshine.html, accessed 23/11/12.

15 De Sica, interviewed in 1954, quoted in Christopher Wagstaff, *Italian Neorealist Cinema*, p 316.

16 André Bazin, *What is Cinema?* Vol 1, p 50.

17 As he was described by Jean Cocteau. Quoted in James Monaco, *The New Wave*, p 15.

18 Astruc did not invent auteur theory out of thin air: the concept was almost as old as cinema itself. George Méliès wrote about the necessity of the filmmaker being 'the author, director, designer, and often actor if he wants to obtain a unified whole' as early as 1906. The idea reappeared in the writings of Louis Delluc and others in the years following the First World War. See Richard Abel, *French Film Theory and Criticism 1907–1939, Vol I 1907–1929*, pp 41 (Méliès) & 203 (Delluc).

19 Le Festival du Film Maudit, whose name translates more literally as the Festival of Ill-fated, or Cursed, Films. It ran from 28 July to 5 August 1949.

20 Richard Neupert, 'The French New Wave', *Traditions in World Cinema*, p 41.

21 Don Allen, *Finally Truffaut*, p 19.

22 Truffaut, *Hitchcock*, p 537.

23 He did in fact return to genre with his last film, *Finally Sunday* (*Vivement Dimanche!*, 1983), another noir.

24 The title refers to a photographic filter that enables night scenes to be shot during the day, hence 'day for night', or, as the title literally translates, 'American night', as the device was frequently identified with Hollywood movies.

25 Kristin Thompson and David Bordwell, *Film History: An Introduction*, p 525.

26 Originally published in *Gazette du Cinéma* 3, September 1950, the essay is reprinted in *Godard on Godard*, pp 16–17.

27 Quoted in *Godard on Godard*, p 16.

28 David Sterritt, *The Films of Jean-Luc Godard: Seeing the Invisible*, p 37.

29 *Cosmo Jones, Crime Smasher* (James Tinling, 1943); *I Killed That Man* (Phil Rosen, 1941); *Suspense* (Frank Tuttle, 1946).

30 As James Monaco notes, 'If Truffaut had made the film... *A bout de souffle* would have paid much more attention to character; it would have had an altogether quieter, softer, and more compassionate mood. Yet the conceptual structure so evident in the final film is clearly present in Truffaut's scenario.' Monaco, p 118.

31 Neupert, p. 210.

32 Ibid, p. 211.

33 Raoul Coutard, 'Statements: Raoul Coutard', in *Breathless*, ed Dudley Andrew (Rutgers University Press, 1995), quoted in Neupert, p 210.

34 Neupert, p 211.

35 The detractors in this case being Claude Autant-Lara, who had been one of Truffaut's targets in his groundbreaking 1954 essay, 'A Certain Tendency of the French Cinema', and the critic Robert Benayoun, who was writing for the rival magazine, *Positif*. See Autant-Lara, 'La nouvelle vague: un préjudice énorme', in *La nouvelle vague 25 ans après*, edited by Jean-Luc Douin. Paris: Les éditions du Cerf, 1983; pp 203–207; Benayoun, Robert, 'Breathless', *Positif* 46 (June 1962), p 27.

36 Sterritt draws numerous parallels between Godard and the Beats in his book *The Films of Jean-Luc Godard: Seeing the Invisible*, particularly in Chapter 2.

37 Neupert, p 214.

38 Ibid.

39 Ibid, p 215.

40 Ibid, p 216.

41 Ibid.

42 Ibid, p 211.

43 Monaco, *The New Wave*, p 98.

44 Quoted in Monaco, p 273.

45 Quoted in Monaco, p 274. The quote comes from the 1970 interview from *Positif* (see below).

46 Chabrol relates the delights of working with Colonel Rémy in Michel Ciment, Gérard Legrand and Jean-Paul Török, 'Claude Chabrol Interviewed', *Positif*, 115, Winter 1970–1971. As for directing whilst 'comprehensively refreshed' (to use Bill Bryson's term), Chabrol was famous for his love of good food and wine – and the general bonhomie of his shoots – and was said to have chosen Alsace for the location of one of the Decameron films (*Ten Days' Wonder*) simply because he wanted to sample the local cuisine. In the case of *La Ligne de démarcation*, however, it may well have been the pressure of working with the Colonel as much as the local food and wine. See Austin, p 6. For those wishing to conduct further research into the areas of directing and alcohol, see the chapter 'Drunk or Sober?' in Andrzej Wajda's *Double Vision: My Life in Film*.

47 Neupert, p 160.

48 Guy Austin, *Claude Chabrol*, p 5.

49 Neupert, p 133.

50 Monaco, *The New Wave*, p 21.

51 In keeping with the biographical uncertainty surrounding Rohmer, the novel's title is sometimes given as *Elizabeth*.

52 Graham Petrie, 'Eric Rohmer: An Interview', *Film Quarterly*, Summer 1971.

53 Apart from the cook, who received a small fee and, apparently, served cast and crew the same meal every day (minestrone) during the shoot. She also took a small role in the film.

54 Eric Rohmer, preface to *Six Moral Tales* (novelisation).

55 Unifrance press release, June 1970. At this point, Rivette had only made three features, and had just started editing his fourth. He finally did make ten films, the tenth being *L'amour par Terre* (1984). (At the time of writing, he has made around 20 altogether, depending on whether you count the shortened versions of some of his films, such as *Out One: Spectre* and *La Belle Noiseuse: Divertimento* as separate works, and also whether his two-part film about Joan of Arc, *Jeanne la Pucelle*, is really two films, or one long one.)

56 Pierre Marcabru, review of *Paris nous appartient*, *Combat*, 16 December 1961.

57 Carlos Clemens & Edgardo Cozarinsky, 'Jacques Rivette' (interview), *Sight and Sound*, Autumn 1974.

58 At Le Havre, on 9 and 10 September 1971. Rivette didn't have enough money to get a new print made, so the cutting copy was screened. The film went unseen for many years, until finally being revived in 2006.

59 Losing, in the process, as Rivette later described, 'ten-minute takes of the actors... cracking up rather spectacularly'. Interview by Carlos Clarens, Edgardo Cozarinsky, *Sight and Sound*, Vol 43, No 4, Autumn 1974, pp 195–8.

60 The film was to have starred Jeanne Moreau and been set in the world of *fin de siècle* Parisian theatre.

61 David Thomson, *Biographical Dictionary of Film*, p 761.

62 Resnais cut Varda's first feature, *La pointe courte*, and Truffaut's first short, *Une Visite* (1955).

63 Alison Smith, *Agnès Varda*, p 100.

64 Fragola/Smith, *The Erotic Dream Machine*, p 5.

65 M B White, 'Marguerite Duras', Film Reference.com. http://www.filmreference.com/Directors-Du-Fr/Duras-Marguerite.html, accessed 11/08/09.

66 Ibid

67 Resnais, quoted in *Traditions in World Cinema*, p 48.

68 Richard Neupert, 'The French New Wave', *Traditions in World Cinema*, p 48.

69 See Bondanella, *Italian Cinema: From Neorealism to the Present*, pp 142–44 and Mary P Wood, *Italian Cinema*, pp 14–21.

70 Truffaut commented that the term 'new wave' 'never really corresponded to reality in the sense that... there was an association of French directors who got together regularly and had a plan, a common aesthetic, when in fact there was never anything like that and it was all a fiction, made up from those outside [i.e. the media]'. Interview in *France-Observateur* 501, 3 December, 1959, cited in Michel Marie, *The French New Wave: An Artistic School*, p 9.

71 Bondanella, *Italian Cinema: From Neorealism to the Present*, p 144.

72 The Cannes Film Festival was founded in 1939 to combat Venice's drift to the right. The first festival was scheduled to start on 1 September of that year, but events in Poland put a stop to the festival on the first day. It resumed in 1946, as did Venice.

73 Robin Buss, *Italian Films*, p 14.

74 Ibid, pp 39–40.

75 Cowie, *Revolution!*, p 6.

76 'My intention... was to translate the beauty of this world, in which even the factories can be very beautiful... the line, the curves of factories and their smoke-stacks, are perhaps more beautiful than a row of trees – which every eye has already seen to the point of monotony. It's a rich world – living, useful.' Bondanella, *Italian Cinema*, p 218, quoting Andrew Sarris, *Interviews with Film Directors* (New York: Avon, 1969), p 23.

77 Bondanella, *Italian Cinema*, p 225.

78 Statement released at Cannes in 1960, Bondanella, *Italian Cinema*, p 218.

79 Mary P Wood, *Italian Cinema*, p 123.

80 The film is generally known by its Italian title, which does not translate well into English. It literally translates as 'big calves', a reference to the fact that Moraldo and his friends are, to use a phrase unknown in Italy at the time, slackers – that is, big calves who are old enough to be oxen, but haven't yet faced up to the responsibilities of adulthood. 'Vitelloni' is also a pun on the dialect word 'vudellone', which means 'large intestine', the inference being that the group of friends are like those who eat too much, only living for the pleasures of the table. As Fellini's co-writer, Ennio Flaiano, later admitted, 'It was a way of describing the family son who only ate but never "produced".' Tullio Kezich, *Fellini: His Life and Work*, p 132.

81 *La Dolce Vita* gave us the words 'paparazzi' (plural) and 'paparazzo' (singular) – they are derived from the film's character Paparazzo (Walter Santesso), who is a photographer. Fellini got the name from the Italian word for mosquito, implying that celebrity photographers were just as annoying.

82 In between the two features, Fellini contributed the episode *The Temptations of Dr Antonio* to the portmanteau feature *Boccaccio '70*; the other directors were De Sica, Visconti and Mario Monicelli.

83 Peter Bondanella, *The Films of Federico Fellini*, p 26.

84 Ibid, p. 69.

85 Ibid, p. 133. Elsewhere, Fellini spoke of the need for film to go in the direction of poetry: 'Movies have now gone past the phase of prose narrative and are coming nearer and nearer to poetry. I am trying to free my work from certain constructions – a story with a beginning, a development, and an ending. It should move more like a poem with meter and cadence.' Federico Fellini, quoted in Robert Richardson, 'Waste Lands: The Breakdown of Order', *The New Yorker*, 30 October 1965, p 66.

86 Fellini, quoted in Buss, p 141.

87 Bondanella, *The Films of Federico Fellini*, p 66.

88 *Fellini on Fellini*, edited by Costanzo Costantini, p 50.

89 Bondanella, *The Films of Federico Fellini*, p 67.

90   Extracts from the dream diaries have now been published as *The Book of Dreams*.

91   Federico Fellini, *Comments on Film*, pp 161–62. The irony is, of course, that the rest of *8½ isn't* autobiographical.

92   Visconti worked on *A Day in the Country* (*Une Partie de Campagne*, 1936), *The Lower Depths* (*Les Bas-Fonds*, 1936, aka *Underworld*) and *Tosca* (*La Tosca*, 1940). He also worked as a set and costume designer in Italy around the same time, graduating to directing for the stage in 1945 with a production of Cocteau's *Les Parents Terribles* at the Teatro Eliseo in Rome.

93   Laurence Schifano, *Luchino Visconti: The Flames of Passion*, p 234.

94   Ibid, p 235.

95   The main characters are all played by stars; the only non-professionals in the film being some of the minor characters.

96   Schifano, p 321.

97   Luchino Visconti, letter to the Italian Minister of Culture, 24 October 1961, quoted in Schifano, p 322.

98   Luchino Visconti, interviewed by Derek Prouse, *The Sunday Times*, 8 July 1962; quoted in Gaia Servadio, *Luchino Visconti: A Biography*, p 177.

99   Servadio, p 177.

100 Ibid.

101 *The Damned*, review by Pablo Vargas, from http://www.thespinningimage. co.uk/cultfilms/displaycultfilm.asp?reviewid=1670, accessed 15/11/11.

102 The families concerned apparently being Kirdorfs and Thyssens (steel), Voeglers (steel), Schnitzlers (I G Farben, the chemists who made Zyklon-B, the gas used in the death camps), Rostergs and Diehns (potash), and Schröders (bankers), Monica Stirling, *A Screen of Time: A Study of Luchino Visconti*, p 192.

103 Vargas, op cit.

104 Stirling, p.194.

105 Luchino Visconti, quoted in Schifano, p 324.

106 Bondanella, *Italian Cinema: From Neorealism to the Present*, p 179.

107 Ibid, p 180.

108 Pasolini originally didn't intend to direct, but only did so after Fellini, for whom Pasolini had been a screenwriter, turned the script down.

109 Bertolucci, cited in Naomi Greene, p 21.

110 Gino Moliterno, 'Pier Paolo Pasolini', http://www.sensesofcinema.com/2002/ great-directors/pasolini/, accessed 24/01/11.

111 Moliterno, op cit.

112 Something of an about-turn for Pasolini, as his episode in the 1963 portmanteau feature, *RoGoPaG*, had caused controversy by showing an actor playing Jesus in a film, and actually dying on the cross – due to indigestion caused by eating too much ricotta for lunch. The film was banned and Pasolini received a four-month suspended prison sentence.

113 The title's colloquial Italian could perhaps be better rendered in English as 'Big Bad Birds and Little Birds'.

114 Mino Argentieri, 'Uccellacci e Uccellini', cited in Greene, p 80.

115 Adelio Ferrero, *Il cinema di Pier Paolo Pasolini* (Venice: Marsilio, 1977), p 68, quoted in Greene, p 81.

116 Bondanella, *Italian Cinema: From Neorealism to the Present*, p 283.

117 Rumble, p 63.

118 Bernardo Bertolucci, quoted in Enzo Ungari, *Scene madri di Bernardo Bertolucci* (Milan: Ubulibri, 1982), p 31, cited in Tonetti, pp 16–17.

119 Bertolucci, Ungari, p 35, cited in Tonetti, p 27.

120 Carl Jung, *Memories, Dreams, Reflections*, Chapter VI: Confronting the Unconscious (New York: Vintage Books, 1989; Richard and Clara Winston, tr), p 176.

121 Tonetti, p 33.

122 Geoffrey Nowell-Smith, *Making Waves*, p 157.

123 Bondanella, *Italian Cinema: From Neorealism to the Present*, p 297.

124 See Wood, pp 21–29.

125 Bondanella, *Italian Cinema: From Neorealism to the Present*, p 304. Bertolucci arranged to meet Godard immediately after the Parisian premiere: 'He doesn't say anything to me. He just gives me a note and then he leaves. I take the note and there was a Chairman Mao portrait on it and with Jean-Luc's writing... The note says: "You have to fight against individualism and capitalism." That was his reaction to my movie. I was so enraged that I crumpled it up and threw it under my feet. I'm so sorry I did that because I would love to have it now, to keep it as a relic.' 'Films are a way to kill my father', *The Guardian*, 22 February 2008.

126 Gino Moliterno, 'Francesco Rosi', from http://www.sensesofcinema.com/2003/great-directors/rosi/, accessed 16/11/11.

127 Ibid.

128 Ibid.

129 Millicent Marcus, 'Francesco Rosi', in Geoffrey Nowell Smith, James Hay and Gianni Volpi, *The Companion to Italian Cinema*, p 102.

130 Ibid.

131 Bondanella, *Italian Cinema: From Neorealism to the Present*, p 167.

132 Ibid, pp 168– 9.

133 Marcus, p 102.

134 Moliterno, op cit.

135 Francesco Rosi, quoted in Gary Crowdus, 'Investigating the Relationship between Causes and Effects: An Interview with Francesco Rosi', *Cineaste*, Vol 20, No 4, 1994, p 26.

136 François Truffaut, *Hitchcock*, p 170.

137 Gavin Lambert, 'Introduction to Lindsay Anderson's "John Ford"', *Cinema* 3, Spring 1971, p 22, quoted in Hedling, p 21.

138 *Sequence* 3, Spring 1948, pp 7–10, quoted in Hedling, p 11.

139 Gavin Lambert, *Mainly About Lindsay Anderson*, p 71.

140 *Sight and Sound*, Autumn 1956, reprinted in Paul Ryan (ed), *Never Apologise: The Collected Writings of Lindsay Anderson*, pp 218–32.

141 Eva Orbanz, Gisela Tuchtenhagen and Klaus Wildenhahn, 'Lindsay Anderson', in *Journey to a Legend and Back: The British Realist Film* (Berlin: Volker Spiess, 1977), pp 46–7, quoted in Hedling, p 42.

142 Karel Reisz, interviewed by Peter Cowie, *Revolution!*, p 52.

143 Reisz interviewed by Peter Cowie in London, 9 May 2002. Cowie, *Revolution!*, p 58.

144 Aside from Amis himself, the Movement included Thom Gunn, John Wain, Philip Larkin, Peter Porter, Donald Davie, Elizabeth Jennings and D J Enright. The titles of Gunn's first two collections, *Fighting Terms* (1954) and *The Sense of Movement* (1957), almost sound like manifestoes for a new wave film.

145 Tony Richardson, *Long Distance Runner: A Memoir*, p 97.

146 Ibid, p. 111.

147 Neil Sinyard, *Jack Clayton*, p 38.

148 Jack Clayton, interview in the *Oxford Mail*, 24 February 1962, quoted in Sinyard, *Jack Clayton*, p 12.

149 The phrase – and story – comes from Sinyard, *Jack Clayton*, p 31.

150 Clayton had in fact directed one prior film, *Naples is a Battlefield* (1944), a documentary he made while serving with the RAF Film Unit.

151 Sinyard, *Jack Clayton*, p 35.

152 *The New Statesman*, 10 December 1955.

153 Sinyard, *Jack Clayton*, p 37.

154 'The Way Things Are: Jack Clayton in an Interview with Gordon Gow', *Films and Filming*, April 1974, pp 11–14, quoted in Sinyard, *Jack Clayton*, p 39.

155 Alexander Walker, *Birmingham Post & Gazette*, 23 January 1959, quoted in Sinyard p 37. For the relationship between *Room at the Top* and *Brief Encounter*, see Sinyard, *Jack Clayton*, pp 58–59.

156 Dilys Powell, *Sunday Times*, 25 January 1959, quoted in Sinyard, *Jack Clayton*, p 37.

157 A note, written in Truffaut's imperfect but passionately felt English, delivered to Clayton in a restaurant where the two auteurs were dining in the early 1980s. Quoted in Sinyard, *Jack Clayton*, p 81.

158 Sinyard, *Jack Clayton*, p 82.

159 Jack Clayton, in *Sight and Sound*, Spring 1959, p 9.

160 Karel Reisz, Jack Clayton – Obituary, *The Guardian*, 25 March 1995.

161 Sinyard, *Jack Clayton*, p 83.

162 James M Welsh, 'Running the Distance', in *The Cinema of Tony Richardson: Essays and Interviews*, p 6.

163 Tom Maschler, 'Introduction', in *Declaration*, ed Tom Maschler, pp 7–9 (London: MacGibbon & Kee, 1957).

164 Lindsay Anderson, 'Get Out and Push!', in *Declaration*, pp 153–78; reprinted in *Never Apologise: The Collected Writings*, pp 233–51.

165 Tony Richardson, 'A Free Hand', *Sight and Sound*, Vol 28, No 2, Spring 1959, pp 60–64.

166 Isabel Quigly, *The Spectator* review, June 1959, quoted in John C Tibbetts, 'Breaking the Proscenium', in *The Cinema of Tony Richardson*, p 69.

167 Tibbetts, p 68.

168 David Robinson, 'Look Back in Anger', *Sight and Sound*, Vol 28, Nos 3 & 4, Summer/Autumn 1959, pp 122–125, pp 123–124, quoted in Taylor, p 41.

169 Richardson, *Long Distance Runner*, p 108.

170 Alexander Walker, *Hollywood England: The British Film Industry in the Sixties*, p 76.

171 Richardson, p 108.

172 Ibid. He notes that Olivier was very tired on the shoot, due to his also playing Coriolanus in Stratford, and commuting to locations in Morecambe and Bradford by ambulance, which enabled his chauffeur to maintain a cavalier attitude to the speed limit – a trick discovered by Orson Welles in New York in the late 1930s, who faced the challenge of going from radio to theatre commitments, usually with minutes to spare and the challenge of Manhattan's traffic to deal with.

173 Penelope Huston, 'The Entertainer', *Sight and Sound*, Vol 29, No 4 (Autumn 1960), pp 194–195.

174 Karel Reisz interviewed at home in London, 18 January 1997, from John C Tibbetts and James M Welsh, 'Let's Talk About Tony: Interviews with Colleagues', from *The Cinema of Tony Richardson: Essays and Interviews*, p 27.

175 Quoted in Colin Gardner, *Karel Reisz*, p 105. As was common practice at the time, Trevelyan often read scripts before they were shot. He read the script for *Saturday Night* in October 1959, as the film was going into pre-production.

176 Trevelyan, quoted in Gardner, p 105.

177 Gardner, p 104.

178 Forbes's screenwriting of this period also has a new wave edge to it: he wrote the script for Basil Dearden's *The League of Gentlemen* (1960), in which a group of disaffected ex-soldiers decide to get their revenge on the establishment. The irreverent tone of the film is certainly more 1960s than 50s, and contains such memorable lines as Race (Nigel Patrick) asking Hyde (Jack Hawkins) if his wife is dead: 'No,' comes the reply, 'I'm sorry to say the bitch is still going strong.'

179 British Board of Film Censors' letter to Bryan Forbes, 11 April 1962, quoted in Bryan Forbes, *A Divided Life: Memoirs*, p 360.

180 Forbes, p 361.

181 Ibid, p 362.

182 Ibid, pp 361–362.

183 B F Taylor, *The British New Wave: A Certain Tendency?*, p 106. The visual clues throughout the film are, Taylor argues, based on the positioning of actors within the frame, Tom Courtenay in particular.

184 Ian Buruma, *Conversations with John Schlesinger*, p 78.

185 Walker, *Hollywood, England*, p 23.

186 Lambert, p 61.

187 Erik Hedling, *Lindsay Anderson: Maverick Film-maker*, p 54.

188 Hedling, p 55.

189 Alexander Walker, *Hollywood, England*, p 173.

190 Ibid.

191 Paul Ryan, 'Introduction: A Revolutionary Solider', in Lindsay Anderson, *Never Apologise: The Collected Writings*, p 18.

192 Ibid, pp 18–19.

193 Lambert, *Mainly About Lindsay Anderson*, p 93.

194 *Evening Standard*, 24 December 1963.

195 Ryan, *Never Apologise*, p 19.

196 Skinner, *The British New Wave*, p 38.

197 Neil Sinyard, *Jack Clayton*, p 13.

198 Truffaut was a huge admirer of Bill Douglas's work. His celebrated trilogy – *My Childhood*, *My Ain Folk* and *My Way Home* – was complete and being shown internationally by 1979. One assumes Truffaut was no longer subscribing to the belief that 'Britain' and 'cinema' were incompatible terms by this time.

199 The first films made in Bohemia were by Jan Kříženecký, such as *Dostavenícko ve mlýnici* and *Smích a pláč* (both 1898).

200 Incidentally, yet another major talent to emerge from the Max Reinhardt school, studying under him in Berlin.

201 The full modern name for the school is Filmová a Televizní Fakulta Akademie Múzických Umení V Praze (Film and TV School of the Academy of Performing Arts in Prague).

202 Peter Hames, *The Czechoslovak New Wave*, p 29.

203 In fact, the nearest Trnka seems to have come to official censure was the banning of two episodes of *The Czech Year* – 'Spring' and 'The Legend of St Prokop' – as Church propaganda. They remained proscribed until the Velvet Revolution of 1989.

204 Hames, *Czechoslovak New Wave*, p 37.

205 *Film a doba*, No 4, April 1959, p 219.

206 Hames, *Czechoslovak New Wave*, p 29.

207 Ibid.

208 Ibid, p 46.

209 Vláčil said that this was partly because he didn't want to burden his child actors with the necessity of learning too many lines and thereby risk false and unconvincing performances; it also fits squarely into his aesthetic as a whole.

210 Hames, *Czechoslovak New Wave*, p 55.

211 Ibid.

212 Ibid, p 46.

213 Miloš Forman and Jan Novak, *Turnaround: A Memoir*, p 129.

214 Ibid, p 135.

215 Ibid, p 140.

216 This actually was the starting point for the idea of the film, being based on Forman's own recollections of seeing a girl lugging a suitcase along a Prague street in the late 1950s.

217 Hames, *Czechoslovak New Wave*, p 83.

218 Josef Škvorecký, *All the Bright Young Men and Women: A Personal History of the Czech Cinema*, p 113.

219 Ibid, pp 120–121.

220 Škvorecký, *All the Bright Young Men and Women*, p 121.

221 Ibid, p 123.

222 Ibid, p 126.

223 Ibid.

224 Ibid, p 129.

225 Ibid, pp 129–130.

226 Ibid, p 129.

227 Hames, *Czechoslovak New Wave*, p 187.

228 Philip Bergson, from the DVD booklet essay, *Intimate Lighting* (Second Run DVD).

229 Krzysztof Kieślowski, quoted in *Projections 4½*, edited by John Boorman and Walter Donohoe (London: Faber & Faber, 1995), pp 102–104.

230 Antonín J Liehm, *Closely Watched Films*, p 384.

231 Menzel, quoted in Hames, *Czechoslovak New Wave*, p 158.

232 Ľubica Mistríková, 'A Shop on the High Street', in Hames (ed), *The Cinema of Central Europe*, p 97.

233 Liehm, p 175.

234 Hames, *The Czechoslovak New Wave*, p 61.

235 Vláčil, speaking to Antonín J Liehm in the spring of 1969. Liehm, pp 175–6.

236 Hames, *Czech and Slovak Cinema: Theme and Tradition*, p 85.

237 Liehm, p 132.

238 Škvorecký, *All The Bright Young Men and Women*, p 264.

239 Ibid, p vii.

240 Liehm, p 133.

241 John Cunningham, *Hungarian Cinema*, p 10.

242 Tom Levin, 'From Dialectical to Normative Specificity: Reading Lukács on Film', *New German Critique* 40, Winter 1987, p 36.

243 Cunningham, *Hungarian Cinema*, p 10. Like Curtiz, Korda was to become an expat, moving to England and changing his name to Alexander, where he became one of Britain's most successful and influential producers.

244 John Cunningham, *Hungarian Cinema: From Coffee House to Multiplex*, p 93.

245 Jörg K Hoensch, *A History of Modern Hungary: 1867– 1994* (London: Longman, 1995), p 234.

246 Cunningham, p 96.

247 András Bálint Kovács, 'The Round-Up', in Hames, *The Cinema of Central Europe*, p 108.

248 Ibid, pp 109–110.

249 Peter Cowie, *Revolution!*, p 142.

250 András Gervai, 'A Screen Moralist', review of József Marx's *István Szabó* (Budapest: Vincze Kiadó, 2002) from http://www.hungarianquarterly.com/ no168/15.html, accessed 07/06/11.

251 Richard F Shepard, 'A Charmer: Szabó's *Father* Tells of Need for Heritage', *New York Times*, 29 September 1967.

252 Cunningham, p 94.

253 Andrzej Wajda, Cowie, *Revolution!*, p 10.

254 Ibid.

255 Ibid, p 15.

256 Ibid, p 16.

257 Ibid.

258 Ibid.

259 Chris Fujiwara, 'The Brief Career of Andrzej Munk', *Boston Phoenix*, September 12–19, 2002.

260 Christopher Sandford, *Polanski*, p 90.

261 Roman Polanski, *Roman by Polanksi*, p 156.

262 Andrei Tarkovsky, *Sculpting in Time*, p 29.

263 Ibid, p 213.

264 Josephine Woll, *Real Images: Soviet Cinema and the Thaw*, p 185.

265 Ibid, p 186.

266 Seven episodes in the original 205-minute version of the film. See my *Andrei Tarkovsky* for a fuller treatment of the film's history.

267 It was not his first arrest: he had been detained on similar charges (homosexuality) in 1948. Parajanov was re-arrested in 1982 on charges of bribery. He finally won his freedom in 1983, and was able to return to filmmaking with *The Legend of the Suram Fortress* (1984), on the proviso that he had a 'baby-sitter' as co-director to make sure nothing ideologically unwise happened. Happily, Parajanov's 'minder' was his friend, Georgian actor Dodo Abashidze, who was of a like mind to Parajanov and allowed him a free hand, doing no directing himself.

268 Jeanne Vronskaya, *Young Soviet Film Makers*, p 41.

269 Moscow features so heavily in the film that it almost becomes another character, giving *I Am Twenty* an interesting psychogeographic dimension.

270 Josephine Woll, *Real Images: Soviet Cinema and the Thaw*, p 173.

271 Jeanne Vronskaya, p 38.

272 Woll, p 218.

273 Vronskaya, p 39.

274 Ibid, p 36.

275 Woll, p 195.

276 Tarkovsky, *Sculpting in Time*, p 149.

277 Andrew Horton, *The Films of Theo Angelopoulos: A Cinema of Contemplation*, p 75.

278 Ibid.

279 Ibid, p 3.

280 Ibid, p 93.

281 Dan Georgakas, 'Angelopoulos, Greek History and The Travelling Players', in Andrew Horton (ed), *The Last Modernist: The Films of Theo Angelopoulos*, p 35.

282 Ibid.

283 Ibid, p 36.

284 Ibid, p 27.

285 Ibid.

286 Ibid.

287 Roger Ebert, review of *Z*, *Chicago Sun Times*, 30 December 1969. From http://rogerebert.suntimes.com/apps/pbcs.dll/article?AID=/19691230/REVIEWS/912300301/1023, accessed 23/09/12.

288 Ibid.

289 Mary Anne Weaver, 'The Greek Who Filmed His Country's Tragedy', *Washington Star*, 25 April 1976, p 14.

290 Ibid.

291 Costa-Gavras, Franco Solinas et al, *State of Siege* (published screenplay), p 156.

292 Ibid, p 147.

293 Ibid, pp 154–5.

294 Ibid, p 142.

295 Ibid, p 148.

296 Ibid, p 156.

297 Ibid, p 158.

298 The Chilean coup was addressed in Costa-Gavras's 1982 film *Missing*, starring Jack Lemmon and Sissy Spacek. The United States' history of supporting dictators and non-democratic governments since 1945 is, frankly, appalling. For more on this most lamentable episode in the history of democracy, see Stephen E Ambrose and Douglas G Brinkley's *Rise to Globalism: American Foreign Policy Since 1938* (Harmondsworth: Penguin Books, 1997); William Blum's *Rogue State* (Monroe, ME: Common Courage Press, 2000), and Noam Chomsky's *Hegemony or Survival: America's Quest for Global Dominance* (London: Penguin Books, 2004), amongst others.

299 Actually, the very first films ever made – although much less well known than those of the Lumières – were those by Augustin Louis Le Prince, a Frenchman based in Leeds, and they were also 'documentaries', or documents. His earliest surviving film, shot in 1888, shows his family in the garden in their house in Leeds. It is known as the Roundhay Garden Sequence. Another, slightly later, fragment shows traffic crossing Leeds Bridge. For more on Le Prince, see Christopher Rawlence, *The Missing Reel – The Untold Story of the Lost Inventor of Moving Pictures* (London: Collins, 1990).

300 'Of course, *Moana*, being a visual account of events in the daily life of a Polynesian youth and his family, has documentary value.' Grierson, writing as 'The Moviegoer', *New York Sun*, 8 February 1926.

301 Quoted in Patricia Aufderheide, *Documentary Film: A Very Short Introduction*, p 28.

302 It has to be said that Grierson was not entirely motivated by a fear of reds under the bed. His father had been a Calvinist minister, and the young Grierson had frequently taught the value of good works, etc, in his capacity as a school teacher.

303 Quoted in Aufderheide, p 35.

304 Ibid.

305 John Grierson, review of Robert Flaherty's *Moana*, *New York Sun*, 8 February 1926, cited in Hardy, *Grierson on Documentary*, p 11.

306 Unedited footage. Also known as 'dailies' because such screenings would be held every day, as soon as the processed film was back from the lab.

307 Basil Wright, interviewed in *Film-Maker's Newsletter*, November 1975, Vol 9, No 1.

308 Humphrey Jennings, letter to Cicely Jennings, Easter Monday 1941, quoted in *The Humphrey Jennings Film Reader*, Kevin Jackson (ed), (Manchester: Carcanet Press, 1993), p 16.

309 Like Flaherty – and, it has to be said, countless other documentarians – Buñuel was not averse to intervening in events. When told that the villagers in a particular area only ever ate a goat if it fell from a mountain, Buñuel realised he did not have the time to wait around for a goat to miss its footing and fall to its death, so the goat we see falling in the film did not fall by accident: Buñuel shot it – his gun is just visible in the corner of the frame.

310 An earlier film, *La chevelure magique* (*Magical Hair*, 1946), also shot in Africa, has been lost.

311 Quoted in Aufderheide, p 112.

312 Jean Rouch, interviewed by James Blue, *Film Comment*, Vol II, No 2, Spring 1964.

313 Jean Rouch, interviewed by G Roy-Leven in 1969, quoted in *Imagining Reality: The Faber Book of Documentary*, Kevin Macdonald and Mark Cousins (eds), p 265.

314 Aufderheide, p 52.

315 Richard Leacock, speaking in *The Louisiana Story Study Film* (George Amberg, 1962), quoted in Erik Barnouw, *Documentary: A History of the Non-Fiction Film*, p 236.

316 Erik Barnouw, p 236.

317 Ibid.

318 Pennebaker actually breaks his own rules at the very beginning of the film, in the pre-credits sequence showing Dylan holding up cards that contain phrases from 'Subterranean Homesick Blues', while the song plays on the soundtrack. This obviously staged scene – apparently shot in an alleyway in Croydon – has the virtue of being, at the time it was shot, the first pop promo. Pennebaker has since made many more films about musicians, including *Monterey Pop* (1968), *Sweet Toronto* (1988) and *Down from the Mountain* (2000).

319 Barnouw, p 244.

320 Ibid, p 248.

321 Thompson & Bordwell, pp 581–582.

322 *Godard on Godard*, p 171, cited by Rascaroli, p 84.

323 Thompson & Bordwell, p 563.

324 From *Pravda* (1969), also cited by Hames, *Czech New Wave*, p 4. To which arrant nonsense we need to propose the formula, 'Godard + Mao = Merde'.

325 Thompson & Bordwell, p 563. Peter Cowie is less polite, dubbing Godard's late 60s work 'self-referential drivel'. Cowie, *Revolution!*, p 241.

326 Chris Marker, interviewed by Dolores Wallfisch, *Vertigo* 7, Autumn 1996, p 38, quoted in Sarah Cooper, *Chris Marker*, p 3.

327 Kevin Macdonald and Mark Cousins (eds), *Imagining Reality: The Faber Book of the Documentary*, p 241.

328 David Thomson, *The New Biographical Dictionary of Film*, p 578.

329 Ibid, p 579.

330 Cooper, *Chris Marker*, p. 44.

331 Ibid.

332 Ibid, p. 52.

333 Paul Cronin (ed), *Herzog on Herzog* (London: Faber and Faber, 2002), e.g. pp 303–326.

334 Werner Herzog, in Cronin, pp 238–240.

335 Amos Vogel, 'On Seeing a Mirage', in Timothy Corrigan (ed), *The Films of Werner Herzog: Between Mirage & History*, p 46.

336 Cronin, p. 241.

337 Ibid.

338 Ibid, pp 69–70.

339 Thomas Elsaesser, 'An Anthropologist's Eye: *Where The Green Ants Dream*', in Corrigan, p 150.

340 Both quotes from *Herzog on Herzog*, p 240.

341 See Micheál Mac Liammóir's *Put Money in thy Purse* (London: Columbus Books, 1988) for a brilliant account of the four years it took Welles to make his version of *Othello* between 1948 and 1952 across Europe and North Africa.

342 Manny Farber, 'Underground Films' (1957), in *Negative Space: Manny Farber on the Movies* (New York: Da Capo, 1998), p 12.

343 Jaglom directed *A Safe Place* (1971), starring Orson Welles, Tuesday Weld and Jack Nicholson, for BBS. He also played a major part in getting *Easy Rider* down to a releasable length from Dennis Hopper's original five-hour cut.

344 Gene Fowler, Jr interviewed by Gary Fishgall, 1993. Gary Fishgall, *Against Type: The Biography of Burt Lancaster* (New York: Scribner, 1995), p 224.

345 John Cassavetes, *Cassavetes on Cassavetes*, ed Ray Carney p 123.

346 Martin Scorsese, *Accidental Genius: How John Cassavetes Invented the American Independent Film*, Marshall Fine, cover blurb.

347 Joan Didion, *The White Album* (London: Weidenfeld & Nicolson, 1979), pp 100–101.

348 Peter Biskind, *Easy Riders, Raging Bulls*, p 49.

349 Ibid, p 18.

350 The whole campfire scene is:

> George: You know, this used to be a hell of a good country. I can't understand what's gone wrong with it.
>
> Billy: Huh. Man, everybody got chicken, that's what happened, man. Hey, we can't even get into like, uh, second-rate hotel, I mean, a second-rate motel. You dig? They think we're gonna cut their throat or something, man. They're scared, man.
>
> George: Oh, they're not scared of you. They're scared of what you represent to 'em.
>
> Billy: Hey man. All we represent to them, man, is somebody needs a haircut.
>
> George: Oh no. What you represent to them is freedom.
>
> Billy: What the hell's wrong with freedom, man? That's what it's all about.
>
> George: Oh yeah, that's right, that's what it's all about, all right. But talkin' about it and bein' it – that's two different things. I mean, it's real hard to be free when you are bought and sold in the marketplace. 'Course, don't ever tell anybody that they're not free 'cause then they're gonna get real busy killin' and maimin' to prove to you that they are. Oh yeah, they're gonna talk to you, and talk to you, and talk to you about individual freedom, but they see a free individual, it's gonna scare 'em.
>
> Billy: Mmmm, well, that don't make 'em runnin' scared.
>
> George: No, it makes 'em dangerous.

351 Biskind, p 118.

352 Ibid, p 132.

353 Peter Cowie, *Coppola*, p 25.

354 Pye and Myles, *The Movie Brats*, p 76.

355 Pollock, *Skywalking*, p 4.

356 Lucas on Coppola, *Skywalking*, p 88.

357 Kerry O'Quinn, 'The George Lucas Saga', *Starlog* 48–50, July–September 1981, quoted in Sally Kline (ed), *George Lucas Interviews*, p 121.

358 Cowie, *Coppola*, p 61.

359 Stephen Farber, 'Coppola in Hollywood', *Los Angeles Magazine*, 23 September 1972, quoted in Schumacher, p 134.

360 Drew Casper, *Hollywood Film 1963–1976*, p 26.

361 Ibid, p 27.

362 Ibid.

363 Pollock, *Skywalking*, p 123.

364 There is some controversy as to the origins of *Apocalypse Now*, and its relation to Conrad's *Heart of Darkness*. See Cowie, *Coppola*, pp 116–117, for a summary.

365 Pye & Myles, p 132.

366 Pollock, p 139.

367 Vincent LoBrutto, *Martin Scorsese: A Biography*, p 51.

368 Ian Christie and David Thompson, *Scorsese on Scorsese*, pp 13–14.

369 Ibid, p 14.

370 Vincent LoBrutto, *Martin Scorsese: A Biography*, p 84.

371 Ibid, p. 91.

372 Ibid.

373 *Scorsese on Scorsese*, p 25.

374 Ibid.

375 LoBrutto, p 84.

376 Weill's English-language version of *Cahiers* ran for 12 issues in 1966–67.

377 Roger Ebert, review of *I Call First* [*Who's That Knocking at My Door*], *Chicago Sun-Times*, 17 November 1967.

378 Ibid.

379 *Scorsese on Scorsese*, p 26.

380 Scorsese's other Low Countries connection from this period was Jacques Ledoux, curator of the Cinémathèque in Brussels, who funded Scorsese's 1967 short, *The Big Shave*. Ledoux had, of course, also appeared in Chris Marker's *La Jetée*.

381 Pye and Myles, p 196.

382 The anecdote, and its variants, are recounted by Vincent LoBrutto in *Martin Scorsese: A Biography*, pp 129–130.

383 Scorsese interviewed in *Scorsese on Scorsese*, p 47. 'Emotional violence' for Fuller didn't necessarily mean actual fisticuffs, more a sense of psychological

turmoil: he famously thought David Lean's *Brief Encounter* (1945) was one of the most emotionally violent films he had ever seen. See Lisa Dombrowski, *The Films of Samuel Fuller: If You Die, I'll Kill You!* (Middletown, CT: Wesleyan University Press, 2008), p 13.

384 *Scorsese on Scorsese*, p 48.

385 Ibid.

386 Ibid, p 45.

387 Roger Ebert, 'Mean Streets', *Chicago Sun-Times*, 31 December 2003.

388 *Scorsese on Scorsese*, p 48.

389 T H Guback, *The International Film Industry* (Bloomington: University of Indiana Press, 1969), p 125. Quoted in Julia Knight, *New German Cinema*, p 8.

390 Knight, *New German Cinema*, p 7.

391 Ibid, p 9.

392 Isabel Quigly, *The Spectator*, 25 May 1957, quoted in John Sandford, *The New German Cinema*, p 156.

393 Thomas Elsaesser, *New German Cinema*, p 20.

394 Knight, *New German Cinema*, p 2.

395 Edgar Reitz, quoted in J Dawson, 'A Labyrinth of Subsidies', *Sight and Sound*, 50, 1, 14–20, p 17.

396 Julia Knight, *New German Cinema*, Ch 2, especially pp 46–89.

397 In addition, there was also a smaller, less well-known group of films that dealt with workers who were German nationals, including Fassbinder's *Eight Hours are Not a Day* (*Acht Stunden sind kein Tag*, 1973) and Christian Ziewer's *Dear Mother, I'm OK* (*Liebe Mutter, mir geht es gut*, 1972), but the genre died out after 1976.

398 Thomas Elsaesser, *New German Cinema: A History*, p 185.

399 John Sandford, *The New German Cinema*, p 18.

400 Ibid.

401 Ibid.

402 Ibid, p 17.

403 Jean-Marie Straub, *Enthusiasm*, No 1, Dec 1975, p 31 (quoted in Sandford, p 35).

404 Richard Roud, *Jean-Marie Straub*, p 44. Roud was present at the screening, and seems to have been one of the few people to actually like the film. His book on the Straubs, published in 1972, was the first in English to champion their work.

405 Straub, from an interview with *Film* magazine, April 1968; quoted in Byg, p 53. Byg (Ch 3) details the problems the Straubs had in the 13 years it took to get the Bach film financed.

406 Thomas Elsaesser, *New German Cinema: A History*, p 77.

407 Straub, quoted in Roud, p 71.

408 Christian Braad Thomsen, 'Five Interviews with Fassbinder', in Tony Rayns (ed), *Fassbinder*, p 82.

409 Christian Braad Thomsen, *Fassbinder: The Life and Work of a Provocative Genius*, p 66.

410 Ibid.

411 Ibid, p 78.

412 Robert Katz & Peter Berling, *Love is Colder Than Death: The Life and Work of Rainer Werner Fassbinder*, pp 38–39.

413 Ibid, p 81.

414 Ibid, p 44.

415 Ibid, p 50.

416 Julia Knight, *New German Cinema*, pp 30–31.

417 Katz & Berling, p 63.

418 Ibid, p 64.

419 Thomsen, p 25; Fassbinder quote from an interview with Dieter Schidor in the film *The Wizard of Babylon* (*Der Bauer von Babylon*, 1982).

420 Katz & Berling, p 57.

421 Ronald Hayman, *Fassbinder: Film Maker*, p 8.

422 Thomsen, *Fassbinder*, p 69.

423 The other two were *Blood on the Cat's Neck* (*Blut am Hals der Katze*), staged in Nuremberg in March 1971, and *Bremen Freedom* (*Bremer Freiheit*), staged in Bremen in December 1971. The latter also became a film, shot the following September in Saarbrücken. The stage version of *The Bitter Tears of Petra von Kant* opened in Darmstadt in June 1971.

424 Andrew J Mitchell, 'Rainer Werner Fassbinder: The Subject of Film', in *Cinematic Thinking: Philosophical Approaches to the New Cinema*, James Phillips (ed), p 128.

425 Katz & Berling, p 71.

426 Rainer Werner Fassbinder, *The Anarchy of the Imagination: Interviews, Essays, Notes*, p 28.

427 Katz & Berling, p 100.

428 Thomsen, *Fassbinder*, p 189.

429 Ibid.

430 Thompson & Bordwell, p 576.

431 Veronika was based on Sybille Schmitz, star of Carl Dreyer's *Vampyr* (1932). Fassbinder originally wanted Schmitz to play the role of Petra von Kant's mother, unaware that she had committed suicide in 1955.

432 Thomsen, p ix.

433 Quoted in William Van Wert, 'Last Words: Observations on a New Language', in Corrigan, *The Films of Werner Herzog*, p 63.

434 *Herzog on Herzog*, p 42.

435 Ibid, pp. 56–57.

436 Ibid, p 77.

437 Ibid.

438 See *Herzog on Herzog*, pp 89–91 for the death threat story.

439 *Herzog on Herzog*, p 84.

440 Ibid, p 79.

441 Ibid.

442 See Louise S Milne's *Carnivals and Dreams: Pieter Bruegel and the History of the Imagination* (London: Mutus Liber, 2007), Ch 3, for more on the World Turned Upside Down.

443 *Herzog on Herzog*, p 80.

444 Ibid, p 81.

445 Ibid, p 112. This theme recurs in the second film Herzog made with Bruno S, *Stroszek* (1977). The film (which has nothing to do with Peter Brogle's character in *Signs of Life*) is set in contemporary Germany – a first for the director – and follows the fortunes of Bruno, a street musician and former convict. When he and his girlfriend are harassed by lowlifes, they decide to move to America, ending up in the desolate wastes of the Midwest in winter. Bruno S essentially plays himself in the film, lending it considerable power. Eva Mattes and Herzog regular Clemens Scheitz co-star.

446 *Herzog on Herzog*, p 127.

447 Herzog, speaking at the end of *Burden of Dreams*, Les Blank and Maureen Gosling's film about the making of *Fitzcarraldo* (both films 1982). The interview is also reproduced in the *Burden of Dreams* book, pp 61–62.

448 *Herzog on Herzog*, p 128.

449 *Woyzeck* (1979) was made back-to-back with *Nosferatu*, and again stars Klaus Kinski in one of his finest roles. Eva Mattes co-stars as his doomed girlfriend Marie in a performance that won her a Special Jury Prize at Cannes in 1979.

450 *Herzog on Herzog*, p 151.

451 Ibid, p 152.

452 Ibid, p 153. The respect was mutual. Herzog was Eisner's favourite of the New German directors. When Fritz Lang complained that there were no more German films, Eisner urged him to see *Signs of Life*. When Herzog heard, in 1974, that Eisner was ill and might die, he resolved to walk from Munich to Paris, where Eisner lived, convinced that if he could make the entire journey on foot, she would survive. The walk took three weeks (and is recounted in Herzog's book, *Of Walking in Ice*). Herzog arrived to find Eisner on the mend, and she lived for another nine years.

453 An ending reminiscent of Polanski's *The Fearless Vampire Killers*. Although not intentionally a comedy, *Nosferatu* does contain some wonderfully absurd exchanges. For instance, Van Helsing's arrest at the end of the film:

Town Official: Arrest this man!

Clerk (the incomparable Clemens Scheitz)*:* Arrest him? I can't arrest him.

Town Official: Then get the police.

Clerk: The police don't exist anymore.

Town Official:	Then take him to prison.
Clerk:	There's no one there to guard him.
Town Official:	It's your duty as a town employee to handle it.
Clerk:	I don't have a weapon.
Town Official:	I don't care! I want you to arrest this man!
Van Helsing:	Where will you take me, then?

(They look at each other)

Clerk:	I don't know where I'm taking you.
Van Helsing:	Take me wherever you want.

Van Helsing is led out.

454 *Herzog on Herzog*, p 152.

455 Franklin, *New German Cinema*, p 56.

456 The Hamburg Declaration, quoted in Franklin, p 56.

457 J Hoberman, 'Listen, Turkey', *Village Voice*, 23 November 1982.

458 Kiarostami also shot the documentary *ABC Africa* (2001) on palmcorders, and went even further than *Ten* in *Five* (2003), a sequence of five long takes in which nothing much happens, where digital cinema becomes very close to gallery installation work.

459 François Truffaut, interview, *France-Observateur*, 3 December 1959, quoted in Michel Marie, p 9.

460 Mark Betz, 'Beyond Europe: On Parametric Transcendence', from *Global Art Cinema*, eds Rosalind Galt and Karl Schoonover (Oxford: Oxford University Press, 2010), p 31.

461 Dziga Vertov, Provisional instructions to Kino-Eye Groups, 1926.

462 Cowie, *Revolution!*, p 103.

463 Makavejev, interviewed by Cowie, 23/24 April 2001, quoted in *Revolution!*, p 103.

464 Ibid.

465 Thompson & Bordwell, p 554.

466 Cowie, *Revolution!*, p 184.

467 Erik Barnouw, *Documentary: A History of the Non-Fiction Film*, p 249.

468 Biskind, p 17.

469 *Please Kill Me*, p 381.

470 Amos Poe, interviewed by Glenn Andreiev, 2011, from http://www.filmsinreview.com/2011/04/07/interview-amos-poe-and-the-no-wave-cinema/, accessed 28/11/12.

471 Ibid.

472 Glenn Andreiev, in the Amos Poe interview, from http://www.filmsinreview.com/2011/04/07/interview-amos-poe-and-the-no-wave-cinema/, accessed 28/11/12.

473 Franklin, *New German Cinema*, p 164, originally from an interview with John Pym, *Sight and Sound*, Vol 46, Autumn 1977, pp 227–30.

474 Franklin, *New German Cinema*, p 167.

475 From: http://sensesofcinema.com/2009/52/jean-marie-straub-and-daniele-huillet/#1, accessed 31/08/09.

476 Katz & Berling, p 203.

477 The name derives from the 1956 film *Season of the Sun* (*Taiyo no kisetsu*), directed by Takumi Furukawa. Like 'nouvelle vague' in France, the name initially applied to a youth, rather than cinematic, subculture. The *taiyozoku* could be seen as being the equivalent of the Beats in America, rockers and greasers in Britain, and the *stilyagi* in Russia.

478 Thompson and Bordwell, p 469.

479 Nagisa Oshima, *Cinema, Censorship and the State*, p 48.

480 Thompson and Bordwell, p 468.

481 Audie Bock, *Japanese Film Directors*, p 293. The quote comes from a 1965 *Cahiers du cinéma* interview with Imamura.

482 Thompson and Bordwell, p 470.

483 Carlos Diegues, 'Cinema Novo', quoted in Johnson & Stam, *Brazilian Cinema*, p 65.

484 Ibid.

485 Johnson & Stam, *Brazilian Cinema*, p 33.

486 Glauber Rocha, 'An Aesthetic of Hunger', quoted in Johnson & Stam, *Brazilian Cinema*, p 70.

487 Ibid, p 69.

488 Ibid, p 70.

489 Glauber Rocha, 'The Tricontinental Filmmaker: That is Called the Dawn', *Cahiers du cinéma*, November 1967, quoted in Johnson & Stam, *Brazilian Cinema*, pp 76–80. The essay was written after Rocha heard the news of Ché Guevara's death (which occurred on 9 October 1967).

490 See Johnson & Stam, *Brazilian Cinema*, p 40, for a discussion of these utterly dire films.

491 Hamid Dabashi, *Makhmalbaf at Large*, p 11.

492 Such an apparently 'safe' subject became known as the 'child quest' genre, spawning later films such as Jafar Panahi's *The White Balloon* (*Badkonake sefid*, 1997, written by Kiarostami) and Samira Makhmalbaf's *The Apple* (*Sib*, 1997).

493 Quoted on the cover of Alberto Elena's *The Cinema of Abbas Kiarostami*.

494 Bernardo Bertolucci, interviewed 3 February 2003, quoted in Cowie, *Revolution!*, p. 223.

495 Martin Scorsese, interviewed in 2005, *Antonio das Mortes* DVD.

496 Glauber Rocha, 'An Aesthetic of Hunger', quoted in Johnson & Stam, *Brazilian Cinema*, p. 70.

INDEX